Crime Prevention Through Physical Security

OCCUPATIONAL SAFETY AND HEALTH

A Series of Reference Books and Textbooks
on Occupational Hazards • Safety • Health •
Fire Protection • Security • and Industrial Hygiene

Series Editor

ALAN L. KLING

Loss Prevention Consultant
Jamesburg, New Jersey

1. Occupational Safety, Health and Fire Index   *David E. Miller*
2. Crime Prevention Through Physical Security   *Walter M. Strobl*

Additional volumes in preparation

Crime Prevention Through Physical Security

WALTER M. STROBL, CPP
President
Strobl Security Service, Inc.
Memphis, Tennessee

MARCEL DEKKER, INC.   New York and Basel

Library of Congress Cataloging in Publication Data

Strobl, Walter M.[Date]
    Crime prevention through physical security.

    (Occupational safety and health ; v. 2).
    Bibliography: p.
    Includes index.
    1. Industry--Security measures. 2. Retail trade--
Security measures. 3. Public institutions--Security
measures. 4. Crime prevention and architectural design.
I. Title. II. Series: Occupational safety and health
(New York) ; v. 2.
HV8290.S84   364.4   78-15329
ISBN 0-8247-6722-5

MARCEL DEKKER, INC.
270 Madison Avenue, New York, New York 10016

Current printing (last digit):
10 9 8 7 6 5 4 3

PRINTED IN THE UNITED STATES OF AMERICA

For my wife, Carolyn

Foreword

Crime Prevention Through Physical Security is a unique combination of
technical information and professional experiences that will be valuable to
a broad range of security interests. The book will be valuable to the security generalist who needs a solid introduction or review of the technical
aspects of security hardware and will be a practical guide to the analysis
of security problems and the application of solutions.

Mr. Strobl's extensive use of personal experiences lends credibility to
his recommendations and instructs through example how initiative, innova-
tion, and pragmatism are required to construct workable security programs.

But the author does not treat only practical matters in this volume. He
also addresses an issue that must be faced by private and public decision
makers—the right of privacy versus the right to protect company and personal assets.

In encouraging police crime prevention personnel to acquaint themselves
with fire prevention activities, the author has helped close a communications
gap that sometimes exists between police and fire services.

Crime Prevention Through Physical Security is required reading for
newly appointed security directors. It is a solid review for the experienced
and could serve as a textbook for practice-oriented college and university
security courses.

Wilbur Rykert
Executive Director
National Crime Prevention Association
Washington, D.C.

v

Preface

During the past 2 years, I have had numerous discussions with professional security experts and police officers assigned to crime prevention units concerning the need for a comprehensive book on establishing security programs for specific facilities and situations. The majority of these conversations inevitably led to discussions about the need for a sophisticated reference book on the subject of physical security. Specifically, more detailed information is needed by the security professional in the security industry, the police officer assigned to a crime prevention unit, and those individuals employed at different facilities who may "wear many hats," one of which is to ensure that the facility's physical security program is adequate and regularly updated to meet changing requirements.

On September 16, 1975, Richard Velde, Administrator of the Law Enforcement Assistance Administration, speaking at the annual meeting of the International Association of Chiefs of Police in Denver, declared that America simply cannot afford two competing systems of crime prevention—public and private. He told the gathering of national police chiefs that they should learn to cooperate more fully with the private security industry, which in many metropolitan areas outstripped the police departments in terms of financial and manpower resources.

Most major city police departments have organized or are in the process of organizing crime prevention units. The obvious need for this police service should not be underestimated, because police departments should participate in planning decisions in new construction within their jurisdiction, whether this construction is a high-rise apartment complex, a condominium housing project, a shopping center, or an urban renewal project. I feel there is an obligation on the part of police departments to assist in these areas as well as to survey and give advice to the builders, owners, or operators of all types of business, both government and private, when they are requested to do so. The basic concept of crime prevention must start with the establishment of physical security of the facility or area to be protected.

One need only consider the 18 percent increase nationwide in overall crime that occurred in 1975, remembering that this increase was directed against both persons and property.

Facts are irrefutable. Between December 1973 and February 1974 the Federal Aviation Administration required airport management and airline management to tighten security for the protection of passengers and aircraft crews. It appeared incredible that persons and hand-carried luggage would be subjected to thorough searches before boarding any aircraft departing some 531 airports throughout the United States. The program, as we are now all aware, has been successful within the United States. The search of both persons and baggage is accomplished through the use of electronic devices and physical searches by trained personnel.

The recent increase in kidnappings, bombings, and other terrorist activities in the United States dictates that security personnel review their current programs and expand their protection plans to include executive personnel and their families. There is a need for tighter security in their computer operations and a general tightening of all security measures to ensure adequate protection of property and safety of personnel.

Top management in the private sector and in municipalities and their police departments must take a more realistic look at their protection programs. There is no reason to believe that crimes in the nation will decline appreciably in the next few years. Certainly there is no expectation that crimes against persons will decline in the near future.

With these conditions in mind and in view of the apparent need for more information in developing security programs for specific installations, personnel protection, and the like, I have assembled, in this book, detailed information that will assist individuals in better discharging their security responsibilities.

The need for tighter security on our college campuses, in our high schools, and in our grade schools has increased dramatically in the past couple of years. There is hardly a school district in the nation that has not been plagued with costly vandalism inflicted by the student population and outsiders. Therefore, I have included a chapter that discusses numerous changes in design, material used in building construction, and organization of the complexes' parking lots, sidewalks and athletic fields, which will in many cases deter vandalism or otherwise decrease the cost of damage repair caused by vandals.

To write about or discuss physical security without including a discussion of the basic principles is quite impossible, because these principles apply in all situations to some degree. They are merely tailored to provide the degree of security required in each situation. It is therefore impossible to write a book such as this without discussing these principles and their application in the overall security plan.

I wish to thank all my associates and good friends in the private security industry and police department crime prevention units for encouraging me to undertake this project so that this material can be shared with all who have the responsibility for protecting property, lives, and assets.

Special thanks to my wife, Carolyn, for her inspiration, dedication, and confidence in me. My appreciation also to the many persons and companies who have so generously provided the photographs that appear throughout this book and to Eddie Hamilton, retired fire chief, Memphis, Tennessee, for his assistance with the material in Chapter 10. Thanks also to Caril Magdefrau for contributing his talent in the field of closed-circuit television systems.

Finally, my most sincere appreciation to Kathie Wilson, who, I believe, sometimes neglected her family to spend long hours at her typewriter to complete the manuscript.

Walter M. Strobl

Contents

FOREWORD   v

PREFACE   vii

1
EVALUATING THE SECURITY REQUIREMENTS   1

2
DEFINING AND ANALYZING EXISTING HAZARDS   4

3
SECURING THE FACILITY'S PERIMETER   25

4
SECURITY OF OPEN AREAS   45

5
ILLUMINATION IN THE PROTECTIVE PLAN   53

6
INDUSTRIAL BUILDING SECURITY   70

7
DOCK, WAREHOUSE, AND CARGO SECURITY   93

8
LOCK IDENTIFICATION, KEY SYSTEMS, AND KEY CONTROL   111

9
IDENTIFICATION AND CONTROL
OF PERSONNEL AND VEHICLES   147

10
THE FIRE PROTECTION PLAN   175

11
SECURITY THROUGH ELECTRONICS   214

12
SURVEILLANCE THROUGH CLOSED
CIRCUIT TELEVISION SYSTEMS   237

13
PHYSICAL SECURITY OF A COMPUTER AREA   256

14
HIGH-RISE BUILDING SECURITY   269

15
HOSPITAL AND HEALTH CARE SECURITY   286

16
BANK AND FINANCIAL INSTITUTION SECURITY   312

17
THE RETAIL INDUSTRY PROTECTION PLAN   331

18
REDUCING VULNERABILITY
OF THE CONSTRUCTION SITE TO THEFTS   356

19
INDIVIDUAL AND GROUP THEFT CONTROLS   365

20
MINIMIZE THE BOMB THREAT—PLAN AHEAD   379

21
THE EMERGENCY CONTROL PLAN   388

22
THE EMPLOYEE SECURITY EDUCATION PROGRAM   399

23
DESIGN TO REDUCE SCHOOL PROPERTY LOSS   403

24
THE EXECUTIVE PROTECTION PLAN   414

BIBLIOGRAPHY   419

INDEX   425

1
Evaluating
the Security Requirements

To establish an economical, workable, and effective security program at any type of facility requires first that an in-depth study of the facility be conducted. This study must then be analyzed and a determination made of the degree of security that is required for the protection of property, lives, and assets.

It is not difficult to determine whether protection of property and assets must be increased. High losses and depressed profits indicate that either internal or external thefts are being committed or perhaps a combination of both. In order to reduce these losses and increase the organization's profits, it is essential that a security study be conducted.

Depending on the type of commodity being handled, the high public visibility of the organization, and the notoriety that chief executives may be creating for whatever reason, protecting the life safety of management personnel and their families may become increasingly more important. The fact that the company may have multinational operations adds to the possibility of attempted attacks and most certainly tends to make assets more vulnerable.

Initially, a number of assessments must be considered in developing an overall security program. Generally, those assessments fall into ten basic categories.

1. Surrounding terrain. This is of particular importance when the facility is located in suburban or rural areas, where special precautions must be taken or where existing conditions may be used to the advantage of the security planner. If the surrounding terrain is unlikely to affect the overall protection of the facility, then disregard it. However, in most instances, particularly in the industrial sector, surrounding terrain will present the security planner with areas that require special treatment.

2. Economic status of the area. This requires careful study, particularly in urban areas where crime rates are high. In these areas, unemployment, inadequate education, and other unstable conditions are likely to result in overt or covert attacks against the facility being protected.

3. Sociological conditions and psychological outlook. Unfavorable social conditions and psychological outlook of the surrounding community can present special problems and may already have had some effect on existing

operations, because local residents probably are a substantial part of the work force. When planning new construction, site-selection teams must fairly evaluate sociological and psychological conditions, because they will have a definite bearing on the security of future operations. Therefore, any organization planning construction of a facility at a new location would be well advised to include a security representative as a member of the site-selection team.

4. Labor conditions. Labor conditions in the community as well as conditions in established facilities may well dictate the degree of security that will be acceptable. Planners must give consideration to employee-management relations, union agreements, and the severity of violence that may have occurred in past labor disputes. Perhaps now is the time to effect greater protection for the transformer banks, gas metering equipment, or other critical equipment that suffered physical damage in past disputes because of the vulnerability of its location.

5. Location of fire and police departments. The size and proficiency of these departments and the response time when summoned will certainly influence the security plan. For example, if the fire department is made up entirely of volunteers, surely the fire-protection plan of the facility will need to be strengthened by an increase in manpower, by better training, and, in all probability, by the purchase of fire-fighting equipment that ordinarily would not be required.

6. Operational flow plan. The operational flow plan and the number and category of employees will certainly have an effect on the overall plan. The study of this area must consider density of employee population in the various departments or on various floors. Consideration should also be given to the rate of annual employee turnover in all categories; administrative, hourly, technical, supervisory, and so forth. Any contemplated changes in employee strength usually attributed to seasonal production and the effect of these changes in population density throughout areas is of equal importance. The number of employees on each operational shift and shift-change times must be studied. These conditions will almost always have an effect on the parking plan and the location and number of authorized employee entrances. One can easily see that the size and deployment of the security force may well be determined by this one item alone.

7. Criticality and vulnerability. By criticality we mean the importance of certain functions to the continued successful operation of the organization and the vulnerability of these functions to successful attack. An example might be a computer operation located at ground level on the periphery of the building with expansive plate glass areas that expose the operation unnecessarily. The computer operation is critical, and the location makes the operation quite vulnerable to attack. This type condition may require protecting the window openings or moving the entire operation elsewhere.

8. Natural phenomena. The vulnerability of the facility to damage or destruction by natural phenomena must always be considered, particularly

by those who are selecting sites for new construction. This part of the study will require securing past weather data from the government weather service and local chambers of commerce. Studies of topographical maps are a must when the facility is located in suburban areas. United States Army Engineers can offer much assistance in this area relative to drainage conditions and past flooding conditions. A small stream near an industrial park may become a raging torrent when hurricanes or heavy rains occur. The possibility of such phenomena as tornadoes, hurricanes, earthquakes, and even heavy snows will surely require special training for emergency squads of employees and the security force. An evacuation plan will have to be set up, and special equipment may have to be purchased. Weather conditions will have a direct effect on any plans being formulated. We shall discuss later the effects of heat, cold, and darkness in creating favorable climates for the perpetration of thefts and other crimes against people and property.

9. <u>Vulnerability to theft and pilferage</u>. The security of all entrances to property and buildings and control of personnel and vehicles fall into this category. In a given facility, the product being manufactured and its susceptibility to easy removal, personal use, or quick resale will always dictate the degree of security that must be developed in quality-control operations and in areas where the finished product is stored and displayed.

10. <u>Manpower requirements</u>. Finally, the actual manpower that will be required to execute the security plan that has been formulated will have to be determined. The following items must be considered: (a) the economy of the overall program; (b) the legal aspects of certain restrictions; (c) the effect of the new or revised restrictions on employee morale; and (d) the calculated risk that management is willing to accept in lieu of obtaining maximum security as determined by the study.

After all of the above conditions have been studied, data accumulated, and the analysis of each condition made, how the program will be implemented must be decided upon. Certainly it is human nature to resist changes, particularly when such changes may cause some inconveniences heretofore not encountered. The security planner must, therefore, attempt to anticipate the problems and find means to incorporate the program into the overall operational procedures of the facility so that it is at least reasonably acceptable to the majority of the population affected by it.

The success of the security program is related directly to the employee educational program, which should be started well in advance of inaugurating any changes. The informed employee is a more satisfied, cooperative person. If management is in tune with the spirit of the program, acceptance by the employee is that much more assured.

2

Defining
and Analyzing
Existing Hazards

The first step in any study is to determine what is to be accomplished, what present conditions are, and how these conditions can be altered to best satisfy requirements.

The same is true of the security study—or survey, as it is normally referred to. However, before starting this study, the surveyor must be able to identify those obstacles, including those that may surface later, that will have to be overcome. The obstacles are security hazards. The degree of danger these security hazards present will depend on numerous factors that are usually grouped under two general terms: criticality and vulnerability.

What, then, is a security hazard, regardless of the type facility or area being surveyed? By definition, the hazard is any act, omission, or condition which would seriously impede continuous successful operations, cause the loss of assets, compromise proprietary information or cause loss of life or serious injury to personnel—either employees or others temporarily on company property.

Industrial complexes, for example, are often the target of attack merely because of the product they manufacture, or the computer complex is attacked merely because of the information stored that pertains to persons. It is likely that attacks will soon be attempted against computer operations involved in the National Crime Information Centers, not necessarily to destroy records, but perhaps to secure information on individuals that would be used for extortion or perhaps merely to distort factual information.

It is a proved fact that it is far more economical to deter or attempt in some manner to prevent illegal and unsafe acts from occurring than it is to apprehend and prosecute individuals after the acts have been committed. Furthermore, it is also a fact that the employee, regardless of his or her rank or category, who feels secure in his or her position, both physically and financially, is a more productive and accurate worker. One must also consider that embarrassing or undesirable notoriety caused by the peers of the employees have a direct effect on the morale of the employees as a group, even though they may not be directly involved.

4

It is often not possible to eliminate all hazards to security for numerous reasons, but usually because management considers the reduction unwise or unjustifiable economically or because the restrictions on movement of personnel or material would impede operational efficiency and cause the loss of time and money. When this occurs, calculations of the risks involved must be defined, and management will then have to decide the degree of risk it is willing to assume.

One cannot discuss the major hazards to security without examining in some detail the human element. Until quite recently, this aspect of security was concerned almost entirely with the illegal actions of employees alone or in concert with outsiders and fell into the category of "natural hazards" that will always exist to some degree. We now must expand the human category to include the "bomber," the "extortionist," the "kidnapper," the "assassin," and the "terrorist."

NATURAL HAZARDS

Actually, the natural hazards to security are nothing more than acts of nature or natural phenomena that occur and are usually peculiar to a particular area. Weathermen will refer to regions in the United States as the "Hail Belt" or "Tornado Alley," and certain geographical locations are more apt than others to have earthquakes. All of the natural hazards present their own peculiar problems, some more frequent and more severe than others.

Site-selection teams for construction of new facilities or major expansion at present locations must be clearly aware of the local destructive phenomena that could occur. In California, for example, building codes in many localities include specific design to reduce damage should an earthquake occur.

There is little that individuals or groups can do while some of these phenomena—for example, an earthquake—are occurring. The loss of lives and property, however, can be minimized by prior planning, including the preparation of written plans that are tested and updated regularly. There is much that can be accomplished in reducing damage due to natural hazards if the security plan includes a well-organized, trained, and supervised security force whose effectiveness can be measured only by their involvement in the overall disaster or emergency plans that have been formulated.

Natural hazards most often discussed are the following: heat, cold, darkness (these three being by far the most common and troublesome), fires, explosions, floods, hurricanes, tornadoes, and earthquakes. Other less frequently discussed destructive phenomena include hail, ice storms, and the occurrence of "pot holes" in some sections of the country. The largest "pot holes" occur when the surface of the earth caves in as a result of subterranean erosion, the work of underground rivers. However, such occurrences are unpredictable and infrequent, and so the security analysis rarely, if ever, considers them.

Darkness

It is an old adage that thieves do not like to "work" during the hours of daylight or in areas that are sufficiently illuminated to expose their illegal activity to observation.

Because periods of darkness occur regularly during every 24-hour period with a predictable by-the-minute increase or decrease in duration, the surveyor must be ever mindful of this occurrence. Not only is the engineering and installation of the interior and exterior protective lighting system directly affected, but equally involved are closed circuit television systems, foot and motorized patrols, location of truck parks inside the perimeter, and practically every other item or condition that will be examined in determining and planning the security requirements for any facility.

Although a properly engineered protective lighting system will eliminate many of the hazards that exist, during the hours of darkness one cannot rely entirely upon the system alone. Remember that every physical device designed to increase protection has a certain vulnerability to being defeated. The power lines serving the lighting system and each individual luminaire or group of luminaires are highly vulnerable to successful attack by the very nature of their location. Therefore, the defense of the entire system must be planned in depth. For example, the effectiveness of the chain-link-type perimeter barrier at any facility is immediately reduced when darkness occurs unless it is adequately illuminated. Also, peripheral lighting equipment is extremely vulnerable, and this vulnerability is increased if there is no chain link fence to protect it. Therefore, one technique or device to establish physical security at a facility is compatible with one another, and one will directly affect the effectiveness of another.

The following incident will give you some appreciation for the immense problems that darkness can cause. Recently, I was involved in planning security protection during the construction phase of the trans-Alaska oil pipeline. I had an assistant fly to the Prudoe Bay area installations in the month of January to carry out various tasks, including photographing a typical installation and some typical terrain. The photography part of the mission was a complete flop because during that time of year the area is in almost total darkness 24 hours per day, and only 1 day was scheduled for completion of the mission.

Heat

These hazards to security, like darkness, will vary in severity and duration depending upon the geographical location of the facility to be protected. Protection against the effects of heat, including the high temperatures that result from some manufacturing processes, require that adequate natural ventilation or some other cooling system be planned during construction, especially for areas where high temperatures are likely. When employees become uncomfortable in the work areas, they or management will open windows, doors, and other peripheral openings to reduce this discomfort.

It is obvious that when this occurs the probability of incidents of pilferage and thefts will rise. Not only is one faced with a rise in losses, but the unprotected openings become invitations for the outside intruder to enter without even needing to use force. Therefore, when these conditions do exist, it is imperative that the openings be further secured by screens, metal bars, or chain link fencing. It should be kept in mind, of course, that if any of these openings are intended as exits in emergency situations, the protective coverings must have the capability of being quickly removed from within the building. I shall have more to say on this subject in Chapter 6, which deals with building security.

I recall conducting a survey of a manufacturing plant that produced small kitchen appliances; coffee pots, blenders, cooking utensils, and the like. These items had a personal use and quick resale value when stolen, and stolen they were. The survey revealed excellent employee control as well as control of others who were authorized from time to time to be in the production and warehouse areas. Doors were well secured and were protected by alarms where necessary. Controls in the warehouse and on the shipping docks were satisfactory. Outwardly, it appeared that existing physical security was adequate.

The personnel manager of the facility was also responsible for security. The losses continued, and he was stymied. However, our detailed survey uncovered two areas through which losses of the finished products were occurring.

1. Trash was being removed from the facility with a $1\frac{1}{2}$-ton stake-body, company-owned truck driven by a company employee who exited the protected area through an unguarded gate and dumped the refuse on company land about 400 yards from the plant. The company dump was unprotected, and it was evident that both vehicles and persons on foot were entering the dump from a nearby county road.

2. Ventilation was furnished for the entire production area by open windows on the south side of the building, and the windows were adequately protected by chain link screens. On the north side, installed near the floor was a series of electric fans that were also covered with an adequate heavy-guage metal screen on both sides to prevent injury to personnel. This screen, however, was installed on the metal frame surrounding the fan, rather than permanently secured to the building walls. There were no third-shift operations, and during this time we examined each of some two dozen fans and found that three nearest the quality control area could easily be removed, leaving an opening about 2 feet in diameter.

We placed two undercover agents in the plant, one near the quality control area, the other as outside grounds maintenance man. As we suspected,
within a week they verified that four employees in production and quality
control were passing appliances through the openings after the fans were
removed and that driver of the company trash truck was picking them up
and placing them at the trash dump where he and/or the others would
recover them after darkness. Needless to say, the security plan was
considerably altered in numerous areas.

Cold

Although a definite hazard that must be studied, cold does not present the
surveyor with as great a number of possible problems as heat. Here again
the severity of possible problems can be measured only by the type and
geographical location of the facility being protected.

The primary hazard emerges from the heavier outer garments that are
worn by personnel authorized in the protected area. Obviously, this additional clothing (and additional pockets) increases the opportunity to hide
items from the exit guards because seldom do conditions allow complete
"shake downs," or body searches, if you will. We discuss searches in
detail in Chapter 19 and examine some electronic devices that may be used
for this purpose.

Cold weather also increases the possible loss of assets through the
higher exposure to fires because heating systems, boilers, individual
electrical heaters, and, in all probability, many more electrical coffee
pots are being used. A malfunction of the heating system can be damaging
if it overheats and causes fires or if it fails to function and causes water
pipes, including automatic wet sprinkler systems to freeze.

During freezing weather, employee absenteeism always increases, and
roadways, stairs, and walkways within the protected area become more
dangerous to use and are more likely to cause injury and/or accidents
involving personnel and vehicles.

Fires and Explosions

Fires and explosions, although classified under natural hazards, are
closely linked to human hazards and indeed often are the result of carelessness or ignorance on the part of individuals.

A great percentage of fire losses sustained by industry are the result of
storms, floods, or other natural hazards that occur and for which no plan
of combat or remedy exists. The lack of such a plan or the failure of
individuals to act in time and correctly often results in the greatest losses.

Fires and explosions that occur together, though still a threat, have
been substantially reduced in recent years as the result of new mandatory
safety measures established by the Occupation Safety and Health Act. Also
contributing to this reduction are the more frequent, detailed, and probably
more professional inspections.

The subject of reduction of fires through fire protection and preventive inspections is covered in greater detail in Chapter 10. However, those readers who are specifically charged with fire protection and prevention and who do not have expertise in this area or who are not familiar with requirements should secure two sets of books from the National Fire Protection Association (470 Atlantic Avenue, Boston, MA 02210). One set is known as the National Fire Codes and consists of 15 volumes. The other set referred to is entitled "Guide to OSHA Fire Protection Regulations" and consists of five volumes. These codes and regulations should be a part of every security manager's library. Familiarity with local fire codes obviously is a must. Local fire department inspectors are usually available to offer their expert assistance.

Floods, Tornadoes, Hurricanes, and Earthquakes

These natural phenomena are referred to in the profession as "acts of God." Although their occurrence and magnitude can quite accurately be forecast, with the possible exception of earthquakes, there is no control over them, and should they occur, one must take the corrective action that hopefully has been preplanned. Flooding, in spite of present-day controls, still can and does occur in some sections of the nation. If the possibility of flooding exists, the overall protection plan is not complete unless it includes action to be initiated when such flooding occurs.

Tornadoes present a greater danger than hurricanes, because they are spontaneous and cannot be as accurately forecast. When weather conditions exist that are likely to spawn tornadoes and the weather service has issued warnings, employees and other personnel in the buildings should be notified. This is particularly true if the local security plan includes evacuation of personnel to shelters or more secure areas within the structure where they are working. Often building occupants are not aware of weather conditions because of their location within the building or the absence of windows. Keeping people informed of existing conditions will perhaps unconsciously prepare employees psychologically should evacuation be required. It will at least cause them to think of the "plan"—shut down the machine, close the gas valve, secure the fire door, or take any other required action which, if accomplished properly, will minimize loss of life and property.

HUMAN HAZARDS

In discussing security hazards in the past, most experts discussed the category of human hazards first. This, I think, was because security personnel have always felt that those unfavorable and illegal incidents that occurred and had to be dealt with more frequently usually involved employees acting either alone or in groups, or in conjunction with noncompany employees who were authorized within the protected area; any or all of those individuals involved would probably remove, or play a part in the removal of, property being stolen.

The attitude of certain employees also presented problems when they became disgruntled for any number of reasons and deliberately caused the loss of, or damage to, company assets. After World War II, the possibility of espionage and sabotage was almost forgotten. Conditions have drastically changed in the last couple of years, and now we are faced with the possibility of kidnappings of executive personnel, receipt of letter bombs through the government mails, threats upon the lives of families of executives and employees alike unless an extortionist demands are met, and numerous other crimes to be discussed later in this chapter.

Whatever turn these latest attacks upon private industry and public service departments take, whether they increase, decrease, or disappear mysteriously, security personnel will still be faced first and foremost with the problems and crimes perpetrated by the employee and his or her fellow conspirator.

Human hazards are usually considered to be pilferage, theft, careless-ness, disloyalty, dissatisfaction, sabotage, and espionage. Although these will be discussed, they will be covered rather generally because in most instances they can be effectively dealt with by means of electronic aids, closed circuit television, and the security techniques discussed in later chapters. Depending upon each local situation and the degree of security in effect, these hazards can usually be eliminated entirely.

Because the hazards just listed are perpetrated within the area being secured, it is most always advisable to employ one or more undercover agents in the initial effort to overcome these hazards. Information supplied by the undercover agent will usually result in pinpointing the individual or individuals and the area or areas where illegal acts are being committed. It is well established that the use of undercover investigators, although they will usually be contracted for from an outside source, is the most economical and efficient method to employ to eradicate or bring under control internal stealing, accidents, damage to property, drinking on the job, or any other type of activity that causes or is likely to cause loss of assets.

Pilferage and Theft

Pilferage and thefts are the most annoying incidents for the security manager. In addition, these illegal acts often are the most costly to private industry, whether the facility is a department store, a supermarket, an industrial plant, or high-rise office building.

The Casual Pilferer. The pilferer can be categorized into two groups: the casual and systematic pilferer. The casual pilferer, as the name implies, steals when the opportunity presents itself, and when he or she can be reasonably certain of not being detected. The pilferer's conviction that his or her action will go undetected is an important condition and should always be kept in mind by supervisors, department heads, and others responsible for the actions of people and the security of property. Remember—the casual pilferer steals only on occasions and not on a regular basis. Therefore, if the temptation is removed, in all probability a basically honest person will remain honest. I experimented once by leaving an expensive pair of garden pruners (my own) at a truck dock and then wagering that they would be stolen before I completed that particular survey. They disappeared within the first 3 hours and were never recovered. The size of my wager, however, covered the cost of replacement of the pruners.

The Systematic Pilferer. Although control of the casual pilferer can be effectively established with comparative ease, the systematic pilferer is another breed of thief. Obviously, this individual has developed a system. He or she has organized several people inside and outside the facility into a cohesive unit usually referred to as "a ring." Ali Baba was a fortunate man, indeed, in that he had only 40 thieves to contend with, all of whom were known to him.

On occasion, the systematic pilferer may work alone at the scene of the thefts. However, these are rare occasions, because the objective of this type of thief is the accumulation of wealth for one reason or another, and this dictates that large quantities of goods be removed in short periods of time.

How does one determine the amount of losses being suffered? Usually through an annual inventory long after the loss. There are other methods to determine the extent of losses or even if they are occurring. One, and probably the most effective and economical is employing the undercover agent, male or female depending upon existing conditions. The second method is to watch for warning signals. Detailed inspections by security personnel, particularly security supervisory personnel, will detect abnormal conditions or activities that are overlooked by employee supervisors.

These warning signals may take numerous forms depending upon the type of facility. These signals, or deviations from the norm, may take the form of unlocked doors that should be locked, alarm systems that have been tampered with, files that are missing or documents that have been altered, frequent carton or container damage, excessive mileage recorded on interplant company vehicles, and hundreds of other indicators. Many more of these warning signs will be covered in Chapter 19 in a great deal of detail.

The systematic pilferer is a clever fellow, and his plans often call for changes in his modus operandi to relieve pressure or to divert suspicion from his group. Some plan their strategy well and will create incidents to throw suspicion on innocent parties.

A large appliance wholesaler was losing an alarming number of items as determined by an annual inventory. An undercover investigator, working as an order picker and truck loader, quickly learned that an employee with

some 20 years service with the plant was placing small appliances, particularly portable color TV sets, inside chest-type freezers that were to be
delivered to a distributor some 600 miles from the wholesaler. The pilferer
used two employees to assist him (one, the undercover agent). However,
none of the truck drivers, who were employed by common carriers, knew
they were part of the scheme being used.

The methods used to remove stolen property from a facility successfully
are too numerous to attempt to tabulate. Chapter 19, however, lists in
detail the most common ones used in various types of industry. One must
remember that the most effective methods used to prevent pilferage today
may need to be altered in the future. Successful thieves are resourceful
and often ingenious in their planning and will not hesitate to remove a large
quantity of items or material and then stop completely for a few weeks or
even months, if necessary; they can usually well afford a "vacation."

Carelessness

Carelessness of an employee or employees can create as great a security
risk as employing a known thief. Injuries to personnel directly affect losses;
however, carelessness in leaving doors unlocked, leaving truck seals exposed
instead of secured, leaving item or carton count up to the truck driver, and
failures properly to perform assigned functions of this nature soon are discovered, particularly by the systematic pilferer, and these careless practices soon are incorporated into the pilferer's permanent plans. The best
remedy for carelessness insofar as security is concerned is a well-planned
and executed security education program. This program should receive at
least the same attention as the safety program, using posters and other
visual material, and possibly even more attention.

Disloyalty and Dissatisfaction

Disloyalty and dissatisfaction of employees are closely related. Dissatisfaction is often only temporary and usually occurs because an employee is
disgruntled over being disciplined, having his or her vacation changed, or
being given some assignment, if only for a time, that he or she does not
like. The dissatisfied employee, although posing a threat to security, can
usually be easily identified by changes in attitude and normal facial expressions or even by a deterioration in productivity.

Dissatisfaction can be avoided if supervisory personnel are familiar with
their employee's personality, attitude, character, and, to some extent,
their private lives. However, if a situation cannot be avoided and if the
employee becomes a hazard to the facility and himself, he should be coun-
seled immediately and the unfavorable situation corrected or eliminated as
soon as possible.

Disloyalty, on the other hand, is an attitude developed by an employee
that normally is the result of actions he or she feels are unjust, although

not necessarily directed against him or her personally. This attitude will last longer and in all probability will become worse until resentment can no longer be retained and it surfaces in the form of violence, sabotage of equipment, thefts of material, and other physical actions against the employer. These situations will require expert counseling if the employee is to be retained or immediate discharge if illegal acts have already been committed.

Sabotage and Espionage

If the overall security of the facility has been properly planned and the plan is executed by a highly motivated and well-trained security force, sabotage by nonemployees can be effectively controlled. However, even if an adequate perimeter barrier is constructed and if illumination of the barrier and inside areas has been properly engineered, poorly planned control of personnel and vehicles at gate locations, with no positive identification system and with untrained or poorly motivated security officers manning the gates, the possibility of sabotage committed by outsiders is greatly increased. One need only visualize such a situation to understand the need for integrating all phases of the security plan into one cohesive protective program, assuring that at every point and area the degree of security required is established and is being maintained.

Granting, then, that the greatest vulnerability to sabotage is the employee, the need to eliminate disloyalty and dissatisfaction assumes greater proportions. Incidentally, the word "sabotage" was coined in France during World War I when industrial workers still wearing wooden shoes called sabots would accidentally drop their shoes into machinery and other manufacturing processes to stop or slow down production. These individuals came to be known as saboteurs and were motivated by personal grudges against the company or individuals or by disagreement with the national policy. Sometimes they were paid by foreign agents to commit specific acts of sabotage.

A great deal of the sabotage committed today will precede labor negotiations or will occur during labor disputes and strikes. Later chapters will discuss in greater detail the need for increased protection and incorporation of special procedures during times of stress or disaffection between management and workers, whether it is imaginary or not.

Espionage, on the other hand, is less likely to occur and almost always involves "outsiders." Most acts of espionage committed or discovered today probably involve what is referred to as "industrial espionage" or the stealing of a company's proprietary information whether it is their general marketing plans or the development of a new product.

Unless company employees are a part of a conspiracy illegally to obtain this proprietary or secret information, espionage usually takes the form of agents applying for open positions that the company is seeking to fill via help-wanted ads. Because the information being sought may be kept in a

secure area, may be accessible only to certain employees, or may be so
technical that only an expert in the field could properly evaluate or even
recognize its importance, the agent must possess great skill and cunning.
His or her degree of success will be directly related to the company's
financial loss.

The security force can do little to combat this type of espionage agent,
because in all probability he or she will have become an employee with
authority to enter the protected area and often as not will have complete
freedom to enter any time he or she wishes. When personnel controls
include issuance of "access rosters" to the security force, they must be
updated as changes occur and strictly complied with by the controlling
security officers.

The only effective action that can be initiated to reduce the possibility
of an espionage agent's being employed is a thorough background investigation. The more sensitive the position being filled, the more thorough the
background must be checked. This subject will be discussed in detail in
Chapter 9.

THE MORE HEINOUS HAZARDS

The next couple of pages will be devoted to discussing crimes against
personnel and property that are not new by any means, but the frequency
with which they are now occurring dictates that security planners consider
the possibility that these crimes may be committed against the lives and
assets they are being paid to protect. The existing security plan may have
to be altered and tailored to include deterrents and actions to be taken
should any of the following incidents be likely to occur. Some security
managers will need to include preplanned actions covering all of the crimes
listed in the next few paragraphs. I have studied the list of crimes that
follow and have attempted to categorize them by importance or frequency
of occurrence or to put them in some other logical sequence. However,
the attempt has been futile primarily because certain industries, personnel,
or institutions may be more subject by one type of attack than another
depending on the type of facility or even on the amount and kind of current
publicity coverage. I therefore decided to use the public relations approach
and alphabetize them.

Arson

The International Association of Arson Investigators, meeting in Lincoln,
Nebraska, in April 1975, recommended that "the crime of arson" be included
as a Class I crime in the Federal Bureau of Investigation's Uniform Crime
Reporting System and urged that all law enforcement agencies with sufficient
personnel assign one or more properly trained members to arson investigations as their primary duty.

Arson in America causes the death and injury of thousands of persons and results in over $1 billion in property damage annually. Although arson is a violent and costly crime, the arsonist is not being apprehended and/or convicted at a rate comparable to the arson crime rate. Some sources believe only about 4.5 percent of the persons believed to have committed arson in the United States are arrested, and of those arrested, less than 1 percent are ever convicted. In 1975, arsonists destroyed a sponge rubber factory in Connecticut, which the Federal Bureau of Investigation described as "the most costly fire caused by arson that that agency had ever investigated." Fortunately, the arsonists were all arrested, and the majority of them convicted. At least 19 persons perished as a result of the Wincrest Nursing Home fire in Chicago, which police allege was started by a 21-year-old male on January 30, 1976.

The cause of this pyromania is not fully understood. Some psychoanalysts place emphasis on the pyromaniac's sexual needs, others, such as Dr. Peter Barglon of Northwestern University, places more emphasis on a quest for power. Whatever the cause, arson, often referred to as the "forgotten crime," continues to cause devastating losses. Consider the 19-year-old charged with starting the $2 million fire in the 110-story twin towers of the World Trade Center in New York City.

Apprehension of the arsonist is most often the result of police and fire investigators' studies of photographs of crowds that watch fires. Pyromaniacs almost always return to the scene of the fire and often never leave it. Some, in fact, may be hailed as heroes initially because they rushed into a burning structure and saved lives. All of this, of course, was pre-planned by the pyromaniac.

Again, the best defense against the arsonist is tight perimeter security, with equally tight controls at entrances and exits, and through background investigations of employees. Personnel assigned as security officers have not infrequently been apprehended and convicted of setting fire to the structures they are paid to protect.

If closed circuit television systems are in use at the facility, plans to video-tape crowds should a fire occur may prove useful in post fire investigations. Perhaps the fire plan discussed in Chapter 10 should include making still or movie cameras available to the security force with specific instructions relating to photographing crowds and other activities should a fire occur.

Assassination

The assassin will play a part in the security plans of far fewer security managers than will the arsonist. The assassin, however, is a real threat, particularly to public figures and executive personnel of multinational companies with operations overseas. Probably the areas most ripe for assassination attempts at this writing are the industrial South American countries. One need only read current news publications to keep abreast.

President Gerald Ford escaped two attempts on his life in 1975, with both intended assassins being apprehended, tried, convicted, and incarcerated. Just prior to the September 5, 1975, attempt to take President Ford's life, a Dow Chemical Company executive received a phone call at his home from a female who, after identifying herself as a member of the Charles Manson family, threatened his life.

Sandra Goode, a Manson disciple, gave the Associated Press in 1975 a list of 75 persons marked for death by the "International People's Court of Retribution." Two Dow employees' names were included in the list.

Certainly these incidents dictate that plans must be made to protect executives, public officials, and others well known nationally or internationally as well as their families. In addition, the after-the-fact action must be planned, and the everyday security of these personnel must be increased and changed, in all probability almost daily. We shall have more to say on this subject in Chapter 24.

Bombings

I can still recall the first bombing experience that affected my daily activities in 1961 when I was employed by a private security company. A so-called "bomber" had destroyed a couple of microwave towers in our national telephone system and had threatened "to blow up the entire system." Within a very short time practically every microwave tower in existence then was protected by armed guards on fixed posts or by armed patrols on a 24-hour-per-day, 7-day-per-week basis. About a week after the first bombing occurred, the bomber was apprehended aboard an armed yacht in the Gulf of Mexico.

The incidents of destruction by explosives and incendiary bombs today makes these crimes almost commonplace, and, unless it is an "exceptionally devastating attack," these incidents receive little publicity. Perhaps this lack of publicity aids in stopping these attacks, because in the majority of these attacks the real reason is to publicize some warped cause of equally warped individuals and groups.

To realize the potential danger and extent of these attacks, look at the facts. The director of the Treasury Department's Bureau of Alcohol, Tobacco, and Firearms told the Senate Judiciary Subcommittee on International Security in April 1976 that the total number of explosive bombings in the United States increased from 893 in 1974 to 1,313 in 1975. During the same period, deaths attributed to terrorist bombing jumped from 24 in 1974 to 69 in 1975, with property damage almost tripling from $10 million to $27 million. Director Rex D. Davis added, "In the past politically motivated activists using terror tactics tried to avoid loss of life, but now are changing these tactics believing that property attacks are not enough." Davis also indicated that because of this change in attitudes toward avoiding deaths, the number of victims can be expected to rise.

In June 1975, the postal service reported that there had been 15 bomb mailings in the United States during the preceding 12-month period compared with 11 during the previous year. During June 1976, perhaps more than 200 bomb mailings occurred within a 30-day period. Electronic devices available to screen mail in mail rooms in the private sectors should be considered even though the postal service has increased its vigilance in this area. The examination of packages, envelopes, and cartons should be extended to include <u>outside deliveries</u>. It is simple and convenient for a bomber to purchase an item of appropriate size locally, open the package carefully, and, after inserting the explosive device, have it delivered to the intended target.

An executive at a cocktail party was overheard telling a friend that he had the "bombs-by-mail" threat solved. When asked how, he replied he had his assistant open all his mail in an outer office. He overlooked the fact that good assistants are scarce and difficult to get.

A great deal of planning is required to devise an effective bomb-threat plan, keeping in mind that the more information that can be assembled for investigators, the greater chances for success in apprehending the individual or individuals concerned. The subject requires detailed discussion, and an entire chapter, Chapter 20, is devoted to this hazard.

Embezzlement

Embezzlement in 90 percent of the cases is committed by employees. Often these employees are highly paid officials of the organization and long-term, previously faithful employees. However, there is always "the 10 percent that don't get the word." Take, for example, the electronics student who, by tricking the Pacific Telephone Company computers into making available to him a fortune in communication equipment, made himself a teenage tycoon. He is now repaying the company for their losses at $141.50 per month for 5 years. He accomplished this embezzlement merely by clever manipulation of a pushbutton telephone.

Embezzlement and its detection should really be the responsibility of the company financial or auditing department assisted by the security director or security head. Because the crime usually involves manipulation of financial books and figures, the security plan should include recommendations to management that consideration be given to employing internal auditors in whatever strength is required. Do not overlook the fact that alert management familiar with signals that warn of internal dishonesty will greatly reduce the possibility that embezzlement will occur. Suspected cases should be quickly and thoroughly investigated, sudden changes in an employee's lifestyle for the better should come under close scrutiny; recently deceased "rich uncles" who leave legacies to employees should have not only their death confirmed but their financial status as well.

Extortion

Extortion is attempted or accomplished in numerous ways. It may be
committed by obtaining money or information through coercion or intimidation or by using one's official position or power to obtain property, funds,
or patronage to which one is not entitled. However, it also will include
kidnapping or taking hostages if necessary in order to obtain the extortionist's goal.

My local newspaper dated June 24, 1976, contained an article headlined
"Three Youths Sentenced for Extortion Robbery." The three young men,
two aged 16 and one aged 17, were charged and convicted of either extorting
or robbing fellow school students of money. Four other youths were involved
in the same school, but they were fortunate enough to have the original
charge amended to a lesser offense.

In the fall of 1975 several utility companies received letters threatening
murder of company employees unless substantial amounts of money were
paid. These extortionists worded their letters in such a manner that the
threat could be implied to be meant for all employees. It would be practically impossible to protect all employees of an organization receiving
such a threat. What action should be taken if extortion letters or verbal
threats are received? Presume that all threats are genuine, secure as
much information from and about the caller as possible, and notify local
and federal law enforcement immediately. The attempt may be a segment
of a larger conspiracy, and your information may furnish just the information that is necessary to effect arrests.

Again, preplanning must be accomplished. The plans must be updated
as required, and close liaison with local law enforcement officials should
be developed and maintained. Their advice and guidance should be followed
in formulating the plans and certainly must be adhered to should such an
incident occur.

Fraud

Fraud is a crime very closely related to embezzlement, but it is not
necessarily perpetrated by an employee. To the contrary, fraud is committed by deliberate deception in order to secure unlawful gain. Fraud is
accomplished through swindle and trickery by an imposter.

The "pigeon drop scheme" used to bilk money from the elderly and innocent is a form of fraud. This scheme involves "finding" money or other
valuables, showing them to a person, and telling him or her that they can
share the "find" if they can put up earnest money. The fraud is accomplished
by switching the money and giving the victim worthless paper or merely
disappearing, once the earnest money has been received.

Fortunately, security personnel seldom become involved in investigating
fraudulent schemes. However, they should be aware that such schemes can
occur. Security educational programs should definitely include a reminder

that employees can be the subject of fraudulent schemes at work or away from work. Security personnel should be ever mindful that fraudulent schemes could possibly be perpetrated at the facility being protected by personnel authorized to be within the facility. Claims of "good buys" and "easy money" heard during employee discussions should be investigated. Investigation may even lead to uncovering theft rings within the facility.

To assist in reducing the possibility of fraud through the use of official stationery, the security director must ensure that the organization's letterhead stationery is secured. Possibly, a unique type of stationery for executive use should be considered.

Hostages and Kidnapping

Almost any or all of the crimes just listed may include kidnapping or the taking of hostages. Kidnappings usually are planned and deliberate, whereas the taking of hostages may be spontaneous because the criminal has lost the advantage. However, hostages may be selected because of their sex or social prominence. Women have historically been taken as hostages because they are less likely to present a physical threat to their captors. In addition, the cultural assumption that women, and especially children, need to be protected at all cost reduces the likelihood that any assault that may harm the hostages would be attempted if female hostages were taken.

Rarely will the security manager in private industry play a role in incidents involving the taking of hostages. If the property being protected is successfully penetrated and hostages are taken, local police should be notified and given complete control of the situation. Negotiating successful release of hostages requires specialized training. The New York Police Department has organized a hostage negotiation team, now being used as a model by several other departments. Historically, hostages have been taken in larger municipalities where trained police assistance is available.

One need only remember the Munich Olympic killings in 1972 to realize the intensity and impact upon the whole world that the act of hostage taking can create. My best advice is, where hostages are concerned, notify the police.

The taking of a person hostage by an individual in the course of a robbery is quite another situation, and plans to cope with this type situation are covered in Chapter 16.

Kidnapping is more likely to involve the security manager than is hostage-taking, and almost weekly some business executive or a member of his or her family is abducted and held for ransom. The abduction in almost all instances includes the threat to kill the victim if demands are not met. Demands, in this country at least, usually involve cash ransom payments. Kidnappers in Italy, the country with the highest abduction rate in the world, have been motivated to act merely because of increases in the retail price of beef—and if that is not good enough reason, the retail price of chicken will do.

On September 26, 1975, the body of a furniture executive was discovered in a wooded area on the outskirts of Dayton, Ohio, <u>after</u> the family paid a $400,000 ransom. The victim had been shot in the back several times. The crime involved, among others, a 41-year-old <u>former</u> <u>employee</u> who led the Federal Bureau of Investigation to the body.

The 27-year-old son of an executive of a trucking firm in Washington, D.C. was more fortunate. He was released after 5 days' captivity in January 1976 after a six-figure ransom had been paid.

The incidents above are proof enough that practically anyone with the resources to be "bailed out of abduction" could very well be the target of a kidnapper and that this crime is more likely to occur today than is any of the others discussed earlier. Chapter 24, which deals with executive protection, contains a great deal of information that will assist in developing a plan to deter kidnapping and in furnishing timely information to law enforcement authorities and the security director should an abduction actually occur.

Robbery

A robbery generally takes place during working hours or immediately before or immediately after working hours. Usually robbers are looking for money or small valuables such as jewelry, narcotics, or other things that they can easily carry with them and that will either be of use to them personally or can be quickly converted into cash. Most robberies take only a few minutes.

In the order of magnitude of ordinary crimes, robbery represents the smallest monetary loss. It falls significantly below shoplifting, employee theft, frauds, and burglary. However, the one outstanding factor about robbery is the personal danger to those that are involved, because they are likely to face violence, especially when the robber is armed, which is 95 percent of the times.

Almost universally, police departments advise that the robbery victim should not antagonize the robber. If a robbery occurs, the best thing that can be done is to cooperate fully with the robber's demands. At the same time, however, mental notes must be taken by all individuals involved relating to the robbery, the physical appearance of the robber, and any other information that will be of value to the police in their investigation.

General Measures to Prevent Robbery. It must be remembered that robbers are very observant. They are always looking for an easy, convenient victim. Such things as poor housekeeping and casual cash-handling methods will attract a robber's attention. Some businesspeople show a complete lack of concern because they think no one would ever rob their business. Always be prepared and have a plan devised for action to take in the event a robbery should occur. All it takes to prepare such a plan is a little time, a little common sense, and some action. The greater the deterrent action taken by a business, the greater the possibility that that particular business will not attract the robber. Following is a list of some things that can be done and other things that should not be done in order to deter robberies:

1. Keep the interior, and especially the front and rear entrances that can be seen from outside the building, well lighted.
2. Restrict the amount of advertising and merchandise displayed in the windows. Always keep the windows unobstructed so that a clear view of the inside of the building is possible.
3. Keep all doors that are not in operational use secured with good locking devices at all times.
4. Be certain that any alarms installed are in working order at all times.
5. If you plan to visit the place of business after normal business hours, notify the local police precinct.
6. Always be on the alert for "till tapping." This will usually involve two people. One distracts the cashier's attention while the other steals the money from the open cash register.
7. Keep checks separate from cash, even when making bank deposits.
8. Always keep some marked decoy currency in the cash register that can be given to a robber should a robbery occur. Record the denominations, serial numbers, and the series of these bills.
9. Avoid following easily observed routine procedures in the cash-handling operations, either inside the store or when deposits are made.
10. When making bank deposits, vary the time, the routes, and the routine of the bank trips, make deposits in daylight hours wherever possible, conceal the money and go directly to the bank, never go to the bank alone to make a deposit, and, finally, never leave deposits or withdrawals unattended in an automobile, even in the trunk.
11. Never keep large sums of money in the cash register where others may see it. Frequently emptying the cash register during the business day will assist in deterring robberies.

Anticipating Robbery. In anticipating a robbery, a plan must be formulated, and management must assume that their business can become the victim of a robber. Here are some items that should be considered in anticipating a robbery:

1. Always be alert. Be aware of people attempting to hide in the premises near closing time.
2. If a suspicious person is observed, call a member of the security force or the police. Do so even if the individual is outside the premises but has been observing activities in the premises for a long period of time.

3. Teach all employees to operate the hold-up alarm system and ensure that all employees know the location of the hold-up alarm buttons.
4. Hold discussions with employees and tell them what is expected of them should a robbery occur. Some employees may be more observant than others, and they should be encouraged to be particularly watchful if a robbery should take place.
5. In the plan, designate in advance what actions you would want various categories or individuals to take.
6. Somewhere in the vicinity of the cash register or at the exit doors, measure off distances from the floor, and, using black tape or black paint, indicate various heights from 5 feet to approximately $6\frac{1}{2}$ feet so that as the robber is standing near the cash register or exiting the door a fairly accurate height of the individual can be obtained.

In Chapter 16, which deals with bank security, detailed information will be found on the actions that employees should be trained to take at the time a robbery occurs and immediately after a robbery. These actions pertain as well to the employees of a department store, a drug store, or any type of business that handles cash. For further details on protection of robberies, Chapter 16 should be studied.

Terrorists

On September 5, 1975, a bomb exploded in a seventeenth-floor restroom of the Kennecott Copper Corporation in Salt Lake City, causing $50,000 damage but no injuries. This attack was directed at the corporation, presumably to protest U.S. action in Chile. A bomb threat had been received prior to the explosion, and the security director ordered the building evacuated. There obviously was a plan to cope with bomb threats, and the speedy evacuation of the building certainly contributed to the fact that no personnel were reported injured.

The Nuclear Regulatory Commission called an all-alert from May 27 to June 8, 1976, of all 58 U.S. nuclear power plants because "information had been obtained from the intelligence community that two groups may have plans to take over and occupy one or more of the nuclear power plants." Eighteen previous threats had been received in the first 5 months of 1976. The alert instructions also revealed that the credentials of two Nuclear Regulatory Commission inspectors had been stolen, along with other personal belongings.

New York State and Missouri received equal shares of $5.2 million in federal financial assistance to augment security programs for the 1976 Democratic and Republican National Conventions to deter terrorist activity that had already been threatened.

In all probability, the security manager will receive initial information on possible terrorist activity that could affect his or her facility from law enforcement intelligence organizations. The organization's security plan must contemplate this possibility, and provisions should be made to increase security by the employment of additional personnel and general tightening of all measures to control the flow of personnel and vehicles.

All possible illegal acts that may affect the security of lives and property have not been covered in this chapter. It would be quite impractical, if not practically impossible, to enumerate all conditions that may occur. The acts discussed are possible major occurrences, but the reader should pause briefly to contemplate the types of crimes discussed. In almost all instances, a well-designed security plan following the basic principles that will follow in this text will effectively deter these illegal acts from occurring. No security program can guarantee absolute immunity against these crimes, any more than a maximum security prison can guarantee that no prisoner will ever escape.

Security personnel must remember that the criminal, whether he is a company employee or a "pro" is cunning, daring, and often treacherous. He definitely has one advantage. He knows when he will strike. With the advantage of surprise on his side, any security program must be structured to react quickly to minimize the effects of the illegal incident.

CRITICALITY AND VULNERABILITY ASSESSMENT

To complete the discussion on hazards to security that may be encountered during the survey, one must also have a constant awareness of the critical-ity of the facility as a whole and of portions or areas of the facility that are more critical than others to continued operations. One must also determine how vulnerable the facility or parts of the facility are to possible successful attack by the thief, kidnapper, bomber, or even the embezzler. Defining the critical area will depend upon the type facility being protected. In an industrial plant, the most critical area may be the power plant. In a corporate headquarters located in a high-rise building, the computer area may be most critical; in a school setting, it may be the library or experi-mental laboratories.

To establish criticality requires a careful overall evaluation of the entire facility being surveyed before and during the process. In a multiplant organization, this criticality may be established by the overall contribution of one facility to the successful continued operations to maintain maximum output by the most efficient means. For example, if the pattern-cutting plant of a garment manufacturer were destroyed, the entire process from that point to shipping the finished garment would be halted.

The criticality study must also include accurate estimates of the time needed to restore operations to full production or usefulness. When con-sidering this estimate, the criticality of the points or areas will be deter-mined by a study of four basic groups or categories. These groups are as follows:

1. All the installations whose loss would cause an immediate stoppage of all production because production equipment or parts of production equipment would be lost.
2. That equipment or those areas whose loss would reduce production or operations merely because of a partial loss of this productive equipment or parts of equipment.
3. Those areas where any type of loss would not have an immediate devastating effect on operations or production but where a loss would require additional manpower to maintain operational functions.
4. The areas in which a loss would not necessarily have any direct effect on production or operations; however, a definite loss of assets would be involved.

After the criticality determination has been made, the critical points or areas will have to be ranked in order of their vulnerability. It must be remembered that as physical changes at the facility occur, the assessment in these two areas must be updated. An example: The computer area with one or more sides on the perimeter of a building protected only by plate glass is further protected by replacing the glass with masonry construction. The criticality of the computer operations may not necessarily be changed, but certainly the vulnerability of the computer operations would be. That is, the vulnerability to successful attack would be lessened.

Vulnerability need not and should not be considered only in terms of attack or penetration by outsiders. The area may be vulnerable to theft and pilferage only. The OS&D (over, short, or damaged) area at a trucking terminal would probably be rather low on the list of critical areas but high on the vulnerable area list, simply because of its location within the terminal, lack of adequate physical security, or lack of positive control. Therefore, it is likely that the vulnerability calculations will contain structures, areas, or operations that do not appear on the criticality list. Seldom, if ever, would this situation be reversed, because a critical item must always be assessed as to its vulnerability to successful attack.

3

Securing
the Facility's Perimeter

The physical examination of any facility must start at the perimeter, whether it is an industrial plant, a shopping mall, or a high-rise apartment building. The perimeter may be located some distance from any structures, or the only perimeter may be the peripheral walls of the structure itself. An industrial plant will usually be constructed so that there are large open areas between buildings and the actual property line where the initial protection will be established.

One cannot escape visualizing four separate and distinctly different lines of protection or defense against loss of assets starting with the protection established at the peripheral extremes of the property. These four lines of protection start at the extremes of the property being protected and are generally described as follows:

1. <u>Perimeter barrier</u>. The perimeter barrier may consist of an industrial-type chain link fence, some type of masonry wall, a combination of masonry walls and chain link fencing, or a natural hazard such as a swamp, body of water, or high cliff which would, in all probability, in itself not furnish the degree of security required. The location of this perimeter protection, as previously stated, is normally on the property line; however, in recent years, particularly in industry, large tracts of land are purchased to allow for expansion of the facility, but initially only a portion of the real estate is utilized. In these instances the perimeter barrier, because it is more economical and furnishes more security, should be installed to protect only the area that will be utilized in the immediate future.

2. <u>Area security</u>. In discussing area security, the area involved again could be vast or practically nonexistent. At industrial sites this area lies between the established perimeter barrier and the buildings, storage areas, and other structures that comprise the complex. Security of this area is usually established by installing an adequate protective lighting system and patrolling the area through the use of security guards either on foot or in some sort of vehicle. In many instances, if the area is adequately lighted during the hours of darkness, it is patrolled merely by observation. Research and development in the closed circuit television camera industry and the alarm industry, particularly those alarms that have been developed

and are stable enough for outside detection use, has reduced the number
of guards needed to patrol these outside areas. This has considerably
diminished the cost of security, because the cost of employing a security
guard is undoubtedly the greatest expenditure of any security program.

   3. The peripheral walls of buildings. The walls of high-rise buildings
of various types and buildings in urban areas are actually in most instances
considered the first line of protection rather than the third line. However,
if buildings lie within a perimeter barrier and if some degree of security
has been established in outside areas, the peripheral walls of all buildings
can be considered as the third line of protection. To establish adequate
security of each building, special security measures must be adopted to
protect door and window openings that breach these peripheral walls. The
degree of protection provided these openings will depend upon whether or
not the openings lead outside or inside the protected area. A higher degree
of security need be established for those openings that lead to the inside of
the protected area.

   4. The interior areas of the building. Areas inside the building are
considered the fourth line of protection, and the protection consists of
tailoring whatever security measures are necessary to protect processes,
materials, or activities within these areas. If the criticality and vulnerability study and the analysis was complete and correct, these areas will
already have been defined, and a preliminary determination of the degree
of security required in all probability will have already been made.

EFFECTIVENESS OF PERIMETER PROTECTION

Any barrier, whether it is the peripheral walls of the building or an
industrial-type chain link fence, must accomplish certain functions before
it can be considered an effective deterrent in the overall physical security
plan. Among the most important functions are:

   1. The barrier must be substantial enough to present a physical and
      psychological deterrent to entry into the protected area by innocent
      parties.
   2. The barrier must be physically substantial enough to cause intrusion
      delays and assist in the detection and apprehension of the successful
      intruder.
   3. Properly designed, it should provide an effective, efficient, and
      economical deployment of the security forces in their identification
      and control roles.
   4. It must provide, in conjunction with the above, an effective means of
      directing the flow of personnel and vehicles through manned control
      points without impeding operations or creating delays.

5. Secondary perimeter barriers should be designed so that they
   furnish additional protection of critical and vulnerable structures
   and/or operations within the principal perimeter protection. Some
   of these installations may be power plants, gas metering equipment,
   or outside production areas. The secondary barrier is usually constructed not only to increase the protection of a specific possible
   target, but also to ensure that employees and others authorized
   within the principal barrier are denied access to certain installations.

TYPES OF BARRIER CONSTRUCTION

Perimeter barriers are usually referred to as isolated or nonisolated
barriers. Regardless of the classification of the barrier, in both instances
the barrier obviously must be adequately lighted. A barrier is isolated if
it is far enough from the built-up area so that to adequately observe the
barrier, foot or vehicular patrols must move from the built-up area and
actually patrol in the vicinity of the barrier. A nonisolated perimeter
barrier is one that can be adequately observed by patrolling guards from
their established patrol routes in and about the built-up area of the facility
being protected.

Chain Link Fencing

The material most often used to construct the perimeter barrier is the
industrial-type chain link fence. It is used in probably 95 percent of all
barriers used to protect industrial, commercial, and, to a lesser degree,
institutional facilities.

The chain link fence is manufactured in varying heights and in three or
four wire sizes or "gauge" strengths. The standards or specifications
used by manufacturers today were originated some 35 years ago during
World War II. These specifications were drawn up by the Department of
Defense, and the installation of such fencing was required at all facilities
participating in the defense effort who were producing material or products
that were paid for by the U.S. government. The design and specifications
were effective then and furnish more than adequate perimeter protection
today. The specifications covered installation requirements as well as
manufacturing detail.

Galvanization is a process that involves coating a metal object with a
preservative to keep it from rusting. There are basically two methods
used to galvanize a chain link fence. One method is to weave the fence and
then to galvanize the entire fence by dipping it into the galvanizing vats.
The second procedure used is to galvanize the lengths of wire before the
fence is actually woven. There are many pros and cons as to which method
is the best. The second method discussed produces a fence that is somewhat

more expensive; however, in all of the years that I have spent in inspecting
chain link fencing, I have yet to find that the fence has deteriorated because
the wire has been rusted. The deterioration normally is the result of physical damage to the fence. See Figure 3-1.

The Defense Department standards for the construction of a standard
industrial-type chain link perimeter barrier are generally accepted as
minimum requirements for this type of barrier construction. These
specifications can be found in many texts dealing with perimeter barriers
and are well known to security professionals. These standards and specifications are included in this chapter as a review for some readers and as
new material for others.

1. The size or the gauge of the wire for an industrial-type chain link
   fence to be used in industrial and commercial installations should
   be at least No. 11 gauge or heavier. The lower the gauge number
   the heavier or thicker the wire. I usually recommend No. 9 gauge
   wire in the protection of such facilities as trucking terminals and
   warehousing or distribution center facilities.
2. If a chain link fence is used for perimeter protection, it should be
   at least 7 feet in height. In some instances this height may be
   increased to 10 or 12 feet. I have recommended 12-foot industrial
   chain link fencing to establish perimeters at meat packing plants,
   pharmaceutical manufacturing facilities, and the like.
3. The chain link barrier, in order to provide maximum effectiveness,
   must contain an overhang that is referred to as "cleavage." This
   overhang consists of three strands of ordinary barbed wire that
   are stretched tightly and angled outward and upward away from the
   property that is protected at a 45-degree angle from the horizontal.
   Fence manufacturers provide angle irons for the installation of the
   barbed wire at the top of the fence.
4. The barbed wire cleavage that is installed at the top of the chain
   link fence will increase the overall height of a 7-foot fence to 8 feet.
5. The mesh openings (that is, the openings between the wires) should
   not be larger than 2 inches square. If the security requirement
   demands finer mesh, custom-made chain link fencing will be needed.
6. The fence should be installed to extend to within at least 2 inches
   of the ground when the soil is firm and may be installed below the
   surface of the ground if the soil is sandy, loamy, or otherwise
   easily eroded by the weather.
7. The fence when installed must be drawn extremely taut and securely
   fastened with metal fasteners to rigid metal posts that are normally
   set in concrete. Additional bracing obviously is necessary at gate
   openings and fence corners.
8. If erosion or washouts under the barrier will cause problems,
   culverts or troughs can be constructed to assist in water runoff

and prevent erosion. If any openings under the fence, such as
those made by streams that may run through the property line, are
larger than 96 square inches in area, additional protection must be
provided. This is usually accomplished by driving metal stakes
deeply into the dirt or using metal stakes and barbed wires to secure
the openings.

9. When the barrier is designed and prior to its being installed a study
   must be made to determine the number of openings that are required
   for operational purposes. Openings in the barrier such as personnel
   and vehicular gates must be kept to a minimum consistent with
   requirements. Each gate established in the chain link barrier will
   create a weak point, because only one or two points need to be
   attacked in order to reach the barrier. At a gate, the locking
   device, usually a padlock, is often the only item that needs to be
   attacked or two or three hinges can be removed to gain entry into
   the protected area.

10. No materials should be stacked within 8 feet of the barrier. If
    trees, utility poles, or other structures are within 8 feet of the
    barrier, the barrier should be increased in height. In most
    instances an increase in illumination is also required (see Figure
    3-1).

Should a surveyor need to recommend construction of an industrial chain
link barrier, it is of utmost importance that he cover all of the items just
discussed to ensure that the entire length of the barrier furnishes equal
amounts of protection.

Masonry Barriers

Masonry walls constructed of bricks, cement blocks, cinder blocks, or
even field stone can also be used as an effective deterrent to penetration at
the periphery of the protected area, providing certain precautions and construction details are followed.

Masonry barriers may be considered for perimeter protection in areas
where flooding may be expected. In such instances, the barrier serves a
double purpose; as a "sea wall" during periods of flooding and as physical
protection against intrusion during other periods. Obviously, if the primary
function is to protect against water damage and destruction, the construction specifications must provide for sufficient strength and height to ensure
that the barrier satisfies these initial requirements. Any security appurte-
nances should not interfere with its intended use for flood control.

Commercial establishments, institutions, and high-rise buildings used
as dwelling or office structures can be adequately protected by masonry
walls that will not be objectionable or detract from the architectural or
landscaping effort. In some industrial applications, it may be necessary

Figure 3-1 A 55-gallon drum obviously being used to breach the barrier
in a remote location.

to construct a barrier that consists partially of masonry walls, particularly
in some of the newer industrial parks that restrict the use of chain link
fencing facing the public streets. Masonry walls used in conjunction with
chain link fencing must furnish the same degree of protection as the fence.
    Walls constructed as perimeter barriers must be at least 8 feet in height
and must be topped with some material that would make it extremely hazardous to enter the protected area by climbing over the wall. Broken glass or
nails embedded in concrete are quite effective. If this material is used,
perimeter inspection must include observation of the top of the barrier to

ensure that the nails have not been bent or the glass removed by fracturing it. The possibility of rather serious injury during hasty breaches of the barrier serves as an effective deterrent.

Barbed wire can be considered for installation at the top of a masonry barrier; however, it has been my experience that it is often used as an assist in breaching the wall because the width of the wall at the top will permit a person to stand on it. If barbed wire is used, the configuration used should be in the form of a "Y." The barbed wire should be angled outward and inward to make it equally difficult for the intruder to leave the protected area by the same means used to enter. The enclosed "Y" or diamond shaped cleavage is the most effective deterrent. However, if the wall was used so as not to distract from the aesthetic beauty of the area, obviously even one strand of barbed wire would be objectionable.

Masonry walls are often used in commercial applications to furnish both protection and privacy. In many instances, particularly where masonry walls are constructed around dwelling structures, they will incorporate a geometrical pattern created by using masonry blocks with openings. The design is created by leaving openings between the blocks or the bricks or whatever other material is being used. If any degree of protection is expected from this type of barrier, openings must be too small to insert the toes of a foot or must slant outward and downward to make a firm footing almost impossible.

The use of masonry walls will often assist in increasing the protection of some critical and vulnerable installations or structures that are already inside the primary perimeter barrier.

At one time, we recommended that a large electrical transformer area at an industrial plant be protected further by constructing a masonry wall around it of sufficient strength to stop a bullet fired from a high-powered rifle. The transformer was inside the perimeter barrier, but in a remote corner within 100 yards of a heavily wooded area. Company management decided not to follow the recommendations. Within a year, as a result of a dispute, not only was the transformer fired into, completely severing the electrical supply, but gas metering equipment installed near the barrier and overlooked during the survey because of high grass and weeds was also fired into, causing a disruption of the natural gas supply used in the manufacturing processes and creating an extremely hazardous fire condition. The cost of complete shutdown was higher than the cost of constructing a masonry barrier around the entire facility.

When considering masonry walls as perimeter barriers, particularly where a certain dependence upon public police patrols of the area is considered in the protection plan, the surveyor must keep in mind that observation from the outside, if not entirely impossible, will be considerably limited. This type of situation usually results in the assumption of a certain degree of "calculated risk." Choose the barrier that will most nearly provide the degree of security required.

Secondary Barriers

Already discussed is one instance where a secondary barrier consisting of
masonry walls would have increased the protection. It is also possible to
reduce vulnerability of critical areas or installations by the use of chain
link fencing. Some such areas may be outside storage areas, emergency
water pump houses, artesian wellheads, or even the lowly salvage dump
in order to assist in personnel control when salvage is sold or given to
employees.
    While studying the security requirements of the outside areas—that is,
those areas between the perimeter barrier and the buildings—access to
these areas by the employee will often dictate that secondary barriers be
established. That is, outside lunch areas, smoking areas, or recreational
areas used during breaks should perhaps be separated physically from
other outside areas. For example, the water fountain and pool in a shopping
mall would perhaps need no more protection than a barrier consisting of
pipes or rails to deter accidents and possibly vandalism to the fountain.

PERIMETER PROTECTION BY MEANS OF ELECTRONIC DEVICES

Now that we have discussed perimeter barriers in some detail, it is time
to discuss securing the perimeter barrier itself by electronic means. The
goal is to monitor the perimeter barrier against attempted intrusion.
    As recently as 3 or 4 years ago there were scarcely any stable, depend-
able electronic devices on the market that could be employed by the security
force to monitor conditions at the perimeter barrier except, perhaps, the
use of a closed circuit television surveillance system. The military
operating in South Vietnam required some dependable means to monitor
the miles of chain link fence and barbed wire installations constructed to
protect air fields, ammunition dumps, warehouses, and the like from attack
by foot patrols of the enemy. In this situation, the perimeter barrier lost
much of its effectiveness as soon as darkness fell, for lighting of the barrier
would give the enemy his target location to "home in on." Thousands of
dollars were spent in research by many companies, and as a result there
are available some stable, dependable electronic devices that substantially
increase the security provided by the perimeter barrier, both day and night.
Excluding closed circuit television surveillance systems, which we shall
discuss in detail later, there are three basic technologies that furnish this
perimeter protection.

1. The fence assault system
2. The interrupted beam system
3. The buried line sensor system

The Fence Assault System

The fence assault or tampering system consists in one instance of pairs of wires, high-tension springs, insulators, support posts, and controlled units. The device consists of a field wire electronically charged and a sensing wire connected to an amplifier which monitors and amplifies the signal received. The electronic field can be adjusted horizontally or vertically and installed in different detection patterns in conjunction with a chain link fence or even around the top of a masonry wall or building to detect intrusion. After proper adjustment, the system will sense large objects such as humans but will not be triggered by birds, wind-blown paper, and small animals.

The equipment is easily portable and can be quickly erected for temporary installation at construction sites, supply stockpiles, cargo loading areas, and the like. Installation is economical, because no special treatment is required at corners and the significant cost of grading and trenching between transmitters and receivers as in the case of systems using either light or radar beams is avoided. Maximum span capability for each separate unit is 1,000 feet. See Figure 3-2 for typical detection pattern installations.

Another system of sensors capable of immediately detecting any movement, cutting, tampering, or intrusion of the fence area is available at a reasonable cost. It is advertised that "two men with basic electrical knowledge can secure 800 feet of fence per day." This system consists of a single low-voltage cable, fence clamps, sensors, and receiver-annunciators that can be zoned to specific areas. Installation can cover only a few feet or several miles with zones monitored independently. The system is activated by a motion of the fence and is said to be virtually free of false alarms when sensors are individually adjusted properly (see Figures 3-3 through 3-5).

The Interrupted Beam System

This second category of perimeter protection devices uses a continuous beam, either of infrared light or microwaves whose interruption by a solid object will trigger the alarm. The microwave system for outdoor protection covers maximum linear distance of 500 feet per unit. The height or width of protection offered by microwaves is 20 feet.

Because the system utilizes microwaves, it is not affected by weather conditions, and, if installed inside the perimeter barrier with the detection pattern a couple of feet above the ground, it is quite stable and reliable. The system can also be zoned and corner protection can easily be achieved (see Figures 3-6 and 3-7).

One infrared detection system used in outdoor perimeter protection has a linear coverage of 300 feet for each pair of units. One unit consists of a transmitter, receiver, and monitor. A system may utilize four transmitters

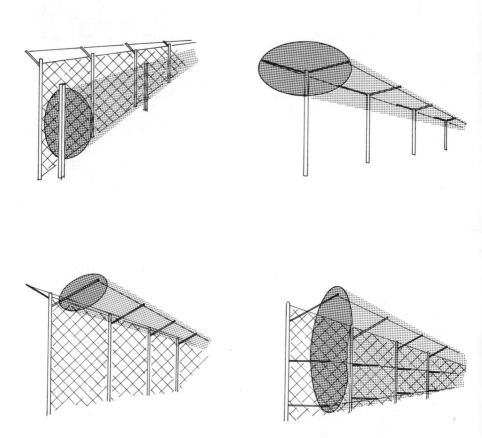

Figure 3-2 This sketch shows four configurations possible with Stellar Systems E-field fence protection. The system is said to be less expensive than microwave or infrared protection. Installation requires no site leveling or trenching and the system can be installed around corners. (Stellar Systems, Inc.)

Figure 3-3 The Perim-Alert is a low voltage fence protection system that provides weatherproof, tamper-proof, around-the-clock protection. (Courtesy of Norton Company, Safety Products Division)

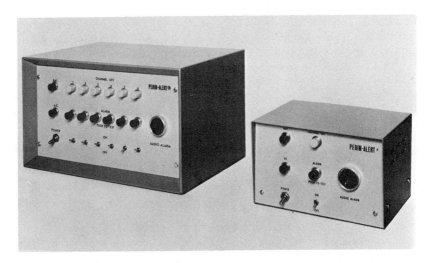

Figure 3-4 The Perim-Alert system is activated by a motion on the fence, with the alarm signal transferred through low voltage wire to the receiver-annunciator which converts the signal to a visual and audio alarm. (Courtesy of Norton Company, Safety Products Division)

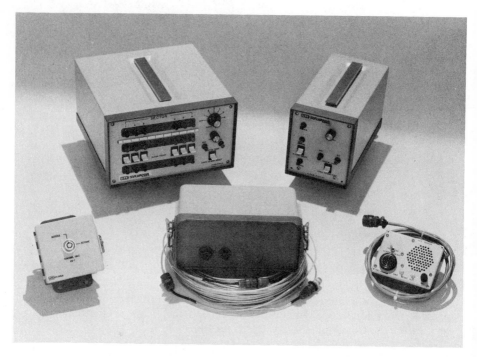

Figure 3-5 Another fence protection system that provides high detection probability. The system consists of a sensing cable that is attached to the fence to detect vibrations and a processor box buried near the fence that analyzes the signal and sends the alarm to a central monitoring station. The six-channel monitor shown at the upper left can monitor up to 6,000 feet of fence. The device on the lower left is a gate bypass unit, and the device on the lower right is used to test the system. (GTE Sylvania, Inc.)

and receivers stacked one over the other. This would furnish protection to a sufficient height to make it impossible for a person to step over or crawl under the light beams. False alarms are minimized in this system by a variable self-adaptive time-delay threshold. In this automatic mode, the system response time varies inversely with the number of beams interrupted. As the number of beams broken increases the response time rapidly decreases (see Figure 3-8). One should remember that any of these devices using a microwave or infrared light source requires that entrenching must be done as part of the installation process. If the terrain is uneven, it may also be necessary to grade or level it to some extent to achieve line-of-sight alignment of the transmitter and receiver. These installations will also require either burying the electrical supply cables

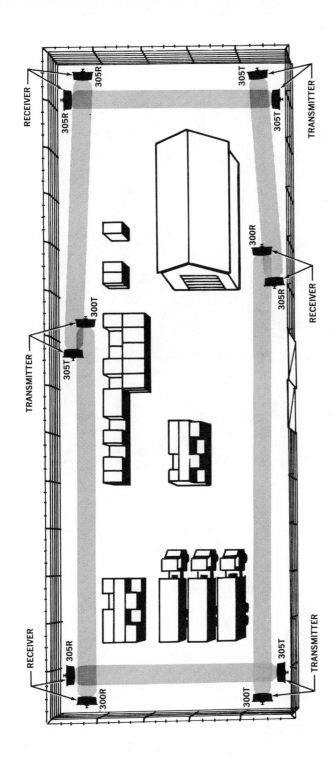

Figure 3-6 Perimeter protection utilizing microwaves. This is a typical installation using some equipment with a maximum range of 150 feet and a second set consisting of a transmitter and receiver with a maximum range of 500 feet. (Omni Spectra, Inc.)

37

Figure 3-7 A close-up view of the use of a 150-foot range microwave link. (Omni Spectra, Inc.)

and monitoring cables or installing them overhead. An electrical supply must be furnished for both the transmitter and the receiver.

Buried Line Sensor System

Probably the greatest advantage of the buried line sensor is that after the ground has been returned to its original state, it is quite impossible for an intruder to detect its location and attempt to avoid it. There are three systems in this family of detection devices, and each can be used in conjunction with a physical perimeter barrier or by itself. The oldest of these systems uses the <u>magnetic stress</u> principle. One of the remaining two operates on the <u>pressure system</u>, and the other is a <u>seismic device</u>. When first developed, the <u>magnetic stress</u> sensing device employed a magnetic loop as a means of detection. These loops, however, gave false alarms during electrical storms. The principle of operation is simply that the device is capable of detecting a change in a steady-state magnetic field that is sensor generated. The system assumes the alarm mode when an object passes through the field and distorts the steady-state field.

In the <u>pressure sensor system</u>, local pressure changes created on the surface of the ground by personnel or vehicles attempting to cross the buried line are converted into alarm signals by the electronic processing units. The area of sensitivity can be controlled jointly by the depth of burial of the detector and by a sensitivity control located in the signal processor. The greater the depth of burial, the wider the zone of sensitivity. This unique detection system consists of five basic components (see Figure 3-9).

Finally, the <u>seismic sensor system</u> utilizes geophones that are connected in series along the line. Geophones used are of a type similar to those used in geophysical studies. The device measures shock waves occurring in the earth in which it is embedded that are caused by objects passing across the zone of protection. These minute disturbances are detected, transmitted to the sensor, and converted into an alarm signal at the monitor.

The three systems just discussed have been designed so that all can now be buried in a narrow slit trench that can be opened quickly and efficiently, whether it is buried under earth or covered by asphalt. The type of sensor used, if any, will depend upon each special requirement and the degree of

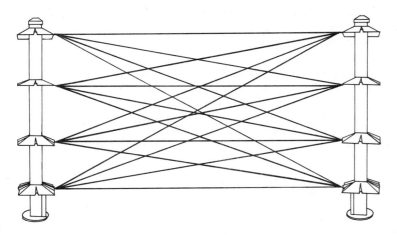

Figure 3-8 Fence protection utilizing infrared interlaced beams that can be used for outdoor or indoor protection. A self-adaptive time delay prevents environmental conditions such as fog, rain, and snow from triggering the device. Range is 300 feet per unit. (Courtesy Applied Metro Technology, Inc.)

Figure 3-9 The BLID (Buried Line Intrusion Detector) is a unique advance-
ment in outdoor security sensors. It can be buried under any paved or
unpaved surface and provides reliable detection by sensing local pressure
changes created on the surface. In the upper left is the buried line intrusion
detector, upper right is a map display, lower left is the base station, and
to the right is the sensor transmitter. At the bottom of the photo are the
cable and sensors. (Courtesy Teledyne Geotech)

security being established. Buried line sensor systems are normally used
in place of a physical barrier. When used in conjunction with, say, a chain
link fence, maximum security will very nearly have been established in
creating the perimeter barrier.

OPENINGS IN THE PERIMETER BARRIER

All openings in the perimeter barriers, whether the barrier consists solely
of the peripheral walls of the buildings or an industrial chain link fence,
should be kept to a minimum consistent with the requirements of operating
the facility.

First, we should examine the need for creating gates in the chain link barrier. Obviously, gates that will be used for operational purposes will be installed without further consideration, <u>except that each operational gate will require that controls be established while operations are in progress</u>.

The location of emergency installations such as servicing fire stations and other vehicular approaches will often dictate that other openings will need to be created. The location of exceptionally hazardous areas in an industrial facility may dictate that emergency gates be created. The existence and size of the street approaches, to a public or private parking lot will influence the location and number of gates required.

It is important to remember that operational gates or openings in the perimeter barrier will require some means of control. Some expense will be involved, even if the opening is remotely observed and controlled. It is equally important to keep in mind that every opening constructed in the perimeter barrier creates a weak point in the barrier. To create an opening large enough for a human to pass through, an intruder need only direct his attack against the locking mechanism installed or the hinges that secure the opening rather than cut through at least nine strands of wire per foot on a chain link fence.

Because all gates used in chain link fencing are custom-made, local requirements will determine the size or width of the opening. The same requirements will dictate whether or not turnstiles will be used instead of gates.

Generally speaking, the principle will apply whether the peripheral walls of a single structure are the first line or become the perimeter protection. One difference is that it is substantially more economical and less difficult to provide greater security to a peripheral opening of a building than to an isolated section of industrial fencing.

Railroad gates in the perimeter barrier of an industrial facility can be as troublesome as the overhead doors of the receiving dock of a high-rise office building. Establishing security in these areas requires studying the existing problems and possible future problems and following the basic principles outlined throughout this text. In this way, the degree of control necessary to minimize loss of assets can be established.

IMPORTANCE OF CLEAR ZONES

If the zone around the barrier is wide and free of undergrowth or any other obstruction that will limit the observation of the barrier, a greater amount of protection can be developed. Such an area around a barrier is called a clear zone. Imagine, if you will, a chain link fence with absolutely nothing to obstruct observation from 20 feet inside the fence and 50 feet outside the fence! Now imagine that the surface at ground level has been graded, paved, whitewashed or painted or perhaps not paved but covered with white pebbles or crushed rock that has been sprayed with white paint or whitewashed. Properly illuminated, a creature as small as an ant could probably be detected crossing the barrier at midnight.

Unfortunately, the value of real estate and the expense of creating this sort of clear zone prohibits such exorbitant preparations. However, only 20 or 25 years ago this was considered standard for clear zones at an industrial facility. In addition to being documented in specifications, I have seen an animated projection of these standards in a World War II plant protection film.

Today we must be more realistic and certainly more economical if we are to survive as security experts and expect to obtain any financial and decision-making support from top management as we plan security of any facility.

It is true that the greater the clear zones inside and outside the perimeter barrier, the more effective the barrier becomes. However, it is seldom possible today to establish a clear zone of any width <u>outside</u> the barrier unless the real estate is owned or controlled by management of the facility being protected. Furthermore, it is economically unwise to consider a clear zone of 20 feet inside any type of barrier.

A clear zone adds to the strength of the perimeter barrier and to stack or pile material against or immediately adjacent to a perimeter barrier and thus obstruct the activity of an intruder and aid him in reaching the barrier is foolhardy. Similarly, to construct a barrier and then obstruct its observation and reduce its effectiveness by landscaping with trees, hedges, or other shrubs is also foolhardy.

Examine closely the area under consideration, apply the principles discussed in assessing criticality and vulnerability, and then decide what size clear zone is <u>really</u> <u>necessary</u> and whether or not the cost can be justified.

BUILDINGS ON THE PERIMETER

Often, particularly in industrial applications, one will find that the walls of some buildings will form a part of the perimeter. At the expense of repeating what security personnel have said for years (this is one of the "old standards" and, though possibly questionable, still cannot be disputed as a sound security principle), any opening greater than 96 square inches in area, less than 18 feet from the ground level, and less than 14 feet from any structure or object outside the perimeter should be further protected.

The overall strength of the exposed peripheral walls of the building should be used to determine the additional security devices that will be installed to protect windows and door openings. The same general principles discussed in the paragraphs pertaining to gates also apply to doors.

Whether securing windows in your own home, a commercial complex, or at an industrial site, keep in mind that fire emergencies or, in industrial instances, a multitude of equally hazardous conditions can occur. Window protection should be designed so that fire fighters can enter and occupants can exit if conditions require.

Numerous means can be employed to secure windows and other peripheral openings, ranging from the use of chain link fencing to specially designed and manufactured wrought iron devices.

When building walls and chain link fence meet to form a perimeter barrier, consideration must be given to increasing the height of the fence nearest the building. If window ledges, drain pipes, or other objects are in close proximity to this junction, the height of the fence should be increased. In most instances this can be accomplished by erecting a fan-shaped section of chain link fence that is approximately 6 feet higher than the fence at the building edge and extends approximately 8 feet from the building along the top of the existing barrier. All of this additional fencing should be securely anchored to the building and to the barrier.

ATTRACTIVE NUISANCES

Almost every type of facility has as a part of the overall complex some installation that could legally be considered or classified as an "attractive nuisance." The settling basic at an industrial plant, the gravity tank of a small rural community, or the attraction of the open, unused parking lot at a shopping mall to the go-cart enthusiast may all be considered attractive nuisances.

Areas or objects that may be classified under this heading should be considered for further protection. Such areas may never be found on the criticality or vulnerability assessment list, but experience has proved that it is far more economical to establish "legal deterrents" than to ignore these conditions, to say nothing of the moral responsibility for the protection of life of those still not conscious of the dangers of living.

EXISTING BREACHES AT THE PERIMETER BARRIERS

Although I cannot list all the possible breaches of the barrier, the subject of existing breaches must be discussed briefly. By existing breaches I refer to sidewalk elevators and utility tunnels in urban areas, storm sewers, and the like. Examination of existing perimeter barriers or a study of the location of future barriers obviously must include natural and man-made breaches that could be utilized by an outsider intent on penetrating the protected area. The type of barrier construction and the purpose and seriousness of the breach will determine what measures will need to be initiated to secure that particular area to ensure that every foot of the barrier furnishes exactly the same degree of protection.

In conclusion, there is no doubt that the perimeter barrier, the first line of protection, is in all probability the most important part of the entire security system. It is here that the overall degree of security is established, the control of personnel and vehicles originates, the flow of supplies into the facility and the flow of finished products is finally regulated, and the effectiveness of the security force is tested on a day-to-day if not hour-by-hour basis.

To overlook an important control procedure at the perimeter barrier is to invite disaster and possibly a complete disintegration of the overall protection plan.

4

Security
of Open Areas

The discussion relating to establishing area security will be devoted mainly
to protection of industrial plants and parking lots. Commercial installations will have scarcely any outside areas where material is stored or
where activities would be exposed, thus requiring further protection.

Institutions will always require that some special techniques be applied
to ensure that open areas such as sports fields, botanical gardens, and
park settings are safeguarded for the preservation of life and property.

Construction sites during the initial phases could be considered one
large-area security problem because special techniques must be used in
these instances. The problems of establishing adequate security are covered
in the chapters dealing with these types of installations.

The areas we are concerned with here lie between the perimeter or the
perimeter barrier and the structures comprising the total facility being
secured. As stated previously, we shall discuss primarily the industrial
complex.

Probably the hazard more often encountered in the initial stages of the
security study is the height and density of the grass and other undergrowth
throughout the area. This undergrowth provides numerous opportunities
for concealment of the intruder and/or of material being stolen that will
eventually be thrown over the perimeter barrier to be recovered later.
One can visualize the use an intruder will make of heavy undergrowth once
he has penetrated the perimeter barrier and progresses toward his target,
whether it be an outside storage area or an area within the structure. Give
him a further advantage by not illuminating the area, and the perimeter
barrier now becomes nothing more than a part of an "obstacle course."

All outside areas must be kept clear of undergrowth during the growing
season. In addition to creating a security hazard, undergrowth left to die
and dry in the fall of the year creates an unnecessary fire hazard. This
situation becomes potentially more dangerous if dried heavy undergrowth
and brush is allowed to build up beyond the perimeter barrier in areas not
under control of the facility management.

LANDSCAPING

Landscaping may be defined as an adornment or improvement of a sector of ground by contouring the land and planting flowers, shrubs, or trees. Landscaping is designed to make the grounds aesthetically pleasing.

Landscaping must come under close scrutiny of the security surveyor. It will often be impossible to convince management that a bush or hedge must be removed to ensure maximum area security, and, often as not, it is difficult to justify its removal. One just would feel better "if the damn thing would never have been planted in the first place." Established landscaping that really presents a problem but cannot be eliminated or changed may become less of a risk if illumination in the area is increased. If this cannot be accomplished, either outside patrols will need to include these areas in their field of observation or actual physical patrol of the areas must be accomplished.

HOUSEKEEPING

Housekeeping of outside areas appears to be a nemesis of the American people. Any drive through practically any section of this nation will reveal that farm buildings, corners of wooded areas and ravines or gulches are littered with unused machinery, automobiles, and other worthless junk that should be removed, if for no other reason than to improve appearances.

With few exceptions, the industrial and commercial facilities I have surveyed hold literally tons of scrap machinery, wooden pallets, and old salvage strewn haphazardly throughout outside areas or merely thrown into a remote corner. These conditions create numerous unnecessary security and safety hazards in addition to reducing the effectiveness of a well-engineered protective lighting system.

Who, then, is responsible for creating conditions and allowing them to persist? In most instances, the maintenance crews create the hazard as they repair or replace machinery. For some reason unknown to me, maintenance personnel will hold or store unsalvageable items rather than removing them from the facility. Management and security personnel are responsible for permitting the conditions to persist. If items have a salvage or reuse value, the economy of operations should dictate that they be properly stored and protected from the weather. The security personnel that allow these conditions to exist are grossly negligent in their protection duties. In many instances, I have found that top management at the plant was not aware of these conditions and, when told of the hazard, immediately directed its elimination or reduction.

OUTSIDE STORAGE AND PRODUCTION AREAS

At some industrial facilities, outside areas are used for the production of
certain items, or, in some instances, the entire item is produced in open
areas not otherwise protected. These areas normally will require little
or no protection from the security force while operations are in progress,
because these types of outside production areas will normally be restricted
to operations such as processing lumber, constructing prefabricated buildings, and the like. However, when valuable products or materials are being
processed, in all probability security force posts and patrols will have to
be established on a 24-hour-per-day, 7-day-per-week basis. If these
outside production areas are near truck or rail shipping or receiving operations, it may be necessary that additional fencing be installed to protect
the processes and the material against theft and pilferage by employees
and others operating at shipping docks.
 In almost all industrial facilities, in a great number of commercial
facilities, and occasionally at institutional facilities, material will be stored
in outside areas or in buildings that provide only a roof over the material,
with all sides exposed. If material stored in outside areas differs in value,
the items of greater value should be stacked nearest the bottom of the pile,
whenever possible. This makes it all the more difficult to remove the more
expensive or more desirable items from the stacked material.
 Outside storage of material other than lumber is usually protected from
the weather. Tarpaulins or heavy plastic covers may be used. If such
covers are used, they should be of the type that can be secured to the ground
or to the storage platform by fastening the grommets to eyes embedded in
the cement storage bases, with locks or seals being used to fasten the cover
in place over the anchor-type eyes. The use of locks or seals will help the
patrolling guard to determine immediately whether or not the stored material
had been tampered with. Additionally, such devices will ensure that the
flexible covering will not be blown off the material during inclement weather.
 Whether or not the material is stored under a roof, consideration should
always be given to at least palletizing the material and strapping it to the
pallets so that again the guard patrolling the area can easily detect whether
or not the material has been tampered with.
 Probably the most important goal in establishing security of outside areas
when storage is involved is to ensure that all material is stacked or piled
neatly and uniformly. Aisles between the stacks should be kept clear of
debris, undergrowth, and other material and should be wide enough for the
guard to be able to patrol freely and to observe clearly the areas between
the stacks of material. The proper organization of outside storage will also
assist in increasing the protection provided by the protective lighting system
because as many heavily shadowed areas as possible will be eliminated.

RECREATIONAL FACILITIES

There is a trend today toward establishing small recreational areas at
industrial facilities and in some commercial facilities. These recreational
areas may be nothing more than a place for the employees to play horse-
shoes, volleyball, or similar games during their lunch or coffee breaks.
In other instances, facilities have created a picnic area in outside areas
by planting trees and providing benches and tables where the employees
can eat their lunch when weather permits.

Those employees intent on stealing or pilfering products from the facility
will take whatever advantage these recreational or lunch areas provide.
Therefore, it would be practical wherever possible to keep these areas as
far from the perimeter barrier as possible and even to consider installing
fencing to separate the areas from the remainder of the outside areas. If
this is not possible or if the fencing is considered to be unsightly, guards
should be assigned to the areas while activity is in progress and/or should
patrol through the areas immediately after the activities have ceased.
These guards should make a visual search to determine whether or not
items have been secreted in or near the area for later recovery.

EXCESS REAL ESTATE

Excess real estate is not uncommon and is found in institutional, commercial, and industrial settings. It is more the rule today than the exception
for management to purchase larger tracts of land than they need at that
particular time. The long-range plans of almost every type of business
include plans for expansion. Because of this, and because the price of real
estate continues to rise, it is more than likely that more acreage will be
purchased than will be needed in the immediate future, that is, if the real
estate is available.

When there is excess real estate, the perimeter barrier is usually
designed to protect only the property that will be developed in the near
future. If so, outside maintenance must include the removal of undergrowth
beyond the perimeter barrier to a distance of 40 or 50 feet, not only for
security purposes but for fire protection as well. This is so that any fires
that occur in the dried undergrowth in the fall or winter months of the year
are arrested before they reach the perimeter barrier and move on into the
protected area.

If the perimeter barrier is installed at the property line and if vast
expanses of unused real estate exist between the barrier and the portion
of the property being used, all grounds must be maintained in such condition that all fire security and safety hazards are reduced or eliminated
entirely.

Often, when large areas are not being used inside the perimeter barrier, facility management will authorize employees to park trailers, boats, and campers inside the area merely as a convenience for the employee and to protect these vehicles against theft, damage, or vandalism if they were parked on the street or in the yards at employees' homes. If so, employees should not be authorized to move between their vehicles and the facility unless accompanied or observed by a member of the security force. For practical purposes, such areas should be fenced in such a manner that ingress and egress can be controlled by a member of the security force who would have a key to open and close the gates as these vehicles are moved in and out of the area.

PARKING LOTS

Employee parking lots should not be constructed within the primary perimeter barrier of any type of facility. If all owned real estate is enclosed with a perimeter barrier and sufficient area exists to construct an employee parking lot, the area to be used should be fenced from the remainder of the area creating, in effect, an outside parking lot. Where the configuration and size of the property will permit, entrances and exits from the lots should be through the perimeter barrier rather than into and through any portion of the remainder of the property being protected.

It is important that in planning parking facilities consideration be given to installing a hard surface so that whatever parking plan is adopted, parking stalls can be adequately marked and arranged to suit the pattern of traffic flow. There are four basic parking lot layouts. These are shown schematically in Figure 4-1 and are furnished here primarily for informational purposes. It is usually far more economical and certainly will result in a more efficient utilization of all available space if the project of creating a parking lot is out-contracted to an organization specializing in this field. At an industrial site, the security force will control ingress and egress of employees' automobiles and in all probability will also "police" the parking lot to ensure that proper parking procedures are maintained, that restricted parking regulations are observed, that unsafe driving habits are corrected, and that the employees' vehicles are protected against theft, vandalism, and repossession. Protection of employees' automobiles should include security of perimeter gates between shifts and the requirement that persons with authority to repossess an automobile confront the employee involved. Repossession should never be authorized without the employee's being made aware of the action beforehand. One of the most prized possessions of almost all Americans is his or her automobile. If an automotive parts and accessories thief is able to spend only 10 minutes in an unprotected parking lot, he can effectively lower or destroy the morale of a half dozen employees.

Control systems for parking lots connected with commercial establishments may be totally lacking or may include assignment of attendants when

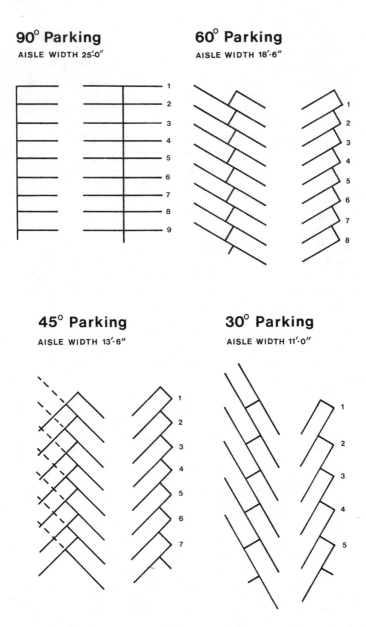

Figure 4-1 Typical parking lot layouts showing four possible variations. The layout of stalls and aisles will depend upon available space and approaches to the parking area. All stalls are 19 feet deep and $8\frac{1}{2}$ feet wide. Note that aisle widths vary depending upon the angle of parking.

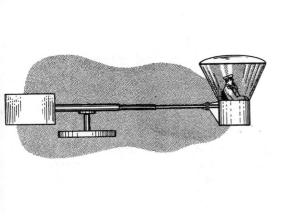
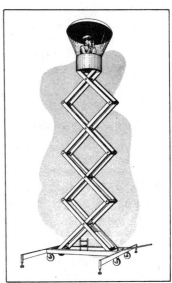

Figure 4-2 The R-Bar surveillance capsule may be ordered in a variety of configurations for various applications, for example, (left) the wheeled mobile unit is ideal in large industrial situations, and (right) the unit is useful for wide visibility in high crime and traffic areas.

Figure 4-3 An effective way of directing the flow of traffic is through the use of this spike device. The device can be lowered and raised either manually or electrically. A warning sign and illumination must always be used in conjunction with this device.

the lot is being used by customers. Parking lots at hospitals and sports arenas, schools, and other installations used by the general public are often operated by professional parking lot management organizations.

In other instances, parking may be controlled by automatic parking equipment that is installed to restrict parking either to certain authorized individuals or to anyone who has the correct amount of change. Here again, each specific situation or condition must be evaluated to determine the most economical, effective controls to establish.

SECURITY PATROLS

There are seldom outside areas at an industrial plant that can be considered secure, particularly during the hours of darkness, without active patrolling by the security force. Occasionally, when outside areas are restricted in size and illumination is adequate, the security force can "patrol by observation" from within or near the buildings. This, however, is the exception and not the rule.

Whether foot or vehicular patrols are established would depend upon the size of the security force, their deployment, their assigned functions, local present conditions, outside material storage, and the overall size of the area to be secured. Whether foot or vehicular patrols are employed, at least "after-the-fact supervision" must be considered by requiring the patrolling guards to "clock in" at predetermined points using fixed watch-clock key stations or at electronically supervised stations that are monitored by other security personnel. The frequency of, and routes established for, the patrols will depend upon whether or not outside storage areas are being protected and upon the condition of the perimeter barrier and the overall adequacy of the protective lighting system.

A new interesting concept in patrol deployment is high-vantage-point, fixed observation posts that offer extensive observation, protection from the weather, and economical hard-line communication. One such effective deterrent is a recently patented device called the R-Bar. The portable version (Figure 4-2) has many use possibilities, ranging from temporary parking lot surveillance at state fairs to observation of crowds of demonstrators who gather spontaneously. The device, when permanently mounted on a building or other support, may be utilized at traffic control points, for perimeter or area observation, and for surveillance of large open areas used for storage. This device is depicted in Figure 4-2.

It cannot be overemphasized that, in almost all instances, security of outside areas, whether these areas lie between the perimeter barrier and the built-up area or between a hospital building and a public parking lot, requires the use of security force patrols. If no perimeter barrier exists, the need for the patrols is even greater.

In the construction of parking lots, whether accomplished by company personnel or by professionals, security personnel should supervise the work and ensure that barriers are installed so that vehicles cannot strike and damage the fence.

5

Illumination
in the Protective Plan

A grocery store had been the target of several burglaries and was regularly
checked by the police officers in the city. Although there was a storage bin
for merchandise in the rear of the store, the owner disconnected the exterior lighting, leaving the area in darkness. A police officer was making his
nightly search of the back of the store when he was fatally shot by a burglar.

The widow of the police officer filed suit against the store owner, alleg-
ing that the owner was negligent in disconnecting the outside lights. This
lack of adequate lighting, according to the complaint, created an area of
darkness in which a burglar could conceal himself. The owner, the widow
contended, was negligent in imperiling the safety of an invitee, a police
officer whom he knew regularly checked the burglary-prone store. The
local county circuit court, however, entered judgment for the store and
dismissed the complaint.

The deceased policeman's widow appealed to the state appellate court,
which reversed and remanded the decision in favor of the plaintiff, holding
the store owner negligent for the lack of lighting and security consciousness. The court based its reversal on two previous cases of similar
circumstances, and the store was found liable for the officer's death, and
the case was remanded for damages. The average award for damages in
the case of the wrongful death of an adult married male in the state in
question is $65,000 when childless and $200,000 with children.

This incident demonstrates without a doubt that protective lighting
systems, or even single lights, are not installed and illuminated solely
to deter the criminal, who unquestionably prefers to work under cover of
darkness. It also is stark evidence that a properly engineered system will
increase the personal safety of those individuals whose responsibility it is
to protect the property.

The Illuminating Engineering Society has established the American
National Standard Practice for various types of protective lighting, both
indoors and outdoors. The Practice for Protective Lighting should be
consulted for detailed specifications and industrial applications, and when
new systems are to be installed or where major changes are necessary in
an existing system, illuminating engineers should be employed to design
proper lighting. However, security personnel and those responsible for

studying the overall security of an installation must have at least a basic working knowledge of the available types of luminaires and reflectors, of the basic designs of the systems, of the methods of control, and of the approximate cost differentials between lighting systems.

Facilities, whether industrial, commercial, or institutional, will differ widely in their need for protective lighting. In addition, the amount and type of illumination will also differ depending upon any inherent hazards. At institutional and commercial installations, consideration may also be given to blending luminaires in with the architectural design and/or landscaping.

There are some techniques that can be used as a guide when considering a protective lighting system. These guidelines are sufficiently general so that they can be referred to in the study of protective lighting in practically all types of installations.

EFFECTIVE PROTECTIVE LIGHTING

A protective lighting system at any facility is generally designed to illuminate the boundary approaches, the perimeter barrier, the area between the perimeter barrier and the structures, and the structures within the protected area.

Any protective lighting system must accomplish certain purposes if maximum effectiveness is to be obtained, and these purposes should be kept in mind during the examination and analysis of the protective lighting system or protective lighting requirements.

1. The protective lighting system must be so designed that the illumination is sufficient to discourage and deter illegal entry.

2. The intensity of the illumination must be sufficient to make detection certain should surreptitious entry be accomplished.

3. The individual luminaires must be installed so that there is no glare in the eyes of security personnel; however, glare should be cast in the direction of the possible intruder. Caution must be exercised to avoid directing glaring lights into adjacent streets or highway traffic areas, and the lighting should not be annoying to occupants of neighboring buildings or any neighboring facilities. This may require that shields be fabricated and installed on some of the lights to ensure that the glare in any particular direction is reduced. Every effort should be made when installing the system to attempt to direct the glare in the direction of the intruder which obviously will handicap him and reduce his ability to see both the patrolling security guard and his intended target.

4. The exterior protective lighting system must be designed to provide complete reliability; that is, failure of any single light for whatever reason should not plunge an area into intense darkness. The lights

on the perimeter, in particular, should be installed so that the cone of the illumination overlaps. With the use of this overlapping method, the failure of any one light would still not plunge any portion of the area into complete darkness.

5. The system must provide a means for convenient control and maintenance of the system as a whole and individual luminaires.

6. Adequate illumination must be provided in each specific area. The amount of light that is required in a particular area will depend upon the criticality of the installations in the area, the vulnerability of these installations, and whether or not a closed circuit television surveillance system will be used after the hours of darkness. The system as a whole must be so engineered as to eliminate entirely any heavily shadowed areas that obscure easy observation of an intruder.

7. In engineering the system, provisions must be made for increasing lighting in certain areas and for the installation of special lighting in such areas as railroad sidings, water approaches, truck loading areas, and, in particular, at points of ingress and egress on the perimeter barrier that will be operational after the hours of darkness.

8. A complete effective protective lighting system will provide for supplementary lighting, or portable lighting, as it is often referred to, that can be turned on by the security forces when emergency conditions exist. This supplementary lighting ideally should generate its own power so that it is operable when the normal utility supply is not available.

9. The exterior protective lighting system will have some luminaires mounted on the sides of buildings. Some luminaires will be mounted on poles, and others will be mounted on the roofs of buildings and directed outward and downward toward the area to be illuminated. To provide maximum security to the system as a whole, all of the luminaires should be located inside the perimeter barrier and far enough from the perimeter barrier so that the luminaires will not be easily damaged or destroyed. Luminaires used on the perimeter areas of a facility should be protected by polycarbonate shields. In some instances where the incidence of vandalism is high, it may be desirable to increase the intensity and the height of the luminaire to make it that much more difficult to damage or destroy.

10. The security force must make daily inspection of every luminaire in the entire protective lighting system inside and outside the buildings and all outages should be reported. When the outage is reported, it should be corrected before the next nightfall.

The principles just listed must all be met if maximum effectiveness is to be obtained. The following points are also particularly important.

1. Bordering areas and approaches to the border of the protected area or the perimeter barrier if one exists should be fully illuminated.
2. Patrolling security forces, particularly at industrial and commercial facilities, should remain behind the luminaires so that they cannot be easily observed.
3. Wherever needed and whenever possible, a high contrast should be created between an intruder and his or her background. This may be accomplished by increasing the amount of light or by brightening the background. (The clear zone should be covered with whitewashed or light-colored gravel.)

LIGHTING SYSTEM CONTROLS

Four methods (three standard and one emergency) are employed to illuminate the protective lighting system and turn it off again at specified times. Usually a combination of at least two methods will be found because a great deal of the protective illumination in the building is controlled manually, whereas outside systems are operated by electronic devices and are illuminated and extinguished automatically. Do not rule out the possibility that all three standard methods may be employed at a single facility. Vapor-type lights may be automatically controlled individually by a photoelectric device, incandescent luminaires may be controlled by a timing device, and still other lights may be operated manually. Obviously, those operated electronically furnish the greatest reliability because the chance of human error through forgetfulness is eliminated. The fourth method of illuminating the protective lighting system or portions of the protective lighting system is by tying the system into an alarm device which, when activated, in addition to possibly activating a siren, will also illuminate the area being violated. The four primary methods of illumination, then, are as follows.

1. Photoelectric devices. These are automatic controls that illuminate an individual luminaire or a group of luminaires as darkness occurs and extinguish them again when sufficient daylight is available. These controls are merely photoelectric cells, and the control is activated by the change in the amount of light passing through the cell. Occasionally, the photoelectric cell control will become stuck either in its open or closed position when dirt or other foreign matter obstructs the infrared ray of light and causes a malfunction. To reduce this condition merely requires that the device be cleaned. This type of device is shown in Figure 5-1.

2. Timing devices. The second most commonly used method of controlling the protective lighting system is by a timing device which automatically engages a switch at a given time of the day, illuminating the system and extinguishing it at a specific time. This device is similar to an alarm clock, and setting the device is very similar to setting an alarm clock. When timing devices are used to illuminate and extinguish the protective

Figure 5-1 Outside protective lighting may be actuated by natural daylight passing through a photo control device with time delay. (Courtesy of Tork Time Controls, Inc.)

lighting system, changes in time must be made in the spring and fall of the year so that the lights are illuminated at darkness and again extinguished as daylight occurs. This is normally done by making adjustments approximately every two weeks using the weather bureau's local time of sunrise and sunset (see Figure 5-2).

3. Manual devices. Manual operation is no different than the method used to turn the lights on and off in the home, with the exception that switches at industrial, commercial, and institutional facilities will probably illuminate a great many lights rather than merely one or two. The manual electrical control switches, if the system is engineered properly, will all be grouped in one area. This will assist in reducing as much as possible human error in not illuminating a part of the protective lighting system. In other instances where the original protective lighting system has been increased, manual switch boxes will be found in several different locations. These protective lighting systems are usually illuminated by the security force and/or maintenance personnel of the organization and often, because of carelessness and forgetfulness, the systems are either not illuminated on time or energy is wasted because the systems remain illuminated after daylight occurs.

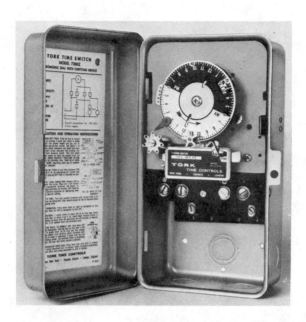

Figure 5-2 A dial time switch including a day-omitting device for automatic control of outdoor lighting. The day-omitting feature keeps the system from being illuminated on selected days. (Courtesy of Tork Time Controls, Inc.)

4. Emergency illumination. This illumination system, as previously stated, will normally be tied in to some type of anti-intrusion or other electronic protective device, and the protective lighting system in a particular area is illuminated only when that area is violated. Sometimes this system may be tied into a timing device, and the luminaires may be turned on and off at different intervals several times throughout the period of darkness to create the impression that activity in the area is in progress from time to time. This is similar to timing devices that are used extensively in residential areas to illuminate and extinguish certain lights inside the home while the home is unoccupied.

There has recently been developed a device that can be classified under the fourth method of control. This control method is used primarily to test and illuminate emergency lighting by microwave principle. The system operates on the same principle as garage doors that are operated electronically. Battery-powered emergency lights can be tested by security personnel regularly to ensure they are operable. An advantage of this control system is that the lights can be illuminated and extinguished as the guard passes the luminaires on his patrol routes.

TYPES OF LAMPS

Four basic types of lamps can be used in the <u>planned protective lighting</u> <u>system</u>. These same types may be used to illuminate operational processes, and the spillage from these luminaires, for economical purposes, may be used as part of the protective lighting system. When this is done, the security analyst must ensure that illumination is available during the entire period of darkness on all days, including Saturdays, Sundays and holidays, that the illumination furnished by this spillage is adequate for security purposes, and that the light controls are not operable by the employees working in the area because they would have the option of extinguishing the lights whenever they desired.

The four basic types of lamps or luminaires are listed below with a brief description of their value in the protective lighting system and their method of operation. These are not necessarily the only luminaires used in all protective lighting systems, but they are the basic types that are generally used for protective illumination.

1. <u>Incandescent lamps</u>. An incandescent lamp or bulb is the sort of luminaire found in lamps used in homes and in table lamps and floor lamps used in offices and installations of this type. Some security personnel prefer this type of illumination in the protective lighting system because when the power is applied, illumination is instantaneous; however, incandescent lamps consume more electrical energy than the remaining three and therefore have been losing their popularity as part of a protective lighting system.

2. <u>Sodium-vapor lamps</u>. The sodium-vapor lamp is becoming more and more popular as a protective lighting luminaire. These lamps are manufactured in both high- and low-pressure versions, and their color is amber, rather than white. The lamps require a great deal less electrical power for the same amount of wattage output, and, because of the peculiar amber color of the light, the ability to see and observe activities from a greater distance is possible. This amber or yellow light also has a greater penetrating power than a white light during rainstorms and snow storms and during periods of fog. This is because the amber light is not reflected by these elements. Many automobiles are equipped with amber lights or lights with amber lenses that are mounted at about bumper height and are used during periods when fog reduced visibility. Sodium-vapor lights are being installed in numerous cities throughout the United States for street lighting, with excellent results being reported.

3. <u>Mercury-vapor lamps</u>. These lamps are similar to sodium-vapor lamps, except that the mercury vapor emits a white light, either directly or indirectly. Light is emitted when mercury and other gases are activated by an electrical current. These lamps have been used for many years in the illumination of parking lots and are quite frequently found in protective lighting systems. Even though they are popular, primarily because of the

clear white light emitted and because they do not consume the amount of
energy that an incandescent lamp consumes, they are somewhat limited
in effectiveness because they require an initial warm-up period. In addition,
in the event of a temporary power outage while the lamp is still warm, the
ability of the lamp to reignite is somewhat retarded, thereby extending by
some minutes the temporary period of darkness.

    4. Quartz lamps. These luminaires emit an extremely bright, high-
intensity white light and ignite as instantaneously as an incandescent bulb.
The quartz lamp is suited to very high wattage, which is normally 1000
watts or more per lamp. It is not uncommon to find 1500- or 2000-watt
quartz lamps in a protective lighting system, particularly if the luminaires
are mounted on the building and are intended to illuminate an area some
distance from their actual location. These lamps can be used effectively
to illuminate parking lots, outside storage areas, or the perimeter barrier;
however, the amount of energy these lamps consume is resulting in the loss
of their popularity as a protective lighting luminaire.

    All outside luminaires—in particular, those near the perimeter boundary
that may be subject to damage by vandals or intruders in their attempts to
breach the perimeter barrier—should be equipped with polycarbonate shields
in lieu of glass. This is also obviously true in areas where vandalism is
high, whether the luminaires are used in parking lots to illuminate roadways or other areas outside or near the perimeter barrier. One should
also remember that when glass shields are broken, it usually results in a
broken luminaire and damage to the ballast and the reflectors. Research
continues in the use of polycarbonate shield for outdoor luminaire protection
because ultraviolet light will cause polycarbonate shields to become brittle
and discolor to some degree.

    As of this writing, to the best of my knowledge, the General Electric
Company has manufactured the only luminaire that can be converted from
mercury vapor to sodium vapor. This requires that the ballast, lens, and
power supply doors be replaced. Changing from mercury vapor to sodium
vapor may appear to be costly when considering hardware change only.
There are numerous plus factors, not only in energy-cost savings, but in
the increase of light output with the same or less wattage consumption (see
Figures 5-3 and 5-4).

    One more word about sodium-vapor lights. Until fairly recently they
were not used to any great extent in the United States even though they have
been used in street lighting in European countries for a much greater length
of time.

    The popularity of sodium-vapor lamps for street lighting is increasing.
The District of Columbia, as an example, converted about 22,000 lights to
sodium vapor in 1972, and the latest figures available now indicate that
over 56,000 lights in the District of Columbia have been converted. In
high-crime areas, the decrease in crime after increasing illumination was
between 30 and 35 percent, with even higher reductions in the area of less

Figure 5-3 A high-pressure sodium-discharge lamp provides excellent outdoor illumination in the protective lighting system. (General Electric Lamp Division)

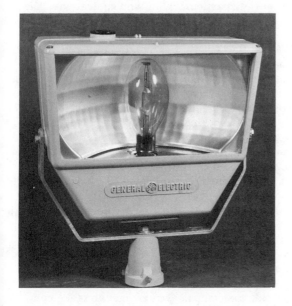

Figure 5-4 The multivapor lamp also provides excellent outdoor illumination at a cost, including installation, that is far less than in the case of incandescent or mercury-vapor lamps. (General Electric Lamp Division)

crime concentration. These statistics also indicate that criminal activity
did not move to other areas not as well lighted.

As an example of the economy in the reduction of energy used, here are
some statistics. In replacing a 400-watt mercury-vapor luminaire with a
400-watt sodium-vapor luminaire, 62 percent less electricity is consumed,
with a reduction of 26 percent in light. In exchanging a 175-watt mercury-
vapor luminaire with a 150-watt sodium-vapor luminaire, 14 percent less
electricity is consumed with 106 percent more light being produced. Another
example: By replacing a 400-watt mercury-vapor luminaire with a 250-watt
sodium-vapor luminaire, 37 percent less electricity is consumed and 18
percent more light is produced. The best mast height for 400-watt sodium-
vapor luminaires is 45 feet. This height also increases the protection
against damage or destruction by vandals.

The low-pressure sodium-vapor light in use in Europe and Canada for
many years and now in extensive use throughout the United States is the
most efficient light available. There are some problems because of inaccu-
rate color rendition, and for most people, the amber color of the sodium-
vapor light causes color changes. For example, reds become blues.
However, police investigators have found that this phenomenon has little
effect on descriptions that they would normally expect to receive from
witnesses of any type of accident or violent incident or crime because,
psychologically, accurate descriptions are almost impossible anyway.

Recently, the shortage of energy, particularly oil and natural gas, has
received a considerable amount of publicity. As a result of actual reductions in electrical, gas, and oil supplies, many installations have reduced
the effectiveness of the protective lighting system by eliminating luminaires.
These reductions increase the calculated risk assumed, and, in many
instances, because of the lack of security expertise on the part of individuals
making the decision to reduce lighting, wrong lights were extinguished. I
have found that a thorough cost analysis in many instances indicated that as
great a savings could have been realized if certain lamps were replaced
with ones of lower wattage without creating as great a security risk.

For example, parking lots at an industrial plant properly organized by
shift may have certain areas not utilized on second and third shifts. In
this case, illumination could be decreased or eliminated in a parking lot
protected by a well-constructed and maintained perimeter barrier without
creating a major hazard or have too great an effect on employee morale.
It is this type of thinking that hopefully this chapter will stimulate.

I know of an industrial plant in the northeast section of the country that
is located in an area surrounded by middle-class and upper-class residences.
The plant employs hundreds of local residents; however, when company
management was negotiating with city officials about 10 years ago when the
plant was going to be constructed, the company was obliged to make certain
concessions if the plant would be located there at all. One was a restriction
in outdoor lighting of all types to 2-footcandle maximum. At ground level,
2 footcandles is slightly better lighting than bright open moonlight. Other

Figure 5-5 A Smith and Wesson Star-tron Model 303-A with 135 mm, f/16 objective lens: for possible use by security forces and also usable with still cameras and motion picture and TV cameras. The night-vision device is said to intensify moonlight and starlight up to 50,000 times. Used extensively by the police, the units are compact, lightweight, and highly portable. (Smith and Wesson)

restrictions at this location included the location and type of perimeter barrier that could be erected. To overcome these unavoidable risks, a closed circuit television system was installed that required the use of expensive television cameras to operate at that lower light level of illumination. The security force was also issued night-vision devices to increase the effectiveness of the external patrols (see Figure 5-5).

It is interesting to note the percentage of use of all available electrical power in the nation. Commercial establishments consume a total of 49 percent of all energy use when outdoor advertising and other outside applications are added. Residential areas use approximately 20 percent of all the energy consumed in lighting, and the industrial community uses a like percentage. The institutional community uses approximately 7.5 percent, and street and highway illumination consumes the remaining 3.5 percent of all the energy used for illumination.

TYPES OF SYSTEMS AND POWER SOURCES

The protective lighting system may consist of one or more general methods used to apply the intensity of illumination necessary at any given predetermined point and time. Should unpredictable circumstances arise, all of the accepted methods may be employed. In the industrial community, most systems are considered highly effective and have available the necessary equipment to implement lighting of areas by any one or all methods. In commercial and some institutional facilities, no emergency lighting is available and management will rely on lighting equipment employed by the police and fire departments when emergencies occur. Hospitals will in all cases have emergency standby generators that have the capability of producing enough energy to continue operations indefinitely.

In most of the larger cities where well-equipped fire departments, emergency squads, and police organizations are available, there is a complete reliance upon these units for emergency lighting except for interior emergency lighting required by local fire and safety codes.

The following four systems are the generally accepted types or methods used.

1. Continuous lighting method. This method is the most common type of protective lighting system and consists of a series of fixed lights designed to provide a continuous flood of light to a given area. The beams of light will overlap to ensure that individual outages do not disrupt the accurate observation of the area being illuminated.

2. Standby lighting. This lighting differs from continuous lighting in that it is not normally used in the protective lighting plan on a regular basis. The lights are fixed, either installed on buildings or poles; however, they are not continually lighted. A standby lighting system could be illuminated by the activation of an alarm or by manually throwing a switch. Standby lighting could be likened to the light in a refrigerator or freezer that remains extinguished until the door is open and is then illuminated and remains in the illumination mode until the door is again closed and the light switch disengaged.

3. Movable lighting. Movable lighting normally consists of a combination of searchlights and floodlights. Movable lighting is the type of lighting that is found in municipal fire and police departments. It is used to supplement either the continuous or standby lighting system, or, if a particular emergency exists, it may be the only illumination that is available for a period of time. Movable lighting normally is installed on fixed mounts that can easily be moved from point to point, either merely by being pulled or in some instances, if the light is large enough, it may be mounted on the motor-driven vehicle and moved in this manner.

4. Emergency lighting. Emergency lighting is installed in all buildings used by the public and in all industrial, commercial, and institutional buildings. Emergency lighting obviously is used only during an emergency and usually employs batteries of one sort or another as a power source. Such lighting is usually tied directly into the utility power source servicing the building, and a continuous trickle charge ensures that the battery is at full capacity constantly. The mechanism is so arranged that when the utility power source is no longer available, the light illuminates immediately,

using the battery as its source of energy. These lights will normally have at least a rating of 4 hours continuous lighting.

To ensure complete reliability of the protective lighting system, an auxiliary power source should be available in the event the primary public utility supply should fail. In hospitals, as we mentioned previously, adequate auxiliary power capabilities will always be found so that the hospital can continue operations and, if necessary, execute the emergency and disaster plan. However, the auxiliary source seldom provides power to maintain illumination of outside areas. When this condition exists, security plans must provide for increased manpower in patrol and control activities.

PROTECTIVE LIGHTING SYSTEM EQUIPMENT

The type of equipment used in developing the protective lighting system will depend upon the character of the facility, the contour of the terrain, the natural barriers or hazards that exist, the location of the facility in relation to adjacent activities, and numerous other conditions that may dictate the intensity and the type of lighting required. The equipment will range from the lighting units required to the type, size, and number of auxiliary power sources required. Our discussion will be confined to the general classification of lighting units that are suitable for installation in the protective lighting plan and a short description of each.

1. Floodlights. These luminaires are designed to form the light into a beam so that it can be projected to distant points and is used for area illumination. Floodlights are specified in wattage and beam width. The beam width is expressed in degrees, and this will define the angle included by the beam. A rough classification of floodlights, according to beam width, is to use the terms narrow, medium, or wide. Floodlights are manufactured in two types—one that is considered open and the other closed. The closed fixture is equipped with a cover or door constructed of glass or polycarbonate that protects it from rain and dust. Therefore, enclosed floodlights are preferred for a protective lighting system because the lamp and the reflecting surfaces are protected from damage due to inclement weather. Floodlights can be used to illuminate outside areas, buildings, and perimeter barriers and are also used for special lighting of critical and vulnerable structures or vital areas within the perimeter barrier.

2. Street lights. We have already discussed the mercury-vapor and sodium-vapor lamps—both high and low pressure—that are in use for street lighting and the fact that their popularity, particularly of the sodium-vapor luminaire, is increasing. The type of lights usually referred to as street lights are used for numerous applications, including the illumination of parking lots, interplant roadways, storage areas. They can be used wherever the need for illumination exists.

3. <u>Fresnal luminaires</u>. Fresnal luminaires are used in the protective
lighting system and are highly effective in isolated areas. This luminaire
delivers a fanlike beam of light that is approximately 180 degrees horizontally and anywhere from 50 to 30 degrees vertically. They are generally
used in isolated areas because they project the light outward and into the
eyes of the intruder while the patrolling guard under or behind the light is
in relative darkness. Lamps commonly used in fresnal luminaires are the
300- or 500-watt incandescent type. Some manufacturers manufacture this
type lighting using a quartz bulb.

4. <u>Searchlights</u>. Searchlights can either be fixed or movable and are
seldom found in any industrial or commercial facility or at institutions.
They are normally employed as emergency lighting or can be found in fixed
positions in remote areas along waterfronts where the security force will
from time to time illuminate the searchlight and sweep a given area to
observe whether or not any activity exists.

5. <u>Spotlights</u>. Spotlights are used to illuminate peripheral windows or
doors, and in some instances they are the sole luminaire used to illuminate
small parking areas. These lights are very fragile and easily destroyed,
because the entire fixture is normally manufactured of glass. In only a
very few instances is the spotlight protected by any metal or polycarbonate
covering. The spotlight has limited use in the protective lighting system;
however, it is used extensively for residential protection and in the protection of small stores, shops, and so on.

ILLUMINATION TECHNIQUES

1. <u>Perimeter barrier</u>. The intensity of illumination of the perimeter
barrier will depend upon whether or not it is isolated or nonisolated.
Normally when a barrier is not within observation from a point in the
built-up area, lighting is increased as a further deterrent to attempted
breaches.

Nonisolated barriers can be adequately lighted by installing light poles
inside and at least 8 feet from the barrier. Pole height will vary with the
type of luminaire being used as will the distances between the light poles.
A rule of thumb is that poles are approximately 15 feet in height and spaced
about 150 feet apart.

Security personnel should have in their library the various national
standards of protective lighting that are issued in pamphlet form by the
Illuminating Engineering Society of America, the address of which can be
found among the sources at the end of this book. Perimeter barrier illumination includes the lighting of openings on the perimeter barrier that are
used operationally.

Intrafacility roadways obviously need to be illuminated, particularly if
operations are in progress after the hours of darkness, and these roadways
are illuminated in a manner similar to the illumination of public streets.

Figure 5-6 Illumination of the interior of truck trailers being loaded or unloaded will deter, if not eliminate, pilfering small items from cartons. (Courtesy Pheonix Products Company)

Areas inside the protected area such as storage areas also require that special techniques be applied to ensure that adequate illumination exists.

2. <u>Waterfronts, piers, and docks</u>. Special illumination is required when piers and docks are used operationally after the hours of darkness. The illumination of docks, for example, will include illumination of the underside of the docks and sufficient illumination of the dock surface and surrounding areas, including roadways, to permit operations to be conducted after the hours of darkness. The system should furnish a sufficient amount of light so that the security force can observe these operations and the dock area after operations have ceased. Truck docks, railroad docks, and open

Figure 5-7 The extended arm of the dock light is used effectively here to illuminate the inside of a railroad car. Note the large opening between the railroad car and the face of the building. (Courtesy Phoenix Products Company)

docks also require special illumination techniques. Figures 5-6 through 5-8 will indicate methods and techniques for illuminating these areas.

In conducting a survey of any type of facility in order to assess the effectiveness of the protective lighting system, the surveyor must conduct a study of the facility after the hours of darkness. Seldom will the security surveyor require light measurements, and he should be concerned primarily with whether or not he, as a patrolling guard, has adequate illumination for good observation of all areas that the security guard is responsible for protecting.

If special lighting is required, the local utility company should be contacted and illuminating engineers should make the study. This service normally is provided without charge, and once the study is completed and

Figure 5-8 This dock light is being utilized to furnish added illumination of an open dock that remains operational after the hours of darkness. Note the open unprotected door to the warehouse area and the unprotected windows on the right. (Courtesy Phoenix Products Company)

a decision made on whether or not the additional illumination or special illumination will be installed, the engineer who conducted the study will also supervise its installation to ensure that the correct equipment is properly installed.

This chapter should furnish the security surveyor sufficient information so that he can make an intelligent study and analysis of the protective lighting system in an effort to determine whether or not additional illumination is needed and, if so, the type.

6

Industrial
Building Security

This chapter will discuss the protection plan as it applies primarily to buildings in industrial and commercial complexes. Developing the protection plan for high-rise buildings differs greatly because in almost all cases little or no security can be established in outside areas or at the property boundary to assist in establishing a program of protection for the building.

The protection of buildings that lie within an area surrounded by a perimeter barrier of one type or another simplifies the analysis somewhat in that the effort can be directed toward security of, and controls at, the building openings—the windows and doors. Other openings that are no longer or seldom used cannot be overlooked in older structures because the intruder, like flowing liquid, will glide from one point of entry to another until a weak point is discovered. Then, like water seeping into the building, he penetrates the barrier and effects his entry.

As in all other facets of the security study, an assessment of each building being protected must be made to determine its criticality and vulnerability. Without this assessment, it will not be possible to determine the degree of security that is required for the overall protection of the building and areas or points within the building.

The lack of an intelligent assessment of security needs will result in either not enough or too great security measures being established. In the first case, hazards would not be reduced, controlled, or eliminated, and, in the second, an added unnecessary economic burden would impede efficient operations or slow down work because the unwarranted restriction has adversely affected employee morale.

The previous chapters were devoted to securing the perimeter or boundary of the facility and the establishing secure areas between the outer barrier and the buildings. Included in these measures is provision of a sufficient amount of illumination to deter illegal entry and, if illegal entry is successful, to make detection of the intruder almost a certainty. If these basic principles are properly analyzed and applied to the protection plan, with controls established at the perimeter openings, the amount of security needed for the protection of the buildings within the protected area may be somewhat lessened.

Nevertheless, even though outer walls of most buildings can be easily breached with tools as simple as a hammer and masonry chisel, our efforts will be directed toward fortification of the peripheral openings of the building. It must be remembered that equally as important as keeping the intruder out is keeping company property in and, even more important, establishing positive control over the movements of personnel and material through authorized avenues of ingress and egress.

DOORS

Doors are installed in all buildings to serve a specific purpose. If existing doors that previously served a useful purpose are no longer needed, consideration should be given to removing the door and permanently closing the opening. Look, if you will, at the modern telephone switching stations. Most are windowless, one-story buildings with only one or two personnel openings, an overhead door or two at the service dock. Usually the entire building or at least the rear of the building is further protected by chain link fencing. Air conditioning and ventilation openings are usually within the perimeter barrier or otherwise protected.

There are literally thousands of industrial and commercial structures in the nation today that have been expanded and/or whose interior operations have been changed so as to require reassignment of employee population. Either or both of these changes affect the intended use of the original doors and windows, and rather than eliminating them the openings remained. These openings are usually in remote areas, and most are not properly secured, inspected, or controlled by the security force. Perhaps this is just another nemesis of American industry in that it is similar to allowing junk and scrap to accumulate in the far corners of the protected area.

Security personnel involved in planning building expansion or major operational changes should always reevaluate their security requirements and recommend changes that are required to ensure that they are included in the budgetary planning.

Studying the Use of All Doors

Assume that no doors any longer exist that are not required for some purpose. Also remember that the peripheral walls of buildings that form a part of the perimeter barrier have already been discussed. The logical sequence, then, in commencing the building protection study is to assign a priority of importance to these openings depending upon their purpose and frequency of intended use.

Employee Entrances and Exits

There is no doubt that this category should receive first priority; however, this category can be divided into two groups, each being as important as the other. The first is employee entrances. These must be designated as such and controls established, whether the controls are through the use of electronic devices, security personnel, or merely a receptionist.

There are few industrial or commercial buildings that do not have a second entrance in addition to the main employee entrance. The second one is used by officials, management personnel, administrative or office personnel, and usually visitors, whether they are sales personnel or any other category of nonemployee. This type of entrance quite frequently is not protected by the perimeter barrier because the "face" or front of the building usually faces toward the main arterial approach. The entrance door at this point is more likely than not constructed of plate glass set into metal frames. Locking devices used to secure these doors should be· of the type intended for this use, and because these doors are easily "spread" they should be secured by a horizontal dead,bolt near the center of the door and vertically locking bars at the top and at the bottom. The horizontal dead bolt and the vertical locking bars can be operated by two different locking devices or both can be attached to one common locking device in the center of the door. Control of the doors can be assigned to a reception-ist, a switchboard-receptionist, a security guard or a combination of any of these. Low-traffic entrances, such as the entrance used by office em-ployees may be controlled remotely through electronic locking devices, closed circuit television surveillance systems, and audio arrangements.

The main employee entrance used by hourly or production employees · presents quite another problem, primarily because of the large numbers of individuals and secondly, of equal importance, because controls must ensure that no "time stealing" or "double carding," if you will, occurs. In addition, security must ensure that company property, raw materials, or the finished products that this category of employee is exposed to are not removed without authority. Obviously, if personnel controls are estab-lished at the perimeter barrier or somewhere near the perimeter barrier, the controls exercised at the building entrance can be relaxed.

All employee entrances must be considered to be emergency exits and therefore should not be secured while employees are in the building in a manner that would interfere with rapid emergency egress. Usually the security devices used on other emergency exits can be equally as effective at these points.

Emergency Exit Doors

All doors intended as emergency exits only obviously should receive the next priority in the study of the door arrangement of each building. Gene-rally these doors are not intended for operational purposes, and because they would be used only during emergencies, they should be equipped with either local alarms or an alarm system that can be monitored elsewhere on the property. The installation of local alarms usually will effectively discourage employees from using the doors surreptitiously. Because

emergency exit doors are not used for operational purposes, further security
may be established by removing the door handles, door knobs, or any type
of locking device installed on the outside of the doors. If emergency exit
doors are not equipped with any type of alarm, after-the-fact supervision
of these doors can be effected merely by installing a screw eye in the door
and the door frame and using either a railroad-type seal or other type seal
and fastening it through the two eyes. Inspections by the security force will
quickly determine whether or not the doors have been used surreptitiously.
If a railroad-type seal is used, a record can be made of the number of the
seal to ensure that it is not removed and replaced by another of similar
manufacture. If it is discovered that the seals are broken and that the doors
are used surreptitiously, further precautions must be taken. Some type of
alarm device must be installed so that the security force is alerted immediately when the door is used surreptitiously.

Fire Doors

Fire doors installed throughout industrial and commercial buildings are
designed to close automatically should a fire occur. For example, fire
doors located in hospital corridors are normally held in their open position
by electromagnets that are electronically tied into a fire alarm system.
When a fire occurs anywhere in the area, the current to the electromagnets
holding the doors in their open positions is severed and the doors then
automatically close. The obvious purpose of such doors is to halt the spread
of fire and prevent fluing the fire through the corridors and up stairwells.

In industrial facilities, fire doors are often found in openings in fire
walls that are constructed between various departments, usually between
warehousing, shipping and receiving areas, and the production areas.
These fire doors are normally kept in their open position by the use of a
fusible link that is destroyed when the heat at the location reaches a certain
temperature. The doors then close automatically because they are installed
on a track that would automatically cause the door to glide to its closed
position. Sometimes the rupture of the seal may release a counterweight
that, in conjunction with the slanted rail on which the door rides, automatically closes the door swiftly. Fire doors may be used for operational
purposes and in many instances, particularly when they are installed between operational departments and warehousing operations, they are closed,
locked, and used for security purposes during second and third shift operations, providing the operational schedule does not require that products be
moved into the warehouse or into the shipping area.

Dock Doors

The doors at shipping and/or receiving docks normally consist of overhead
and personnel-type doors. Obviously the overhead doors are used for
shipping purposes and the personnel doors are normally used by truck

drivers and helpers to enter the building. Both types of doors must be secured when not in use.

Overhead doors will normally have a locking bar installed during manufacture which will lock into both tracks in which the door rides. These bars are usually secured in place at the center of the door. These locking devices are usually of poor grade and are unsatisfactory as a security locking device. If the overhead doors are equipped with locking bars, adequate security can be obtained by drilling a hole through either or both locking bars that protrude through the slot in the track and locking the bar into the track by placing a padlock through the holes that have been drilled. This arrangement is effective whether or not there are one or two locking bars on the overhead door. If the door does not have locking bars, adequate security can be obtained by drilling a hole through the door track near the bottom roller and inserting the hasp of a padlock through the hole, locking it in place. This makes it impossible to roll the door up further than about 1 inch from the surface.

Personnel doors should remain locked at all times in all dock areas and can be controlled either manually at the door location or remotely by an individual assigned to the shipping and/or receiving department. However, if this system is used, some means of positive identification of the individuals desiring to enter the building must be possible and observation of the individuals departing the building is a necessity. This can be accomplished in one of two ways. The most economical is obviously a direct line of sight observation of the door and the individuals using the door. If the door is located so that it cannot be observed directly, a closed circuit television camera monitored by the individual operating the remote electrical latch may be used. To ensure proper identity, a two-way audio system can be installed so that the individual operating the door can communicate with the individuals desiring ingress or egress.

Doors Separating Warehousing and Production Departments

These doors should receive the next priority because in almost all industrial establishments some warehousing activity and shipping exists in the same area where production is in progress. In most instances shipping is done on a one-shift basis; however, production may continue during second and third shifts. To ensure that the finished material is not unnecessarily exposed, these doors should be secured during second and third shift operations. If the quantity of production is great enough, it may require that the finished product be stored in the warehouse. In these instances, keys to the doors should be issued to selected individuals and the doors opened and closed only when ingress or egress to the warehouse is required. If operations are of such magnitude that the warehouse requires the same number of personnel during second and third shift operations as they did during the first shift, no special precautions need be taken that are not already in effect during first shift operations.

If doors between production areas and the warehousing operations will
be closed and secured during second and third shift operations, management
must be absolutely certain that no emergency exits from the warehousing
area are intended for use by those in production. In some instances, it
may be necessary to create an additional emergency exit in the production
area to ensure rapid evacuation of production employees, even though the
warehousing section may be secured.

Doors Between Working and Idle Areas

It often occurs that during second and third shift operations all departments
are not in operation. If departments are physically separated with fire
walls or otherwise, consideration should be given to securing those departments that are idle from the departments that are in operation. This may
be accomplished if the departments are separated by a fire wall by closing
and securing the fire door that breaches the fire wall. However, caution
should be exercised to ensure that personnel working in active departments
are not required to evacuate through emergency exit doors in idle departments. Each department must be studied, and consideration must be given
to the work schedules of all departments within the facility. If this is not
included in the study and analysis, a disaster could occur if assigned emergency exit doors in the escape route have been cut off.

DOORS TO WARM WORKING AREAS

In many industrial plants, particularly during the warm months, doors are
left open either between departments or on the peripheral walls of the building for ventilation purposes only. Often these doors are emergency exit
doors that have never been intended for operational use. However, during
the warm months they are open and unguarded merely for the purposes of
supplying ventilation (see Figure 6-1).
   If such opening of doors is necessary, additional protection must be
installed over the openings. This protection is normally a door constructed
of chain link fence of a gauge similar to that used on the perimeter barrier.
The door should be equipped so that, if it is an emergency exit, speedy
evacuation can be effected should an emergency occur. This will usually
require that any protection be hung or hinged at the end of the doorway that
is opposite from where the regular solid door is hinged. Because it is an
emergency entrance, both the solid door and the security protection installed
to secure the opening during hot weather must open outward.
   The security force must conduct a study of all openings, doors and windows, that are likely to be opened during the warm months to furnish ventilation to ensure that a hazard is not created during these periods. In some
instances, where closed circuit television surveillance systems are already
installed, it may require nothing more than scanning these openings with

Figure 6-1 An open, unprotected freight dock door with bagged chemicals exposed to theft.

the television cameras installed for other purposes to ensure that the doors are not used for unauthorized purposes. When these conditions are established, all employees should be notified that although the doors are open and unprotected, they are constantly observed through the closed circuit television system by a member of the security force.

DOORS SEPARATING PRODUCTION AND OFFICE AREAS

All too often the doors separating production and office areas contain either an inadequate locking device or no locking device whatsoever. If there is no activity in the facility except during first shift operations, this arrangement may suffice; however, if second and third shift operations are in progress when the administrative offices of the facility cease operations, it is mandatory that locking devices be installed so that these doors can be secured to prevent hourly employees who have no reason to be in the office areas from entering them. The control of these doors by the security force will assist in controlling custodial personnel who are cleaning the office areas of the building. Establishing a schedule for cleaning personnel is a must if the trash accumulated in the office areas is brought into the production areas to be disposed of. This will enable the security force to ensure that no property in the plant offices is being removed and that no property from the production areas is being moved into the office areas and removed the following day by one of the office employees in collusion with the custodial worker.

If it is necessary for certain supervisors and other personnel assigned to night management to move into the office areas, keys should be issued to these individuals only. The keys issued to them should permit them to enter only those areas where they are actually authorized.

Locking devices installed on doors separating the office areas from the production areas should be of the cipher type. This would require that no key be issued, and, should line supervision in the production area be changed, the combination of the lock can be changed in a matter of minutes. It must be remembered, however, that if custodial personnel are being controlled through the use of a locking device on these doors, the cipher lock will not suffice because such a lock is operated by depressing selected buttons on the outside (the production side) of the door and can be opened from within without the use of a key or the knowledge of the combination. All that is required to withdraw the dead bolt or latch bolt is to turn a thumb latch, and, unless the lock is left in its open position, the individual moving from the office to the production area will not be able to return unless he has knowledge of the combination.

DOORS TO DANGER AREAS AND RESTRICTED AREAS

Normally doors that secure danger areas or restricted areas are of solid construction and in addition are often covered with metal as further protection against fire. Doors to danger areas and restricted areas should remain secured at all times, and the keys to these areas, particularly during the second and third shifts, should be assigned to the security force only because few should have the need to enter these areas.

If transformer banks are installed on the protected property and further protected with either a masonry wall or a chain link fence, the gates leading into these areas should remain secured at all times and the keys controlled by the security force and perhaps the maintenance department supervisor. However, because the maintenance supervisor normally is not available during second and third shift operations, keys to these areas must be in the possession of the security force.

If the need for security in quality-control areas, research and development areas, and areas housing pilot projects is high enough, it may be desirable that these areas be secured with two locking devices requiring two separate keys to be used in order to gain entrance. In these instances, a key to each of the locks would be assigned to two individuals with authority to enter the area. Both individuals would have to be present before access to the area can be gained. In the research and development area or a pilot project area, for example, these persons would normally be the engineers

in charge of the operations in progress. This procedure establishes a
further deterrent against the possibility that material or documents will
be removed by an employee assigned to the project who has authority to
enter it.

DOORS TO TOOL ROOMS, STORAGE AREAS, AND SUPPLY ROOMS

Experience has shown that the doors that open into areas such as these
should be of the "dutch door" variety. That is, the doors should be cut
approximately at the center with a locking device to secure the top half
and the lower half. If the door is used to issue items, it will usually also
contain a shelf at the upper part of the lower door. The lower door remains
secured at all times and acts as a deterrent to unauthorized entry. However, my experience has been that if this type of control is necessary, it
is far better to secure the lower half of the door and to cover the upper
portion of the door with a locking chain link type barrier with an opening
large enough to conduct business. This will ensure that surreptitious entry
is not gained while the individual in charge of the area and responsible for
the security of the area is some distance from the door securing supplies.

DOORS TO SECURITY AREAS

The security areas we refer to are often called "hot item" storage areas.
These areas are found at shipping and receiving docks, particularly in
truck terminals, where cartons have for one reason or another become
broken and the material inside exposed. These security areas or rooms
may also be used to store valuable shipments rather than to allow them to
remain on the dock. The shipment is removed directly from the security,
or "hot item," storage room to the transport that will move it from the
property. This is often required, particularly if a facility is producing
classified items for the government that require that a specific degree of
security be maintained on the item from the time it is assembled or completed until it is shipped.

VAULT DOORS

Walk-in vaults are infrequently found in industrial facilities; however, with
the advent of computerization and computer installations, walk-in vaults
are used more frequently today for the storage of tapes, records, and other
valuables that require a higher degree of security than that obtained by
merely locking a door to a room. In industries using precious metals such
as gold, silver, or mercury, vaults are usually provided to secure this

material. These vaults are normally locked with a combination-type padlock and, in some instances, may even contain a "day gate," a day gate being nothing more than a gate constructed of tool-resistant steel that is operated with a key. During operations, the vault door is opened and remains opened; however, the day gate is closed and remains locked, the key being issued to those individuals who are authorized to enter the vault. The day gate originated at banks where vault doors weigh upwards of 20 to 30 tons. Although vault doors are extremely easy to move, if moved too fast they can cause damage or injury because it is almost impossible to stop a door of this weight once it gains momentum. Vault doors that are not of this heavy construction may not need a daygate; however, it would impede operations if the combination had to be operated each time the vault had to be entered. It would also either tie up one or two individuals if they alone had knowledge of the combination or lessen the security of the vault if too many employees were given the combination.

DOOR LOCKING SCHEDULES

We shall discuss the various types of locks and methods of key control in another chapter in this book; however, any time that locks are used to secure one or a hundred doors, a locking schedule must be established to ensure that the door is locked at a specific time and opened at a specific time, if the lock is to be as effective as possible. In addition, the locking schedule ensures that only those individuals who have authority to open or close the area being guarded are in possession of the key or have knowledge of the combination if a cipher lock is used.

The locking schedule should ensure that certain individuals are assigned to lock specific doors; usually department heads secure the doors in their departments, and certain office personnel secure the doors in their office areas. However, regardless of who is responsible for securing one or all of the doors, the security force must check all doors that are on the locking schedule to ensure that doors are not left open through error or carelessness.

Cleaning crews may be given keys to certain doors, particularly in office areas that they are to clean, with instructions to secure the doors later. Rather than issue the keys to the cleaning personnel and leave them in their possession for a matter of a few hours, I have always recommended that the security force unlock the doors of the areas to be cleaned and secure them again when cleaning has been completed. It is not difficult for a cleaning crew to establish a cleaning schedule that would require the door to be opened only during the period when cleaning is actually in progress. Securing these doors by the security force does not necessarily create any additional patrols, because schedules can normally be established by the security force supervisor and the supervisor of the custodial personnel to ensure that the doors remain open for only short periods of time once cleaning has been completed.

Any door, whether it is installed on the peripheral walls of the building or used to secure an interior area, should be installed so that the hinge pins of the door are not exposed to the outside. If existing doors that will be locked have the hinge pins exposed to the outside, it is not necessary to rehang the door. The pins may be welded to the hinges or a duplex nail or metal pin may be installed in the hinge side of the door with a hole drilled into the frame. When the door is closed, the protruding nail or pin will be seated in the hole or recess, making removal of the door impossible even. though the hinge pins have been removed. Locking devices manufactured specifically for certain types of doors constructed with metal frames, for sliding doors, and for other nonstandard doors, including time-recording locking devices are discussed in Chapter 8.

When examining any door in any facility, the door structure and overall strength must be assessed to determine if it will furnish the degree of security required. A hollow-core door, even though equipped with a maximum-security locking device, furnishes little security against a determined attack. On some doors, I have seen locking devices that were more costly than the door itself.

The door frame is the next item to consider in determining the overall strength of the door. Most interior and many exterior doors, particularly those installed in structures using lumber for the skeletal structure, can easily be "spread" from the door frame.

During construction, to ensure proper fit, wooden wedges are used between the wooden upright and the wooden door frame. These wedges are normally inserted above and below the locking device so that a·"bridge" is formed to accommodate the lock face plate. Very little pressure needs to be applied between the door and the frame at the lock location to "spread" the frame from the door, a distance of usually less than $\frac{1}{2}$ inch being all that is necessary.

Doors containing windows of ordinary glass or doors within 40 inches of a window constructed of the same material must be secured with a lock containing a keyhole both inside and outside. A hand-operated latch on the inside, generally speaking, is unacceptable for any peripheral door because persons hidden in the building can exit at will, and persons who enter the building at another point can exit wherever the lock does not require a key to open it. Why 40 inches? Beyond 40 inches the lock cannot be readily operated by the normal individual without some tool to extend his reach.

WINDOW SECURITY

Windows are installed in a building for three reasons: to permit light to enter; to observe the outside areas or the inside of the building; and for ventilation purposes. Whatever the reason, a window creates a weak point in the periphery of the building and, in most instances in industrial and commercial facilities, requires more protection than that furnished by the breakable glass regardless of the size of the opening.

I was once asked to conduct a security study in a facility that manufactured men's and women's shirts. In this facility, all of the windows in all of the warehousing and production areas were adequately protected, with the exception of a small window in one of the ladies' restrooms, which was immediately adjacent to the public street. One of the peripheral walls of the building formed a part of the perimeter barrier. For one reason or another, the restroom window was overlooked in past security studies of the building. During the new survey, undercover agents had been employed in three of the departments in the production area, and one undercover agent was employed in the warehousing area.

In starting my survey, I used my usual style and started at the perimeter and worked in. On my first tour around the portion of the building that formed a part of the perimeter barrier, the unguarded window was extremely obvious, especially because all of the other windows along that side of the building and along the public street were adequately secured with fencing of small gauge. I made my report of my findings verbally that evening to the client during dinner and he said that he would have this deficiency corrected the following day.

I arrived at the facility at approximately 8:00 the following morning and was met by the client with whom I had dinner and was told that we were a day late. The undercover personnel had discovered that two employees, one of them a member of the security force, were throwing shirts through the window in cartons containing a dozen shirts each to an accomplice on the street who loaded them in an automobile and drove off. When the security audit was completed, it was revealed that this unprotected opening was practically the only way that any large amount of the shirts could be stolen and had it been protected like the other windows, the losses in all probability would not have occurred. My immediate thought was that perhaps the individual who, in the past, was responsible for security might possibly have been in collusion with employees in committing thefts and removing the property from the building in this manner. Fortunately, the individual who had been responsible for security had departed some 2 or 3 years previous to the survey being conducted.

The simplest method to increase security at the window openings is to install a screen, metal rods, or chain link fencing. Whatever material is used, it must be firmly attached to the window frame or adjoining wall.

In analyzing each such opening for further security, one must include a determination of whether or not the protection can be permanently installed or must be movable should an emergency occur. Such movability can usually be accomplished by means of hinges, hasps, and padlocks or hasps and padlocks alone, making it possible to remove the entire additional protection. If the window will not be used during emergencies, permanent installations should then be made.

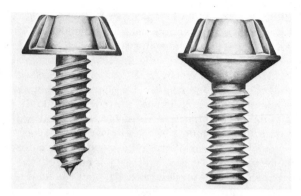

Figure 6-2 Tamper-proof fasteners such as these machine screws or wood
or metal screws require a special tool without which it is virtually impossible to extract them. They will increase door security when used in hedges
and will make virtually impossible the removal when used in metal window-
protection installation. (Courtesy Jefferson Screw Corporation)

   Whether screens or chain link fencing will be used, it will usually be
necessary to tailor protection for each window, and the size of the mesh
or openings will depend upon the degree of security to be achieved. Some
windows used for ventilation are installed so that they swing on an axis
hinge; if so, any protection must be fabricated in "basket" form.
   Several manufacturers produce a polycarbonate or "impact-resistant"
plate glass for use in doors, windows, or other enclosures that furnishes
a higher degree of security than that provided ordinary plate glass but still
less than that obtained from the so-called "bullet-proof" glass. The protective material is manufactured in different thicknesses and, therefore,
different strengths. It is said not to discolor with age. It is in common
use in store fronts, for protection of computer areas, and in financial
establishments, and the like.
   In the chapter dealing with high-rise security, this protection is discussed for special purpose use. It is expensive to install and is used
primarily in security applications in museums, hospitals, schools, prisons,
and similar facilities. If properly installed, this material furnishes excellent protection and should not be overlooked.
   Perhaps the only security precaution that needs to be exercised is to
close, lock, and seal the window in its lowered position and require regular
inspections and reports by the security force. Seals should be of the type
described previously for use on emergency exits and should be installed
in a similar manner. The number of the seal should be recorded by the
security force so that it can be checked to determine whether or not the
original seal was removed and another one installed in its place.

When installing any type of security device on a window or door that requires the use of machine screws or wood or metal screws, those especially engineered to be "tamper-proof" should be used. These may be of the "one-way screw head" type that can be easily installed with a flat-bladed screwdriver but are almost impossible to withdraw with the same tool. Or, the screws could be of the type that require a special tool to install and remove them (see Figure 6-2).

AREAS REQUIRING SPECIAL ATTENTION

In addition to those areas already covered in establishing area and building security, there are necessary activities that, if not given special treatment in the security plan, will almost surely result in loss of assets and lowering of employee morale with its resulting loss of productivity contributing even further to the losses.

Some of the areas listed below will be given only brief mention because the magnitude of the security analysis dictates that these areas be treated separately and in greater detail. Another entire chapter will be devoted to programming security for these installations.

The location of the activity within the building will often have a positive or negative effect upon the overall security program, and it may be necessary that the activity be moved to another location in order to establish the protection required. We shall discuss relocation of activities later in this chapter.

Location of Time Clocks

I have found in numerous production facilities that I have surveyed, particularly larger operations where several hundred employees are involved, that time stealing by double carding was often the rule instead of the exception. By double carding we mean that one employee will punch in other employees' time cards into the time clock when he arrives at work and again when he departs work without the other employees ever being present. This is quite often done when male and female employees are employed at the same facility, with the husband or the wife punching in the spouse who never arrived for that day's work. It may also involve punching in an employee at the appointed hour when the shift begins, whereas the employee, in fact, does not arrive until 2 or 3 hours later.

Wherever possible, all time clocks should be located in one area or clock alley, the obvious position being near the main employee entrance. A security guard should be on duty at the time clock and time card location to ensure that each employee clocks in only one time card.

When employees are authorized to leave the plant during lunch periods, they will normally be required to punch out and again punch in. This gives them a second opportunity of stealing time. If the security guard is at the time clock location only at the beginning and the end of the shift but not during the lunch break, time stealing is almost certain to occur.

Stealing time can also occur when an employee is excused and leaves during the shift for whatever reason. Instead of clocking out, the employee may have a fellow worker clock him out at the end of the shift. I have observed, on numerous occasions, that employees who leave shortly after lunch do not punch out on the time clock even though they pick up their time card and appear to be recording the time on the card. In checking the card, I have found that it was never inserted into the time clock. Instead, a fellow employee will insert it at the end of the shift.

The greater the number of time clock locations in the facility, the more opportunity employees have to punch other employees' cards in and out. This is a particularly troublesome problem in most hospitals, because quite often time clocks are found in individual departments rather than in a group at one location so that controls can be established.

Employee Locker Rooms

Employee locker rooms will often create security problems, particularly if management does not insist that all lockers be secured with some type of locking device. When lockers are not secured, employees will eventually start stealing from one another, and an employee may steal company property and hide it in another employee's locker until he is ready to depart the facility. If an unannounced inspection should be made by the security force and management, the property is found in the innocent employee's locker, thus creating an unnecessary morale problem.

If lockers are available for employees use, they should be assigned by management, usually by the personnel manager. They should be furnished with a locking device, and employees should not be allowed to use their own locking device on the locker. The employee informational pamphlet should contain the company policy that if the employee is assigned a locker and a key to the locking device on the locker, this locker must remain secured at all times. In addition, employees should be told that if locker inspections are conducted at unannounced times and company property is found in the locker, it will be assumed that that employee who has been assigned the locker is the one responsible for the unauthorized material found therein. A policy of this nature will normally ensure that all employees secure their lockers, and notifying employees that unannounced locker inspections may be made is itself a deterrent.

Cafeterias and Lunch Areas

Hot-line cafeterias, vending machine lunch areas, and smoking areas often create considerable problems for the security force and consequently for management. Hot-line cafeterias are normally operated by a concessionaire, which means that additional outside nonemployees with usually a considerable turnover must be controlled by the security force. In addition, even though management of the facility has no responsibility to the concessionaire other than securing the area, theft or damage that occurs when the cafeteria is closed creates problems among the concessionaire, the security force, and management.

If a facility is equipped with a hot-line cafeteria, whether it is operated by a concessionaire or by the company, one individual in charge of the cafeteria operations must be responsible and must become the contact between that operation and the guard force. Guard patrols should include cafeterias and lunch areas on their security routes, and if a concessionaire is operating the cafeteria, he should be instructed by the security force on how to secure the area. The security force should check to ensure that their instructions are being followed on a day-to-day basis.

Another problem is that additional outsiders and vendors must be controlled by the security force as they deliver foodstuffs to the cafeteria. Inherent in cafeteria operations is another hazard—removal of the garbage from the facility. If possible, hot-line cafeterias should be equipped with garbage disposals so that most leftover food can be ground up and disposed of in this manner. If the trash and garbage is removed in cans, the security force should occasionally conduct an inspection of garbage-removal operations by requiring the concessionaire to empty the garbage he is about to remove into a similar-type container so that a visual inspection of the can's contents can be made.

If only vending machines are provided for the employees and lunch areas are established, the problem of control of the vendor serviceman still exists. The security force should inspect the serviceman's carts, boxes, and any other package that he removes from the facility, not necessarily on a day-to-day basis, but frequently and at unannounced times. Vending machine lunch areas, like cafeterias, must be included on the security guard's tours, and the vending machine operators should be advised that management will not be responsible for losses sustained if the vending machines are broken into. However, management should establish the necessary precautions to secure the machines to the degree required.

Whenever possible, if the vending machine lunch area is not within a room in the building but is merely along one wall or in a section of an area, it should be located so that patrolling guards, supervisors, and employees have a clear view of the machines and the areas. This will assist in reducing, if not eliminating, thefts from the vending machines.

Smoking areas quite often are located just outside the building if smoking inside the building is prohibited. If smoking areas are located outside the building, frequent patrols through these areas should be made by the security force. If closed circuit television is being used to observe outside areas, consideration should be given at the time of installation to positioning the cameras so that these authorized smoking areas can be observed if necessary.

If the smoking areas are inside the facility, they do not necessarily create a security hazard; however, if smoking is authorized in the cafeterias or in the vending machine lunch areas, a certain potential for fire does exist, and the security force should check these areas immediately after lunch periods and any breaks.

Pilot Operations and Quality Control

These two operations are grouped together; however, the degree of security established for pilot operations may be greater than that established for quality control. Wherever possible, pilot operations should be located in out-of-the-way areas. That is, in areas that employees normally would not be required to pass by in their day-to-day functions. If the nature of the pilot operations requires an exceptionally high degree of security for proprietary reasons, the entire operation should be separated, if within one of the primary buildings, from the remainder of the operations by means of a temporary wall that completely surrounds pilot operations from floor to ceiling, with only those access doors that are required for operational purposes. Usually, plywood will suffice to secure the area, and special controls should be established at the doors to ensure that only those individuals authorized in the activity are able to enter. This would normally be accomplished with either a card lock or a cipher lock, giving the combination or issuing cards only to those individuals who will have authority to enter the area. Personnel-type doors leading into the area should be constructed with pneumatic door closers to ensure that they are not inadvertently left ajar.

Quality-control departments or areas, on the other hand, normally do not require the degree of security that is assigned to pilot operations. However, records compiled as a result of the quality-control operations should be secured in locked filing cabinets, and the cabinets or security containers that are used should be checked by the security force when the quality-control department is closed down to ensure that the information is adequately secured.

On numerous occasions in the past, a competitor gained a sales edge because he was able to secure data from quality-control departments of his competition. For example, an advertisement might indicate that the item the manufacturer was advertising for sale, although similar to that of his competitor, was of higher quality because only one item out of twenty had to be reworked whereas his competitor's records indicated that one item out of five inspected was returned to the production line to be reworked.

Personnel assigned to quality-control departments are normally technicians of one sort or another and possess skills somewhat greater than the hourly production worker. Therefore, when quality-control personnel are employed, more extensive background investigation should be conducted than that required for an ordinary hourly employee. Similarly, if an hourly employee who has been with the company for some time is assigned to quality control, consideration should be given to conducting another background investigation of this employee in greater depth.

Display Areas

In some operations, the products manufactured at the facility, distributed by the facility, or sold by the facility are displayed in an area that may be open to the public or may be restricted only to sales personnel. If the finished product placed in these areas is of a size that can be readily removed, the display area should be policed, and the personnel moving in and out of the area should be controlled just as they would be in a retail store. Normally the installation of a closed circuit television camera to scan the entire area, including the avenues of ingress and egress to the area, will suffice and will act as a sufficient deterrent against thefts. The installation of closed circuit television is far more economical than assigning a guard to patrol the area during the period that it is in operation. In addition, the closed circuit television camera can be used during periods that the display areas are closed to prevent thefts from occurring by employees operating second and third shifts.

Model Shops

In some industries, particularly the furniture industry, and often in the automobile and aircraft industries, model shops are established where models of the new products being manufactured are created. Security for a model shop should equal the security that would normally be established for the protection of pilot operations, because all the activity in a model shop is proprietary and should not be revealed to anyone who does not have a specific "need to know."

Company Stores

Of all facilities and operations discussed in this chapter, probably the most troublesome to the security force are the company stores. Company stores are normally created as an additional fringe benefit for employees. In company stores, employees can purchase the product being manufactured at a discounted price. In some instances, products that will not be sold to the public because they are considered "seconds" because of some slight flaw in the manufacture of the item are sold at a greatly reduced rate to the employees.

In some instances, the company store may be open not only to the spouses of employees but to the public at large. This often occurs in hosiery manufacturing plants, linen and towel manufacturing plants and, to some degree, in the garment industry.

If company store operations are of any size, consideration should be given to constructing a separate building and locating the retail store there, away from any of the manufacturing buildings.

If this is not considered economical or if the area required does not exist and the company store must be established within one of the buildings, it is normally established somewhere in the vicinity of the warehouse and shipping docks. This is so that the finished product in the warehousing area is easily transferred to the company store.

If the company store is located inside the facility, policies and procedures must be established to ensure (1) that all items moved from the warehouse to the store are accounted for and signed for by the individual in charge, (2) that regularly scheduled inventories are made, (3) that the store hours do not conflict with employees' work hours, and (4) that the employees are not authorized to take the purchases to their work areas, regardless of the type of container they are placed in. Ideally, if a company store is located inside one of the production or warehousing buildings, it should be located near the peripheral wall of the building and the exit used by those patronizing the store should lead outside the plant, even if it requires creating a door in the peripheral wall. In this manner, control is simplified because the employee makes his purchase and is able to take the purchase directly to his automobile without requiring the company to furnish any area where the item may be stored and picked up by the employee as he departs his shift. This arrangement also saves the security force the trouble of having to inspect the package if it were carried from the building through the authorized employee entrances and exits.

Even if there is no company store, scrap and other salvageable items may be sold to employees. This is normally done in outside areas, and the material usually consists of lumber, metal, pipes, scrap machinery, or items that are produced that contain flaws that prevent the item's being sold to the public. Regardless of the items being sold, they must be removed from the plant by the employee, and when the item is purchased and picked up by the employee, a member of the security force or an authorized supervisor should be assigned to the operation. Sales slips describing the item in detail must be used, not only for internal control and cash control, but to ensure that the guard can make an intelligent inspection of the material being removed to ensure that if one item is purchased, only one item is taken out by the employee.

Government Classified Operations

We shall not discuss the security required when government classified operations are in progress because the Department of Defense has published an entire manual on the subject, and a government inspector is responsible to ensure that the degree of security required is being maintained. The security force should be apprised of the classifications of the various operations and storage areas, and obviously they must be assigned to patrol and inspect these areas to ensure that the required degree of security is being maintained.

First-aid Facilities

Since the enactment of the Occupation, Safety and Health Act in April 1971, few problems exist in the area of first-aid stations, because the act is quite clear regarding what is required in various industries insofar as first-aid facilities are concerned.

Generally speaking, first-aid facilities should, in larger operations, be located centrally so that they are equally available to the entire employee population. Quite often, first-aid facilities are located inside the facility's office area, and so employees have to enter the office area when they require treatment. Although this may be the most economical method of operating the first-aid facility for a particular installation, it is usually several hundred feet from the farthest point in the facility. If the injured person is nonambulatory, this means that he or she must be carried the entire distance of the facility to reach the first-aid room.

Whenever possible, the first-aid facility should be located in a central area and near an avenue so that rapid egress can be made should a severely injured employee require hospitalization or outside care by a doctor. Whenever possible, the first-aid facility should be located near an exit door that can be approached by an emergency vehicle. This would eliminate any necessity of exposing the employee unnecessarily during inclement weather.

Credit Unions

Credit unions exist in almost all industrial, commercial, and institutional facilities. Very little cash is handled in the credit union because the majority of the transactions are by check. However, the credit union's information on individual employees should be considered confidential, much the same as accounts in public banks. Even though management of the facility may have no more responsibility for operating the credit union than the moral responsibility of securing the area with the existing security force during and after operations, the credit union area must be included on the guard's tour to ensure that the area is properly secured and that if a break-in occurs, it is quickly discovered.

RELOCATION OF ACTIVITIES

In the past few years, it has become increasingly less difficult to have established activities relocated. One factor in favor of the security planner was the expansion of facilities during the "boom" years of the Vietnam era. The other was the consolidation that occurred during recession that followed our withdrawal from Vietnam.

The security expert who planned his program carefully took advantage of the expansion period and convinced management that if certain activities were also expanded and moved, the overall security would be enhanced.

Later, when unemployment was rising and profit figures were declining, the security plan had to be revised, updated, and, in all probability, reduced in terms of manpower and other expenditures. A thorough study and analysis of changing conditions often indicated that relocation of activities would permit a more economical security program and yet would sustain the approximate degree of security previously enjoyed.

Obviously, any operation within a facility could be relocated for one reason or another, but the following facilities were most often considered for relocation to improve security and reduce its cost.

Personnel Offices

Personnel offices should be located as near to the periphery of the building as possible, and if a portion of the facility office or headquarters building forms a part of the perimeter, the personnel department should ideally be located near an outside entrance. Applicants for employment would thus not be required to walk any great distance through any of the buildings to reach the personnel office. The nearer the personnel office is to periphery of the building, the simpler is the control of applicants and other nonemployees who, for all intents and purposes, are unknown.

One personnel office that should have been relocated but, to my knowledge, still has not been was located in a headquarters building immediately across the hall from the computer operations. The computer operations in this instance were rather large. Immediately outside the computer area in the hallway were several chairs where the applicants for employment would sit and wait their turn to be interviewed and where they would complete the necessary employment papers.

In one 30-minute period, the door leading into the computer room, although locked, was opened a total of 13 times. This door was immediately adjacent to the chairs in which the applicants sat. There were a total of 14 chairs, and during the period of this survey, 10 of the chairs were usually occupied. In addition to unnecessarily exposing the computer room to attack by anyone desiring to walk into the building, there was no security control point, and there was also no control to prevent these personnel from moving down the hall into any one of the other offices or anywhere within the building. In this instance, the personnel office could have been moved into an area approximately 40 feet down the hall where access to the personnel office from the outside would have been through an existing door. It would then have been possible to secure the personnel office so that only individuals that were authorized inside the remainder of the building could depart the office. This, however, was never accomplished.

Computer Rooms

If computer rooms are located on the periphery of the building and their windows open directly to the outside, the operation should be considered for relocation or the windows should be protected with impact-resistant glass or heavy screening. Better yet, the windows could be eliminated entirely by bricking them shut.

It is often difficult and expensive to move a computer room because of the raised floor, the miles of cable, and the carefully engineered electrical system. However, if computer rooms cannot be relocated and they are highly vulnerable, consideration must be given to securing the peripheral walls of the area, preferably by removing all glass.

Display Areas, Sales Areas, and Company Stores

Depending upon the type and category of personnel who will be conducting business in any or all three of these areas, relocation may or may not be justified. Ideally, all three of these operations should be located near the peripheral walls of the building where entrance can be made directly from the outside. This will reduce the need for additional controls to ensure that outside personnel do not wander through any other portions of the building, whether intentionally or because they are simply lost.

Whether or not these areas are located some distance from the peripheral entrances, precautions must always be taken to ensure that finished products are not stolen. As mentioned previously, usually those techniques applied in the protection of property in retail stores will apply to a lesser degree in these areas.

Customer Pickup Stations

Customer pickup stations or "will-call" areas, as they are also referred to, are usually found somewhere in or near the shipping dock areas. They are located in these areas for convenience of operations because the items that are sold are the finished product. "Will-call" windows are often found in meat-packing houses, distribution centers that handle practically any type of commodity, and large department stores.

Too often these areas will consist merely of a desk or two or perhaps a window through which the customer can be serviced. Whenever possible, the area where the customer is actually serviced (the window, for example) should be on the peripheral walls of the building so that the customer is not required to enter the building to conduct his business. I have seen a "will-call" area in a distribution warehouse that advertises that it handles 55,000 different items, from nails to row boats. This "will-call" area always has a huge supply of items stacked on the floor that have been ordered by telephone and are awaiting pickup. All business is conducted over a desk, and no control whatsoever is exercised over the customers. The distance from the peripheral door used by both truck drivers and customers to the "will-call" area is some 150 feet, and as customers walk from the "will-call" pickup point to the door they pass thousands of dollars worth of items that are awaiting shipment by the trucks at the dock.

When these conditions exist, it is obvious that thefts are being committed, and, in all probability, small purchases are made as an excuse to get inside the building. There is no security guard or any other responsible individual to check out the customer as he or she departs the building.

The security of future structures can be increased tremendously with minimum expenditures if security personnel are included during the planning stages. Before the final blueprint is approved, sometimes it may be necessary for security planners to inject themselves into the initial phases of construction plans. It appears that all too often architects and engineers proceed merely on their course, without any thought regarding the security plan. Then they may suddenly realize, for example, that the second story of the guardhouse was never needed. Or even worse, changes may have occurred that required the employee parking lot and entrances to be on the west instead of on the east. Because no one gave a second thought to changing the location of the guardhouse, it is now located in the wrong place. This actually happened. The guardhouse in question a two-story structure some 200 yards from the nearest building having any restroom facilities. Building a two-story guardhouse merely for the purpose of elevating a guard so that he can observe the parking lots in the area must have engrossed the architects so deeply that they forgot to provide for restroom facilities in the "ghost house," as it is now called.

Architects, designers, and engineers must be made aware that their completed edifice will require some degree of security to ensure safety of personnel and protection of company property, and it is my opinion that it is the responsibility of top management and the organization's security official or officials to ensure that the design for security is not overlooked in the planning stages.

7

Dock, Warehouse,
and Cargo Security

There is probably no single area in any type of facility, industrial, commercial, or institutional, that is more often the target of pilferers, thieves, and hijackers than the warehouses where finished products are stored, the docks over which the products are shipped, and the transports that move these products from point to point.

To cover all possible hazards and all actions to reduce those hazards in these areas would by itself require an entire book. A great deal has been written on the subject by experts on warehouse, dock, and cargo security. I have carefully researched and will discuss in this chapter those points considered most important.

The titles of articles, the publications in which they appear, and the names of the authors may be found in the bibliography at the end of this book should readers require more in-depth information in certain areas.

To become aware of the seriousness of the losses in these areas, one need only consider that the average loss of cash in a bank robbery during 1975 was under $4,000 per robbery, while during this same period the average loss due to truck hijacking was approximately $35,000 per occurrence. There are no accurate statistics available on dollar losses of material through thefts perpetrated by collusion between employees and truck drivers, whether or not the drivers are company employees or employees of common carriers.

A recent incident with which I am familiar involved a truck driver, an employee of a common carrier, and employees of a frozen food packing company. The employees in this case were so brazen that they dealt with drivers they had never seen before. The case came to light when an honest truck driver was approached, declined the offer to purchase food at half the retail price, and notified his supervisor, who in turn notified the plant manager.

An undercover agent was assigned to rent a refrigerated truck and, with bills of lading set up for him by management, backed his truck to the dock about 10:00 P.M. As soon as he had left the shipping clerk's office and moved to his trailer to supervise loading and to verify count, a forklift operator offered to sell him food at half price. The agent said he would be interested in buying a few cases of a particular type of food, but the company employee said that if he bought anything, it had to be some of the same product that would be legally loaded because the forklift driver would create suspicion if he went to another reefer and picked up only a few cases of the other product.

A deal was consummated between the agent and the employee, and several cases were loaded. The employee asked the driver when he would return, and the agent stated that his next scheduled trip to this company would be at another plant some distance away. Three days later the agent reported for a pickup at another one of the company's plants and was as quickly approached by a forklift driver who introduced himself by saying, "I understand you are in the market for food." Obviously, a systematic group of interplant thieves had been organized. Of a total of four plants tested, purchases were openly made at three.

PACKAGING FOR SECURITY

Probably the first area in warehouse security to study is the form or type of packaging used. Proper packaging can be a deterrent to pilfering and theft of entire cartons if the true contents of the carton or package are hidden by use of coded outer markings or labels.

Another effective deterrent, to pilfering at least, involves the technique used to close or seal the carton. If access is made difficult, it will not only deter persons from opening the package illegally, but it will make any illegal entry immediately obvious and difficult to conceal. Gluing and stapling can hardly be considered secure methods.

Taping with gummed reinforced tape and banding with plastic or metal strapping is much more effective. If a package thus sealed has been opened, it would require some very obvious actions to reseal it. The manufacturers of gummed tape have recently been promoting the idea of in-plant coding of reinforced sealing tape. The operation merely involves a printing wheel with changeable rubber mats that can be installed in either a tape dispenser or a sealing machine. Ink is applied to the rubber mat or marker, making color coding easy, and the code or mark is transposed to the kraft surface of the tape. This is considered to be an excellent method of sealing.

The type of package-sealing technique used will often be dictated by the packaging material or the items being packaged. Whatever technique is developed or used, the degree of security that will be obtained will certainly be influenced by whether or not the sealing material or tool is available to the pilferer. Sealing equipment must be controlled in a manner similar to that used to secure and account for seals used to seal the doors of the transport vehicle. Unitized packaging furnishes maximum protection against pilferage, whether it involves lockable metal containers or palletized loads. Merely strapping or taping palletized loads will substantially reduce pilferage. However, too much reliance on this deterrent may create a false sense

of security. The very method may create a monster out of a mouse. Instead of a single item being stolen, several may be removed at a time.
Security cannot be relaxed!

As Colin Venning, Director of the Security Council, Ontario Trucking
Association, Rexdale, Ontario, Canada, wrote in BABACO Alarm Systems
News (Summer—Fall 1975): "The battle cry is PREVENTION—ENFORCED,
CONTROLS THE SWORD—AWARENESS IS THE SHIELD. Security must
be in the air—not violent—not suddenly—just there—ALWAYS THERE."

SECURITY IN THE WAREHOUSE

The process of transferring items being manufactured into the package
must be studied so that there is no unnecessary exposure to theft. The
distance between the final manufacturing process and the packaging area
can greatly affect the security of the product, for the greater the distance,
the greater the risk. In today's computerized warehousing operations, the
losses sustained through the physical handling processes have been reduced
dramatically. With computerized handling, losses will generally occur
before the item is packaged or at the time the item is loaded for shipment.
Therefore, it would appear that if the two ends were tied tightly, the material
would be secure as long as it is warehoused. No so!

When computerization first became popular, many truck drivers' honesty
was questioned when they delivered open packages and cartons. After all,
the package was sealed when the computerized machinery placed it on the
shelf. Since then no one handled it until the computer placed it on the loading belt and it was picked up by the driver and stowed on his truck. Drivers
were lulled into a false sense of security because they were "handed the
package by a computer." Little did the driver know of the initial problems
with the machinery and the long hours the product was exposed to theft and
pilferage by maintenance crews who "adjusted, repaired, and stole."

It is true that computerized warehousing today has left most of the
mechanical and electronic deficiencies behind. But collusion between
computer operators, shipping personnel, and truck drivers is still possible.
Perpetual inventory methods will assist in reducing this possibility and may
even reduce losses more if computer operators need not be replaced.

Managers of warehousing operations, whether a separate entity, an
integral part of a manufacturing operation, or a small operation at a hospital called "general supplies," need to observe some basic rules.

1. Allow no one in the storage area who does not work there or have
   a definite need to be there.
2. Recover immediately all damaged cartons and attempt to fix the
   blame for such damage. Repackage or secure the cartons immediately.

3. Whenever possible, store easily pilferable or small items in areas where they will be easily observed by supervisors and other employees.
4. Construct special security rooms or cages for storage items with a high value.
5. Conduct frequent unannounced inspections of forklift trucks and other industrial vehicles that must leave the warehouse proper for refueling, recharging, or repair.
6. Maintain a set pattern for storage of all items. Do not permit employees to change location of items. This will assist in easily identifying items that are out of place, for this may signal preparation for dishonest activity to come.
7. Require inspection of all tool boxes, carts, empty cartons, and the like that are in the possession of outside utility repairmen or maintenance men as they depart the warehousing operation.
8. Plan shelf storage so that as many "hidden areas" as possible are eliminated.
9. Use time-sequence cameras, closed circuit television systems, or even industrial mirrors for more complete observation.
10. If the size of the operation will justify and economics permit, use patrolling guards whose duties also include checking items being moved from the warehouse to the shipping dock.
11. Never allow the warehouse area or dock area to become joined physically. Insist on dividing walls or even chain link barriers to separate the two areas so movement can be channeled through specific lanes for better observation and control.
12. Keep the storage areas neatly organized. Do not allow trash or used packaging material to accumulate or general housekeeping to deteriorate. Organize the removal of trash and inspect these operations frequently.
13. Increase security measures as activities increase as a result of seasonal demands or unusually heavy sales.
14. Require area or department supervisors regularly to conduct a walk-through inspection of their areas of responsibility before departing work.
15. When operations cease, ensure that the responsibility for securing the area is assigned to a specific individual or individuals and, when practical, direct that security measures checked by another or a member of the security force.

The majority of the items just discussed apply to all warehousing operations, whether the facility is a grocery distribution center, a perishable-food distribution center, an automobile-parts distribution center, or a furniture warehouse.

It will be necessary to tailor some of the techniques to fit more closely local situations, and the very nature of an operation requires that common sense be applied and safety measures observed. For example, a few thousand cartons of matches should not be stored in the center of the warehouse, nor should they be stored next to the supply of paper products.

Probably the most perplexing and frustrating problem encountered in manufacturing plants occurs when the manufacturing department works two or three shifts and warehouse-shipping operations work only one. After packaging, the finished products are moved into the warehouse and, because of reduced operations in the warehouse, there is an insufficient number of supervisory personnel to control and observe activities properly. When this condition exists, all peripheral openings from the warehouse must be adequately secured, including any existing skylights. If this is done, employees with access to the warehouse cannot depart the building without moving through the authorized exit control point. Supervisors in such instances should make their walk-through inspections at the beginning of their shifts as well as at the end of their shifts.

DOCK SECURITY

Colin Venning, in BABACO Alarm Systems News (Summer—Fall 1975), stated:

> Security of high value movements such as cigarettes, liquor,
> precious metal, clothing, etc., are they being checked regularly?
> Hustle dispatch to get rid of them. If they remain too long
> "attack," "attack the terminal manager—raise hell at the top
> if you get no action." Every second a load of this type is setting
> on the ground it is giving someone ideas, allowing plans to be
> made—a theft may soon be committed.

A most appropriate statement with which to start a discussion of dock security is the old adage, "Leave something of value lying around long enough and someone will steal it."

One would think that the amount of publicity the thefts of bulk containerized shipments, the truck hijackings, and airport freight terminal thefts have received of late, including the enormous losses sustained, would have led the transport industry and the shipping industry to bolster their defenses by funding architectural studies in an attempt to reduce losses from docks as well as of shipments in transit. Again, Mr. Venning advocates "attack," and in most situations, this is sound advice. Even the military presumes the best defense is to attack! Perhaps when conditions and situations are fluid enough, to attack is the best defense, but what about the static situation that Colin Venning also writes about—when material shipments, if you will, are in a temporary holding position. Once a shipment, regardless of its content, leaves the warehouse, it should for all practical purposes continue to move under documented control until it arrives at its intended destination. The intended destination is the user or the consumer.

What form, then, will defensive tactics take? First and foremost, it is proper design and construction of docks. Everyday truck terminals, 90 percent of the operational square footage of which is utilized as dock space, are constructed using the old design of "open platforms" covered by a roof. There is no physical separation between operational areas. Incoming is on the west, and breakdown of shipment and local or long-distance outgoing are on the east. The only apparent variations are a change in direction. It appears to me that with the advent of computerized warehousing, a modernization in dock construction and distribution procedures, more rapid machine handling of materials, and more closely scrutinized inventory procedures are long overdue.

Docks can be considered either open or closed and isolated or nonisolated. An open dock is an extension of the building and is generally unprotected on three sides. Products awaiting shipment are thus exposed to pilferage and theft by any passersby.

In large cities, docks and entire terminals are often located adjacent to public sidewalks. These installations are constantly plagued by thieves using hit-and-run tactics, grabbing anything they can carry; in most instances, they do not even know the contents. An open dock will always have some type of overhead covering for protection during inclement weather. Often security of this type of dock can be increased by installing a movable or permanently installed chain link fence barrier from the dock floor to the overhead covering. This type of protection is particularly necessary if shipments moved to the dock remain there for some time before loading.

Closed docks are found at most new industrial facilities. The door openings are flush with the face of the outside walls and are fitted with heavy rubber or synthetic cushioning around the outside of the entire opening. This arrangement acts as a seal between the rear of a truck and the building proper and prevents items from being dropped to the ground between the trailer and the building for later recovery.

This arrangement also prevents drivers from entering the dock area by climbing through the opening between their truck and the building. In addition to increasing security, it also acts as a weather seal, keeping out heat or cold. See Figure 7-1 and note the large opening between the truck and the dock door.

Inflatable dock seals are available for installation at both railroad and truck docks. When inflated, these seal building and loading transports even more securely than the permanently installed type. Loading and unloading railroad cars directly from a closed dock will always result in a large opening between the building and the rail car. The inflatable seal

Figure 7-1 Storage nearby an operational shipping door invites the employee to commit thefts. Note that the stairwell leading to the basement
has been left uncovered, creating an unnecessary safety hazard in the work
area. (Courtesy Phoenix Products Company)

eliminates the opening and when deflated and not in use does not create an
obstruction protruding from the building along the rail siding (see Figures
7-2a and 7-2b).

Depending upon several factors such as number of trailers being loaded
at one time and size of the hardtop area outside the dock, it is often possible
to enclose an open dock with masonry material, thus converting it to the
more secure closed type.

A dock is considered <u>isolated</u> if it is physically separated from the warehousing operation with or without controls established at the openings in
the dividing wall. This arrangement also increases fire protection if fire
doors are installed to close the openings, thus reducing fire spread from
the more hazardous dock area.

A <u>nonisolated</u> dock creates many more security hazards and increases
the possibility of theft and pilferage because the dock operations and warehousing operations are not physically separated. There are few controls
on the handling of materials, and it is exceedingly more difficult to control
the movements of personnel, both company and noncompany. In most
instances, it is possible to construct a barrier to separate the operations

Figure 7-2 (a) The inflated air lock secures the opening between the railroad car and the face of the building. Compare this with Figure 5-8 and
visualize the additional security that would be provided. (b) The air lock,
when deflated, does not cause an obstruction or interfere with the movement
of rail cars. (Courtesy Airlocke Division of O'Neal Tarpaulin Company)

and channel activities through definite points; even chain link fence may be
used. Obviously, this material does not furnish the added fire protection
that a masonry wall would.

HOUSEKEEPING IN THE DOCK AREA

Whether the dock is open, closed, isolated, or nonisolated, proper housekeeping of the area will play an important part in reducing thefts and
accidents. The dock area should not be used as a storage area for any
material. When shipping or receiving activities have ceased, at least for
the time being, the dock should be clear. Compare hazards observed in
Figure 7-1 as compared with the unobstructed view and lack of potential
hazards in Figure 7-3.

Figure 7-3 Compare with this dock area the dock in Figure 7-1 and note that no material has been stored in the operational area of the dock. (Courtesy Phoenix Products Company)

Frequent outside inspections of the area under the dock and around the dock are necessary when dock configuration makes it possible to drop items that can be recovered by the driver later or by a pilferer in collusion with the driver. This area must remain free of any type of trash that could be used to hide objects temporarily or that would create unnecessary fire hazards.

Outside patrols should not only ascertain that vehicles are being properly chocked during loading or unloading operations, but they should be particularly observant when drivers remove the chocks, because this is the best time for the driver to recover items that might have been dropped from the dock.

Trash Removal

It always appears that the smaller the dock, the more likely it is that trash generated inside the facility is removed over the operational dock. Trash removal via shipping docks is quite obviously much more likely to involve unauthorized removal of property than is removal via the receiving dock.
If trash is removed over the docks, the thief has two advantages:

1. He can pick up items from the dock and remove them with the trash.
2. He can bring items to the dock in the trash and have them removed by drivers who participate in the theft.

A positive method of eliminating this possibility is to use a compactor to remove trash from the facility. The compactor should be installed so that the loading chute is flush with the peripheral wall. This will eliminate the necessity for any employee in the janitorial crews to go outside the building. Additionally, there is very little material that will still be useful after it has been loaded and compacted into the container. Compactors also reduce the fire hazard always present when combustible trash is collected in containers inside or outside the building.

OS&D DEPARTMENT

Over, short, and damaged (OS&D) items create substantial losses in any shipping operation. A room or area should be constructed at the dock where "hot", "over," or "damaged" items can be secured. Hot items, such as cigarettes or liquor, may be stored in the secured area until actual loading takes place. However, if security rooms are used, absolute control must be established, both at the time the material is placed in storage and when it is removed.
In the BABACO Alarm Systems News (Summer—Fall 1975), Colin Venning aptly discussed the importance of the OS&D department:

Daily contact with the OS&D department is essential. They are the frontline troops in the battle against losses. They should know of every shortage as it occurs. Each day ask if any shortage had occurred of desirable or high-value products (power tools, clothing, cigarettes, liquor, etc.) and has the driver or warehouseman been questioned? The next day inquire if the shortage from the day before had been cleared and wait at night, if necessary, to question the employees involved. Security men must be watching for date, time, commodity, name and location patterns of current shortages and claims.

COLLUSION BETWEEN DRIVERS AND EMPLOYERS

When drivers are allowed to load their own vehicles, an atmosphere is created immediately that will breed collusion between driver and employee in committing thefts. When these conditions exist in conjunction with any of those hazards previously discussed, systematic pilfering in huge quantities will certainly result in staggering losses.

Under some circumstances, drivers must at least be present to verify count during loading operations, because they are ultimately responsible for shortages that may occur. Supervision should be increased and restrictions on the drivers' movements should be made clear to them. Employees should not be allowed to converse with the drivers, and all necessary administrative procedures should be accomplished by shipping clerks or supervisors.

If security forces observe or patrol docks, they must increase their vigilance and concentrate their observations on personnel activities. When the size of the shipping operation permits, loaders should be changed regularly so drivers will not know in advance who will load their trucks, and loaders will not know in advance which trucks they will load.

The use of undercover agents to replace loaders who are on vacation or out sick should be considered wherever procedures or employment practices will permit.

Restroom facilities and driver waiting rooms or areas with vending machines should be made available. If drivers will be permitted to use restroom areas some distance from the dock, the route should be clearly and plainly marked, and the drivers should be cautioned not to deviate from the route. If employee lunchrooms or cafeterias are used by drivers, tables or areas should be reserved for them to ensure that they are separated from the employees. These restrictions will need to be checked by supervisors and/or the security force if they are to be effective for any appreciable period of time.

A few facilities large enough to support dock operations are not sustaining any losses because they have effected the security measures discussed in this chapter. Any or all of the basic principles discussed here can be applied to a single-bay dock in an office building or to a 40-bay dock at a trucking terminal to reduce pilferage.

The items being handled, the type of transportation used to move the items, the organization of, and procedures in use at, the dock, and all other operational conditions will affect the loss experience. Generally speaking, security will have to be tightened in all areas of the dock if it is expected to be effective.

Increasing dock security through redesign or renovation has also been discussed. The cost of reconstruction versus the cost of losses being sustained should be the determining factor affecting the decision to renovate an existing dock. However, losses must be projected into future operations to arrive at a realistic figure to compare.

In one instance, I found that production had outgrown shipping capabilities, and this resulted in large amounts of the finished product being stored in the vicinity of the loading area so that trucks could be loaded rapidly as they were backed to the dock. Simple, inexpensive redesign of the dock eliminated the need to store finished products in the loading area and also doubled the capacity of the shipping operations.

CARGO SECURITY

The security of any load must, of necessity, commence during loading activities and continue during transit of the load to its destination. Cargo losses will actually start during loading operations, as shipping personnel open packages and cartons and remove only some of the packed items. The importance of proper packaging cannot be overemphasized, and records of the identity of employees charged with loading trucks or rail cars must be accurately maintained to ensure a productive investigation when losses are discovered at a later date.

It has been estimated that 85 percent of cargo theft and pilferage is committed by personnel who are authorized to be in the dock terminal or holding yard area. Most losses occur during normal working hours, with hijacking and burglaries outside the protected area accounting for approximately 15 percent of cargo theft losses.

Of the thousands of commodities handled by the transportation industry, only 13 account for 90 percent of all theft-related losses. The top 10 are clothing, electrical appliances, auto parts and accessories, hardware, liquors, food products, tobacco products, rubber and plastic items, instruments of all types, and jewelry. Losses from all causes for all modes of transportation—air, land and sea—total $2.8 billion. This represents 4.5 percent of the entire industry's revenue.

A breakdown by percentage of total losses sustained through theft and pilferage by persons authorized to handle cargo or merely authorized in the area is as follows:

1. Theft of caseloads or more but less than a full trailerload—60 percent.
2. Pilferage of less than caseload quantities—25 percent.
3. Hijacking of full loads, which constitutes grand larceny—10 percent.
4. Burglary theft at stopping points during shipment or from the lot during nonworking hours—5 percent.

Confining our discussion to wheeled, land transport, we should emphasize the importance of adequate lighting of the interior of the transport. The darkened interior of a rail car or forward end of a darkened trailer often offer grand opportunities to pilfer the packages. Loading must be closely supervised at all times, and manifests, bills of lading, and commodities being loaded must be frequently checked.

Once the loading is complete, the vehicle should be moved from the dock immediately; all doors should be closed, and seals and/or padlocks should be affixed. Seals should be used in conjunction with padlocks. One lock manufacturer has produced a fine-quality padlock that can be sealed with an ordinary railway-type seal that will indicate whether or not the lock was opened without authority.

There are many seals manufactured for the express purpose of sealing vehicles used to transport cargo. These devices range in strength and security value from a cable and heavy lead seal requiring a special hand tool for installation and bolt cutters to remove it (Figure 7-4) to a flimsy device often used for this purpose but certainly manufactured for another purpose (see Figure 7-5). Some seals can be opened and again sealed using "home-fashioned" tools without causing any detectable damage (see Figure 7-6).

Probably the most secure seal intended for transport-sealing purposes is often referred to as the "railroad car seal." This seal is shown in its opened and closed position in Figure 7-7. Any tampering with this type of seal can be quickly and easily detected.

Figure 7-4 A seal of substantial strength like this one constructed of cable and a soft metal fastener requires a special tool to place the seal on the trailer and bolt cutters to remove it.

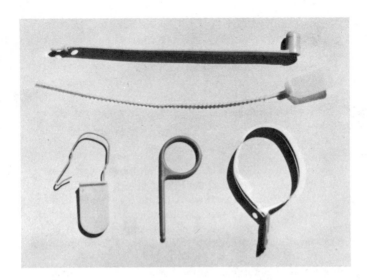

Figure 7-5 A variety of seals not intended for use in shipping and receiving operations. However, some are still occasionally found in use.

In some operations, loads must be discharged at several locations. This is particularly true with shipments of food products and department store commodities, which, incidently, will normally include all top ten items on the priority theft list mentioned previously.

If management or other responsible personnel are available to receive the shipments at these numerous destinations, a seal for each stop is included with the driver's distribution list. The correct seal is listed by number on each successive delivery bill, and the seals are removed and new ones installed by the person receiving the shipment. The driver should not be involved in seal removal or seal installation.

If some items are to be returned, for whatever reason, the person receiving the last delivery should affix the last seal. This seal should be removed by the security guard at the gate control point or by the receiving dock supervisor.

Seals should contain the name or logo of the organization and a control number. They may be painted with a color code to establish still further controls and to ensure easy identification by the security guard.

Seals must be stored in secure containers and controlled by serial number. Frequent, unannounced audits should be conducted by operational or guard force personnel. Broken or damaged seals must also be accounted for and should be destroyed to make their fraudulent use impossible.

Some special measures must be incorporated into the security plan at the facility serviced by rail. Incoming cars should have seals inspected

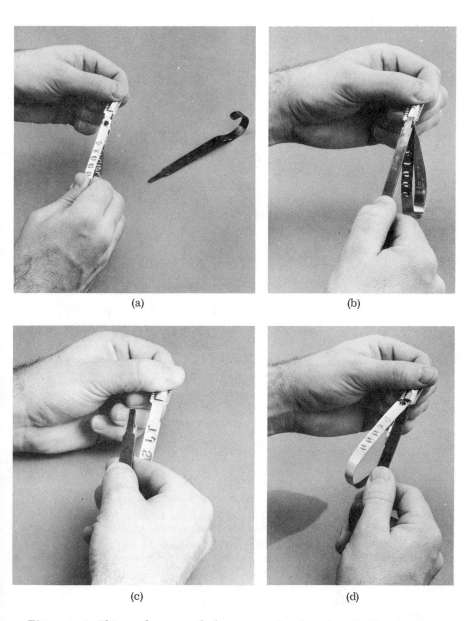

(a)   (b)

(c)   (d)

Figure 7-6 This seal can easily be removed and replaced without any apparent damage to the seal itself. (a) Closing the seal. (b) Inserting a simple tool to remove the seal. (c) The seal reopened. (d) Resealing still without visible damage. (Courtesy the Tyden Seal Company)

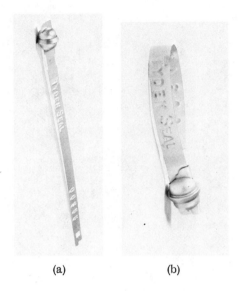

(a)   (b)

Figure 7-7 This Tyden seal, often referred to as railroad seal, has been
in use for many years and is virtually impossible to remove without
destroying it. Shown here in its (a) opened and (b) closed positions.

to ensure that they are intact. Unloaded rail cars that will be removed
empty should be inspected thoroughly by a security guard or a supervisor,
and the door should be closed in their presence and sealed. Seals should
be checked by number and car identity upon departure.

At one facility surveyed a short while ago, a forklift truck was found
to be missing during the period that the survey was conducted. This facility
was serviced by truck and by rail. The rail docks were also used as a
parking area for forklift trucks that were not in use.

The day the forklift truck was found to be missing was also the day that
railroad switching had been effected. Upon checking with the railroad, we
learned that the cars removed from the facility were still in the railroad
yard. Accompanied by a railroad detective, we proceeded to the railroad
yard and found the cars that had been removed from the facility. We checked
all the doors on the cars, and all were still properly sealed with the seals
of the facility. The seals were broken and the doors opened. In one of
the cars we found the missing forklift truck.

Further investigation revealed that the guard, in fact, did inspect the
car when it was empty. However, he was unable to close the door by himself and, as he inspected other cars and patrolled the dock, the forklift
truck was loaded into the box car, the ramp between the car and the dock
was removed, and the door was closed. Upon his return, the guard found
that the door was closed and merely attached the seal.

Several employees were under suspicion; however, no one was appre-hended for the theft. Obviously, someone intended to remove the forklift truck from the railroad car while it was still in the freight yard. This incident points up the fact that the effectiveness of the sealing procedure is lost unless the doors to railroad cars are closed immediately after inspection and the seal affixed in the presence of the individual conducting the inspection.

Unloaded or partially loaded truck trailers should also be sealed if cir-cumstances dictate, and inspection of truck transport must include the side doors of trailers if they exist.

TRUCK PARK SECURITY

Truck parks should be well lighted and patrolled, whether or not the area is protected by a chain link fence. Padlocks should always be used to secure loads, and the keys may be entrusted to the driver or not, depending upon the operational setup and whether or not the vehicle will be required to undergo state inspections at weigh stations during the trip to its destina-tion. Incidentally, when state inspectors break a company seal to inspect a load, it is replaced with an easily identifiable state seal, and shipping documents are usually stamped to indicate that an inspection by the state has been conducted.

Losses can be eliminated from parked trailers at terminals if the trailers are parked close together and with the rear door against or close to a barrier constructed of railroad ties or some other heavy material. In some instances, masonry walls or metal pipes are installed and the trucks backed against these objects to make it impossible for the rear doors to be opened. If side doors exist, the trucks should be parked close enough to-gether so that the doors cannot be opened and items removed.

There are kingpin locking devices that will deter, if not prevent, trailer-load thefts. Trailer-load thefts are usually committed by using stolen tractors. There are also locking devices that can be used to secure the female hitch on tandem trailers.

Drivers should be cautioned to stop at well-illuminated and active truck stops only. If possible, trailers should be parked closely together to deter entry by restricting the distance the rear or side doors can be opened. This is a particularly desirable practice if long rest stops are involved. Drivers should always inspect seals and/or padlocks before they leave their vehicles and after they return.

Some truck stops, particularly in the East, have increased the protective lighting in the truck parking areas appreciably; in some instances, in order to attract more business, some truck stops furnish security guards to patrol the truck parks during the hours of darkness. Some of the larger truck stops that have rooms available for the drivers to rest will have the patrolling

security guards also check the temperature gauges on refrigerated loads.
Truck drivers regularly traveling certain routes should patronize those
truck stops where their loads will be the most secure while they rest, eat,
or sleep.

The field offices of the Federal Bureau of Investigation have been maintaining informal statistics on cargo-theft investigations in designated cities
since September 1975. Of 2,100 complaints of thefts received by the FBI
from September through December 1975, 1,444 were closed without federal
prosecution because of lack of witnesses or identifiable evidence, delayed
reporting by the complainant, or lack of accountability procedures. The
lack of identifiable evidence precluded prosecution in more than one-third
of these cases.

Federal prosecutors declined to initiate formal prosecution in 557 investigations because of low dollar value of the theft, insufficient admissible
evidence, or other problems. It should be noted that an undetermined number of these cases were referred to local authorities for prosecution. Only
155 convictions for violations of federal laws pertaining to cargo theft were
obtained in the 4-month period. Only 12 acquittals were reported.

The Justice Department has instructed U.S. Attorneys to pay particular
attention to the problem of criminal redistribution of stolen goods—that is,
"fencing." Destroying the marketplace for stolen property makes cargo
theft less profitable to the potential criminal. Thus, the Department of
Justice has encouraged the use of court-approved electronic surveillance
and postconviction grand jury proceedings to gather evidence against fencing
operations. Selective use of the immunity statutes has also been suggested
to gain sufficient evidence of these operations to support prosecutions.

A great deal accomplished in the area of preventing cargo thefts, and
readers who desire or require further information should secure a copy
of "A Report to the President on the National Cargo Security Program."
This report was issued by the Secretary of Transportation on March 31,
1976. Copies of this report are available to the public and should be on
the desk of every individual responsible for moving commodities, whether
it be by airline, motor carrier, railroad, or water transport.

8

Lock Identification,
Key Systems,
and Key Control

The Memphis Press-Scimitar reported on August 20, 1976, that a grocery
manager forgot about the numbers jotted on a piece of paper in his wallet,
but a robber was quick to note their significance. The manager told police
that a gunman invaded his San Francisco home and demanded his keys and
wallet, which contained $15. The manager complied and was bound by the
thief. Police said a robber the next day entered the supermarket in which
the manager worked and cleaned out the safe, which contained $1,400.
The manager had forgotten to tell police that the stolen wallet contained
the combination to his safe.

It is an often repeated phrase that "a lock keeps the honest man honest
but merely slows up the professional thief." Security personnel today scoff
at this old adage, for they know that there are locks being manufactured
that are "virtually pick-proof." If these devices are installed on sturdily
constructed doors, the locks will offer maximum security.

Approximately 75 percent of all locking devices are installed on personnel
and overhead doors, and familiarity with descriptive door terminology is
necessary in order to discuss door security and locking devices intelligently.
This common terminology eliminates the possibility that there will be a
misunderstanding between security personnel and the builder. The sketch
in Figure 8-1 depicts a double swinging door with proper terminology
indicated. The same terminology applies to any single door of this type
used by personnel.

In today's modern commercial and institutional construction, the use
of sliding doors is becoming more popular. This type of door offers little
protection if it is not secured in such a manner to keep it from being easily
slid or pried up and out of the track. Terminology used to describe sliding
doors differs slightly from that applied to swinging doors (see Figure 8-2).
Locking techniques used to secure sliding doors differ widely from the techniques usually applied to swinging doors and will be discussed later in this
chapter.

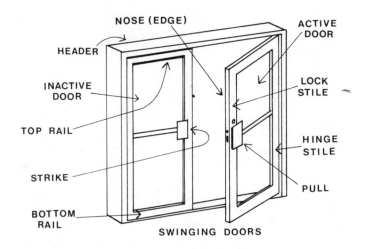

Figure 8-1 The component parts of a single or double swinging door.

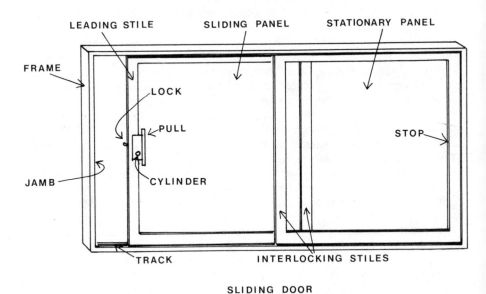

Figure 8-2 The component parts of a glass sliding door.

LOCK SELECTION

Locking devices, whether padlocks or dead bolts, cannot be judged by their weight, size, or appearance. And even though the cost of locks will generally reflect the quality of workmanship and materials used, even price should not be used as the sole criterion in selecting the proper locking devices. A rule of thumb is that when purchasing a lock, you should expect to pay as much or more for the lock as you pay for the door. A key-operated lock will cost from $10 to $175, depending upon the type of construction and design and finish selected. If the security requirement is practically non-existent, a simple passage latch set can be purchased for approximately $10.

Cost of the locking device should be considered on a long-term basis. A quality lock, properly installed and maintained, is said to last the life of the door. A cheaper lock may have a short life and may require considerable maintenance and repair or early replacement. A good-quality lock will usually last 30 to 40 years. If advice is needed, a reputable locksmith should be consulted.

There has been a definite improvement in the workmanship and quality of locks in the last 2 or 3 years, and a considerable expenditure on lock-design research has resulted in locks that are quite impregnable. Obviously, older-style, less secure locks are still available, but these furnish considerably less security than that which is actually required. For example, "light" locks intended for residential use should not be used on commercial structures. Residential locks are usually constructed of metal that is of a much lighter gauge than that required for commercial, industrial, or institutional use.

In a fairly recent study involving 833 of the nation's leading locksmiths, 59 percent of them agreed that better-quality locks should generally be used in commercial and other public buildings. This same survey responded by saying, "There is a great quality difference between the various brands of locks—more so than between the types of locks (mortise versus cylindrical, etc.)."

Total hardware costs in new building construction range from approximately 0.5 to 1.5 percent of the total building cost, and locks make up 25 to 40 percent of this figure. This means that lock cost is from 0.12 to 0.60 percent of the total building cost. These figures may be higher, depending upon the type of building under construction.

TYPES OF LOCKS

There are several types of locks, each using different mechanics to secure the latch or dead bolt in the strike plate in the door frame. Probably the three basic types are the mortise, the cylindrical, and that referred to as

Figure 8-3 The uppermost locking device is of the dead-bolt type and the lower device is known as a cylinder lock. Note that each assembly secures the latch plate metal into metal while also protecting the leading edge of the door. (Courtesy M.A.G. Eng. & Mfg., Inc.)

the "unit" lock. The popularity of the mortise lock has declined in favor of the cylindrical lock in recent years. The mortise lock is costly to install and will weaken the door because it is necessary to mortise out large sections of the door. These locks are seldom used in commercial construction but have a "good track record" in residential and institutional applications. The cylindrical lock is used today in 85 to 90 percent of the instances when locks are installed in commercial buildings. Often referred to as "key-in-knob" locks, they are easier to install and service and can be installed as far as 5 inches from the door jamb.

The <u>unit</u> lock was developed several years ago to overcome installation
difficulties that the mortise locks presented. Figure 8-3 shows a cylindrical lock and a dead-bolt lock. This installation, utilizing special strikes,
was actually made to replace a mortise-type lock. Note also the "dead
latch" on the cylindrical lock. The dead latch prevents the latch from being
withdrawn from the strike by the use of a plastic card or shim.

SEQUENTIAL CYLINDERS

The principle of a construction master-key cylinder is being used in a
relatively new line of cylinder locks that have been developed to permit
changing of a key merely by inserting another key. This line of locks has
been in existence for at least the past 3 or 4 years and is called the <u>sequen-
tial cylinder</u>. The lock can be provided with as many key changes as there
are pins in the cylinder. As an example, a five-pin cylinder could be provided with five different key changes and a six-pin cylinder would be provided with six different key changes.

The first, or number-one, key can be used in the cylinder of this lock
for a certain period of time. Usually this key is used through the construction period and until the peripheral building walls are secured. When a new
combination is desired, for whatever reason, the number-two key can be
inserted and turned, which automatically cancels the operational ability of
the number-one key. Later, number-three key can cancel out the use of
number-two key, and this can be continued until all of the keys that can
change the pin cylinder have been used.

Sequential cylinders are often used by locksmiths when they have a
customer, for example, in an office building, who requires changing combinations quite frequently. The locksmith installs a sequential cylinder
and, when future key changes are necessary, merely inserts one of the
unused keys, which he has retained in his shop, into the keyway and issues
this key with the number of duplicates required. One limitation to the
sequential cylinder is that the cylinders cannot be master-keyed, and re-
cutting keys must be accomplished with great accuracy.

SECURITY CLASSIFICATION OF LOCKS

Each type of locking mechanism provides some protective features not
found in others. The relative security of the lock is based on the amount
of time it would take an expert lockpicker to open it by manipulation of the
mechanism. A warded lock, for example, offers little or no security, a
pin tumbler lock could delay a thief about 2 or 3 minutes, and a maximum-
security lock could be practically invulnerable.

THE LOCK'S MECHANISM

A warded lock offers practically no security and should not be installed
where physical security is a primary requirement. The warded lock is
often referred to as a "privacy" lock because this is all the security it
offers. A typical warded lock was the type of lock installed in most residential doors prior to World War II and could be operated by a skeleton key
purchased at any dime store. This type lock is still in use in many inexpensive padlocks. They can easily be defeated by an amateur with a piece of
stiff wire.

Lever locks, because of the large variety and range of locking mechanisms, are difficult to classify as to their relative security. Some quality
lever locks are now being manufactured, but, generally speaking, they
should not be considered when security is a prime factor. These locks are
used in desks, wooden cabinets, chests, and the like. They are also found
in door locks and padlocks and can be identified by a keyway that will rotate
freely from 25 to 40 degrees without having any effect on opening the lock.

A disc tumbler lock is a lock having a paracentric keyway and a series
of flat tumblers and springs in the key plug. In the locked position the
tumbler springs force the tumblers into a slot in the cylinder shell and
prevent rotation of the plug.

A disc tumbler lock offers only slightly greater relative security than
lever or warded locks. This locking mechanism was primarily designed
for, and is in general use in, automotive door locks. Mass production of
the lock and the soft metals used in manufacturing have substantially reduced
life expectancy. With the brief life expectancy of today's automobiles, such
locks are probably quite suitable for this application. A disc tumbler lock
can be identified by a keyway that will not rotate in the locked position.
This lock should not be used if tight security is desired.

The pin tumbler lock was invented by Linus Yale in 1868. This lock has
a paracentric keyway with upper and lower round pins that are capable of
moving vertically into corresponding holes in the key plug and the shell of
the cylinder. These pins are held downward by the pressure of springs,
and the upper pins engage the holes in the plug. This prevents the lock's
rotation. Pin tumbler locks are best suited for master-keying systems,
and they can be used in door locks, desk locks, cabinet locks, padlocks,
and practically any other locking device used at a facility, all of which can
be master-keyed in one system.

The pin tumbler locking mechanism is acceptable for use in most security
situations, and the security such a lock offers depends upon the configuration
of the drivers and plugs, number of pins, and the number of rows of pins.
The keyway in some pin tumbler locks has been "twisted" (that is, the
regular key is straight along the section and could not be inserted into the
twisted keyway). This configuration substantially increases the security
of the lock. See Figure 8-4 for a cutaway view of pin tumbler lock.

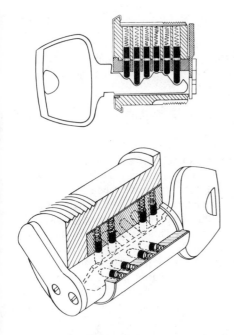

Figure 8-4 A cutaway view comparing a conventional pin tumbler cylinder
and the Sargent maximum-security system cylinder. Note the third row
of pins indicated by the broken line. (Courtesy Sargent and Company)

The mushroom pin tumbler lock utilizes a tumbler pin shaped like a
mushroom. This configuration was adopted to make picking the lock more
difficult.

The barrel or tubular cylinder lock also utilizes pin tumblers; however,
rather than the conventional row of tumblers running from near the entrance
of the keyway to the rear of the core, the tumblers in this lock are arranged
in circular fashion at the rear of the plug. The tumblers are depressed by
pressure being applied to the barrel-shaped key that contains a ridge or
shoulder to guide the key in the keyway. When the circle of pin tumblers
are aligned with the shear line, the lock is opened. The degree of security
offered by this lock is excellent, and defeating the lock by picking is extremely difficult.

The removable-core lock is a locking mechanism in which a control key
can be inserted to remove the entire cylinder. This permits locks fitted
with the interchangeable core to be master-keyed into one system that, if
necessary, can be expanded to meet future requirements. Each of these
cores contain a certain pin tumbler combination, and a single control key
removes any cores within that particular system and can be used to insert

a new core with a new combination. A unique feature of the interchangeable-core lock system is that any lock can be "changed" in a matter of seconds without the requirement of rekeying immediately. Once the core is removed, it can be used elsewhere, still maintaining the relative security of the locking system, or the pin tumblers can be changed either by the facility locksmith or by an outside locksmith.

PADLOCKS

Every major lock manufacturer produces padlocks of varying strengths and designs. All utilize one of the locking mechanisms previously discussed. Styles vary from shackles that are completely protected when locked to shackles constructed of stainless steel aircraft cable covered with weather proofing, which are used in place of a chain and lock to secure gates. One manufacturer produces a "car-seal padlock." This padlock is slotted at the bottom so that it will accept any standard car-seal band. The band is installed in the lock by passing it through the slot that covers the keyway and then securing it. Before the lock can be operated with a key or picked, the band must be removed to expose the keyway. The use of such a seal will indicate immediately whether or not a lock has been opened surreptitiously.

    The strength of padlocks also depends on whether one or both ends of the shackle are engaged when locked (see Figure 8-5). Shackles engaged at one end only are easily defeated by using a wooden hammer handle or

Figure 8-5 A padlock whose body is designed to protect the shackle in the closed position. Note that both sides of the shackle are secured when locked.

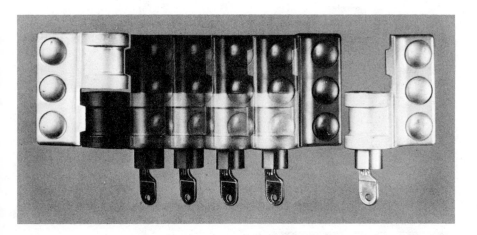

Figure 8-6 This device, referred to as Tuf-Lock, is a unique locking hinge that can be installed on any type of door and can be furnished with a tubular key-type lock or a Medeco cylinder. (Courtesy Security Products Corp.)

similar object and tapping the lock on the side while maintaining pressure by pulling on the shackle.

Padlocks usually require that a hasp be installed. The strength of the metal and the method used to install the hasp will usually determine the relative security of the entire device. To overcome this apparent deficiency, a device can be used that incorporates both the lock and hasp into one unit. Properly installed, this device furnishes excellent security (see Figure 8-6).

MAXIMUM-SECURITY LOCKS

These locks are so named because they provide maximum security in key-operated devices. One such system utilizes three rows of pins containing a total of 12 pins with the rows intersecting on three different axes (see Figure 8-7). The key used to operate this lock is almost impossible to duplicate outside the factory. The key is symmetrical and has a rounded point. The three rows of pins and the design of the key make it possible to insert the key with either edge up, a feature that is found in no other lock (see Figure 8-8). A comparison of the pin arrangement is found in Figure 8-4.

Another relatively new design in cylinder locks furnishing maximum security is the interlocking pin tumbler. The interlocking portions of the driver pins and tumbler pins are designed at a 20-degree angle to the center line of the chisel point of the tumbler pins. The pins must be aligned by a

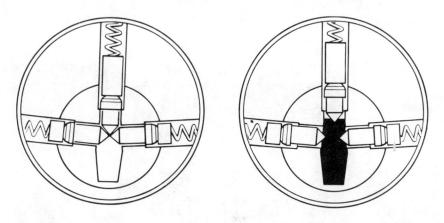

Figure 8-7 The three rows of pin tumblers used in the Sargent maximum-security system shown in the locked and unlocked position. (Courtesy Sargent and Company)

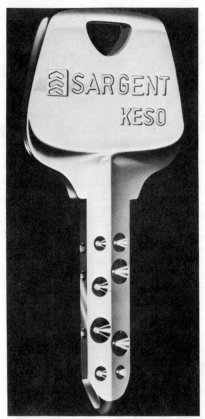

Figure 8-8 Compare the key used in the Sargent maximum-security lock with the key used to operate a conventional cylinder. This key cannot be duplicated in the field on any cutting machines now in use. Duplicate keys are cut with special equipment only at the Sargent plant in New Haven, Connecticut. (Courtesy Sargent and Company)

Figure 8-9 Another maximum-security locking system is the Emhart
System. Shown here is a single pin of a high-security cylinder that shows,
from top to bottom, the driver pin, the master pin, and the tumbler pin.
(Courtesy Emhart Corporation, Hardware Division)

key having a corresponding 20-degree angle. When the pins are thus
aligned, they are in a position that allows the interlocking end of the driver
pins to fit into six circular grooves in the cylinder plug. When this occurs,
the plug can be rotated more than 180 degrees, because the key has slots
corresponding to the grooves in the plug (see Figures 8-9 and 8-10).

ELECTRONIC ACCESS-CONTROL SYSTEMS

These locking systems are called electronic access-control systems because they are designed to offer more than mere door security. Their
unique design makes it possible to control access of personnel into the
protected area effectively and efficiently. There are several manufacturers
of these systems, all utilizing a card rather than the conventional key, with
the majority providing the degree of security expected of these devices.
      One manufacturer of these electronic access-control systems has devel-
oped an electronic interrogation system at a central control location that

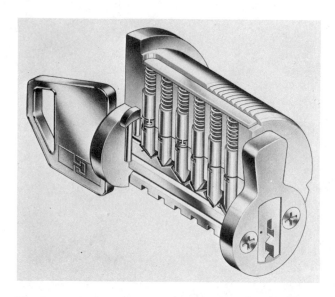

Figure 8-10 A cutaway view of the Emhart high-security cylinder. Note the position of the tumbler pins as they are aligned with the skew-cut bitting at selected 20-degree angles. (Courtesy Emhart Corporation, Hardware Division)

gives maximum-security access control. This system can monitor as many as 128 separate terminals in as many remote locations.

The major part of the system is an invisibly coded card key and an electronic device that "reads" the card to determine the identification number assigned to the card. The data are transmitted to the central control point, and the device known as the "interrogator" evaluates the data, determines whether or not access should be granted, and transmits the appropriate signal to the location where the card is being used. Any attempted entry using an invalid card is immediately displayed on the front panel of the interrogator control and may be seen at a glance. When desired, all cards in use may be displayed. These features enable one interrogator at the central control point to exercise complete control over the system.

Another electronic access-control system operates by means of an electronically coded card that is brought in close proximity (4 to 6 inches) to a sensor located near the door to be unlocked. The sensor is a flat circular disc that is installed in the wall near the door. Therefore, unless its presence is known, there is no indication that this access-control system is used to control this particular door.

The system consists of five basic elements, the first being the command key, which is an electronically coded card that, when brought to within the previously mentioned 4 to 6 inches of the sensor located near the door, activates the system and unlocks the door almost instantaneously.

The second element is the sensor that is installed in the wall near the door. This, as mentioned already, is merely a flat circular disc that is connected to the control unit by a single coaxial cable. When a command key is presented, the sensor reads the key code and sends this information to the control unit for validation.

The control unit, the third element in the system, contains the electronic security, the authorized key code memory, and all the power supplies for the locking hardware. When an authorized command key is used at a door, a signal is immediately sent from the control unit to the sensor at the door, and the door is unlocked by an electrically actuated lock or relay. If the key presented is not authorized, the system merely does not respond, and

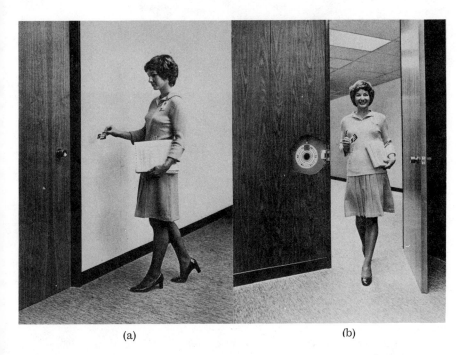

(a) (b)

Figure 8-11 (a) The Schlage Electronic Access Control is not visible and is activated by the use of a command key that is electronically coded simply by bringing it to within 4 to 6 inches of the center located near the door. (b) A cutaway view of the installed sensor. Note the electric latch operated by the sensor when the correct command key has been presented. (Courtesy Schlage Electronics)

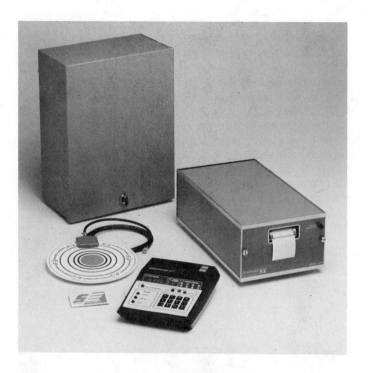

Figure 8-12 The Schlage Electronic Access-Control System consists of
the control unit (upper left); the printer (extreme right), the disc-shaped
sensor (lower left); the system programmer (bottom center); and the command or card key (extreme lower left). (Courtesy Schlage Electronics)

access is prohibited. However, when this occurs, an alarm installed at
the control unit alerts the monitor, and investigative action is initiated.

The fourth element in this access-control system is the systems programmer. This programmer enters the authorized key codes, time codes,
and door codes into the system or voids any key codes that were previously
entered.

The fifth element in the system is the printer. This unit provides a
print out of all accesses and attempted accesses. It records the key code,
the date, the time of entry, and the door number. Attempts at invalid
access print out in red, with an additional code number identifying why the
attempt was not validated. The printer provides all the information that is
necessary on all accesses actually authorized and all accesses that were
attempted but invalidated on the premises being protected (see Figures
8-11 and 8-12).

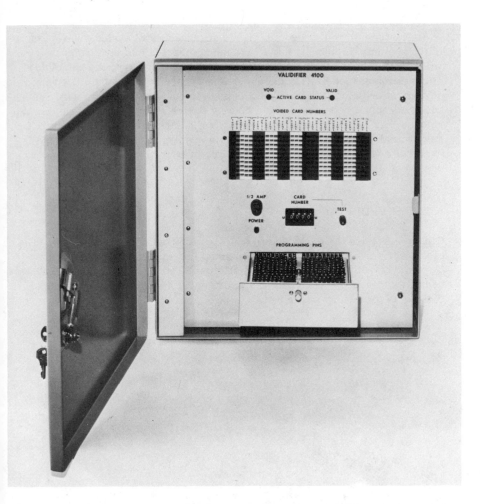

Figure 8-13 A.V.I.D. Enterprises manufactures a Validifier that is used in conjunction with a card reader which accepts coded cards and a control device such as an electric door release. The Validifier determines if the coded card is valid or invalid. If valid, the door release is actuated. If invalid, it denies access and actuates an alarm circuit. (Courtesy A.V.I.D. Enterprises)

As just mentioned, these electronic access-control systems have a capability to verify whether or not a card being inserted into the reader is valid. Even though the design and configuration may vary, the principle of operation of these validating devices is generally the same. The validating equipment depicted in Figure 8-13 is used in conjunction with a card reader which accepts a coded card and a control device such as an electric door release that can be installed on and control a parking gate, an elevator, or any switching circuit. This validator also determines if the coded card is "valid" or "invalid"; the general principle of operation is generally as described above (see Figure 8-13).

KEYLESS SECURITY

Cipher locks are manufactured to operate electronically or manually. The electronic version differs from the manual one in that several doors can be equipped with operating modules all monitored at a central location, usually with a hard-copy read out record being made of each opening and closing as previously described.

Figure 8-14 The card that is used to activate an electric card key lock is a simple instrument that is extremely difficult to duplicate. (Courtesy Cardkey Systems)

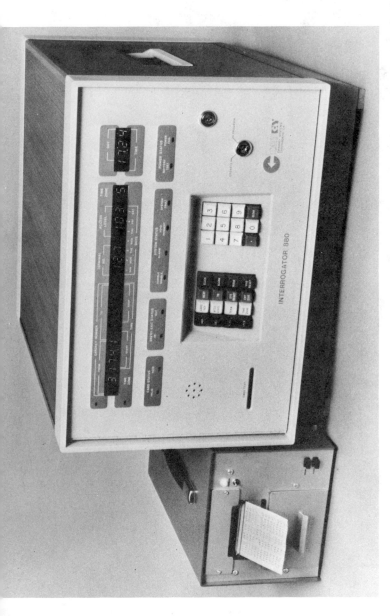

Figure 8-15 This central controller, the heart of the system, can control up to 128 separate card-reader terminals that are located in remote locations. The card reader "reads" the card and transmits the data to this controller. The controller evaluates the data, determines whether or not access should be granted, and returns the appropriate signal to the reader location. Attempted entries by invalid cards are displayed on the front panel. Reader terminals can be located as far away as $1\frac{1}{2}$ miles and can be connected to the controller by two pairs of twisted wires. (Courtesy Cardkey Systems)

Figure 8-16 The Simplex push-button cipher lock and combination spring-latch lock are used extensively where numerous keys would need to be issued. They provide higher security than ordinary pin tumbler locks because they are almost impossible to pick. (Courtesy Simplex Security Systems, Inc.)

Figure 8-17 Another version of the Simplex cipher lock. This style is manufactured for installation on doors having metal frames. (Courtesy Simplex Security Systems, Inc.)

These locks can be used in conjunction with electronically or magnetically impregnated cards. To increase the security when used in conjunction with the card, the record may also reflect the serial number or identity of the card and, therefore, theoretically at least, the cardholder (see Figures 8-14 and 8-15).

The mechanically operated <u>cipher</u> lock requires that a series of buttons be depressed in a preset sequence to release the dead bolt or dead latch, which is then withdrawn from the strike manually. Several styles are manufactured that will blend with practically any decor or fit any door style (see Figures 8-16 and 8-17).

Figure 8-18 Cardkey's mechanical door lock is another high-security device because the card is virtually impossible to reproduce. This lock is designed to be used wherever a standard key-operated door lock could be installed. It requires no external power, no wiring, no electricity, and no batteries. The operation is simple. When a correctly coded card is inserted in the slot, the knob can be turned, the door opened, and the card removed. (Courtesy Cardkey Systems)

The card-operated mechanical lock offers some degree of increased
security over a key-operated lock because the card is more difficult to
copy than a key if it falls temporarily into the hands of an unauthorized
person. Surely it eliminates placing a security key on the same key ring
as the automobile keys and then leaving all the keys in the ignition of a car
at the valet parking garage (see Figure 8-18).

Still in the electronic category but out of the access-control system
class is the electromagnetic locking device. As the name implies, when
the door is secured it is held in place by an electromagnetic device that
requires approximately 1,000 pounds of pressure or pull to break. The
device is used to control a door remotely, usually in conjunction with audio-
visual assistance. Because no key-operated locks are involved, picking
is completely eliminated (see Figure 8-19).

Figure 8-19 The electromagnetic lock can be installed on single or double
doors that can be controlled from a remote location usually in conjunction
with visual and/or audio assistance. When the electromagnetic device is
actuated, it will hold under pressure or pull of 1,000 pounds. (Courtesy
Alpha Components Corporation)

RECENT LOCK DEVELOPMENTS

The electronic padlock, manufactured by Coley Lock Corporation of Memphis, Tennessee, provides the shipping industry much-needed additional security.

Although the padlock is weatherproof and is said not to be affected by extreme weather conditions or road grime, a simple plug is used to prevent foreign material from entering the receptacle. The body and shackle are case-hardened steel to resist filing or being cut by a hacksaw. Shackles of varying lengths and designs are available for appropriate applications.

Figure 8-20 An electronically operated padlock, with the electrical male plug being inserted into the padlock. The electric "key" is hooked to the belt in the inverted position so it can be easily read by the operator merely by holding it in horizontal position. (Courtesy Coley Lock Corporation)

This padlock cannot be picked, because it can be opened only by the use of a specially built and designed "electronic key" that easily clips on one's belt. The "key" plugs into the bottom of the padlock and only from the "key" can the correct electronic data be entered to open the padlock (see Figure 8-20).

One key may service any number of padlocks, yet mere possession of the key by unauthorized personnel will not sacrifice security because knowledge of the correct sequential code is necessary to open the padlock. Because there are millions of possible combinations, the electronic padlock offers unparalleled security.

An electronic padlock can be placed on a truck, boxcar, or container and be opened after the container's arrival at its destination by the consignee with his electronic key. Ideally, the consignee has an electronic key, but if not, one can easily be shipped with the driver, for example, without loss of security, because the code is not known. The correct sequential code can be given to the consignee in advance by bill of lading, telephone, or other means.

DOOR CONTROLS

There are several methods to control use of doors, some of which will furnish printed records of times, openings, closings, and the key number that was used. These locking devices are used frequently when certain individuals are authorized access at specific periods of time—shelf stocking crews at a grocery store, for example, who work other than during operating hours or crews unloading bulk grocery deliveries during nonoperating hours. These devices are usually referred to as time-recording locks (see Figures 8-21 and 8-22).

Electrical strikes are in extensive use in door control during hours of operation. The electrical strike is mounted on the door to restrict access only to those persons otherwise identified by visual or audio means, and the door is released from a remote location. Caution must be exercised when audio identification only is used to make sure that no unauthorized personnel are allowed to enter while the door is open. Another precaution is not to rely upon the individual's self-identification by name or voice alone; code numbers should be assigned to individuals who will have authorized access through openings that cannot be monitored visually.

There is a mechanical locking system, usually referred to as sequential locking, that provides insurance that door locking schedules are properly maintained and that all doors in any given system have definitely been locked at the predesignated time. This procedure requires that doors having the equipment installed must be locked in a specific sequence, and all must be locked before the primary access or egress door can be secured.

Emergency exit doors can be adequately secured against entry into the building, but because of the nature of the intended use, provisions must be

Figure 8-21 This Controlock can be installed on any type of door to be monitored and is electronically wired to a recording unit such as that shown in Figure 8-22. (Courtesy The Silent Watchman Corporation)

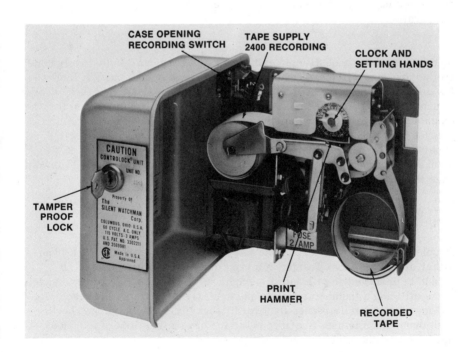

Figure 8-22 The recording unit in its open position. The unit will record the identity of the key, the identity of the door that was used, the date the door was used, and the time of opening and closing. Several Controlocks can be wired to one recorder. (Courtesy The Silent Watchman Corporation)

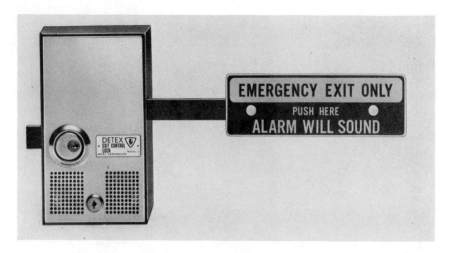

Figure 8-23 A widely used exit-control lock that sounds an alarm locally
when it is unlocked. Such a lock is an effective deterrent and an excellent
device for installation on emergency or remote exits. (Courtesy Detex
Corporation)

made for speedy, unobstructed exit. This category can be effectively controlled and securely locked against entry from the outside merely by not
installing any hardware on the exterior of the door. Control of these doors
is usually established by installing a local alarm and locking device that can
be easily disengaged during an emergency merely by depressing the lock
release bar. When released, a local bell or horn is activated, alerting
supervisors or security personnel that the door has been opened. If the
door is being used surreptitiously, immediate action can be taken to investi-
gage the activity that caused the alarm to be activated (see Figure 8-23).

DOUBLE CYLINDER LOCKS

Double cylinder locks require that a key be used to operate the lock from
either side. This lock is often referred to as the "security lock." It
should be installed on at least all peripheral doors. Reliance on cylindrical
locks utilizing a thumb-turn latch, particularly on doors within reach of a
window, immediately reduce the overall security of the building. Locks
with thumb-turn latches are acceptable for use on inner doors to offices
and in areas where high security is not needed.

MISCELLANEOUS LOCKING DEVICES

There are locks that can be used to limit use of phones, to secure office machinery to desks, to secure filing cabinets with metal security bars, and to lock employee lockers while still giving management the capability of controlling access.

There are various types of electrical switches that have many security and safety uses. These utilize key-operated pin tumbler locks in the locking systems, whether a part of the anti-intrusion alarm system or merely a part of the overall locking system of the facility.

Often safety requirements interfere with the security mission, and sometimes a key to a certain lock must be available for use during an emergency. The key can be adequately safeguarded by a device called the emergency key box. When the box is opened, an alarm is sounded, thereby deterring its unauthorized use and also alerting either supervisors or the security force that the key is being removed from the box (see Figure 8-24).

Even though a lock is large and a certain manufacturer's name may imply quality workmanship, locks will often fail to furnish the relative security

Figure 8-24   The key to an emergency exit or remote nonoperational door is stored in the box. The system uses an electronic circuit, and an alarm is activated at a remote monitor when the door is opened. (Courtesy Fox Police Security Systems)

that may be desired, because they have been altered in one manner or another. Therefore, it may often be necessary to engage the services of a locksmith to examine the interior of a lock or locks when security requirements are high and calculated risks cannot be assumed.

Sliding doors with metal frames will usually require some special locking techniques. The bolts of the locks on these doors have a "hook" shape, and, after being inserted into the receptacle in the jamb, the hook overrides the metal to hold the door closed. The metal used is generally soft, and to furnish any degree of security against "spreading," the metal must be reinforced with a good-quality strike or fabricated metal plate. To add additional strength and to prevent the door from being "spread," a bar is manufactured that is hinged on the stationary side of the door to the frame and can be lowered to a 90-degree horizontal angle and locked into place, making it impossible to slide the door open.

Sliding doors are most often breached by prying them out of their door track. Locking devices of varying kinds are available that, when properly installed, lock the door into its track. A simple screw or pin arrangement from the inside may accomplish the same thing, but the screw or pin is not locked into position and can be easily withdrawn once the glass in the door has been fractured.

I would be remiss if in this chapter I did not discuss briefly what are known as "apartment-house-type cylinders." In many cases, apartment house entrance doors, whether on the periphery of the building or inside the building (for example, a laundry room), may require that many different keys must operate the cylinder. Because of this high usage factor, the cylinders of this type of lock are subject to a great deal of wear. Therefore, locksmiths, instead of filling the cylinder with many small master pins (which, incidentally, does not add to the security of the cylinder), will leave out some of the pins depending upon the number of keys that will operate this cylinder. That is, if the cylinder can accommodate six pin tumblers, perhaps only one, two, or three will actually be used. This will give the cylinder a longer, more trouble-free life and will ensure smoother operation. But these cylinders are simple to pick. I personally know of three apartment houses that have cylinders in peripheral doors that are of the five-pin tumbler type, and yet they utilize only two of the five chambers. This reduces the security of the locking device because it could be picked by a professional within seconds and by an amateur in a matter of only a few minutes.

LOCK PICKING

If a lock can be picked, what type equipment does it take, and what do these tools look like? The tools are called picks, rakes, extractors, and tension bars. The picks vary in design but are similar to the ones shown in Figure 8-25. In addition to the tools, it requires a great deal of instruction and

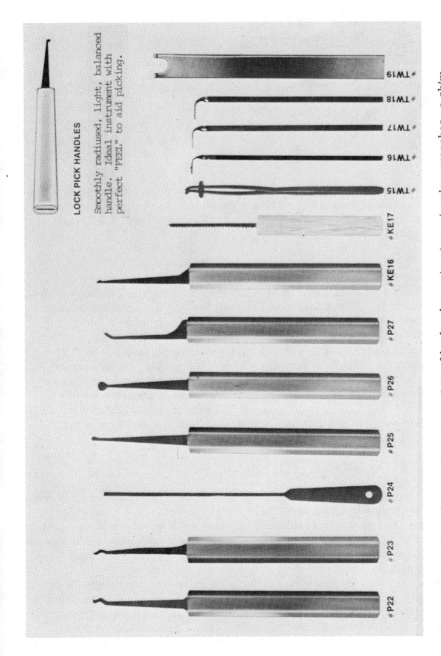

LOCK PICK HANDLES

Smoothly radiused, light, balanced handle. Ideal instrument with perfect "FEEL" to aid picking.

Figure 8-25 Lock-picking equipment consists of broken key extractors, tension wrenches, a shim, feelers, an assortment of picks, and a tiny saw. (Courtesy Dominion Lock Company, Ltd.)

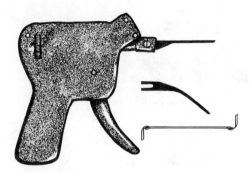

Figure 8-26 The lock-pick gun is widely used by police departments. The pick is agitated by snapping the trigger rapidly. The two picks and the tension bar are the only other items needed. (Courtesy Dominion Lock Company, Ltd.)

experience to become a good lock picker. Possession of lock-pick sets by unauthorized personnel constitutes "possession of burglary tools," and in most states the person possessing such tools illegally is subject to severe penalties.

Law enforcement agencies will often use what is referred to as a "lock-pick gun" to enter buildings during emergencies or investigations. This device has the shape of a hand gun with a needle or pick as the barrel. Snapping the trigger causes the needle to vibrate vertically. The needle is inserted into the keyway and vibrated by means of the trigger while a tension tool is used to exert tension on the plug of the locking device. This is a hit-or-miss operation, but it is fairly effective. See Figure 8-26.

COMBINATION LOCKS

Cipher locks could probably be considered a type of combination lock, but the true combination lock consists of a dial connected to a spindle that operates the internal mechanism which consists of wheels or discs, a bolt connector, and the bolt or bolts. There are numerous types of combination locks, including padlocks, door locks and locks for clothing lockers (see Figure 8-27).

Some security requirements dictate that three-way combination locks be employed, particularly where certain government security classifications are involved. By three-way combination we mean that at least three numbers must be included in the combination before the lock can be opened.

Combinations to operate these locks should be chosen at random without any reference to any other information that could be reduced to numerical

Figure 8-27 A combination lock that can also be opened with a master key in the possession of management is the desired lock to be installed on employees' individual lockers. (Courtesy Master Lock Company)

Figure 8-28 A highly portable magnetic device using a tungsten carbide drill to attack safes or vaults. (Courtesy The Shwayder Company)

Figure 8-29 After drilling, this bore scope can enter a 1/8-inch hole and read the combination directly or a wire filament "feeler" can be used. The lock can be simply dialed open after reading the combination. The hole can be puttied over and, if undetected, can be used again and again for surreptitious entry even if the combination is changed. (Courtesy The Shwayder Company)

form. Combinations that include birth dates, wedding dates, and the like should not be used, because an individual attacking a combination lock will first attempt to open the lock by using a series of birth dates, wedding dates, the date that the store was first opened, and other numerical possibilities that have some special meaning to the owner. Combinations must be given only to those with a need to know and must be memorized. The written record should be secured in the same manner as the highest classified documents or material being protected in the security container.

Combinations should be changed at least semiannually and whenever an individual in possession of the combination no longer needs to know the combination or is no longer employed at that location.

Combination locks obviously eliminate the possibility of picking. There are a handful of individuals, however, who can "pick" a combination lock with their hands, the only tool used being a stethoscope. Safes, vaults, and the like, regardless of size, can be breached in one manner or another. Popular methods most frequently used are litterally "ripping" the safe open, blowing the locking mechanism off, or blowing the entire door off with explosives or simply by drilling (see Figures 8-28 and 8-29).

KEY SYSTEMS

Before discussing the establishment of a typical key system, the names and functions of the keys involved should be clarified, and some familiarity with lock and key terms is necessary. The following terms are used to describe the parts of keys.

1. Bow. The bow of the key is actually the handle of the key or that portion of the key that is used to turn it.
2. Shoulder. The shoulder of the key is the flat portion at the end of the bow. In placing a key into a key-duplicating machine, a locksmith uses the shoulder to hold the key in a set position while other keys are being cut.
3. Shank. The shank of the key is the part between the bow or handle of the key and the wing or bit (see following discussion of keys).
4. Stem. The stem of the key is the rounded portion at the end of a shank of a bit key to which the wing or bit is attached. The part forming the axis on which a bit key rotates in the lock is often also referred to as the post.
5. Post. The post of a key is the round part of a bit key to which the wing or bit is attached.

To aid our discussion of keys and key problems, we should review the types of keys that are in use and some other important terms.

1. Barrel key. This is a key that has a round hollow post and a projecting wing to actuate the tumblers and the bolt of the lock. It is sometimes known as a "pipe key."
2. Push key. This key performs its function of aligning the tumblers with the sear line by inward rather than rotary motion. This key is sometimes known as a "thrust key" and is often referred to also as a "barrel key"; however, the term "barrel key" is not properly applied to a push key.
3. Bit key. A bit key is one having a wing or a bit that projects from the round solid post which operates the tumblers and the bolt of the lock. This key is sometimes referred to as a "wing key." It is

the type of key referred to in the text earlier as a "skeleton key"; these were once popular in earlier locks used in residential buildings.

4. Double bit key. A double bit key is merely an extension of the bit key. Such a key has bits or cuts on two sides that actuate the tumblers of the lock. This key is often found in the less expensive padlocks sold in department stores.

5. Flat key. This is a thin flat key, usually made of steel, that is stamped and has square-cut bittings. The locks that are installed on a great number of the lockers used in industry and schools utilize keys of this type.

6. Warded key. The warded key is one having grooves or notches that are designed to clear the warding of a warded lock.

7. Corrugated key. This is a key that is also often used to operate inexpensive padlocks and has longitudinal corrugations pressed in its shank that correspond to the irregular-shaped keyway. This key, rather than being machined, is usually pressed of steel.

8. Keyway. The keyway is the opening in the plug of a lock cylinder into which the key that operates the lock is inserted.

9. Paracentric. This term is used to distinguish a milled cylinder key from others such as bit keys and flat keys. The word is defined as "deviating from the center." The term describes the irregular shape of keyways used in pin tumbler locks only. The deviation from the center adds to the security of the cylinder, because it makes inserting lock picks difficult, and the bearing surface of the key will assure longer life.

10. Key change number. The key change number is the recorded code number that is stamped on the bow of a key that indicates the key change. For example, in the key change number A-2, A means that the key was assigned to master system A and the 2 indicates the sub-master system.

11. Construction key. Construction keys and sequential cylinder keys are often the same. Locks that are installed on new construction are operated with a key in the possession of the construction personnel. When construction is completed, the owner or operator of the facility inserts a different key into the lock, which changes the pin arrangement in the cylinder and voids the construction key. Now the locking device can be operated only with the key that is given to the owner or operator of the property.

MASTER-KEY SYSTEM

Developing a master-key system involves a careful analysis of company or corporate structure, the lines of authority, the areas of responsibility, and, even more important, a need for access to specific areas or buildings. To reach the objectives of the security required and yet maintain efficiency, several different types of master-key systems may be used. Before discussing a typical master-key system, some clarification of names and functions of the keys involved in the system is needed. Below are listed the names and general descriptions of keys that are involved in any master-key or grand master-key system.

1. Change key. This key is the key that is normally issued when you register at a motel and hotel. It has been referred to variously as the "room key," "guest key," or merely a "door key." It is an individual key to any lock in a master-key system and will normally operate only one lock in the system.

2. Sub-master key. This key is also referred to as a "floor master key" or in years past as the "maid's key." This key is generally used for housekeeping purposes and will open all rooms on a particular floor where one or more members of the housekeeping staff are working.

3. Master key. This key is also known as a "section master key" or "group master key." The key will operate a group of individually keyed locks that are not necessarily on the same floor. For example, a master key may operate all of the guest room doors on all floors of a particular motel and would be issued to the supervisor of maintenance or the supervisor of the cleaning personnel to allow him or her to inspect rooms after they have been cleaned or to allow a maintenance man into the room for repairs.

4. Building master key. In an industrial, commercial, or even institutional complex where several buildings comprise the complex, the building master key will operate all of the locks in any one given building but will normally not open the locks in another.

5. Grand master key. A grand master operates a number of groups of locks, each group under the control of a master key. These locks are not necessarily all in the same building of a project. For example, a grand master key may operate the locks at two different university campuses.

6. Great-grand master key. This key will operate all the locks of the entire system, regardless of the number of buildings or complexes that may be involved.

7. Emergency key. This key is sometimes known, particularly in the hotel/motel business, as the "lock-out key." It is normally used in emergency situations when the door to a hotel or motel room is locked from the inside. When the dead bolt is secured from inside a room, the emergency key is the only key that can unlock the locking device from the outside. It is always used in emergency situations only, and if a door is locked with the emergency key, it cannot be unlocked by any other key. This is where the term "lock-out" key is derived. This term arose some years ago when guests who had failed to pay

their rent left their rooms temporarily. The emergency key was
used to lock out the guest until arrangements were made to fulfill
his or her financial obligations.

8. Individual guard key. This key is often referred to as a "display
   key" and is used primarily in hotels and motels. The key, rather
   than a regular room key, is given to a guest who has samples or
   displays that must be stored in his room. When the individual guard
   key is used, it makes the lock inoperative to all other keys except
   the previously discussed emergency key.

In establishing a keying system, an organization chart must be drawn
up in order to establish the organization's "chain of command." The organizational chart must show the organization that is actually used in operational
situations. Often organizational charts do not reflect the true operational
organization of the facility.

Next, a detailed floor plan must be drawn of each floor of each building
that will be placed into the system. If more than one plant is involved, and
the keying system will include great-grand masters, floor plans of all buildings of all complexes being considered must be included.

The key system that is established must be based on the function of an
individual or individuals and a need for access to the particular area being
secured. Although many management personnel will not agree, a master
key is not a status symbol to be issued to the hierarchy but is rather the
key that is assigned according to a particular function or responsibility.
I have found numerous situations where officers of the company who never
had an occasion to use these keys were issued master or grand master keys
even though they were in the secured area only during normal working hours.
In other situations, presidents of companies who displayed their key rings
for me were unable to identify the majority of the keys on the key ring. In
every one of these instances, the ring included the key to the officer's
personal car or a company-owned car—a clear security risk, as discussed
earlier.

KEY CONTROL SYSTEMS

Probably the most important item relating to key system security is the
control of the keys themselves. Some polls of locksmiths indicate that in
over 90 percent of the cases key control of a new facility is lost or partially
lost within the first 30 days. When this occurs, reestablishing the security
of the key system requires extensive, time-consuming work and is very
expensive. Few building owners really appreciate the value of an effective,
continuing, key control system, and for this reason key control usually is
overlooked regardless of the overall degree of security that theoretically
is established by the present physical security program.

Figure 8-30 Secure key cabinets for any size installation are available for key storage. This system has an exceptionally well designed key control card and envelope system. (Courtesy TelKee Corporation)

Obviously, then, a secure master-keying system must be planned to obtain the greatest security and efficiency that can be obtained. This requires a careful study by someone who has thorough knowledge of any and all factors involved. The expense of contracting out this service, plus the cost of master-keyed cylinders, make it imperative that correct records be established initially and maintained so that the integrity of the entire system is not violated through the loss of one or two sub-master or master keys.

Of still greater importance, the individual who is responsible for key control and distribution of the keys must immediately be made aware of any fact that will necessitate a change to be made in the issuance or possession of keys. For example, he must be notified immediately when an employee departs the facility on a permanent basis, for whatever the reason, so that he may recover any keys that were issued to the individual. Only by using a systemized control record and close coordination between the key control manager and personnel can the security of the keying system at the facility be preserved.

There are several key control systems on the market; however, based on experience, it is my personal opinion that the best system is that manufactured by P. O. Moore, Inc.; this system is known commercially as the TelKee System. It is available in numerous sizes and can be used both in small plants and in huge hospitals or hotels. The security of the keys is maintained primarily by accurate record keeping. But the system also includes a container that is of sufficient strength to secure extra keys and the records of the locking system from all unauthorized individuals (see Figure 8-30).

Master-keying for large facilities, especially hospitals or college campuses, requires the expertise of a trained and experienced professional, and consideration should be given to employing a full-time locksmith who will be charged with cutting the facility's keys as well as key control. Technical manuals are available from lock manufacturers, and when locks are installed in new construction or when major renovation of an existing system is undertaken, the manufacturer of the locks that are being installed will often assist in training the facility's personnel who will be assigned the responsibility of key control.

9

Identification
and Control
of Personnel and Vehicles

In spite of the fact that there is a clear need to strengthen the procedures
to prevent criminals from obtaining personal identification documents,
either under false pretenses by theft or by assuming the identification of
deceased personnel, the Federal Advisory Committee on False Identification has recommended against creating a national identity card. In a statement that the committee made in the Federal Register on June 16, 1976,
they indicated that such a national identification system would have a potential for the abuse of personal privacy, would be expensive, and would not
necessarily guarantee that imposters could no longer obtain false identification.

At a press conference that was called on June 14, 1976, in Washington
to release the committee's findings and recommendations, Assistant Attorney
General Richard Thornburgh, the Justice Department's criminal division
director, called false identification "a growth industry" which costs the
American economy more than $20 billion annually. Some major crimes—
for example, the smuggling of drugs—rely on false identification to ensure
success. Approximately 80 percent of all of the controlled substances
referred to normally as "hard drugs" entering the United States are smuggled
by using false identification. In addition, illegal immigration that is aided
by false identification by itself produces federal, state, and local tax burdens
exceeding $12 billion annually. Almost all fugitives from justice use some
form of false identification to avoid arrest. False identification is involved
in many frauds against business and the government, the losses of which
can be counted in the billions, ranging from multiple welfare payments to
abuses of social security and even the food stamp programs. Frauds
against businesses are estimated to cost business in excess of $1 billion
per year and include the fraudulent use of credit cards and securities fraud.

In its June 14 press release, the committee recommended "That state
laws be enacted to require verification of identity of all persons that are
arrested prior to their release on bond or by increased use of equipment
to speed transmission of fingerprints to law enforcement offices."

Although the National Crime Information Center (NCIC) may be used to advantage in this area, it appears from newspaper articles that can be read every day of the year that suspects, sentenced prisoners, and the like are being discharged from confinement because of false identification or merely because they are able to outsmart the law enforcement agencies by claiming to be someone else. How often have we read in the paper that an individual was released from incarceration merely because he reported to the desk sergeant or the officer effecting the release when the name of another prisoner had been called.

I would recommend that law enforcement agencies require that departments responsible for the identification and control of prisoners adopt a method that is similar to the methods used in identification of patients in a hospital. In hospitals, a plastic band is attached, not only to the wrist of the patient but also to one ankle, identifying that individual. These bands are manufactured to make their alteration almost impossible and their removal quite obvious. This type of identification should be adopted by all law enforcement agencies.

Effective July 1, 1976, the fingerprinting of securities industry employees was required in order to combat the loss of securities by theft; however, the fingerprinting identification system is limited only to new industry workers. It appears that plans are at least on the drawing board to expand these efforts in future years. Someday, the fingerprints of all employees, not only of securities firms but of any cash handling firms such as banks and loan associations, should be checked against the files maintained by the Federal Bureau of Investigation.

The identity check of an individual seeking employment should start as soon as he is considered qualified for the position he seeks. A thorough background investigation of the individual should be conducted immediately. The depth of the investigation should be based upon the sensitivity of the position and may be influenced as well by the overall activity the employee is to be engaged in.

In instances where government classified operations of secret or lower classification are in progress, employees must be "cleared" in accordance with the regulations outlined in the "Industrial Security Manual for Safeguarding Classified Information." The background investigation is referred to as personal clearance—that is, the person is cleared for access and/or knowledge of classified information or material. Why, then, shouldn't any employer establish his own policy on "personal clearances"? The employer will obviously have to pay the cost of the investigation, whereas the government absorbs the expense when national security is involved.

There is no doubt that controlling the movements of personnel from the time they enter the facility until they depart is a most important facet of the entire security plan. It is in exercising these controls that all techniques and aids already discussed are brought together to ensure that only those

personnel who are authorized are admitted. It is obvious, then, that the
identity of the individual must first be established. Is the person actually
who he or she proports to be and have his or her previous activities, residences, and behavioral patterns been factually presented?

Remember also that those individuals who are assigned to conduct applicant background investigations, whether by telephone or by physically
approaching their sources of information, must be capable of some resourcefulness and must in their interviews attempt to uncover any undesirable
qualities that the applicant may possess. Too often the personnel assigned
to conduct a background investigation, particularly if it is restricted to the
use of a telephone only, abuse many principles of investigation. This occurs,
first, because they have never been trained to conduct a background investigation, and, second, because they are a part of the personnel team that
too often is reluctant to conduct a thorough investigation because they think
of their job as furnishing bodies to those individuals who have submitted
their applicant requests.

It is difficult, if not impossible, in today's permissive society to obtain
the criminal records of any individual regardless of the immensity or
enormity of the crimes committed or the amount of time that the individual
spent in prison. It appears, as the press has noted all too often, that the
law is "on the side of the criminal and not the victim." This also appears
to be true when the victim is the employer; however, the government has
insisted on being made aware of the possible criminal background of an
employee who will be charged with the protection of classified material
or with performing operations that may endanger the national welfare.

Why, then, should an individual employer be prohibited from conducting
thorough and accurate background investigations of individuals who, in
many instances, will be placed in sensitive positions? Why should employers suffer loss of assets because criminal acts are committed by
employees whose criminal background was hidden from the employer?
Granted, when the national security is at stake, we are speaking of greater
and more awesome consequences if these activities, material, or operations are exposed to the wrong individual, but individually (or by groups,
at least) the private employer and his employees are exposed as well. If
we are to reduce the ever-increasing crime rate in all areas, I feel that
it is time that criminal records be made available to all employers, if not
the public, as part of the penalty that the criminal must face because of
his chosen position in society. I, for one, do not feel that exposing a
person's criminal record should be considered as an invasion of his privacy,
because the criminal has freely chosen to engage in illegal activity. The
failure to provide this information to employers merely permits the criminal
to commit further unlawful activity.

In pursuing the inequities of the laws that prohibit law enforcement
organizations from releasing information to private industry but yet author-

ize them to release information to government agencies, I shall list the following guidelines recommended by several government publications and that were included in Robert McCrie's Security Letter, volume IV, no. 18.*

A. Be deeply motivated and aware of the responsibility.
B. Be adept at gathering all facts possible.
C. Possess a sense of fairness and respect. Report all facts pro and con.
D. Evaluate the facts carefully.
E. Be a good interviewer. (In some personnel screening units, however, the investigator never personally meets the applicant.)
F. Be tactful, diplomatic, and patient.
G. Put aside personal comparison.
H. Maintain a professional and moral responsibility to the employer.
I. Review the application.
   1. Determine if all information has been provided.
   2. Ascertain if certain information doesn't automatically exclude the applicant for employment consideration.
J. Report derogatory information to the supervisor immediately.
   1. Derogatory information should be fully developed.
   2. The reports should reflect unbiased and complete inquiry.
   3. Information should be immediately evaluated to determine whether investigation is required. (The subjective quality of an investigator is critical in making this decision.)

An outline for a thorough background investigation.

A. General guidelines for a satisfactory investigation.
   1. Advise the interviewee the position for which the applicant is being considered.
   2. Request that all interviews be treated as confidential.
   3. Interview the interviewee in private.
   4. Be sure that the interview is voluntary.
   5. Conduct impartial and unbiased questioning.
   6. Obtain information, don't give it. Avoid character assassination or the spreading of rumors.
   7. Watch the interviewee for reactions to specific questions.
   8. Strive to establish personal contact with the interviewee. Make appointments in advance whenever possible. Telephone inquiries and mail queries can be satisfactory, too.
B. Objectives of the investigative process.
   1. To determine if the applicant is qualified for a position of trust and responsibility.

*Security Letter, Inc., 475 Fifth Ave., New York, New York 10017.

2. To ascertain the applicant's needed qualities for the position
   a. Qualifications and ability.
   b. Character and reputation.
   c. Associates, friends, relatives.
   d. Social adaptability.
   e. Emotional stability.
   f. Health.
C. Areas to investigate (depends widely on the nature of the employing organization, its location, the amount of classified government work undertaken, and its relations with local police, etc.).
   1. Criminal records.
      National Crime Information Center (NCIC) files.
      State/motor vehicle/DL files.
      Sheriff and local PD files.
      County judge's office data.
      Criminal and civil court records.
      Police warrant files.
   2. Personal history (birth, marriage, divorce, etc.).
      Bureau of vital statistics.
      Military or draft board records.
      Civil courts records.
   3. Employment history.
      Dates of.
      Type of promotions.
      Rate of pay.
      Description of duties.
      Abilities (aptitude and initiative).
      Attendance record.
      Recommendations.
      Ability to get along with others.
      Reason for leaving.
   4. Education.
      Dates attended.
      Any disciplinary action.
      IQ rating or testing scores.
      Attendance record.
      Infirmary at school.
      Average grade—standing in class.
      Activities in school—their nature and quality.
   5. Residence and neighborhood investigation—current/previous.
      Emotional stability.
      Drinking habits.
      Ways applicant spends leisure time.
      Ability to budget and live within means.
      Marital problems.

  6. References: personal contact whenever possible.
  7. Military service.
   a. Use VA Form 07-3288, or data supplied by applicant.
   b. Request information from provost marshall (give name, branch, and unit when requesting information).
  8. Financial status.
   Commercial credit ratings.
   Any history of judgments.
   Current and past debts—current payment obligations.
  9. Health.
   Family doctor, hospitals, clinics.
   Cross-check with school/employment data.
 D. Corroborating information in the applicant's application.
  1. County and circuit clerks office, U.S. district court office.
  2. Welfare and health departments.
  3. Utility companies.
  4. Newspaper morgue files.
  5. Chamber of Commerce, BBB, auto clubs.
  6. Employment records—evaluations of fellow workers.
  7. Organization memberships including religious.
  8. Banks and retail businesses patronized by the applicant.
  9. Verification of personal history.
  10. Verification of naturalization, if applicable (will need date and place of entry; date, place, and number of naturalization).
  11. Evaluation by applicant's school/college instructors.
 E. Other supporting information: pointers to remember.
  1. Education: a release form should accompany requests for transcripts and class standing. Some large state universities have permanent written evaluations by instructors that are available.
  2. Credit bureau: may need Social Security number in addition to applicant's name, address, date of birth, etc. (In some cases the parents of the applicant will also receive a credit check.)
  3. Personal references: if derogatory information is received from a personal reference, the association between the applicant and the reference must be established. Developed references should be acquired whenever possible.
  4. Employment: if applicant has been in business for himself, interview competitors. Very important: account for all time of employment and education. Investigate time of unemployment.
  5. Neighborhood: contact landlords, neighbors behind, above, below, across, and either side from the applicant's former residence.

6. Selective service status: determine whether applicant is registered.
7. Military service history: a good opportunity to learn of any
   possible disabilities.
8. Medical: release form normally needed.
9. Foreign travel: determine travel history and purpose.
10. Memberships in organizations: ascertain nature of organization
    and leadership role applicant may have taken within.
11. Search for possible criminal record: if organization does not
    have easy access to NCIC data, have applicant petition local
    police departments where the applicant has lived for status
    reports.
12. Drivers licenses: verify and assure the existence or nonexistence
    of violations.
13. Acquaintances currently employed: consider as developed
    references.

Comment: These guidelines are edited and adopted from a government
security manual. By their nature, they focus on objective facts more
than subjective criteria. Yet these subjective inputs (ability to do the
job well, for example) will be more important to most organizations as
a basis for deciding upon the applicant.

If an investigation into an individual's background covered all of the
items and followed the guidelines just listed, there is no doubt that the
applicant would be thoroughly investigated and a factual evaluation of his
background could be made. However, this type of investigation would be
costly, and there are many items listed above that cannot be obtained by
private industry. As a minimum in conducting a background investigation
of, say, an hourly employee, at least the following items should be checked.

1. Periods of employment or unemployment that lasted 30 days or longer
   for the past 10 years should be checked thoroughly.
2. The applicant should be required to name three personal references
   he or she has known for at least the past 5 years (note the word
   "past"—not any 5-year period).
3. If the applicant has served in the military, regardless of how long
   ago it was, he or she should be required to produce his or her last
   DD Form 214 (Military Qualification Record).
4. A medical examination should be conducted by a doctor selected by
   the company, and the applicant's past medical history should be
   probed by the doctor to determine whether or not any fraudulent
   workers' compensation claims have been made by the individual.
5. Wherever possible, police records should be checked in all places
   of residence for the past 10 years. If a police records check is not

obtainable, the names of neighbors should be secured and an attempt
should be made to contact them to discuss the behavior and living
habits of the applicant.

It should be remembered that the items to be checked during a background investigation listed above would apply normally to hourly employees
who would not be assigned to an overly sensitive position such as research
and development or quality control. The more sensitive the position, the
deeper and more thorough should be the investigation.

In many instances, particularly where the thoroughness of the examination is absolutely essential, employers should consider contracting with a
reputable security firm to have these investigations conducted. Often employers will have a continuing contract with a private security or private
investigation agency with standard procedures to follow; if so, all employee
investigations are made by the contractual service organization. Even
though the background investigation may not be very detailed, having an
outside firm conduct the investigation will ensure that the information received is factual and is not "colored" to ensure the hiring of the applicant,
who could even be a friend of the personnel manager or the person responsible for hiring.

Often identification systems are not established and little or no control
over personnel movements is enforced until losses or other adverse conditions finally force management to change its attitude and policies. When
controls are nonexistent or lax, there is no doubt that personnel previously
authorized to enter and leave will resent and vehemently object to a newly
established identification system.

Identification of individuals at control points will normally entail other
restrictive measures to obtain the degree of security that is necessary.
When this occurs, the objection to change becomes even more verbose.
Here is how one security chief solved the problem.

INITIATING AN IDENTIFICATION SYSTEM

A small industrial plant producing household appliances continued to grow
over the years, and, as it grew, the industrial relations manager, who
wore a second hat as the "plant security manager," organized a guard force,
with one man on duty around the clock.

One of the functions of the guards who were on duty during the first and
second shifts was the identification and control of the employees as they
entered and left through the personnel gate in the chain link fence between
the plant and the employee parking lot. As the plant grew, the guards could
no longer recognize each employee personally because of the additions and
the turnover. Therefore, the plant security manager decided he must have
some means of identifying those that would be authorized inside the protected

area, and so he secured a camera and laminating equipment to prepare identification cards. The personnel manager was directed to issue each individual currently working in the facility an identification card and to issue each employee hired in the future an identification card at the time he or she was placed on the payroll.

The preparation of the identification cards began with a photo session in the plant cafeteria. All employees working the first and second shifts were required to report to the cafeteria as they were called in order to have their picture taken and to sign their card. In a few days each of the employees was issued an identification card. They were told that the card must be shown to the plant security force when they arrived for work at the beginning of their shift. They were further told that lunch boxes, purses, and any bags would have to be opened for the inspection by the security forces.

A number of employees, particularly those with seniority, became irate at these new security measures primarily because of a complete lack of an employee security educational program. The employees should have been told about the additional restrictions before they were actually placed into effect.

What particularly irked the employees was the fact, when they had forgotten their card, they had to wait at the guard house, sign in on a special roster, and have their department foreman contacted before they were authorized inside the area. And secondly, both male and female employees objected violently to having their purses and lunch pails checked by the security force.

After several days of confusion and arguments with employees at the guardhouse, the captain in charge of the security force determined that some other method must be devised to pacify those employees who objected the most and at the same time to enforce the additional security measures outlined by the plant security manager.

The captain, with the approval of the plant security manager, had the toolroom issue him about a hundred metal bolt washers. He took these washers to the maintenance department and had approximately 25 percent of them painted a bright red. He also asked the maintenance department to fabricate a metal tube in which the washers could be placed and then removed one at a time from the bottom of the tube.

The captain now had a device that he could issue to one of his guards who would stand near the time clock and remove a washer from the bottom of the tube each time an employee clocked out. These washers were immediately placed back into the top of the tube. Each time one of the red washers was withdrawn from the tube, that employee was asked to step aside to be subjected to either a purse or lunch box inspection.

Within a day or two, the grumbling and arguing almost ceased at the employee control point, and some employees were noted to be wagering on whether or not he or she would have a red washer withdrawn from the bottom of the tube.

Temporary identification cards were manufactured for those employees who forgot their identification cards. They then were required only to sign in on a separate register with their name and their clock number. The identification card was returned to the guardhouse at the end of the shift.

Although the security chief should be commended on his ingenuity in relieving an irritating morale problem, most of the problem could have been avoided had the security manager initiated an employee security education program prior to commencing any new restrictive security measures. Not only would such an educational program result in a less drastic effect on group morale, but it would assist in making the employees more security conscious, which obviously was also required.

Often it is possible to plan a revitalization or restrengthening of the security program in conjunction with another new procedure, renovation, or other type of activity which would be beneficial to the employees as a group. For example, in one instance the installation of a hot-line cafeteria and opening of this cafeteria in conjunction with establishing the first formal identification program resulted in complete acceptance of the security program without any adverse effect on employee morale.

There are several different levels of access control, ranging from personal identification, which is the most positive means of identifying an individual, to control by electronic means through the use of numerically sequential codes or a card key, or even by comparing fingerprints holographically. The method of identification and control will depend upon such factors as degree of security necessary, number of personnel to be processed during any given period of time, the various categories of personnel, and whether or not personnel not regularly admitted will have to pass through any specific control points.

LEVELS OF ACCESS CONTROL

In examining these levels of control, personal recognition should first be discussed because it is the most positive means of identifying a person. Example: A bank is robbed or a murder is committed and the police have witnesses. The immediate means of identifying the criminal is through a composite drawing of the head, usually with facial features receiving the greatest attention to detail.

If a guard at a control point is stationed there long enough, he could probably be able to recognize 50 or more employees. However, this is not enough. If an employee has been terminated and the guard not notified, the now unauthorized person is passed into the protected area; even though there is no doubt that personal recognition is the most positive means of identifying a person, other factors must be considered in establishing adequate controls.

Some readers may now be wondering how a guard could admit a terminated individual by personal recognition when the employee's identification
card should have been picked up. In instances where personal identification
is used, normally identification cards are not required. On the other hand,
some readers may recall that during their period of military service they
were able, when "downtown," to recognize any member of their organization, even though it may have had 150 or 200 members. However, in the
military, members of an organization eat, sleep, and work together 24
hours a day, 7 days a week, and therefore are able to recognize 150, 200,
or in some instances, particularly where the Navy and Marines are concerned, even more individuals merely because of the nature of the association.

IDENTIFICATION CARDS OR BADGES

An identification card or badge manufactured of metal or plastic is of little
use in properly identifying personnel and should not be considered in the
security plan. A button with a company or facility name or designation and
a control number can be presented by anyone in possession of the device.
Often at construction sites, "brassing in" is the only means of identification.
This system may suffice for payroll purposes but has no security value.
Therefore, if security is not a factor, no identifying media need be used
at all.

A laminated identification card containing certain personal data and a
recent color photo of the bearer is the only accepted means of identifying
individuals where any degree of security is a requirement. The equipment
used to produce the card can be highly portable, is simple to operate, and
has the capability of producing an excellent identification card in about 2
minutes (see Figures 9-1 and 9-2).

There are numerous systems on the market that will produce photographic
identification. Some, although portable, are intended for stationary use.
The type of equipment purchased will depend on the number of cards regularly produced and whether or not the equipment may be used by more than
one unit or at more than one location (see Figure 9-3). A laminated card
should contain sufficient basic information about the facility and the bearer
to ensure its effectiveness. At least the following information should appear
on the card.

1. The name of the company issuing the card.
2. A recent color photo of the bearer. At the time he or she is being
    photographed, each employee should be told that a new photograph
    will be required should the color of the hair be substantially changed
    or should a clean-shaven face suddenly become a mass of hair.

Figure 9-1 The compact, highly portable, and efficient Polaroid ID-3
Land Identification System. (Courtesy Polaroid Corporation)

Supervisors must be required to report major changes in the physical
appearance of employees of their groups to personnel, and all personnel should be notified at the time they are employed that if these
changes occur because of the employee's own desires, the cost of
manufacturing a new card will be borne by the employee.

3. The typewritten name and the signature of the bearer should be
included on the front of the card.

4. The date of birth and the height and weight of the bearer should also
appear; this would normally be placed on the reverse of the card.

5. An identification control number should be assigned to the card or
in some instances, a control number and/or the social security number can be used.

6. The title of the person authorized to validate the card should be
indicated, his name should be printed, and his signature should be
affixed. This signature should not be a facsimile signature that is
affixed with a rubber stamp and ink.

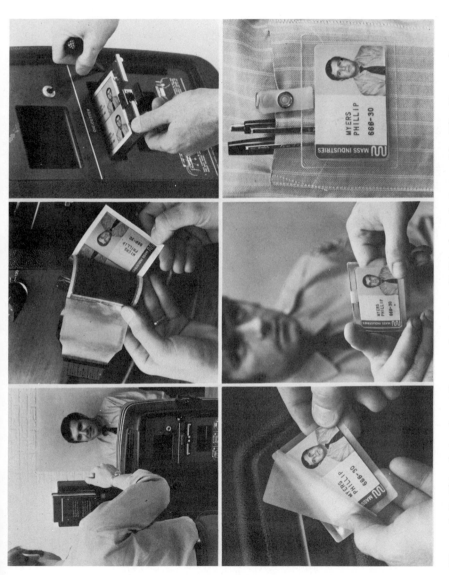

Figure 9-2 This photo shows the speed and simplicity of producing an identification card with the Polaroid system. (Courtesy Polaroid Corporation)

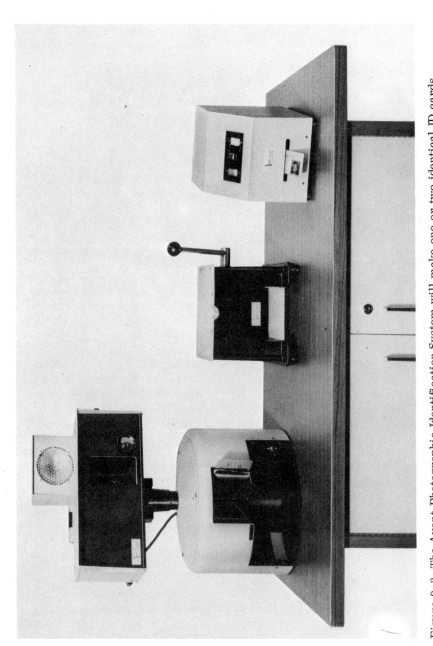

Figure 9-3 The Avant Photographic Identification System will make one or two identical ID cards. Shown here is the Duomatic System. (Courtesy Avant, Inc.)

7. The date of issuance should always be indicated and, if appropriate, depending upon the system used, the date the card will become invalid should be indicated.

In private industry it is of little value to include the thumb print or the fingerprint of the person being identified. In the first place, personnel taking the prints normally will not be trained; therefore, the prints cannot be read and classified. Second, unless a second set of prints is maintained in the personnel file, they are of little use if the employee disappears and the prints are on the card only which probably also disappeared.

COLOR CODING

If the degree of security needed is high enough, it may be necessary to color code the identification cards of personnel who will be allowed within specific areas of the facility.

If color coding is necessary, obviously the identification button is of absolutely no value, even though the button may be manufactured in different colors. Because color coding is done to increase security and usually means a higher budget for manufacturing the identification media, identification buttons that do not contain any personal data or picture of the bearer should not be used just to save money.

Color coding can be accomplished by several different methods. One method is to use a different colored cloth or paper backdrop when the photograph is taken. When complexes are larger and the movement of personnel greater, the basic color of the paper used to produce the identification card may be changed because this permits easier identification from greater distances. In still other applications, where a facility may have numerous restricted or classified areas, the card may contain several color codes. This may be done by placing small squares of solid colors on the front of the card, with each color authorizing the bearer of that particular card to enter a particular area. At operations I surveyed when the Apollo project first came into being several years ago, I saw as many as six colors on one individual's card. Certain portions of project activity were restricted to specific trailers or buildings, and each trailer or building was color coded with a different color. Those individuals who were responsible for the entire project were authorized in all of the trailers and/or buildings, and, therefore, their identification card contained a colored square for each one of the areas they would eventually enter.

Color coding can also be extended when uniforms are issued to personnel. This system is quite frequently used in hospitals where personnel of the various departments that service the hospital are issued uniforms of a different color. As an example, surgical personnel would be issued a green uniform, housekeeping personnel would be issued a brown uniform, dietary personnel would be issued a light blue uniform, and so on through the various service departments. In this way, the security force and supervisors could immediately distinguish whether or not an employee was in an area where they were authorized.

IDENTIFICATION SYSTEMS

Very briefly, three basic types of identification systems can be used for extended periods of time if the system is properly established, adequately safeguarded, and effectively controlled. Depending upon the complexity of the operation, on the need for security, and on the degree of security in various areas, the systems work generally as follows.

1. The single system. This system is normally employed at the average industrial, commercial, or institutional facility. It consists merely of issuing a laminated card to each employee who will be authorized inside the protected area, and the employee carries the card with him or her at all times. The card may or may not be displayed while within the protected area, and the card may or may not be color coded, again depending upon the security requirements.

2. The exchange system. This system requires that two cards be issued for each individual. One card would be of the type referred to above and would be issued to the employee so that he or she could enter the protected area at the initial control point; this card would be retained by the employee. The second card would probably be of a different color and/or different design and would be issued to a guard or receptionist who is securing a specific area. The card would be on file and would be issued to the employee identified on the card only after he or she properly identifies himself or herself. When this card is issued to an individual, the permanent card is left with the control person. When the individual returns from the secured area, the cards would be exchanged again. The employee receives the permanent card, and the second card is returned to the file. Whenever this individual was no longer authorized in the area, the card would be removed from the file and be destroyed.

3. The multiple system. This system is merely an extension of the exchange system. The system is used when there are a number of secured areas in one facility, and one individual may have access to more than one of these areas. The system operates exactly as the exchange system with the exception that there are duplicate cards at more than one control point.

CLOSED CIRCUIT TELEVISION

The use of video to identify and control personnel is becoming more popular in all types of private industry, primarily because the system is inexpensive, easy to install, and capable of positive identification, and can replace guards

at about one-fifth the cost of a guard. A single guard at a master console
is able to control numerous entrances. The system consists of a split-
screen image at the <u>control</u> <u>point</u> through the use of two closed circuit
television cameras at the access point. The person desiring entrance places
the identification card with the photograph at a designated location that is
observed by a closed circuit television camera and looks straight ahead,
usually into a one-way mirror, directly into the lens of a second camera.
The guard monitoring the access control system sees a picture of the person
desiring entrance and a close-up image of their identification card through
a split-image optical system that focuses both on the person's face and the
ID card simultaneously. This process can be accomplished by one system
with only one television camera and still display the split image on a remote
monitor. Obviously this system eliminates the cost of an extra camera and
other equipment. Optional equipment includes a digital time and date clock
that, if video-tape recordings are used, will indicate the exact time and the
date that the tape was made. This system requires that the door be remotely
and electronically controlled so that it can be released when the individual
desiring access is properly identified as authorized within the protected
area (see Figures 9-4 and 9-5).

Figure 9-4 This access-control system utilizes only one camera. The
twin lens and movable mirror produce a clear split image, and the design
offers maximum flexibility. (Courtesy Visual Methods, Inc.)

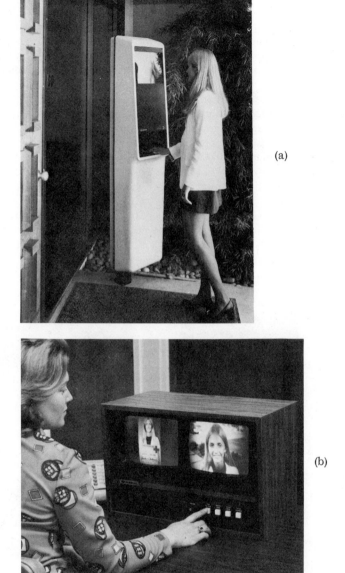

(a)

(b)

Figure 9-5 (a) This identification console utilizes television cameras to observe the individual card bearer and the card for comparison at the monitor. (b) The monitor with two screens where comparison of the bearer and the card is made. (Courtesy Mardix Security Systems)

MAN TRAPS

Man traps, man locks, or special pass-through areas control access through the use of two doors, both of which cannot be unlocked at the same time. A man trap usually consists of a small closet containing two doors. A closed circuit television camera is usually installed inside the closet to assist in the identification. The external door is opened with a cipher lock or a card key lock, and the individual desiring entrance steps inside the small closet where he or she is observed by the guard at the control point. When the individual is properly identified, the guard will then release the second door and the individual passes into the protected area. However, if the individual is not identified as the person having authority to enter, the door that was used to enter the cubicle is electronically secured from the guard's remote location, trapping the individual inside the cubicle until guards and/or investigators arrive.

ELECTRONIC ACCESS CONTROL

We have previously discussed devices that control access electronically, and these devices come in many different price ranges; as the cost increases, so does the sophistication of the equipment. Each increased level of security sophistication will present some trade-offs. Although these electronic access-control devices do offer a great deal of security, the cost of installation and the maintenance must be considered. The more sophisticated the hardware, the more prone to breakdowns and, therefore, the greater expense. Another thing to keep in mind is that these types of access control devices should be purchased from well-established manufacturers to ensure that the equipment is not installed one day and the manufacturer goes out of business the following, resulting in the loss of a source for obtaining spare parts should the equipment require replacements.

On May 17, 1975, the New York Times carried an article that included a report that a patent had been applied for on a special speech recognition apparatus that would be used to identify persons authorized access to restricted areas. To date the equipment has not appeared on the market, but it would appear that utilizing voice comparison would furnish an excellent means of identifying an individual, although such equipment would probably be terribly expensive.

Chapter 8 contains additional information on electronic access controls through the use of code impregnated cards with and without the added security feature that requires that a numerical code be punched manually into the equipment in a specific sequence before access can be gained.

VISITOR CONTROL

The control of visitors presents different problems in different facilities,
even though two facilities may be exactly alike and may manufacture exactly
the same product. Management in one facility may place a higher degree
of security upon a particular area than does their counterpart in another
facility producing the exact same product. The marketing director of one
installation may presume that a high degree of security is necessary for
the protection of the company's product, whereas his counterpart down the
block does not. Therefore, control of visitors is a specialized problem,
and each case must be handled individually, with controls being tailored to
each specific facility that is being surveyed. Visitor control normally will
apply to commercial or institutional establishments only during specific
periods but probably to a lesser degree. In retail establishments, control
is practically nonexistent except where visitors or salespersons are authorized in the facility before or after business hours.

   Therefore, control of visitors in any facility must be determined by the
degree of security that the overall security program will establish. In
some instances, it may be necessary that the visitor be met at the reception
desk or at the guard position and escorted at all times while he or she is
within the protected area. This is particularly true if classified operations
are in progress that must comply with government specifications. In other
instances, control of visitors may be left to the discretion of each department head. This is particularly true, although unwise, in hospital operations.

   Whatever the facility, and regardless of the number of visitors or who
controls them, some procedures and policies must be established by management to guide their subordinates in the control of visitors. If not, the
effectiveness of the entire security program will be downgraded where
personnel controls are overlooked.

   The control of visitors obviously starts at the point of entry to the facility,
and such control may be assigned to a security guard, a receptionist, a
telephone operator, or any other person normally on duty where visitors
enter. In some instances visitors are not required to enter the facility
being protected at a particular point and have a choice of many different
points of ingress and egress. When this occurs, my advice is "forget
security."

   There are literally dozens of methods of controlling visitors to a facility,
and the methods used for control will depend upon the degree of security
that is being established, the size of the facility, and the number or frequency of visits that are authorized at any particular point. In some
instances, the business may thrive on outsiders who visit the facility to
discuss mass purchase of items or to visit the display areas. Visitors,
whatever the purpose of their visit, must be taken into account in measures
to control the entry, activities, and departure of personnel.

In my book Security, I have treated visitor control and the identification of visitors in great detail in the chapter pertaining to this subject. In addition, numerous other publications by respected authors discuss visitor control. Therefore, in this chapter, rather than reiterating all of those recommendations, I shall discuss only those basics that must be observed and that can be expanded upon and tailored to meet the degree of security that is being established in the overall security program.

The visitor's first contact with the facility is when he or she approaches the control point, whether it is the receptionist, a guard, a PBX operator, or whatever. At this point visitors may or may not present their credentials even though they should. Usually (and my estimate is in approximately 85 percent of the cases), no identity is needed other than a business card. However, theoretically at least, a visitor is identified, the person whom he or she wishes to visit is named, and the visitor is required to document his presence on a visitor's log. From this point anything is likely to happen insofar as control is concerned.

If the visitor is not required actually to identify himself, he can merely sign his name on the log using a fictitious company or, on some occasions, even a fictitious name, the time in, the date, and in some instances whether or not he is a U.S. citizen. This is one thing I have never been able to understand—when visitor control is so loose, what difference does it make whether the visitor was a citizen of the United States or of some foreign country. However, the key to the visitor being admitted is the name of the person he wishes to visit. Once this has been accomplished, usually (and I use the word "usually" loosely) the person being visited will be called, and, after a considerable waiting period, the visitor will be given simple rapid directions to the person's office. These directions are understood in only 90 percent of the cases, and from that point the visitor is allowed to roam freely through the facility.

At the very least, a visitors log for nonemployee personnel who will, after proper identification, be authorized to enter the protected area must be established, and certain points in the facility must be designated as those points visitors or nonemployees are authorized to enter and depart. The visitors log should contain at least the following information.

1. The full name and home address of the visitor.
2. The company the visitor represents, if any.
3. The reason for the visit.
4. The person in the facility being visited.
5. The time of entry.
6. The time of departure.
7. A column for remarks that may include the means used to identify the person or safety equipment that may have been issued.

The date of the visit should not be included on the same line the visitor signs in on but should be a part of the log that is completed by controlling personnel.

I am personally against using a ledger-type log in which the pages are sewed or otherwise affixed. I personally prefer that single pages be used on a day-to-day basis; at the end of the business day, these pages should be scrutinized by the security director and filed. My objection to using the bound register is that there is a great deal of information furnished in the register that should not be made available to visitors. For example, a salesman visiting a facility that is in a highly competitive business will ordinarily have the opportunity to leaf through the last pages of the register to determine whether or not his competitor has visited the facility and is already ahead of him. In most instances, salesmen know competing salesmen by name, if not personally, and need merely glance at a page of some 20 or 25 names and in a second be able to identify his competitor.

Whether or not to escort a visitor will usually depend upon the degree of security being planned. However, it is my opinion that if a security program exists, if a visitors log is established, and if some identification media is issued to the visitor, then the security is great enough to demand that the visitor be escorted by the individual he is visiting or that the individual he is visiting report to the lobby of the building or the visitor entrance and conduct his business at this point. Unless it is absolutely necessary for visitors to enter a facility, I prefer to set aside an area, possibly even constructed with small cubicles, where visitors to the plant, regardless of their mission, can discuss their business in private with the person they have come to visit. There is then no need for visitors to venture further into the facility.

In larger operations where government classified information is located or classified operations are in progress, an escort service may be provided. The escorts may be company employees, either male or female, who may or may not be assigned to the security force. After the visitor has been accepted, a member of the escort service escorts the visitor to the office of the individual he is to see and, upon conclusion of the visit, again escorts the visitor to the access point where he is properly documented prior to leaving the facility. This is an extreme method of visitor escort; however, in many instances where government classified operations are in progress, it is a requirement. If the operations of the company are considered proprietary enough to ensure that competitors do not gain access to any portion of the facility, the same system may be established, and the expense may well be justified.

Contractor personnel, vendor servicemen, and utility servicemen who are required from time to time to enter the facility should, in general, be treated in the same manner as are other visitors. However, if visitors are escorted, perhaps this degree of security will not need to be established over utility repairmen, vendor servicemen or contractors, providing positive identification is established at the control point.

It must be remembered that the weakest link in the chain in any identification system is enforcement. The alertness of guards in positively identifying the bearer of a card when the card is presented will determine the effectiveness of the system. The lack of this alertness may well invalidate the most elaborate system that can be designed by the most experienced security personnel. Probably most violations of absolute comparison of individual and the card carried occur because the guard is burdened with so many duties that time just does not permit this identification to be properly performed.

I have often visited facilities after the hours of darkness and have found insufficient illumination for the guard definitely to establish that the individual before him is the one whose card he holds in his hand. I have presented to security guards at institutional and industrial facilities a card that bears my photograph; however, the photograph was taken while I had a cigarette in my mouth and was looking cross-eyed. The card purports that the organization to which I belong is Star Trek Industries, and it would appear that any guard with training and a prudent amount of alertness would certainly suspect that something was amiss when a card of this type was presented to him. However, some guards treated the card as if it were valid.

Establishing an identification system in a high-rise office building with many tenants is probably the most difficult to accomplish, primarily because building management does not want to accept the additional expense or the problem of issuance and recovery of cards. Controls, however, must be established at least after office hours, or thefts, attacks upon personnel, and incidents will certainly occur. If personnel identification and control is not established and the procedures enforced, the remainder of the security procedures already discussed are of little value.

The days when management thought of employees as "the family" are gone, as are, in most cases the businesses that supported this view until the business itself was "carried away."

VEHICLE IDENTIFICATION AND CONTROL

In almost all instances, the discussion in this section of the chapter will pertain to the control of vehicles at industrial or commercial facilities where the protection established commences at a perimeter barrier.

In many commercial facilities and almost all institutional facilities, the identification and control of vehicles is assigned to a private company specializing in vehicle control. In numerous commercial establishments, particularly in the retail industry, little or no control established is over the vehicles that are authorized to enter or depart, even though in some instances protection of the vehicles is established.

However, all vehicles that are to be authorized to enter an area that is protected on the perimeter by a barrier or park on company property must be properly identified and provided with an identification medium, and

accurate records of certain classifications of vehicles must be maintained.
Whether the facility is an industrial plant, a trucking terminal, or a one-
bay dock in a high-rise building basement, it is as important to identify
and control vehicles as it is to identify and control personnel. One not only
complements the other, but both are so closely related that those procedures
outlined previously for personnel control apply to every occupant of every
vehicle that will ultimately be allowed to enter the area.

PRIVATE VEHICLES

Classification of vehicles will vary from facility to facility, but when private
vehicles are discussed, the control measures will apply equally to an industrial plant, a college campus, or an elevated parking garage of a high-rise
office building.

At an industrial facility, private vehicles should be excluded from the
protected area. The employee parking area should be protected, but it
should be separated from the primary secured real estate.

At a commercial shopping mall, the employees should be required to
park their personal vehicles in designated stalls or areas, not so much,
perhaps, to keep them from utilizing prime parking stalls near the building
that should be kept open for customers, but rather for control, particularly
if a security force is employed to enforce a security plan.

At a hospital with or without public parking facilities or whether or not
privately owned parking areas are leased to, and managed by, a professional
parking organization, nurses and hourly employees on the second and third
shifts should park in areas easily observed and patrolled by the security
force. Doctors and other professional personnel will be given special
privileges for parking near the building entrances, just as would the manager
of a trucking terminal.

All private vehicles that will be controlled must be properly identified,
and, to facilitate control, the parking areas must be chosen wisely. It is
not unusual for some employees who commit thefts to use the vehicles of
executives as a means of removing the stolen property. In these cases,
the stolen property may be placed in the automobile trunk or merely taped
under the body and removed later at a location that the automobile is habitu-
ally parked.

A vehicle that will be permitted to occupy specific areas must be identified by a type of decal. The simplest method of controlling and identifying
the privately owned vehicles of employees is to issue a weather-proof decal
that contains the company name and merely a control number. If the installation and the parking area are large enough, and parking is a critical problem,
these decals may also be color coded by shift, by department, or by lot
assignment.

The vehicle identification should be placed on the outside of the vehicle rather than on the inside. If the decal is placed on the outside of the vehicle, the guard force can destroy the decal while the automobile is in the parking lot if an employee is being terminated for whatever reason. Often employees terminated for cause are disgruntled, and if the decal is placed inside the vehicle, either on the front windshield or the back window or on the rear of the rear view mirror and the vehicle is locked, it is impossible for the guard force to destroy the decal, and the employee may refuse to do so.

I have often conducted surveys in small towns and merely through curiosity have strolled through the parking lots of used car dealers. In every instance, without fail, I have found automobiles on the lot for resale that still contained the decals that were issued by a plant in the area, and the decals were still legitimate.

On one particularly difficult survey I conducted that was ordered by corporate management and not necessarily approved by local management, I confronted considerable obstacles from supervisors in the various production, shipping and warehousing departments and even from the plant manager himself. Therefore, rather than receiving the initial administrative information normally freely given to a surveyor, I had to "dig." This digging resulted in my visiting the used car lots, and, after proper identification, I was given permission to "road test" an automobile with the company's parking decal still affixed.

I immediately proceeded to the facility I had already visited, specifically to a control point that I had passed through several times on foot. As I approached the control point in the automobile, I was waved on by the guard merely because the decal was still affixed to the front bumper. In addition, I had learned earlier that the supervisors in the shipping dock area were issued a blue decal. The car I selected at the lot had a blue decal, and so I parked immediately adjacent to the driver entrance door at the shipping dock in an area used by the remainder of the supervisors. I am sure, had I had the desire to continue this hoax, I could have loaded the trunk of my automobile at will and departed without having been discovered.

The above experience is related to point out the fact that the surveyor in his analysis of present conditions must often go further than the perimeter barrier. Certainly, the procedures established at the facility that are given to the security surveyor as "gospel" must be checked and/or tested at least superficially. In some instances, it requires an in-depth investigation to determine the real degree of security that actually exists.

All readers by now will agree that some identification decal must be issued to employees to be affixed to their automobiles if they will be authorized to park on company property and that some procedure must be established to remove or destroy these decals when an employee is terminated.

There is also a need, then, to establish a procedure for the issuance of the decal and the control of unused decals. Control of the vehicles is assigned to the guard force, and the situation that exists will determine the type of control that is needed.

Obviously, in the incident described above, the security force may have better been employed as a janitorial service, and the security director, who had some six or eight other duties assigned that had precedence over security, might well have forgotten about the security program in its entirety. The incident involving the decal on the used car was only magnified in every other aspect of the security program, because the controls that were established did not consider the security that was required. As a result, a group of systematic pilferers in the facility took advantage of the unprofessional manner in which security was being handled.

Controls, then, and procedures must be used in establishing a vehicle identification system. In its very infancy, a control system to identify and control personal vehicles of employees should contain at least the following elements.

1. The controls and procedures established to safeguard and issue identification cards at the facility must be followed as closely as possible. Here again, we repeat that the issuance of identification cards to employees and the control of employees and all other personnel are directly related to the issuance of identification for vehicles and the control of these vehicles that will be authorized ingress and egress to the protected area.

2. The design of the decal should be intricate enough so that it will be difficult to duplicate. However, the overall degree of security being established will determine the intricacy of the design. There would be no point in a great expenditure to provide decals to be placed on the personal automobiles of employees who will park on the property if only plastic identification buttons are being used for the identity and control of the employee himself.

3. Every decal should be serially numbered, and the numbers should be sufficiently large so that they can be easily read from a distance. The control of the decals must be on the basis of the numbers of the decals, and every decal manufactured and received by the facility must be accounted for on a day-to-day basis. Because decals are not normally manufactured by the facility and reliance on outside contractors is a must, any dies that are used in the production of the decals should be purchased by and kept secure by the company having the decals made. Assurance must be received from the manufacturer of the decals that he will not duplicate the design nor sell or give decals to anyone but the authorized representative of the company.

4. Color coding can be considered as previously discussed and should definitely become a part of the vehicle control if the plant regularly works the second and third shifts. If second and third shifts do occur on a regular basis, consideration may be given to the additional expense of having the decals manufactured of a reflective material. This will facilitate a more rapid identification of the vehicle by the guard.

Other Vehicles

Other vehicles that will be authorized to enter the protected area fall into the following categories; visitors, utility vendors, company-owned vehicles, common carriers, company-owned interplant vehicles, and vehicles belonging to the company that are driven by executives. In some instances, executive personnel or officers of the company will be authorized to park within the protected area.

If the basic principles discussed earlier pertaining to vehicle control are applied to one degree or another to these categories of vehicles, adequate and effective control can be established. Usually vehicles that service the facility will be issued temporary identification rather than the permanent type discussed for employees, and these vehicles will be logged in, issued the identification, logged out, and the identification recovered.

The space available for parking of employee and nonemployee vehicles will dictate what controls can be established over the vehicles of nonemployees. In some instances, particularly in urban areas where parking lots restrict parking to employee vehicles only, visitors may be required to park in public parking areas or on the streets wherever parking space can be found.

Normally utility servicemen and vendor servicemen will be authorized to park their vehicles within or next to the protected area to facilitate the rapid completion of their activities. These vehicles obviously must come under the scrutiny of the guard at the control point as they pass through on their departure from the facility.

Common carriers that move the raw supplies in and the finished product out would normally be controlled at the point of ingress and egress with daily vehicle logs maintained containing sufficient information to identify any vehicle of a common carrier and its driver. These records should be maintained for at least 1 year and then destroyed.

Company vehicles such as mail trucks and interplant shipment trucks must be closely controlled. The fact that they are company-owned and company-driven vehicles does not mean that security should be relaxed. To the contrary, these vehicles and their drivers are often the perpetrators of the large thefts that are committed at the facility. Vehicles of this type should be parked in specifically designated areas and should be subject to inspection each time they move into and out of the facility. Interplant shipment trucks should be treated exactly the same as over-the-road carriers. These trucks should be subjected to the same sealing procedures already discussed, and if there is any change from the procedures used to control and inspect the common carriers, the change should mean that security in this area is increased.

Trucks that service a facility, if the facility is of any size, should be issued identification that is placed in the windshield, and, in the security program, different areas of the complex should have different color codes.

That is, if the complex is large, vehicles moving to the receiving docks should be issued an identification of one color, whereas vehicles moving to the shipping dock should be issued an identification of a distinctly different color. Utility trucks, vendor trucks, and other vehicles that will enter the protected area infrequently should be issued identification of a different color. This means of color coding will assist the security force and supervisors in policing and controlling vehicles within the protected area.

More detailed information on control of specific types of vehicles—for example, establishing time distance between points of entry and destination and vice-versa and marking roadways—is presented in my book Security. These controls need not be discussed in this book, because it is designed to be used by persons involved in the application of security systems not only to the industrial facility, but also to commercial and institutional facilities where vehicular control does not present a major security problem.

10

The Fire
Protection Plan

On October 29, 1974, President Ford signed into law the Fire Prevention and Control Act of 1974 (Public Law 93-498).

The administrator responsible for controlling and enforcing this act was directed by the law as being the sole individual responsible for the following.

1. Educating the public in the areas of fire and fire prevention.
2. Conducting a continuing program of fire technology development.
3. Establishing a national academy of fire prevention and control.
4. The establishing and operating a national fire data center.
5. Establishing a program to encourage state and local government to develop master plans for fire prevention and control.
6. Setting up a procedure for reimbursing fire service units for costs of fire fighting on federal property.
7. Setting up a system to review state and local fire and building codes.
8. Establishing necessary guidelines in fire safety effectiveness.
9. Organizing or at least participating in an annual conference on fire prevention and control.

In addition to the above, the act established the prerequisites for awards, the requirements for annual reports to Congress and the President and other activities that can generally be described in the following four categories.

1. The Federal Fire Prevention and Control Act established two classes of honorary public safety awards. These two awards are public safety awards and are to be presented to public safety officers for distinguished service in the field of public safety.
2. The act also requires that the Secretary of Commerce make an annual report to Congress and the President.
3. The act establishes a Fire Research Center within the Department of Commerce's National Bureau of Standards. This is probably the most important of all of the provisions of the act.
4. Finally, the act requires the Secretary of Health, Education, and Welfare to establish an expanded program of research on treatment of burns within the national institutes of health.

This Federal Fire Prevention and Control Act of 1974 established the
National Fire Prevention and Control Administration (NFPCA) with a
separate administrator who reports directly to the Secretary of Commerce.
This was done to ensure that the NFPCA programs would be highly visible.
The National Fire Prevention and Control Administration, which is modeled
after the existing National Oceanic and Atmospheric Administration, imple-
ments all sections of the fire program with the exception of the Fire Research
Center in the National Bureau of Standards. The Fire Research Center will
not be controlled by the administrator of NFPCA, but he is to be consulted
on content and priority of the research program.

Finally, the act states in part, "The administrator is authorized to take
all steps necessary to educate the public and to overcome public indifference
as to fire and fire prevention. These public relations efforts must include
programs to provide specialized information for those groups of individuals
who are particularly vulnerable to fire such as the young and the elderly."

Police crime prevention units and professional security personnel should
be conversant in the purpose of the National Academy for Fire Prevention
and Control, since it was developed to advance the professional development of fire service personnel and other persons engaged in the fire prevention and the fire control activities. It is the intent of Congress that the Fire
Academy be modeled after the FBI Academy and have a rather small campus
with a full-time staff with first-class teaching facilities available.

Thus was provided the much-needed federal backing in the area of fire
protection, prevention, and control (the funding of the act provided for
$18,500,000 for the fiscal year ending June 30, 1975 and $27,000,000 for
the fiscal year ending June 30, 1976), and a public awareness program was
included. It is my feeling that police department crime prevention personnel
and most certainly all security personnel must have more than a conversa-
tional knowledge of fire protection and prevention procedures. They must
have a well-rounded knowledge of the equipment available for fire protection,
prevention, and control systems and its mode of operation.

It is, therefore, the intent of this chapter to provide those responsible
for conducting physical security surveys in an effort to deter crime, including arson, with a working knowledge of fire prevention. This is so that
he or she may better understand the potential effect of the equipment available if this equipment is properly installed, located, and brought into action
at the appropriate time.

The loss of life and assets due to fire is staggering. In 1976 fire claimed
about 8,800 lives in the United States. This represents approximately an
increase of 200 over the number of fire-related deaths in 1974. Deaths in
dwelling fires totaled 6200 in 1976. Dollar losses were $3.4 billion, down
sharply from the 1975 total of $4.4 billion.

Even though inflation continues to be a factor in our economy and in the
rising property loss figures, the inflated dollar alone does not necessarily
account for such a large increase in one single year.

The largest property losses from fire in 1975, according to the National Fire Protection Association study, were the fires that occurred on February 27 in New York City at a telephone exchange and on March 22 at Brown's Ferry Nuclear Power Plant in Tennessee. Loss in each of these fires was more than $70 million.

The Southwestern Insurance Information Service reported in 1975 that in Texas there were 2,202 incidents of arson, compared to 1,658 incidents of arson in 1973. Jerry F. Johnson, President of the Southwestern Insurance Information Service, stated, "Each year in Texas we set an increase of approximately 12–15% in the number of arson cases. It is one of the most despicable crimes Texans must suffer."

Dallas arson investigator, Chief J. E. Tuma, indicated that while 579 incendiary (deliberate) fires occurred in Dallas in the first eleven months of 1974, only 468 incendiary fires occurred in the first eleven months of 1975. Chief Tuma said the decrease in fires was accompanied by greater financial loss. The 570 fires in 1974 caused $2,417,175 in damages, whereas the 468 fires in 1975 caused $2,555,233 in damages.

The real tragedy of a fire is often referred to as "hidden losses," some of these which are the following.

1. The loss of wages and possibly jobs by number of employees.
2. The loss of business for suppliers of raw materials and their services.
3. The loss of stock values and dividends to stockholders of the institution that has been destroyed by fire.
4. The loss of products for customers who require the products successfully to continue their businesses.
5. The loss of circulation of employee payroll dollars within the community.
6. The increased burden on unemployment funds in the community which, as a result of a large fire, may now have several hundred additional unemployed persons.
7. The possible increased burden on welfare funds of the community affected by the fire.
8. The loss of the labor market.
9. The loss of taxes that were derived from the destroyed property.

It is estimated that of those businesses that have major fires, 60 to 70 percent of them either never reopen or will completely close their business within 3 years. Knowing this, it is not hard to visualize the effect of a fire on people who are dependent to some extent on a particular business. Even those businesses that survive a major fire are left with scars and may never fully recover.

If a fire should occur, effective emergency planning as well as good fire prevention and protection practices will minimize the chances for the losses

we have discussed. All that is left is to motivate people to use these tools.
This is probably most difficult and most important job in private fire protection organizations, for the best tools are of little value unless people
are convinced that a problem exists and are motivated to do something about
it.

ARSON

Arson has been an ever-increasing cause of fire in the past 3 or 4 years.
The horrible effects of the crime of arson were clearly demonstrated in
the fire bombing of the Sponge Rubber Products Company in Shelton, Connecticut, a few years ago. The fire completely destroyed the plant, and some
900 employees in the small town of Shelton were suddenly out of work. This
arson was well planned, but the arsonists were caught. A New Haven,
Connecticut, jury convicted six individuals on at least two counts of arson.

The crime prevention specialist or the security specialist should also
be aware of the psychological and physiological effects of fires on human
beings. As Ann Wight of Phillips, Maryland, Surgical Research, writes
in a paper prepared for the Civil Defense Preparedness Program, "In the
presence of fire and smoke, man is a fragile being, prone to confusion,
injury and perhaps death from a multitude of causes. His capacity to survive depends on his age, his physical and mental fitness, his reaction time,
his education, and many other factors over which he may have little or no
control."

The air we breathe normally contains about 20 percent oxygen. If the
oxygen concentration falls below 16 percent, a person may make irrational
or ineffectual efforts to escape. A person may claw at a door instead of
turning the knob, or he may waste vital seconds saving items of little or
no consequence.

Carbon monoxide formed by smoldering fire robs those who inhale it of
the means to transport oxygen to their tissues. Oxygen is normally carried
from the lungs to the tissues via red blood cells containing the hemoglobin
that travel through the circulatory system to the tissues, where the oxygen
is dropped and carbon dioxide is picked up. The carbon dioxide is carried
to the lungs and exhaled, leaving the red cells ready for a new load of oxygen.
If there is carbon monoxide in the inhaled air, it competes with oxygen for
positions on the hemoglobin molecules. Some hemoglobin has a stronger
affinity for carbon monoxide than for oxygen, and so carbon monoxide inhala-
tion blocks the ability of oxygen to join with hemoglobin.

A less commonly understood cause of delayed evasion of the danger of
fires is the inability to react which often accompanies an emotional shock.
Usually following an accidental fire, the shock state is fleeting. Everyone
is stunned for a moment or two, but then each pulls himself or herself
together and responds to the emergency. In a disaster, however, some

people may remain in a state of helplessness, totally withdrawn from reality. In mass disasters, roughly 25 percent of the disaster population assesses the danger correctly and takes the important instant corrective action.

In numerous instances, however, people who are able to respond in a fire emergency will do the wrong thing because they have never been taught to do otherwise or because they do not understand or remember the instructions that have been given them. When asked what they would do if the house caught fire at night, many people, both adults and children alike, say that they would hide under the bed or in a closet, which is exactly where the fire fighters find their bodies. Others, asked what they would do if trapped in a fifth floor room with smoke pouring under the door, say that they would jump from the window, instead of plugging the crack under the door and yelling for help from a window, which would give fire fighters a chance to rescue them.

It is astounding how many people, security professionals included, do not even think of the basic elements that cause a fire to occur, the stages through which a fire progresses, and the type of extinguishing agents generally available and their effects upon a fire. When discussing fire protection and fire control with others, certainly the security official must be conversant in this basic knowledge, if he will command any respect and interest from the individuals with whom he is speaking. It is also astounding that people in general think merely of a fire as a fire and give no thought to the fact that if the fire department does not arrive, the fire eventually will become a conflagration consuming huge amounts of combustible material with split-second timing, reducing a recognizable physical object to ashes within minutes. Let us then get on with the basics and carefully weave our way through the technology, not so that we become experts, but so that we can better understand and discharge our assigned functions.

ELEMENTS THAT CONTRIBUTE TO STARTING A FIRE

There are only three elements that are necessary and that must be present at the same time in order that a fire may occur. These three elements, listed in their obvious sequence, are as follows.

1. Fuel or some sort of combustible material that can burn must be present for the fire to consume.
2. Oxygen must be present in sufficient quantities, for it is necessary for the fire to feed upon oxygen. Oxygen must remain present in varying degrees if the fire is to be sustained. The larger the fire grows, the greater quantity of oxygen it consumes. Therefore, if a fire can be confined to a single room, for example, where the windows and doors are tightly sealed, a fire started inside would soon consume the available oxygen and, without oxygen, would smother and go out.

3. Heat or some type of friction is the third element that is required to start a fire. There must be an ignition source, and these ignition sources can range from unseen overheated electrical wiring to friction caused by improperly oiled bearings in an electrical motor.

FOUR STAGES THROUGH WHICH A FIRE PASSES

Fires, regardless of their source or of the fuel being consumed, will pass through four stages. The rapidity with which each stage is completed will depend upon many factors, ranging from the type of fuel beginning to burn, the amount of oxygen present in the air, the movement of the air, and the gases that may be created by the burning fuel. The four stages are as follows.

1. Incipient stage. At this stage no smoke is visible, and so obviously there is no flame and no significant amount of heat has yet developed. A condition already exists, however, that can generate a sufficient amount of combustible particles that have mass but are too minute individually and collectively in size to be visible to the human eye. The number of these particles will rise quickly, although the incipient stage of the fire will usually consume an extended period of time, lasting from several minutes or hours to, in some cases where spontaneous combustion is involved, a number of days.

2. Smoldering stage. This is the second stage of a fire and is often referred to as the smoke stage. This condition arises when the quantity of combustion particles has increased to the point where their collective mass now becomes visible. During this stage only smoke will be visible and flame and heat are not yet significant.

3. Flame stage. The fire condition has now developed so that actual ignition occurs. Infrared energy is now developed by the flames, and, when this occurs, the level of smoke normally decreases and the amount of heat developed increases.

4. Heat stage. This stage is often referred to as the conflagration stage, and it occurs as the final stage of a fire when tremendous amounts of flame, smoke, heat, and toxic gases are produced. During this stage the fire will develop very quickly and usually follows the flame stage by only a few seconds. During this stage of the fire, if it is in a confined area, it would still "burn itself out" when all of the oxygen in the area was consumed. However, as in most hotel fires, doors to corridors are opened or in older buildings, transoms that are left open or constructed of glass will fracture, and the fire, being fueled by new oxygen, travels rapidly up and down the corridors and as doors between the corridor and rooms are opened, the fire rushes into the room in a manner similar to a liquid seeking its own level.

FIRE CLASSIFICATIONS

Fires are divided into four categories based on the type of combustible
material being consumed. The classifications are primarily a means of
identifying the particular class of fire with a specific type of extinguishant
that is most effective in extinguishing that fire. This is because the effectiveness of specific extinguishants on fires always depends upon the class
of material that is being burned. If an extinguishant is to be effective, it
must remove at least one of the elements mentioned above that are necessary
to sustain a fire, but this does not necessarily mean that each extinguishant
removes or destroys only one of the elements. In some cases more than
one of the elements will be removed or reduced at approximately the same
time.

Each of the four classifications of fire has been assigned a letter, a color
code, and a symbol. These are used to identify the type of extinguisher to
be used to attack that particular fire.

1. Class A fires. These are fires which occur in ordinary combustible
material such as wood, cloth, paper, and other highly combustible materials.
A Class A fire is identified by a large "A" inside a green triangle. Fires
in ordinary combustible material are best extinguished by quenching them
with water. The water lowers the temperature of the burning mass below
the kindling point necessary to sustain fire action. Extinguishers containing
extinguishants other than water may be successfully employed to extinguish
a Class A fire; however, water produces the best and most effective immediate results.

2. Class B fires. These fires occur in flammable liquids such as cooking fats, oils, paints, and petroleum products. These types of burning
liquids are best extinguished by a smothering action to cut off the oxygen
supply; an attempt to bring the burning mass below its kindling point, as in
Class A fires, usually is not effective. Dry chemical and foam extinguishers
are the most effective on Class B fires. However, water may be used if
the water pressure is high enough and the nozzles are designed to create a
"fog" by breaking the stream of water into minute droplets. A Class B fire
is signified by a "B" in the center of a red square, the square being the
symbol and the color being the code.

3. Class C fires. These fires occur in live electrical equipment, most
often in electrical motors, switches, and appliances that generate heat in
one form or another. The type of extinguishing agent used to "knock-down"
a Class C fire must be nonconducting; that is, the extinguishant cannot in
itself conduct electricity. Obviously, if a conducting extinguishant were
used on a live electrical fire, the individual handling the extinguisher would
receive a tremendous electrical shock. Carbon dioxide or general or special
purpose dry chemical extinguishers are most suitable for extinguishing a
Class C fire. The carbon dioxide extinguisher is by far the most desirable;
unlike dry chemicals, it does not leave a residue. A vaporizing liquid agent

may also be used to extinguish a Class C fire; such extinguishants are effective because the rapid vaporization of the liquid as it comes in contact with the burning material creates a smothering effect. A Class C fire is identified by a "C" in a blue circle.

4. Class D fires. These are fires that occur in various types of flammable metals. Magnesium, for example, and other exotic metals will burn when chemical changes occur at the proper temperature and in correct proportion. Powdered graphite was for years the favorite extinguishant to be used on this class of fire; however, there are now special purpose dry chemicals and other specially prepared agents that can be used successfully in extinguishing a Class D fire. This class of fire is identified by a "D" inside a yellow five-pointed star.

PORTABLE HAND EXTINGUISHERS

The following paragraphs will be devoted to a brief discussion of the types of hand (or first aid) fire extinguishers that are available, the type extinguishants used for the various classes of fire, and some relatively new hand extinguishers and extinguishants.

1. Fire pails, tanks and barrels with pails. These containers are filled with a small supply of water that is applied to a Class A fire; however, they are limited as far as fire-extinguishing value is concerned because of the limited supply of water and inability to direct the water at the base of the fire and then cover the fire systematically. Additionally, the pails placed on the larger water containers are often removed and used for other purposes, even though they may be painted bright red with the word "fire" stenciled in large letters on the outside with a contrasting colored paint. Without the pails to apply the water from the storage tanks, it is practically impossible to use the water effectively.

2. Pump-tank extinguishers. This type of extinguisher also uses water as the extinguishant and is used primarily on an ordinary combustible or Class A fire. The tank, as the name indicates, is nothing more than a water pump; as the pump is operated, the water is forced through a hose that can be directed at the burning material. This extinguisher is somewhat more effective than the barrel and fire pail; however, when used in freezing climates, the water must be mixed with antifreeze solution to ensure that the water does not freeze. This is true of all water-base extinguishers to be used in extremely cold climates.

3. Soda-acid extinguishers. These extinguishers are also water-type or water-base extinguishers and again are primarily used on Class A fires. The water in these extinguishers is expelled by mixing bicarbonate of soda, which is dissolved in the water in the extinguisher shell, and a premeasured amount of sulfuric acid, which is placed in an internal bottle; intermixing these produces a chemical reaction that creates pressure to expel the water from the extinguisher.

Figure 10-1 A pressurized $2\frac{1}{2}$-gallon water fire extinguisher for use only on Class A fires. (Courtesy Casco Products Corp.)

   4. <u>Stored-pressure extinguishers</u>. This is also a water-type or water-base extinguisher, and the extinguishant used is ordinary fresh water and antifreeze, if necessary. The stored pressure or air in the container expels the water when it is released through an arrangement of valves that are opened by hand (see Figure 10-1).
   5. <u>Foam extinguishers</u>. These extinguishers are actually water-based; however, the chemicals used in these extinguishers are sodium bicarbonate with a foam stabilizing agent, which is dissolved in the water in the outer

compartment of the extinguisher, and aluminum sulfate, which is dissolved
in the water in the inner compartment of the extinguisher. Intermixing of
these agents causes foam to be produced under pressure that is expelled
through the hose and nozzle of the extinguisher. This extinguisher can be
used on Class A or B fires effectively.

6. Loaded-stream extinguishers. These extinguishers also use a water-
base extinguishant and utilize an alkali metal salt solution which will not
freeze. These extinguishers usually are of the cartridge-operated or stored-
pressure type.

7. Carbon dioxide extinguishers. These extinguishers use liquid carbon
dioxide under its own pressure and are usually stored at room temperature.
The carbon dioxide agent is self-expelling and is discharged by operating
a valve which causes the carbon dioxide to be expelled through a hose and
a horn in its vapor and solid state. These extinguishers are most effectively
used on Class C fires (see Figure 10-2).

8. Dry chemical extinguishers. Dry chemical extinguishers are for use
on Class B and C fires. The extinguishant used is a specially treated material in a very finely divided form with other components for producing free
flow and water repellancy. These extinguishants are formed with a sodium
bicarbonate base, potassium bicarbonate base, potassium chloride base,
or potassium bicarbonate urea base. These extinguishers can be of the
stored-pressure, cartridge-operated, or disposable, nonrefillable type
(see Figure 10-3).

9. Multipurpose dry chemical extinguishers. These extinguishers are
designed to extinguish Class A, B, and C fires, with the extinguishant being
specially treated materials, again in a finely divided form. The primary
base is ammonium phosphate with other components that produce free flow
and water repellancy, as in the dry chemical extinguisher described earlier.
These extinguishers may also be of the stored-pressure or cartridge-
operated types (see Figure 10-4).

10. Dry powder extinguishers. These extinguishers use a dry powder
extinguishant for metal fires and are suitable for use in extinguishing a
Class D fire. The extinguishant can either be placed in an extinguisher or
in pails or drums and applied to the fire by scoop or shovel. Each such
extinguisher will contain a nameplate indicating the type of extinguishant
in the container or extinguisher with the recommended method of application.
Usually these nameplates will also indicate the limitations of the extinguishant.

11. Halon 1301 extinguishers. These extinguishers are technically
referred to as bromotrifluoromethane extinguishers. The agent in these
extinguishers is self-expelling and is discharged through a horn, again by
the operation of a valve. A booster charge of nitrogen is used at low temperatures to improve operation.

12. Halon 1211 extinguishers. These extinguishers are technically
referred to as bromochloriodifluoromethane extinguishers. The agent in

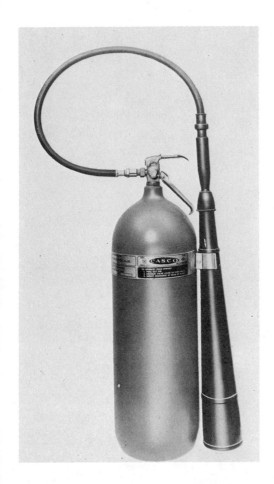

Figure 10-2 A 20-pound carbon dioxide fire extinguisher designed for use on Class B and C fires; however, in an emergency, this extinguisher could be used to fight a small Class A fire. (Courtesy Casco Products Corp.)

these extinguishers is also self-expelling, but it requires a booster charge of nitrogen, regardless of the temperature, to ensure its proper operation. Both the Halon 1301 and the Halon 1211 extinguishers do not leave a residue and are used in Class C fires in highly sophisticated machinery. Halon does not rob the air of oxygen as does carbon dioxide and is often used in the protection of computer areas (see Figure 10-5).

Figure 10-3 A dry chemical extinguisher designed for use on a Class B and C fire. (Courtesy Casco Products Corp.)

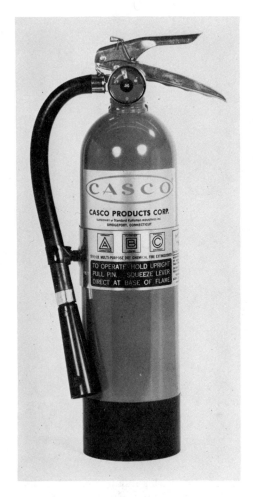

Figure 10-4 A multipurpose dry chemical extinguisher designed for use on Class A, B, and C fires. (Courtesy Casco Products Corp.)

Figure 10-5 This is a comparatively new fire extinguisher containing the extinguishing agent Halon 1211. This is a 9-pound unit that is classified by U.L. as 1A-10B:C. Interestingly, the boiling point of Halon 1211 is a low 25° Fahrenheit and the freezing point -256° Fahrenheit. (Courtesy Graviner, Inc.)

METHOD OF EXTINGUISHER OPERATION

The methods of operation of extinguishers are classified according to the means by which the extinguishant is expelled. There are six methods of expelling the extinguishant now in common use.

1. Self-generating. These extinguishers are actuated by intermixing chemicals that cause gases to be generated in the shell. These gases then provide the energy to expel the extinguishant.
2. Self-expelling. These extinguishers operate because the agents have a sufficient amount of vapor pressure at normal operating temperatures to expel the extinguishant themselves.
3. Gas operated or cylinder. These extinguishers are operated by gas that is stored in a separate pressure bottle or container until the operator releases the gas to pressurize the extinguisher shell. This same principle is used to produce soda water from fresh water in a soda bottle found in the home bar.
4. Stored pressure. The extinguishant in these extinguishers is expelled by a gas, usually air, that is stored in the same container as the extinguishant.
5. Mechanically pumped. This extinguisher will be one of two types. In one, a pump is operated, forcing air into the shell and expelling the extinguishant, which, in most cases, is water. In the second type, a vaporizing liquid is used, but the same principle is used to expel the extinguishant.
6. Hand propelled. Obviously, the hand-propelled method is simply to use a pail or bucket when liquids are involved and a scoop or shovel when dry chemicals are involved, particularly those dry chemicals and graphite that are used in extinguishing Class D fires.

MARKING AND PLACEMENT OF HAND EXTINGUISHERS

All personnel interested in the subject of hand-operated fire extinguishers should secure a copy of NFPA Publication #10 (1974) entitled "Portable Fire Extinguishers."

This publication outlines in detail the standards for the installation, maintenance, and use of portable fire extinguishers. Experience has indicated that some precaution should be exercised in the marking and location of fire extinguishers in certain circumstances to ensure that the extinguisher can be readily located and to minimize the chance that an extinguisher will be damaged by being accidentally struck by industrial vehicles operating within buildings.

Generally speaking, marking the location of an extinguisher and the classification of the type of fire it is to be used on by including in the marking the symbol, letter, and color code is sufficient. However, if extinguishers are mounted on walls, columns, or other uprights in areas where a considerable amount of machinery is located or, as in warehouses, where material is stacked rather high, it is probably desirable to mark the location of the fire extinguisher not only where it is actually mounted, but also near the top of the wall, column, or upright. This is so that the extinguisher's location can be seen from all points in the area in which it is to be used. This is particularly true in storage and warehousing operations and in areas where stored material is piled high and may be moved on a day-to-day basis. Under these conditions, the fire extinguisher itself may be visible throughout the area on one day, whereas on the next it can be seen only by personnel in the immediate vicinity.

    This method should also be used to mark the location of standpipe hoses to ensure that the standpipe hose location can also be seen throughout the area it is intended to service. It may also be advantageous to store a fire extinguisher in the immediate vicinity of the standpipe hose as is often the practice in hotels, motels, and office buildings. However, this does not necessarily mean that only one fire extinguisher will be made available in

Figure 10-6 The "quarter horse" fire truck has numerous applications in the fire fighting field and has a capability of traversing rough terrain. It is an excellent vehicle in which to move fire fighting equipment in large industrial or institutional facilities. (Courtesy Promark Products Corporation)

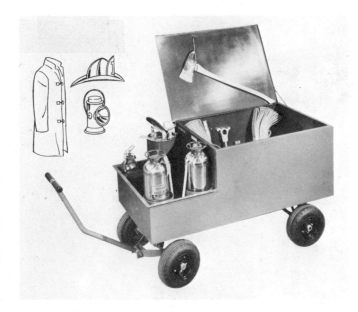

Figure 10-7 The hand-drawn fire truck is used to store an array of fire fighting equipment that can be quickly pulled by fire brigades to the fire location. (Courtesy Brennan Equipment & Manufacturing)

the area serviced by a specific length of standpipe hose. Technical data should be consulted to determine the correct type and number of fire extinguishers required for various types of environments.

Often it is desirable to have a group of extinguishers of the various types discussed and other fire fighting equipment available and mobile enough to permit one or two persons to move all of the equipment to a fire emergency area where the remainder of the fire fighting organization has assembled. The mobility of this equipment also provides a means of easily moving fire equipment to construction areas, welding areas, or other activities that may increase the fire potential only temporarily (see Figures 10-6 and 10-7).

DETECTION DEVICES

As important as equipment to fight fires is equipment to detect fires before they get a chance to become serious. The fire and smoke detectors that are discussed here are not the only ones that are available on today's market. The only difference between devices described here and other

Figure 10-8 The ionization fire detector can respond to the invisible combustion products that are generated during the incipient stage of a fire.
(Courtesy Pyrotronics, Inc.)

devices is in the packaging of the operational components. The basic principle of detection remains the same.

1. <u>Ionization fire detector</u>. The ionization fire detector has recently
come under attack by Ralph Nader's Consumer Service Group which claims
that a small amount of ionization is released constantly into the surrounding
atmosphere. However, this ionization detector, although not relatively new,
is one of the latest detectors developed and operates by means of a small
current that is passed through the air between two plates. Hydrocarbons
and other invisible products of combustion that are emitted during the incipient stage of a fire will interrupt this current and cause an alarm to be
activated. These detectors are extremely effective because they can detect
a fire during the incipient stage, thereby furnishing early warning (see
Figures 10-8 and 10-9).

2. <u>Photoelectric detector</u>. This detector is commonly referred to as a
"smoke detector." Outwardly it appears similar in configuration to the
ionization chamber detector; however, because it is a smoke detector, it
is somewhat slower to detect a fire. Because the fire detected has already
passed through the incipient stage and is now producing visible masses of

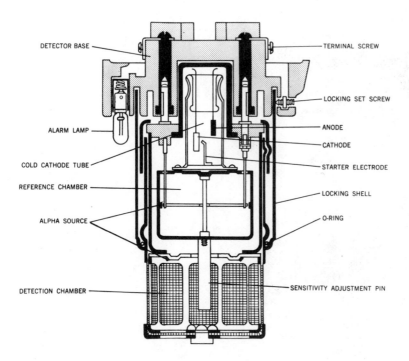

DETECTOR BASE

TERMINAL SCREW

LOCKING SET SCREW

ALARM LAMP

ANODE

CATHODE

COLD CATHODE TUBE

STARTER ELECTRODE

REFERENCE CHAMBER

LOCKING SHELL

ALPHA SOURCE

O-RING

DETECTION CHAMBER

SENSITIVITY ADJUSTMENT PIN

Figure 10-9 A cutaway view of the ionization fire detector. (Courtesy Pyrotronics, Inc.)

particles of combustion (that is, smoke), the fire has progressed to a point where it will soon produce flame and heat. The photoelectric detector assumes its alarm mode when the smoke obscures a small beam of light, breaking the circuit (see Figure 10-10).

    3. <u>Infrared flame detector</u>. This detector operates on the principle that all fire emits infrared rays. The detector is designed to assume an alarm mode during the third stage of a fire when flames actually exist. Therefore, this is third in line of the detectors discussed so far (see Figure 10-11).

    4. <u>Thermal detectors</u>. The thermal detector can be of the fixed-temperature or rate-of-rise type detection device. The fixed-temperature thermal detector will normally be preset at 135° Fahrenheit, and when heat in the protected area rises to that temperature or beyond, a piece of metal used to close the circuit is separated, and the device assumes its alarm mode. The rate-of-rise thermal detector reacts to an unusually rapid rise in the temperature. Often these two thermal detectors are used in one fire protection plan with the fixed temperature detector being used in those areas where there are rapid temperature fluctuations which would

Figure 10-10 The photoelectric smoke detector will respond to the visible smoke that occurs during the second, or smoldering, stage of a fire. (Courtesy Pyrotronics, Inc.)

make the rate-of-rise detector impractical for installation (see Figure 10-12).

    5. Air duct detector. These detectors consist of small hoses or air-tight tubes which are installed throughout the protected area. These tubes are then tied into a detector which measures the pressure in the tube. When the pressure in the tube increases to a preset height, the pneumatic detector is activated by the built-up pressure in the hose, releasing an electrical switch connection and placing the detector head in its alarm mode (see Figure 10-13).

    6. Supervisory alarms. There are several supervisory alarms used in the fire protection system, and obviously each performs a particular function. These alarms generally fall into five categories.

    a. Temperature supervision alarms are found in automatic sprinkler systems and warn when the temperature of the auxiliary water in the supply tanks or pipes is near freezing.

Figure 10-11 The infrared flame detector responds during the third, or flame, stage of a fire. (Courtesy Pyrotronics, Inc.)

Figure 10-12 The fixed-temperature and rate-of-rise thermal detector responds during the fourth stage of fire when heat energy increases. (Courtesy Pyrotronics, Inc.)

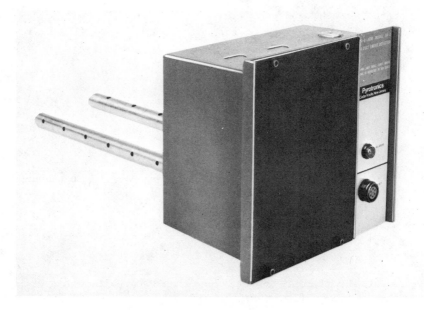

Figure 10-13 The air duct smoke detector is installed in heating and air-conditioning ducts and is activated when smoke in the ducts is sensed. (Courtesy Pyrotronics, Inc.)

    b. Air pressure supervision alarms are found in the dry pipe sprinkler system and warn when the air pressure drops below a predetermined level.

    c. Water level supervision alarms are found in either elevated or suction tank systems and warn when the level of water drops below an established minimum.

    d. Post indicator valve supervision alarms are placed on the post indicator valve and warn when the main water supply to the sprinkler riser has been shut off.

    e. Valve supervisory alarms are those mechanical devices that are installed on the various gate valves, outside, screw, and yoke (OS&Y) valves, to warn when either the secondary or primary water supply valves have been shut off. This type of supervision should be installed at least on each OS&Y valve of all automatic sprinkler risers.

    7. Fire alarm stations. Three types of fire alarms stations can generally be found in a fire protection system of a building. These stations are wall mounted and are usually classified as pull boxes—that is, a lever or trigger that is forceably being held in place must be released and the small rod or handle manipulated either by hand or through a spring installed

to automatically manipulate the seal, lever, or rod which then will automatically sound the intended alarm. These fire alarm stations are classified
into three categories.

a. Local alarm stations are identified by overprinting the word "local"
in bold letters, usually in black, so that they stand out against the red color
of the alarm station. The local alarm does not transmit a signal to a fire
department. It usually transmits the signal locally by activating a bell in
the immediate area and by alerting either the guard force or the fire brigades assigned to the property.

b. Remote signal stations that, when activated, transmit a signal
directly to the area where the signal is monitored. This may be at the
local fire department or at a privately operated central station that monitors several different properties. The person on duty at the monitor then,
in turn, notifies the servicing fire department. The remote signal station
is usually painted red and is labeled as a fire alarm; however, the word
"local" will not be found. This does not mean, however, that a bell is not
rung locally, even when the remote signal stations are located inside the
building.

c. Fire department telephone jacks are found extensively throughout
California in public buildings and in many other modern structures. These
are used by fire fighters to communicate with one another from one area
or from one level to another by means of special telephone lines. These
lines normally remain intact even though the utility telephone lines servicing
the building from outside are inoperable.

ZONES AND CODES

Facilities covering several thousand square feet or multiple story buildings
will normally be zoned into areas that are identified by numbers and audible
codes that are transmitted to personnel in the area through a series of rings
on a bell or blasts on a horn. Procedures are established that require
personnel in affected zones to evacuate or perform fire protection functions
when the audible codes are signaled in their zone. Most modern fire protection systems will be coded so that in the event a sprinkler syster is
activated in a particular area, the code for that particular zone will be
sounded and the personnel in the affected area will then perform protection
functions or evacuate.

Bells or horns coded to specific areas are more desirable than the public
address system that is used on a day-to-day basis for normal communications, because those employees not normally concerned with these communications will ignore a warning that a fire emergency exists when the
public address system is used.

AUTOMATIC SPRINKLER SYSTEMS

A report in the March 1976 <u>Fire</u> <u>Journal</u> describes a fire in a clothing warehouse that occurred on September 17, 1975, in Indianapolis, Indiana. The
article, entitled, "Plant Fire Brigade Functions Well," reads in part:

> Employees in areas not affected by the fire noticed a fire on the
> lower tier of one of the storage racks. One employee notified the
> guard who called the public fire department. Two sprinkler heads
> below the grating fused, and employees helped to control the fire
> with a small diameter hose line. One man noted that the fire was
> climbing above the grating. He fused the sprinkler head with his
> cigarette.
>   When the fire department arrived, the fire was out. The plant
> emergency organization functioned well, controlling and extinguish-
> ing the fire (with the help of the sprinklers), monitoring the sprinkler
> valve, venting smoke, and salvaging the stock.

Quite obviously, the fact that this incident resulted in a relatively small
loss when compared to the overall loss potential is directly related to two
major factors.

1. Organization and training of employees and the guard force in fire
    fighting and use of available equipment.
2. Presence of an automatic sprinkler system.

The greatest advantages of an automatic sprinkler system are, first,
that it removes the possibility of human error during an emergency, and,
second, that the system will continue to function under conditions of heat,
smoke, and gases that would be intolerable for a human being.

I have often found security personnel, maintenance personnel, safety
personnel, and even management personnel who were aware that their
facility was "sprinkled" but didn't know where the <u>riser was located</u>. Even
worse, they didn't have the slightest idea of what it was or what part it
played in making their "sprinkler" an <u>automatic sprinkler system</u>.

In years of instructing security personnel in fire protection and prevention, I am convinced that here again the most logical and easily understood
sequence to follow is to start at the "periphery of the subject and work
inward." Therefore, because water is of primary importance in the functions of the automatic sprinkler system, the discussion will begin with the
primary water source. When we have traced the water to the riser, we
shall examine the type and operation of the sprinkler system.

Components of the Sprinkler System

1. The city hydrant. The city hydrant is used only by the public fire
department drawing its water supply from the public main and is tied
directly into hand-held hose lines that are used to fight the fire or tied
by hose lines into a pumper truck to ensure that maximum water pressure
is maintained in the automatic sprinkler system.

2. Siamese connection. Hose lines from the pumper trucks are tied
directly into the sprinkler system through an outside connection that is
known as the Siamese connection. This component is connected directly
to the automatic sprinkler system and supplies water to the sprinkler risers.
Under pressure built up by the pumper truck, water pressure is maintained
uniformly throughout the automatic sprinkler system. Even though all
sprinkler heads in the system may be operating at the same time, the pressure supplied by the pumper truck will ensure that all sprinkler heads will
operate at their full rated capacity.

3. City valve. This valve controls the supply from the city branch mains
and is installed primarily so that the water supply can be controlled should
a major break in the private system occur for whatever reason.

4. Check valve. Several of these valves are found throughout the system
of pipes. They are so designed to permit water flow in one direction only.
Should the water reverse or back up, the valves will close and prevent the
water in the system from flowing back into the branch or city mains.

5. Post indicator valves. These valves must be operated manually and
must remain open at all times. They are closed only to prevent any water
from entering the automatic sprinkler system should a particular riser or
pipes within that system rupture and result in water damage. The name of
this valve comes from a small window installed in the valve through which
can be seen words that indicate that the valve is either open or closed.

6. Private hydrants. These hydrants are similar in construction to the
public hydrants or city hydrants; however, they are installed on the property
and are owned by the property owner. They are normally not used by the
public fire department. They are used primarily by the facility's fire brigade and will normally be located in or near a hose house that has sufficient
hose available to attack a fire in a predetermined area.

7. Sprinkler shutoff. This valve is installed directly on the riser and
is referred to as the OS&Y valve, or outside, screw, and yoke valve. This
valve is controlled by a large wheel that may be located inside the protected
area or may protrude through the peripheral walls and on the outside of the
building. When the large screw is exposed, the valve is opened, and when
the screw cannot be seen outside the wheel controlling the valve, the valve
is closed. The OS&Y valve should remain open constantly unless that particular riser or sprinkler system is being repaired.

8. Pump shutoff valve. This valve is used to shut off the flow of water to the system from the auxiliary water supply, whether it is a suction tank or a gravity tank, when the water supply is no longer needed.

9. Pump check valve. These valves are similar to the check valve described above and prevent the water in the system from returning or emptying back into the auxiliary water supply source.

10. Auxiliary pump. The auxiliary pump is used to maintain constant water pressure at a set level to ensure that all sprinkler heads in the system can operate at full rated capacity. All sprinkler systems require that an auxiliary pump be available if the system is to be effective.

11. Suction tank pump. The function of this pump is simply to pump water from the auxiliary source, which is usually at ground level or below, into the water supply system supplying the automatic sprinkler system in a sufficient quantity to ensure the system's efficient operation. All pumps in the system are designed to start automatically when the pressure drops below a specified number of pounds per square inch.

12. Tank check valve. The function of this valve is exactly the same as that of the check valve and pump check valve. It prevents the return flow of water to the source.

13. Tank control valves. These valves control the flow of water from a gravity tank and are usually of the post indicator valve type so that the condition of the valves can be easily determined.

14. Water tank or tower. The gravity tank or water tank also contains an auxiliary supply of water for the system. This auxiliary water supply enters into the system initially by gravity and then the pressure is increased by the auxiliary pumps.

The above 14 items are basically all of the components of an ordinary automatic sprinkler system. A dry system or a deluge system or a specially designed system will contain at least all of the components described above and may, in some circumstances, have additional special equipment to ensure that the system produces the protective effect desired.

Five Types of Automatic Sprinkler Systems

The Wet Pipe System. The wet pipe system has water available at the sprinkler head at all times. It is the fastest reacting sprinkler, because when a fire occurs, there is no time lag between the moment that the sprinkler head is fused and the start of water flow. There is no size limitation placed on a wet pipe system except that the maximum area protected by any one system on any one floor cannot exceed 52,000 square feet. Based on this, a building several stories high could be protected by one wet pipe system, providing that the area on each floor does not exceed 52,000 square feet. Sprinkler heads may be installed in either the upright or pendant position, and hose connections for fire fighting may also be attached to the system (see Figure 10-14).

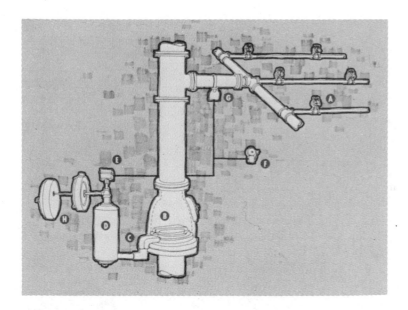

Figure 10-14 The wet pipe sprinkler system. When the sprinkler (A) opens, the discharging water lifts the clapper (B) from the seat in main alarm valve which opens the auxiliary valve (C). Water flows to the retarding chamber (D), building up pressure under the switch (E) and sounding the electrical alarm (F). The water flow indicator (G) also activates the alarm. Water flows to the water motor alarm (H) sounding the mechanical signal. (Courtesy The Viking Corporation)

The Dry Pipe System. The dry pipe system is installed in areas where freezing is likely to occur. The water used by the system is held by a valve in the sprinkler riser, and the riser is located in a heated "riser room." The reaction of this system is slightly slower than the wet pipe system, because when a head is ruptured, the air in the pipes holding the water in the riser by a valve under air pressure must first escape. As the pressure of the air decreases below the pressure of the water, water flows into the entire system.

Once the system has been activated and the fire emergency is placed under control, the entire system must be "bled" and returned to its original dry mode.

The delay between sprinkler fusing and water discharge can often be shorted by installing quick-opening devices. When over 400 sprinkler heads or a capacity of over 500 gallons exist, it is mandatory that such quick-opening devices be installed.

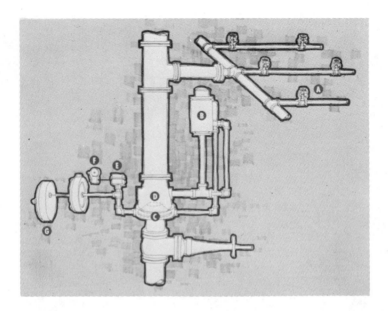

Figure 10-15 The dry pipe sprinkler system. When the sprinkler (A) fuses,
air pressure falls actuating the accelerator (B) which forces air into the
intermediate chamber (C), opening the clapper (D) immediately. Water
build-up under the pressure switch (E) actuates the electrical alarm (F)
and water flow operates the mechanical alarm (G). (Courtesy The Viking
Corporation)

A dry pipe system has the same floor area and fire section limitations
as does the wet pipe system. Sprinkler heads are normally installed in an
upright position. However, if pendant heads are required, they must be
approved dry pendant type to prevent freezing of any trapped water or
moisture. An air supply capable of filling the system to 40 pounds per
square inch in 30 minutes is also a requirement. These conditions are
some of the reasons why the cost of installation of a dry sprinkler system
is somewhat higher than for a wet system (see Figure 10-15).

The Deluge System. The deluge and preaction systems are similar in
design. They both use automatic detection systems and the same main
valve.

Deluge systems with the open sprinkler heads are used for fast total
application of water in extremely hazardous areas and are also used in
water spray systems, which will be mentioned in the following section on
the cost of systems. Deluge systems are limited to 225 sprinklers, which
may be installed either upright or pendant.

The Pre-action System. The pre-action system will operate faster and reduce both fire and water damage when compared to a conventional dry pipe system. These systems are limited to 1,000 sprinkler heads, and if pendant sprinklers are used, they must be of an approved dry pendant design, if the area in which they are installed is subject to freezing temperatures.

Operation of a typical pre-action system involves sprinkler heads that are closed and a check valve which would be installed on the output side of the deluge valve. The primary difference between the deluge and pre-action system is that the deluge system uses open sprinklers to apply water immediately, whereas in the pre-action system application begins only after the sprinklers fuse.

The Firecycle System. The firecycle sprinkler system is the Viking Corporation's trade name for a specially designed system that operates through the use of heat detectors and electrical controls. This system has the capability of continued on and off cycling while controlling fire; it also shuts off water when the fire is extinguished. This system is widely used wherever water damage must be kept to a minimum. Water cannot flow unless initiated by the detection system; therefore, in this system accidental water damage is completely eliminated. Because water is not turned off for maintenance or after a fire, the danger of water being unavailable for subsequent fires is also eliminated. This system may be zoned as other systems are.

The system operates when a detector senses temperature rise above a set point. A solenoid valve opens, and water from the upper chamber vents, reducing pressure, opening the control valve, and supplying water to the sprinkler heads. The sprinkler heads fuse, and water is applied. When the temperature drops below the set point, the detectors that initially triggered the action signal a timer that delays valve closure for a preset period of time. The water then shuts off; should the temperature again rise, the system recycles.

The Cost of Sprinkler Systems

To provide further information to the surveyor and to assist him in answering some obvious questions relative to cost of sprinkler systems, I have listed below some rule-of-thumb estimates that may be useful. These costs will increase or decrease, depending upon the economy of the country or the particular area in which the facility being surveyed is located.

1. The average cost of installing a wet pipe system is approximately 75 cents per square foot being protected.
2. A dry pipe system costs only slightly more because of the added cost of the pump and compressor used in this type system.
3. When a dry pipe system, such as those installed in an office, requires that dry pendant sprinklers be installed, the cost will increase

approximately 15 to 25 cents per square foot. The total cost will
then be from 90 cents to $1 per square foot being protected.

4. A typical deluge system will cost approximately $1.20 per square
foot.

5. Systems that require special hangers and framing to establish a
water spray system will cost approximately $130 per nozzle or
sprinkler. In this case, cost per square foot is not applicable because water spray systems coverage is three-dimensional.

6. A firecycle system will cost between $1.50 and $2.50 per square
foot, depending upon the size of the area to be protected and the
complexity of the system.

The Sprinkler Head

The sprinkler head, the so-called workhorse of the automatic sprinkler
system, is the device that is designed to distribute water in a specific
pattern over a predetermined area. The pattern is determined by the configuration of the area to be protected. The normal "closed sprinkler head"
consists basically of four parts: deflector, struts, frame, and fusible link.
Starting at the opposite end from the water supply or feed line pipes is the
deflector. The deflector can be designed in several different shapes, and
its primary function is directing the flow of the water being discharged.

The next part of the sprinkler head is the frame that is used primarily
to hold the deflector and the struts in the correct position. The frame is
made in one piece and is connected permanently to the head seat that is
screwed into the water supply pipe, with the deflector head at the opposite
end.

The struts consist of two pieces of metal that act as stoppers on the
side opposite the deflector; they are held in position by a fusible link. This
link is manufactured of a soft metal which will melt at a predetermined
temperature. When this predetermined temperature is reached and the
link melts, the water pressure forces the struts from their aligned position
inside the frame and then the water, unobstructed and under pressure, is
forced to the deflector head and deflected in a specific pattern toward the
area being protected.

Eight types of sprinkler heads are generally considered for installation
in an automatic sprinkler system, depending upon the type of protection
required.

1. Standard upright sprinkler. The standard upright sprinkler distributes
water at a 180° angle, giving excellent area coverage. They are used primarily for installation where exposed piping is not objectionable (see Figure 10-16).

2. Standard pendant sprinkler. The pendant sprinkler is for use in the
wet pipe system when piping is not concealed or where exposed piping must
be installed close to the ceiling. The pendant sprinkler covers a floor area

Figure 10-16 A standard upright sprinkler. Note the design of the deflector to direct the water downward. (Courtesy The Viking Corporation)

Figure 10-17 The standard pendant-type sprinkler is used where piping is concealed or where piping must be close to the ceiling. The deflector head is designed to cover a floor area approximately 16 feet in diameter with a directional spray. (Courtesy The Viking Corporation)

approximately 16 feet in diameter with a directional spray (see Figure 10-17).

3. <u>Sidewall sprinkler</u>. The sidewall sprinkler is unique in that it contains a directional deflector that permits the sprinkler to be installed horizontally along the sidewalls or exposed beams in corridors, hallways, and small rooms where structural or other conditions do not readily permit standard sprinkler installation. This type of sprinkler is found in many hotel and motel rooms, with the water directed to cover the bed or beds. They may be installed on either wet or dry pipe systems (see Figure 10-18).

4. <u>Window sprinkler</u>. Window sprinklers are open at all times and are used for the protection of outside walls and windows against exposure fires. They are installed on all deluge systems and provide a 165° fan-shaped flat directional flow of protective water (see Figure 10-19).

5. <u>Deluge sprinkler</u>. The deluge sprinkler obviously is used in the dry pipe system and is similar to the window sprinkler in that it is open at all times and directs a protective sheet of water to the area being protected (see Figure 10-20).

6. <u>Spray nozzle sprinkler</u>. The spray nozzle applies water in the form of a fine conical directional spray to protect such areas as outdoor storage tanks, transformers, oil quench tanks, and spray booths or other areas where flammable liquids or solids are processed or stored. The discharge capacities and spray angles vary and can be designed to meet practically any requirement (see Figure 10-21).

Figure 10-18 The sidewall sprinkler is installed horizontally along the sidewalls or exposed beams in corridors, hallways, and small rooms where structural or other conditions do not readily permit standard sprinkler installations. Note the configuration of the deflector head. (Courtesy The Viking Corporation)

Figure 10-19 The window sprinkler is open at all times. Used in the dry
pipe system, it furnishes a 165° fan-shaped flat directional water flow
which provides a protective sheet of water. (Courtesy The Viking Corporation)

Figure 10-20 The deluge sprinkler is used on the dry pipe system only
and remains open constantly. It directs a heavy stream of water in a predetermined direction. (Courtesy The Viking Corporation)

Figure 10-21 The spray nozzle applies water in the form of a fine conical directional spray to protect outside storage tanks, transformers, and other areas where flammable liquids or solids are processed or stored. (Courtesy The Viking Corporation)

Figure 10-22 Grinnell's "Aquamatic" is designed to open at a predetermined temperature and close when the fire is out, reducing water damage. The sprinkler is Underwriters' Laboratories and Factory Mutual approved. (Courtesy Grinnell Fire Protection Systems Co., Inc.)

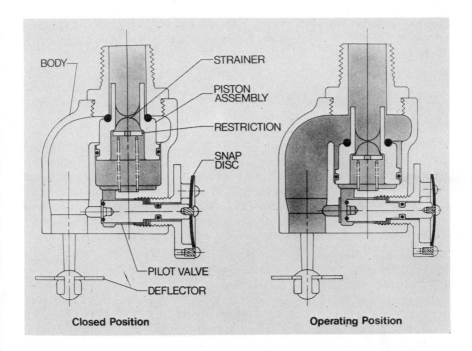

Figure 10-23 A cutaway view of Grinnell's on-off sprinkler showing the closed and operating positions. (Courtesy Grinnell Fire Protection Systems Co., Inc.)

7. Exposure sprinkler. Exposure sprinklers are designed for installation with manually controlled dry pipe or automatically operated deluge systems. They provide uniform water coverage with sufficient velocity to overcome updrafts created by fires. When using a wetting agent, exposure sprinklers give double-glazed tempered glass a 45-minute fire wall rating. They are designed to protect windows with a maximum of 48-inch and 60-inch widths. Where wider widths need to be covered, multiple-exposure sprinkler heads must be used.

8. On-off sprinkler. This sprinkler is referred to as the Aquamatic and is manufactured only by the Grinnell Fire Protection Systems Company, Inc., of Providence, Rhode Island. The sprinkler is made with a temperature rating of 165° Fahrenheit. When this temperature is reached, water is released through a snap disc that opens the pilot orifice which releases pressure on a piston assembly. The piston assembly then opens the main valve, and water is discharged into the fire through the main port. When the heat subsides, the disc snaps into place again and closes the pilot orifice. When this happens, water pressure builds up in the pressure chamber and

pushes the piston assembly closed. The flow of water is stopped, and the sprinkler is automatically set to be released again (see Figures 10-22 and 10-23).

OTHER ELEMENTS OF THE FIRE PROTECTION SYSTEM

Water Motor Alarm Bell

This alarm bell is generally located outside the building and is a foolproof mechanical-type alarm. Water-pressure operated, the standard water motor alarm is adjustable and can fit through walls with special piping that is up to 30 inches thick. The pressure of the water strikes a rotor which, in turn, turns the bell on the shaft, striking the alarm drum.

Engineered Extinguisher Systems

When the fire potential is greater in some areas than in others because of the particular manufacturing process, the need for specially engineered fire systems exists. For example, carbon dioxide or Halon extinguishing systems are usually engineered and designed for the protection of computer areas. When such systems are designed for the protection of large machines, such as printing machines, they may actually be installed on the machines themselves.

Engineered systems are also used in large kitchen operations where either dry chemical, foam, or carbon dioxide may be used in the protection of cooking stoves and other specially designed appliances using oils or fats heated to extremely high temperatures.

Stored Extinguishants

In some applications it may be desirable to store extinguishants in various quantities in locations where there is high potential for fire in small areas. The stored extinguishant could be of any of the types previously mentioned and could be automatically released through heat and flame detection devices (see Figure 10-24).

Fire Doors

Fire doors are normally installed in openings in a fire wall or in such a manner that when closed they prevent the spread of fire in hallways and corridors. These doors normally are left open for operational purposes and are held in the open position by a combination of weights and counter-weights that are released when a fusible link is fused. This allows the door automatically to roll on an angled track to its closed position. These types of fire doors are normally found in industrial facilities.

Figure 10-24 Fenwal's agent-storage container is used for special fire protection situations and can be used with various types of extinguishants and in single or multiple installation. (Courtesy Fenwal Incorporated)

Fire doors to individual rooms or those that close automatically to prevent the spread of fire in a hall or corridor also will remain open for operational purposes and can be automatically closed by several devices. One is commercially known as the "Smok-Chek." It operates on the principle of a photoelectric cell. When smoke is detected by the cell, the door is automatically released and closed with a pneumatic closer (see Figure 10-25). Another device is the electromagnetic fire door holder. This device is tied into a fire or smoke detection device located remotely. When

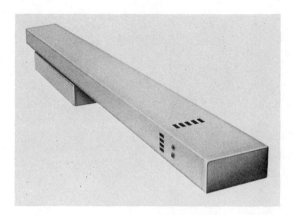

Figure 10-25 The Smok-Chek IV is mounted on a door frame to detect
smoke. It holds the door open until a trace of smoke passes through the
opening and is detected, releasing the hydraulic door closer. (Courtesy
Rixson-Firemark, Inc.)

the device detects fire or smoke, the electrical circuit holding the door
open is automatically broken, the electromagnet is deactivated, and the
doors are closed automatically with pneumatic door closers.

Hose Houses

Hose houses are normally found in outside areas at industrial, commercial,
and institutional facilities; however, they will be found more often at an
industrial facility than at any other type of structure. The hose house is
normally constructed over, or is adjacent to, a yard hydrant and contains
a specific amount of fire fighting equipment, depending upon the requirement at each hose house site. The National Fire Protection Association
(NFPA) lists in their standards for hose houses the minimum amount of
equipment that is required. The list, however, can be modified depending
upon local requirements.

Hose cabinets are somewhat similar to hose houses, with the exception
that they normally are not used to store the amount of fire fighting equipment found in a hose house. Hose cabinets are located in hallways, corridors, and fire wells of commercial and institutional buildings and are
designed so that a specified length of hose attached directly to the standpipe
can be stored in the cabinet. The cabinet usually contains a fire extinguisher
or two, an adjustable fog nozzle, and possibly a crowbar and a spanner
wrench.

Hose houses and the hose cabinets are designed for each specific application and NFPA references or local fire codes should be checked to determine

the minimum amount of equipment and the size and length of hose that is required.

Housekeeping

It is an old adage with fire fighting personnel and security personnel that "a clean facility seldom burns." In recent years the Occupational Safety and Health Act has assisted considerably in cleaning up numerous facilities. The act itself was not primarily concerned with the potential of fire in a facility where poor housekeeping prevailed, but rather with the safety of individuals because poor housekeeping also breeds safety hazards, particularly in the slipping and tripping category, injuring thousands of employees annually. When the requirements to increase the quality of housekeeping to reduce safety hazards became effective in 1971, the clean-up campaigns reduced potential fire hazards in addition to reducing physical safety hazards. However, there are facilities where poor or inadequate housekeeping still exists, particularly in those areas where employees seldom need to travel. These areas have an exceptionally high fire potential, and the surveyor, during his study of the facility, should seek out these out-of-the-way places, including little-used fire stairwells, janitor closets under the stairwells, and areas where through traffic seldom occurs.

This chapter has covered fire protection, fire protection equipment, and fire control in a general way only. The information contained in the chapter is sufficient to permit the surveyor, whether a crime prevention unit police officer or a security specialist, to make an intelligent evaluation of the fire protection and control that exists at the facility being studied. Fire protection is as much a part of the overall security program as is safety to personnel, door locking schedules, anti-intrusion alarms, and those other security measures that are covered in this text.

11

Security
Through Electronics

Recently an article appeared in a Memphis, Tennessee, newspaper bearing the headline, "Rendezvous Hit in $5,500 Theft." A synopsis of the article is as follows. Burglars broke into the office of the owner of the Rendezvous Restaurant and took about $5,500 in cash. An assistant burglary squad commander said that several items of value were bypassed by the burglars who also avoided an electronic alarm system in entering the restaurant. "They entered through an exhaust vent on the south side of the building and were able to enter undetected because of the construction work in that area," the assistant burglary squad commander said.

He also said that the restaurant normally is protected throughout with alarms, but that some of the system had been disconnected while construction work was in progress. The restaurant was closed about 6:30 P.M. Monday and the burglary was discovered when it reopened at 8:13 A.M. the following day.

In another instance in New York City, alarm systems protecting businesses in a three-city-block area were successfully breached, and over $1 million in jewelry was stolen from one establishment. The system was deactivated in such a professional manner that the central station monitors were not aware that anything was amiss.

It would seem from these incidents that alarm systems are rather ineffective in the property protection role. This is not true, but these incidents are dramatic evidence that the criminal element cannot be underestimated. As security devices become more sophisticated, the successful thief must expand his knowledge to stay in business.

In the first instance $5,500 was lost. Had the owner hired a temporary security guard for approximately $5 per hour for the period stated in the news release above, it would have cost him about $5,450 less. In the second instance, the criminals, who, to the best of my knowledge, have never been apprehended, had to have knowledge of proprietary central station information and, in all probability, assistance from one or more of the central station company employees.

Alarm systems properly selected, correctly installed, and professionally monitored by adequately trained personnel are effective. It is of utmost importance that the proper alarms, like the proper locking devices, are selected to obtain required degree of security.

There are literally thousands of alarm manufacturers today who produce every type of device conceivable and as many amateurs to install them. The increase in property crimes, including burglarizing of residences, has created a demand for these devices, and the homeowner and small business-person are constantly being "ripped off" by purchasing the wrong equipment, which is often improperly installed, and in many instances merely plugged into a wall electrical outlet.

Since 1968, crimes of all types have increased approximately 30 percent in the United States, with daylight burglaries increasing 56 percent. Some security analysists and researchers estimate that burglar alarm sales to residential users and small businesses will soar from about 120 million in 1975 to over 700 million by 1982. The businessperson and homeowner need some professional advice in this field.

In this chapter we shall describe the types of alarms available, their capabilities and their limitations, and the method by which these alarms are monitored. We shall also discuss line supervision and space protection patterns.

UNDERWRITERS' LABORATORIES

In any discussion of alarm systems or alarm products, there are usually some misconceptions that occur regarding the role of Underwriters' Labora-tories and the standards that are set for such equipment. Obviously, there is no need to emphasize the importance of Underwriters' Laboratories in its effort to set up objective sets of standards for all classes of anti-intrusion or burglar alarm equipment. To understand the role of the Underwriters' Laboratories in achieving this goal is important.

The Underwriters' Laboratories set standards in the very beginning and then revised them from time to time. These represent the minimum acceptable standards for design and performance of anti-intrusion alarm equipment for a specific application. These standards are the foundation or framework upon which the industry is based. Quite often product design and performance of the product will exceed these standards; therefore, it is possible that one system is far superior to another by actual performance standards, even though each is rated equally under the standards set by Underwriters' Laboratories. There are standards that are issued by the Underwriters' Laboratories Burglary Protective Department for various phases of the alarm industry. These standards will be found in the follow-ing pamphlets or bulletins.

Pamphlets #609 and #610—Burglar Alarm Systems, Local Monitoring
Pamphlet #611—Burglar Alram Systems, Central Station Monitoring
Pamphlet #636—Hold-up Alarm Systems
Pamphlet #681—Installation, Classification and Certification of Burglar Alarm Systems

The standards listed above represent specifications and conditions within which those devoted to the protection of commerce and industry against burglary must operate in order to receive UL approval. Some industrial and military security applications, because the requirements are beyond standards of ordinary alarm defenses, demand much higher standards in specific areas of operations.

Some equipment not listed or approved by Underwriters' Laboratories may equal or excel UL standards, but because of the manner of installation, this equipment may not come within the recognized categories. The standards written by Underwriters' Laboratories are comprehensive and well prepared and were essentially written for the commercial alarm industry. The standards are valuable in serving as a guide to determine whether or not an alarm system can or will provide the minimum protection that is considered generally acceptable in the alarm systems industry.

TYPES OF ALARM SYSTEMS

There are basically four alarm systems that are available for the protection of life and property. These four basic systems are: (1) anti-intrusion or burglar alarm systems; (2) hold-up alarm systems; (3) fire protection alarm systems; and (4) process or supervisory alarm systems.

TYPES OF PROTECTION

There are three types of protection that can be developed with devices available for anti-intrusion or theft prevention alarm systems.

1. Spot or point protection. This type of protection is usually applied to the protection of files, safes, vaults, or other individual small areas within the building.

2. Perimeter protection. This protection, often referred to as the peripheral protection, consists of installing devices to detect intrusion at the perimeter by preparing doors, windows, and other openings with electronic devices in such a manner that breaches of these openings can easily be detected. In some systems, the peripheral protection will be extended to include exterior industrial-type fences, gates, and other outdoor accesses to include the burial of certain electronic and pneumatic systems that detect intrusion by seismic processes.

3. Area or space protection. This is the protection of all or part of a room or building by bathing the protected area in ultrasonic waves, radio waves, microwaves, or infrared radiation. Any or all of these types of protection can be tied into a monitor that will respond to a violation of the protected area, either through a proprietary, central, or remote security monitoring panel or annunciator.

TYPES OF ANTI-INTRUSION ALARMS—THEIR CAPABILITIES AND LIMITATIONS

Over the years, huge expenditures in research and development have resulted in a family of alarms that are quite stable and very reliable. It must be emphasized that the proper alarm for the specific application must be chosen, properly installed, and properly adjusted after installation is made. The principle of operation of the devices, discussed in the following paragraphs of this chapter, have not appreciably changed in several years. The outward appearance or package has been changed, but the basic principles of operation, although refined, remain about the same.

An alarm is nothing more than a device that is triggered to respond because a stable set of electronic circumstances have been upset or thrown out of balance. This activation is transmitted usually by hard wire to a monitor or annunciator, and an operator at this point determines that an intrusion or an invasion of the protected area has occurred and activates preplanned defensive actions in response.

Premise Alarms

A premise alarm consists of various types of devices for the protection of all peripheral doors, windows, and other accessible openings normally in excess of 96 square inches which could be used to enter the protected area. This protection is established by electromagnetic contact devices, switches, vibration detectors and, in some instances, metallic foil tape. Devices referred to as screens, which are constructed of wooden dowels that are wired in a continuous closed circuit group connected to alarm relays, are often used to protect the windows and similar type openings instead of metallic foil tape. The wooden dowels must be broken for entry to be gained through these protected points, and when the dowel is broken, the thin wire in the dowel is also broken, breaking the continuous closed circuit loop and causing an alarm to be activated.

Advantages of Premise Alarms.

1. This is a relatively simple trouble-free system if the metallic foil tape is properly installed.
2. Installation costs are usually low unless the windows being protected are of the multipane type or if the protection must be extended.
3. It may be considered adequate in only low-risk applications.

Disadvantages of Premise Alarms.

1. This system of devices is quite easily compromised because unprotected, easily breached walls or ceilings can be penetrated and access to the protected area gained without disturbing the alarm system.

2. If the system is removed, there is little salvage value, because the major cost of installation is not recoverable.
3. A minimum grade of recognized protection is established with this type system. The grade, as listed under UL standards, is Mercantile No. 3.
4. This system will not spot or detect "stay-behinds" until they are ready to depart the premises and violate the system during exit.
5. Although this system may be upgraded by addition of other protective equipment that is installed on the walls, floors, and ceilings or with space detection devices, the increased cost is considerable.

Premise alarm protection consists of one or all of the following type devices: Electromagnetic switches; electromechanical switches; pressure switches; metallic foil tape; taut wire or floor traps; and vibration devices (see Figure 11-1).

Capacitance or Capacity Alarms

Capacity alarms are used to protect points or spots; the object being protected acts as a part of the capacitance of a tuned circuit similar to a capacitor or condenser. When a change occurs near the protected object such as an approach by an individual or an animal, there is a definite change in the capacitance of great enough magnitude to throw the system out of balance and cause an alarm.

In the protection of safes and files, the capacitance system is flexible enough that it may be used to connect several files in the same general area to one system, and, unlike space alarms, the protective field on the file is usually kept down to within a few inches from the surface of the safe or file being protected. This reduces false alarms by authorized persons passing within a few feet of the object being protected without any intent of intrusion. However, close proximity or actual physical contact with the protected object will upset the electromagnetic field and activate the alarm.

Advantages of Capacitance Alarms.

1. This alarm system is simple to install, adjust, activate, and deactivate.
2. The system provides for an invisible field of protection, making it difficult to determine whether or not an object is protected.
3. The system is extremely flexible and can be used to protect file cabinets, windows, doors, safes, practically any object found in an office building, and even partitions between rooms. Any ungrounded metallic object within the maximum tuning range of the system may be protected.
4. The equipment is compact in size, easily dismantled and reinstalled; therefore, it has a high salvage value.
5. It provides a high degree of stable security.

Figure 11-1 The "Window Bug" detects breakage of window glass and all types of silicon glazing. It detects breakage by use of a tuned fork and cavity, tuned to the frequency of breaking glass. It is not classified as a vibrator, and one such unit can protect a glass surface 4 feet by 8 feet. (Courtesy United Security Products, Inc.)

Disadvantages of Capacitance Alarms.

1. They can be installed only on ungrounded objects or equipment.
2. False alarms can occur if the protected object is carelessly touched or approached too closely by janitors or custodial personnel.

Photoelectric Alarms

A photoelectric alarm, or, as sometime referred to, an electric eye, is a device that can be used in both the anti-intrusion protection system and the fire protection system, because the basic principle of operation is the same. The device is usually used in conjunction with other forms of anti-intrusion alarm equipment. It operates by an interruption or breaking of a beam of light between a small projector or transmitter and a light-sensitive receiver that is installed in a direct line of sight some distance away. When the light is no longer received by the receiver, a relay is actuated in a control cabinet within the secured area, and an alarm is sounded.

The beam of light used is infrared, particularly for security alarm installations, because a white light could easily be detected. These protective devices are difficult to hide or disguise and can easily be located by the professional. When located, they can be compromised merely by introducing a substitute source of illumination which permits penetration of the system without causing an alarm.

Some installations may employ mirrors, thereby utilizing the capabilities of the equipment more efficiently. The mirrors are used to crisscross the infrared light pattern for better coverage; however, when mirrors are employed, detection of the system and mirrors now becomes easier because the equipment is difficult to conceal.

Photoelectric units are often used in combination with other protective alarms and are often used as "man traps." By this we mean they are installed in rooms inside a building protected by premise alarms. If the perimeter is violated, the intruder can be trapped by the strategically located photoelectric unit installed in areas where no alarms may be suspected.

Advantages of Photoelectric Alarms.

1. Photoelectric units can be used to cover driveways or open portals where the installation of physical obstructions cannot be tolerated.
2. When used as a "man trap," this alarm makes it difficult for persons who are concealed and stay behind in the premises to operate without being detected.
3. These alarms have a great advantage in actuating other security devices such as cameras or closed circuit television systems.
4. They can increase the effectiveness of the mercantile premise alarm installation and when properly installed can be awarded a Mercantile 2 classification.
5. Almost all of the equipment is recoverable; therefore, the alarm has a high salvage value.
6. An added feature of the device is that should a fire occur, smoke breaking the beam could be detected.

Disadvantages of Photoelectric Alarms.

1. A substitute light source can be used to defeat the system.
2. It operates only on 110 volts, and 110-volt standby power supply is required if UL approval is desired.
3. It is not the type of device to be installed in smoky or dusty atmospheres because the smoke or dust may break the beam and deposits of soot and dirt on the lenses and mirrors can cause malfunctions.

4. Because the beams are narrow, they may be located and avoided by a careful intruder who may either step over or crawl under the beam.
5. When used in outdoor applications, they are subject to a high degree of false alarms because they may be triggered by heavy rains, fog, or heavy snow.
6. Because the system's receiver, transmitter, and mirrors, if they are included in the system, must be installed precisely on a line-of-sight basis, a great deal of calculation and careful planning are required to obtain effective coverage.

Space Alarms

Space is protected by alarms using either infrared radiation, sound waves, radio waves, or microwaves. A microwave is electromagnetic radiation in the region between infrared and shortwave radio wave length. See Figure 11-2 for typical passive infrared protection patterns. Figure 11-3 shows a passive infrared detector and Figure 11-4 shows typical passive infrared detection patterns.

Ultrasonic Space Alarms. The protection of an enclosed space can be effectively achieved by use of an ultrasonic alarm system. This system also consists of a transmitter and receiver and operates on a principle known as the Doppler effect.
The transmitter generates a series of high-frequency waves which will completely fill an enclosed area with a pattern of standing waves. The receiver is connected to an electronic amplifier which picks up these waves, and so long as the waves sensed by the receiver are of the same frequency

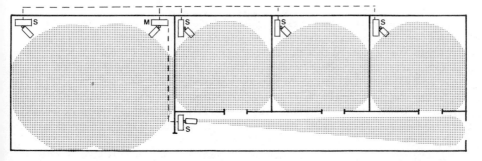

Figure 11-2 These are typical installation patterns of Raytek's Model 8200 Master and 5 Slave passive infrared intrusion detectors. In the illustration, the unit marked "M" is the master unit with the remaining units of the system being tied into the master. The unit can operate from -20° Fahrenheit to 140° Fahrenheit. (Courtesy Raytek Division of Optical Coating Laboratory, Inc.)

FUSE — SIREN MODULE — SIREN HORN

PASSIVE INFRA-RED DECTECTOR HEAD

TAMPER-PROOF LOCK

SOLID STATE CIRCUITRY INCLUDING 15 MINUTE ALARM TURN OFF AND RESET AND BATTERY CHARGING CIRCUIT

STANDBY POWER BATTERIES

Figure 11-3 This self-contained alarm system is activated by the heat of a human body. The passive infrared detector only senses body heat. Once activated, a person within a 1600-square-foot area will trigger the device which is highly portable and includes standby power. (Courtesy The Silent Watchman Corporation)

as the sound emitted by the transmitter, the system is considered stabilized. However, any motion within the protected area will upset the waves and return a wave pattern that differs in frequency from that originally stabilized into the equipment. This change in frequency is detected and amplified in the control unit, and an alarm signal is activated.

This system, as are other space protection systems, is designed to protect a specific number of cubic feet of space, and multiple transmitters and receivers can be operated from the same control unit for coverage of large or broken areas.

Because the system will detect any type of motion, it will also detect air currents, animals, moving machinery, and even venetian blinds that may be flapping, thus causing false alarms. When the system is stabilized, all ambient noises in the area are usually ruled out; however, an unusual noise such as a clap of thunder or someone striking the wall of the room or a pane of glass on the peripheral wall of the room being protected will upset the sound waves and activate the alarm.

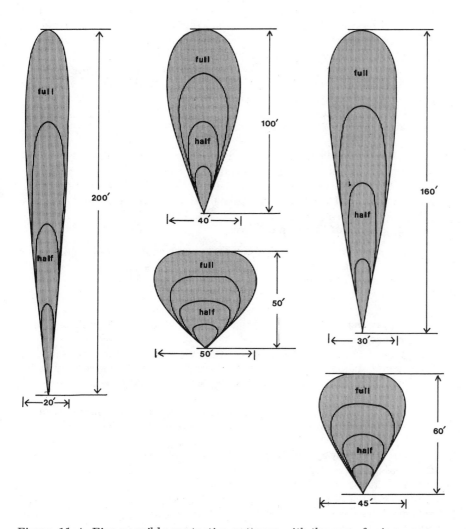

Figure 11-4 Five possible protection patterns with the use of microwave detection devices. The patterns result from the use of different types of antennas. (Courtesy Advanced Devices Laboratory, Inc.)

Advantages of Ultrasonic Alarms.

1. Because the protective field is not visible, it is difficult to detect the presence of the system, and it is almost impossible to compromise the system through slow movements in the area.
2. The system is reasonably flexible for interior protection.
3. Because the system utilizes the principle of space protection, it is effective against "stay-behinds" or intruders that are concealed inside the facility.
4. Most models are highly portable and can be moved easily from area to area.
5. Because the equipment can be removed and relocated easily, the equipment has a high salvage value.
6. If a fire occurs in the protected area, the heat will change the wave pattern, and the fire, in all probability, will be detected.

Disadvantages of Ultrasonic Alarms.

1. If presence of the alarm is known and movement through the protected area is extremely slow (that is, slower than a step per second), intrusion may not be detected.
2. The sensitivity of the system may have to be reduced to overcome other disturbance factors in the area being secured.
3. As previously stated, the system can be actuated by loud external noises.
4. Its use in high sound-absorbing areas such as dry cleaning establishments, baled cotton warehouses, and fur vaults is not recommended.
5. Installation requires expertise in planning if any satisfactory results are expected.
6. The system may not detect penetrations of walls or ceilings if the penetration is made behind large objects close to the wall or ceiling.

Radio Frequency Space Protection. These alarms emit radio frequency waves and utilize a transmitter and receiver. The pattern of protection emitted is highly elliptical, and it is difficult to adjust to cover a room entirely because of this inherent pattern. Usually, when adjusted so that the radio waves are not emitted beyond the walls of the protected area, the corners of the rooms are unprotected. If the system is not properly adjusted, and the radio waves penetrate the walls of the protected area, false alarms occur by persons or objects passing through the radio frequency pattern that exists outside the protected area.

Advantages of Radio Frequency Alarms.

1. The system can be used effectively in high sound-absorbing areas and inside vaults or other areas shielded by metal.

2. The system, when activated, will detect "stay-behinds."
3. The system can be installed in one room and adjusted to protect out-
    side corridors, closets, or adjacent rooms; therefore, the system
    would be difficult to detect if it were installed in the room immedi-
    ately adjacent to the room that is actually intended for protection.

Disadvantages of Radio Frequency Alarms.

1. When set up inside a square or rectangular room, the corners of the
    room are normally left unprotected.
2. If improperly adjusted, false alarms occur when movement outside
    the protective area upsets the radio frequency waves.
3. Extremely slow movement through the protected area will not neces-
    sarily be detected.
4. Because there has been little or no research in this area in recent
    years, the alarms that are available today are very unstable.

Radar or Microwave Alarms. Since radar was developed, there have
been numerous attempts to devise a space alarm using these techniques.
Some attempts have achieved some success, and, in all probability, future
research will result in an alarm with numerous indoor and outdoor installation capabilities.

The principle used in the radar or microwave system is basically the
same as that used in an ultrasonic system. As mentioned previously, radio
waves are highly penetrating and are difficult to confine within a closed
area. As in the radio frequency principle, a train of radio waves is produced by the transmitter, and this is at least partially reflected back to the
antenna. All objects within the range of the waves must remain stationary,
and the reflected waves must return at the same frequency. If they do not,
an alarm condition exists. If these waves strike a moving object, they are
returned to the antenna with a different frequency. This frequency is detected, and an alarm condition is actuated.

Advantages of Microwave Alarms.

1. As in the radio frequency alarms, the equipment has a high salvage
    value and is easily portable.
2. The system is not affected by noise, light, sound, or movement of
    air currents.

Disadvantages of Microwave Alarms.

1. The coverage is not easily confined within the desired area.
2. The stability of this equipment is still questionable.
3. It may be tripped accidentally by other radio transmitters operating
    in the area at frequencies close to the frequency generated by the
    equipment (see Figures 11-5 through 11-7).

Figure 11-5 This ceiling-mounted microwave intrusion detector is easily disguised and when mounted at the normal 8-foot ceiling height will cover an area 24 feet by 36 feet. (Courtesy Racon, Inc.)

Figure 11-6 A wall-mounted microwave intrusion detector is available to protect an area in a conical pattern from 10 to 200 feet in length. (Courtesy Racon, Inc.)

Figure 11-7 This Racon long-range microwave transmitter is capable of
outdoor protection for a distance of 1500 feet. The pattern of protection is
symmetrical, both horizontally and vertically. At 1500 feet, the pattern
is 40 feet horizontally and vertically, at 1000 feet, 26 feet horizontally and
vertically, and at 500 feet, 14 feet horizontally and vertically. (Courtesy
Racon, Inc.)

Audio Alarms. Also in the family of space protection devices are protective systems that emit no type of light beams, ultrasonic waves, radio
frequency, radar, or microwaves. These systems are referred to as audio
systems and generally use open or closed microphones.

These audio systems, unlike ultrasonic systems, can and do tolerate
rapid air movements and other types of motion that are not accompanied by
a high decibel of sound.

The sensitivity of these systems can be adjusted to detect small or large
amounts of noise; however, the more minute the adjustment to pick up small
noises, the more false alarms that will occur.

The open microphone system is monitored at the annunciator location by
a speaker, and all the noise or sound within the area being protected can
be heard.

In the closed microphone or impact microphone system, the microphone
remains closed and is adjusted to rule out all ambient noises. When a noise
or sound occurs creating decibels beyond that to which the microphone is
adjusted, the system then is opened and the person monitoring the system
at the annunciator can detect and "read" the activity that is occurring in
the area being protected.

Impact microphones used in conjunction with premise alarms (that is, alarms installed on the openings to the room, building, or other structure being protected), if monitored by properly trained experienced personnel, will rule out false alarms almost entirely. Because an attack upon the periphery of the protected area will activate the microphone, the monitor can listen and detect the type of intrusion being attempted. If the intrusion is successful, the monitor will receive a second alarm that is activated when the premise alarm on the window, door, or wall is violated. The monitor then is positive that an intrusion has occurred. After alerting the responding individual or agency, the monitor can, through radio communications, "talk" the individuals responding into the situation because he is able to identify the location and activity of the intruder constantly.

Advantages of Audio Alarms.

1. The system is relatively inexpensive and difficult to detect.
2. The system can be used to protect an entire facility and shunted off the main system in certain areas.
3. The system, when properly monitored and "read," rules out false or nuisance alarms.
4. The system can be used in connection with any other premise protection device, and when installed in this manner can be 100 percent free of false alarms.
5. Used widely in school buildings and warehouses, the system has resulted in tremendous reduction of losses due to vandalism and burglary.
6. The system can be used to "back up" the fire alarm protection system. By installing a "listening" device near a fire alarm horn or bell, the person monitoring the system will be alerted when the sound activates the system.
7. Because the system, properly monitored, is free of false alarms, police patrols alerted to an intrusion respond more quickly and use more caution in approaching the violated premises.

Disadvantages of Audio Alarms. If properly installed, there are no disadvantages worthy of mention, and the system, with the exception of used wire, is 100 percent salvageable (see Figures 11-8 through 11-10).

Sound Discriminators. Sound discriminators are occasionally used in conjunction with audio alarms in an attempt to rule out ambient noises that are common in the area but that vary in decibels. That is, a sound discriminator may be used when an audio detection system is installed on a building near a heavily traveled street. The sound discriminator properly adjusted assists in shunting out of the system different levels of noise that may occur. Care must be exercised to ensure that sensitivity in the system is not lost.

Figure 11-8 The Sonitrol Audio Detection Device shown in its open and closed position. The system is virtually false-alarm free and is used extensively in school districts throughout the United States. (Courtesy Sonitrol Corporation)

Figure 11-9 The Sonitrol Control Module that is located in the central station. Many school districts protecting over 100 buildings establish their own central station. Note that the module not only monitors the audio detection device but peripheral or point protection as well. (Courtesy Sonitrol Corporation)

Figure 11-10 A typical central station monitoring Sonitrol systems throughout a given area. Note the direct–line telephones to police and fire departments, the recording instruments, and the police–band radio used to monitor
communications between police dispatcher and the patrol car responding so
that the dispatcher can be notified of moment–to–moment activity in the violated area and "talk" the responding police into the current situation. (Courtesy Sonitrol Corporation)

    I once examined an audio detection system in the kitchen of a very fine
restaurant. The entire restaurant was protected with premise protection
devices and was not zoned. All of the devices were connected to a telephone
dialer so that regardless of where an intrusion was attempted, the owner of
the restaurant, who lived approximately 15 miles away, was alerted through
the telephone dialer. If called, the only information he had was that the
alarm system at his restaurant had been activated for one reason or another.
    The audio detection system in the kitchen was not the Sonitrol system but
one that had been put together by the alarm installer. False alarms were
continually being activated in the system, and 99 percent of the alarms
resulted from the automatic ice-maker. On Saturday and Sunday evening,
for example, the owner received more false alarms than he did during the
first 2 or 3 days of the week. What was occurring was that on Saturday and

Sunday nights the large number of customers required the use of a great deal of ice, and at the end of the business day the automatic ice-maker located in the kitchen was almost empty. As the ice was manufactured and automatically dropped into the storage box, it obviously made some noise, but the emptier the box, the louder was the noise. The sound discriminator had been adjusted on a weekday; therefore, no allowance was made for this particularly high noise level after busy Saturdays and Sundays.

Sound discriminators may be of value in some installations; however, it has been my experience that they cause more problems than they actually reduce.

MONITORING OR ANNUNCIATOR SYSTEMS

Five methods are used to monitor anti-intrusion and fire protection alarm systems. Obviously, when protective alarms are installed, they must not only be monitored, but there must be a means of rapid response once an alarm is activated. Without the capability of immediate response, the value of the alarm system is considerably reduced. Therefore, one must generally consider that any proprietary protective alarm system will undoubtedly require two individuals to ensure that the system retains its effectiveness— one individual to monitor the system, and the second individual to investigate when the system indicates trouble.

Listed below, in order of importance, are the five methods of monitoring any type of alarm system. Described briefly are the location and some advantages and the disadvantages. These monitoring panels or consoles are often referred to as annunciators because they in fact do announce when the protected area has been violated.

1. Proprietary monitoring. Proprietary monitoring, as the name indicates, is a system of monitoring protective devices on the property being protected. This obviously is by far the best method of monitoring these devices because response to alarms is immediate and rapid.

A proprietary monitoring system may monitor more than one building or one complex. For example, if there were ten stores in a shopping center, all protected with anti-intrusion and fire protection alarms and monitored from a single location in the mall, the monitoring station would still be referred to as a proprietary system rather than a central system.

2. Central station monitoring. Central station monitoring systems are commonly used in high-density areas where private protective alarm companies will have numerous clients. All of the facilities protected are monitored at a central location that usually is a considerable distance from the property being protected. The signal is received at the central station via a pair of leased telephone lines. The size of the central station (that is, the number of monitoring panels or annunciators that are involved) will determine the number of personnel that are required to monitor effectively

all of the facilities being protected. Upon receiving an alarm, the individual monitoring the panel will usually, by radio, direct a vehicular patrol to respond to the area where the alarm occurred. In addition, he may also notify the police department or the fire department, depending upon the type of alarm received. Often these privately owned central station companies do not have their own patrolmen to respond, and the only action they take upon receiving an alarm is to notify either the police or the fire department. Alarm installations of this type can be UL approved only when the premises that are protected are no further than 10 minutes average traveling time from the central office. That is the primary disadvantage. The second disadvantage is that in the case of an anti-intrusion alarm being received, the police may not necessarily give this response any priority, and it may be several minutes or longer before any investigation is made to determine whether or not the protected area was, in fact, violated.

3. Local monitoring. A local monitoring system requires no sophisticated annunciators or monitoring panels. An alarm that is installed on any one door and activates a bell or horn at that immediate location when the door is opened is considered a local alarm.

In many of the larger cities, older "burglar alarm" installations in stores and often in the older banks were merely tied into a loud bell located on the outside of the building. If a violation or false alarm occurred, the bell on the outside of the building would ring until the system was reset. Such a system depended upon passersby hearing the bell ringing and notifying the police. In some cities, these installations are still in evidence, particularly in the smaller towns of the West and Midwest.

The most common local alarm systems are alarm-equipped locking devices that are installed on emergency exits to deter the unauthorized or surreptitious use of the exit. In order to be effective, someone in the area must be able to hear the alarm and must respond to determine the cause of the alarm. Obviously, the biggest disadvantage here is that they are impractical for use in fire stairwells or on doors that exit to the outside of the stairwell, unless the alarm bell or horn is located in an area some distance from the alarm where it can be heard and will generate a response. The greatest advantage of these devices is that they are an excellent deterrent and are inexpensive to install. However, they furnish inadequate protection against the determined intruder.

4. Remote monitoring. These systems are often referred to as the police or fire department connection because some years ago fire protection systems or anti-intrusion alarm systems were tied into the local fire or police departments. Although still used in some small towns, this method of monitoring a protective alarm system is almost history because police and fire departments will no longer accept or allow the systems to be monitored in their headquarters. The primary reason that this practice has been discontinued is the number of false alarms that have been received in the past.

I recall conducting a survey at a clothing manufacturing plant in the Mid-South that had both an anti-intrusion alarm system and a fire protection alarm system installed on the property. Both of these systems were monitored in the nearby town by the personnel of a 24-hour ambulance service. If an alarm was activated, the ambulance service employee would notify either the police or fire department, whichever system had been activated. However, no one took into consideration that no one would be present to monitor either if the only employee on duty between 8:00 P.M. and 6:00 A.M. was called out on an emergency. How simple it would have been for an individual planning an attack on the installation to create a false emergency or merely to report an emergency to the ambulance service office and request assistance. During the time that the driver was out on call, a thief could merely move into the building through a window or door and remove whatever was to be stolen.

5. <u>Telephone dialer monitoring</u>. Telephone dialers are normally used in residence protection. However, they are effective in monitoring anti-intrusion and fire protection alarm systems at small businesses. This device requires that a coupler be installed on the telephone line to ensure that destructive surges of electricity do not damage telephone company switching equipment. The telephone dialer is nothing more than a sophisticated tape recorder. Messages are placed on a tape in a cassette, and these messages are then placed in the automatic telephone dialer. The equipment is adjusted to dial specific numbers, usually neighbors, or in the case of a business, the owner's home. When an intrusion is detected by the system, the dialer automatically dials the number set in the equipment until the telephone is answered, and then the canned message is transmitted. The equipment can be installed to distinguish between activation of an anti-intrusion alarm and of a fire protection alarm. Usually these telephone dialers are limited to three numbers; however, it is possible with adjustments to use more than three numbers.

The greatest advantage of the telephone dialer is that it uses existing lines; that is, lines do not need to be leased from the telephone company.

Telephone dialers are also used to monitor security guard patrols in remote locations. Electronic guard-reporting stations are installed throughout the protected area and are designed to transmit an alarm from these stations to a central monitoring point through a telephone dialer if the guard does not reset each station during a specified period of time. For example, the system that is installed may be activated at 8:00 P.M., and the patrolling guard is required to conduct patrols periodically. The system is preset to whatever schedule is developed. The guard, as he conducts his patrols and visits these electronic stations, inserts his key, and, rather than transmitting a signal, he merely resets that particular station. If he fails to reset the station before a certain time, the station automatically sends a signal to the telephone dialer; the telephone dialer, using existing lines, dials the central station, notifying the individual monitoring the guard's

(a)   (b)

Figure 11-11 (a) The Tourkey is carried by the guard with a safety strap
to prevent accidental dropping. The wall station is "punched" by inserting
the Tourkey. All stations, passive and active, must be visited by the guard
for proper reporting. (b) The new Sentry electronic guard-supervision
system. Includes the Tourkey carried by the guard, passive and active
wall stations, and the Sentry delinquency-reporting transmitter. Two
24-hour timers allow programming of different weekday and weekend check-
in schedules. (Courtesy Sentry Technology, Inc.)

activities that he has, for one reason or another, failed to arrive at that
particular station. Theoretically, with this system it would be possible
for an individual in Chicago, for example, to monitor protected facilities
throughout the United States. Providing that all guards being supervised
by this system conduct their patrols as scheduled, hundreds of installations
could be monitored long distance without cost. If the guard in New Orleans
failed to reset a particular station, the telephone dialer, either through
regular long-distance dialing or an 800 telephone number arrangement,
would dial the office in Chicago and report the discrepancy. The system
is marketed by Sentry Technology, Inc., 222 Mt. Hermon Road, Santa
Cruz, California 95066 (see Figure 11-11).

The type of monitoring system to be used and numerous other factors
will determine how the alarm can most effectively be monitored. For
example, the Sonitrol audio system is used quite extensively in the premise-
protection role in school facilities. In numerous cities, the entire school

district is protected with these devices, and the districts purchase them
outright. The monitoring system is installed on school property, and the
individuals assigned to monitor the alarms are school district employees.
This type of system may be considered a cross somewhere between a central
station and a proprietary station. I know of one school district that monitors
over 160 school buildings with this equipment. The personnel on duty at the
monitoring board have a direct line to the city's police and fire departments.
The phone is merely picked up and a direct connection between the police or
fire dispatcher is made.

LINE SUPERVISION

Any alarm system is vulnerable if the system transmits signals over lines
that are outside the protected area, unless these lines are provided with
sufficient electrical sensitivity to detect even an expert attack on the lines.
Almost any alarm can be defeated in one manner or another, regardless of
the effectiveness of its triggering devices.

In the beginning of this chapter we told of a system that was compromised
through line tampering. Successful tampering with alarm lines may often
be prevented by using annunciator panels that have low line tolerance.

Line tolerance is the ability of the alarm transmission circuits to detect
any tampering. This can be defined as the amount of change which the relays
installed in the annunciator or monitor will accept before a trouble or tamper
alarm is sounded. The changes are expressed often in percentages and
depend upon the normal line current of a given system. A normal line current of 20 milliamperes that was overloaded at 30 milliamperes would cause
the load relay in the annunciator panel to signal an alarm. The same would
occur should the current drop below the 20 milliampere range. When the
normal load drops, the underload relay at the annunciator will drop out and
activate an alarm.

Obviously, where alarms are monitored by telephone wires which extend
beyond the protected area, the alarm is considerably more vulnerable to
successful attack than are those monitored by proprietary monitoring systems. This is particularly true for a system that is monitored by an automatic telephone dialer. It is obvious that if the telephone lines leading into
the protected structure are cut, the entire system is deactivated, and so
the criminal is safe to take all the time needed to obtain whatever he is after.
However, if the entire circuit is protected with low line tolerance and the
line is cut, the underload relay should drop out at the annunciator panel and
cause an alarm and ensuing investigation.

A word about the use of radio transmissions to monitor a protective alarm
system. Devices are available that can be used to monitor protective alarm
systems at a central location if the protected area is not beyond 20 to 25
miles from the monitoring station. The principle of operation here is to

transmit the signal by radio frequency waves rather than telephone lines when an alarm is activated at the protected property. However, because radio frequency waves are involved, the system is rather unstable, and alarms can be triggered by police cruisers transmitting near the protected area. Recently, because of the tremendous increase in the use of citizen's band radios, false alarms have been occurring. In all probability, further research into this area of alarm transmitting will result in an effective stable method of signal transmission. Radio transmission of the signal will certainly increase the effectiveness of any alarm system because even though storms, accidents, or other activity may cause telephone line outages, obviously the signals transmitted by radio would not be affected.

In any type of security or fire protection alarm system, it is extremely important that some type of standby power be made available in the event the AC utility power should fail. If standby power is not included as a part of the system, the premises being protected obviously will be unprotected if the power fails. Therefore, standby power must be furnished and is required if UL approval of a central station system is being sought.

Normally commercial dry-cell batteries are used as standby power; however, these batteries must be replaced from time to time because they have a very limited shelf life. If the batteries are not used at all for an entire year, they require replacement with fresh batteries.

Various kinds of rechargeable batteries are available today. Some are wet cells similar to the type used in automobiles, and others are gel cells and nickel cadmium batteries. These batteries are continually kept charged by the electrical control circuitry, and so they are always ready to offer standby power. Unless damaged, they seldom need to be replaced.

Regardless of whether dry cells or rechargeable batteries are used, the circuitry in all protective alarm systems must be designed so that should an AC power failure occur, the system will be automatically switched to these batteries.

Dry cell batteries are normally considered to be effective for a period of at least 4 hours continuous operation of the alarm system; that is, the alarm circuitry remains in a state of readiness, and if an alarm in the system should be triggered, the signal would be emitted to a proprietary monitor, to a central station monitor, or through a telephone dialer.

12

Surveillance
Through Closed Circuit
Television Systems

The full potential of closed circuit television in establishing security programs has not yet been realized. If used in conjunction with a security force in any given facility, closed circuit television not only reduces manpower requirements but also increases the overall effectiveness of the security plan. For example, using closed circuit television, a shopping mall with only two guards on duty during business hours could not only monitor activity in the mall but could closely observe thousands of square feet of parking lots as well as activity in the shipping and receiving dock area.

A closed circuit television surveillance system, in order to be effective, must be constantly monitored, and immediate response to unfavorable activity observed must be possible. This arrangement requires radio communication between security personnel, and, in most instances, will also require a vehicle for rapid response. The deterrent value of this type of security organization can, by itself, justify the cost of the program.

The use of closed circuit television in conjunction with control of personnel and vehicles has already been discussed. Additional security applications of this device depend on the security functions to be accomplished and are limited only by the expertise and ingenuity of the planner. Closed circuit television, like electronic alarms, can be used to monitor operations, hazardous areas, or processes during operational periods and then revert to a security role once operations have ceased. Proper planning and placement of the closed circuit television cameras, to including selection of the proper control equipment, makes it possible to use a closed circuit television surveillance system 24 hours per day, 7 days per week. Unless the system can be used at all times, it is difficult to convince management that the cost of the system can be justified.

A warehousing operation can use a closed circuit television system to reduce damage to material and property, to prevent industrial vehicle accidents and injury to personnel, and to deter pilferage. When operations cease, the security force can use the system to guard against intrusion and to prevent thefts by "stay-behind" employees who leave through a remote door or window. Fire protection is also increased through constant observation of an area.

LIGHTING REQUIREMENTS

The question of the amount of illumination needed is usually the opener when closed circuit television systems are discussed. As a rule of thumb, the amount of light needed by human beings to see will be sufficient to ensure a clear picture on the monitor. Obviously, the type of camera and accessories will determine whether or not existing illumination is sufficient.

Some cameras require less light than that required by the human eye, and these cameras will produce a high-contrast, detailed image even of a dimly lighted area (see Figures 12-1 and 12-2).

The illumination level required by the camera depends upon the lens stop and whether or not a remotely controlled or automatic iris is used. The specifications of all cameras will include the amount of required illumination for any given application.

Figure 12-1 Motorola's low-light-level closed circuit television camera can be compared to the human eye in its ability to adapt automatically to light variations from full daylight to darkness. (Courtesy Motorola Communications and Electronics, Inc.)

Figure 12-2 Typical image seen by Motorola's Model S1171B low-light-level camera with double intensifier and automatic iris zoom lens. The incident could not be seen by the unaided eye from the camera position. (Courtesy Motorola Communications and Electronics, Inc.)

TELEVISION CAMERA VERSUS STILL CAMERAS

Whether closed circuit television or still cameras will be used in bank protection or other covert surveillance will often be governed by the cost and/or duration of the surveillance. Still cameras are far less costly than a television camera, and installation of a still camera is also simple and inexpensive because the camera need only be mounted on a bracket and connected to an electrical supply. In contrast, the television camera requires not only the above, but, in addition, coaxial cable needs to be installed from the camera to a monitor, and if images are to be recorded, a video-tape recorder is required.

Still cameras are seldom mounted so that they can be panned and tilted and obviously need no monitoring. However, once the camera is activated, the film must be removed and developed, and pictures must be printed. The

Figure 12-3 A camera that is electronically activated on command from a
holdup button, a photo cell, a money clip switch, or similar device. (Courtesy CFI Camera Division, Schirmer-National Company)

still pictures will not detect peculiarities in movement of individuals that
may help to identify them (see Figures 12-3 and 12-4).

Television video-tape recorder systems produce moving pictures
instantaneously, whether the camera is on a fixed mount or equipped with
pan and tilt capabilities controlled either manually or automatically (see
Figure 12-5). Another economical advantage of the television camera is
the ability to erase the tape and use it again and again.

In covert surveillance situations, the television camera can be disguised
or hidden and can be left in an operational mode completely unattended for
up to 12 hours without a tape change. The 12-hour tape can be screened
in about an hour. Both still cameras and television cameras can be used
in inactive areas and may be set up to be triggered by an anti-intrusion
alarm. The triggering device activates the electric motor of the still
camera or the entire closed circuit television surveillance system.

Video motion-detection systems are also available. This device is a
minicomputer that creates point protection by setting the shape and position

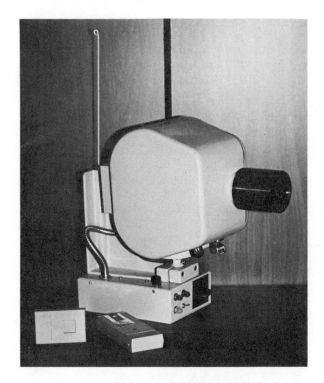

Figure 12-4 A radio-controlled camera that is activated on command from an RF transmitter. The advantage here is that an individual in personal possession of a transmitter can activate the camera without any physical movement. (Courtesy CFI Camera Division, Schirmer-National Company)

of a "window," or detection area, on the monitor screen. The device can detect movement and light changes, and when the changes occur in the predetermined area, the operator is alerted visually and audibly. One device, which is said to be able to distinguish between movement and light change, will reduce false alarms immeasurably (see Figures 12-6 and 12-7).

CAMERA HOUSINGS

In most instances, cameras need to be protected from environmental conditions and against tampering. Cameras installed inside buildings should be mounted as high as possible to deter tampering with the camera or blocking its view.

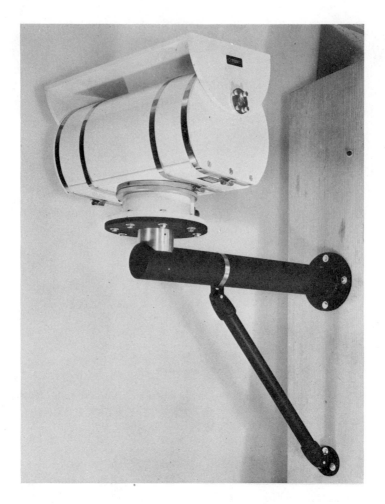

Figure 12-5 Pelco's outdoor pan and tilt unit ready for mounting a camera inside an environmental housing. (Courtesy Pelco Sales, Inc.)

Figure 12-6 RCA's Video Motion Detector is a minicomputer that can distinguish between movement and light changes. When movement is detected an audio beeper alerts the operator at the monitor. (Courtesy RCA Closed-Circuit Video Equipment)

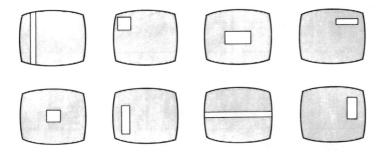

Figure 12-7 A sketch showing the various shapes and locations of the sensing "window." (Courtesy RCA Closed-Circuit Video Equipment)

Figure 12-8 A close-up view of an indoor tamper-proof housing. (Courtesy Cunningham Corporation)

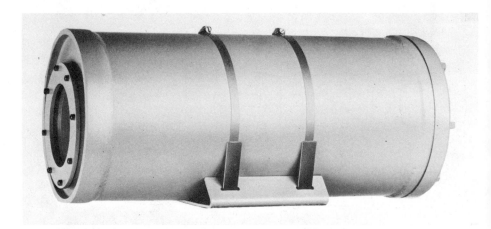

Figure 12-9 A close-up view of an explosion-proof housing. (Courtesy Cunningham Corporation)

When cameras are likely to be subject to vandalism, they should be enclosed in a tamper-proof housing (see Figure 12-8). A strong housing and sufficiently high installation are the best defenses against attack on the equipment. If cameras are tampered with or destroyed outright, the patrolling guard must move to the area quickly to attempt to apprehend the attacker.

Environmental housings are available to protect the camera against extremes of heat and cold, dust, inclement weather, or explosions. The area being observed and the environmental conditions will dictate the type of housing and system accessories that are required. Figure 12-9 shows

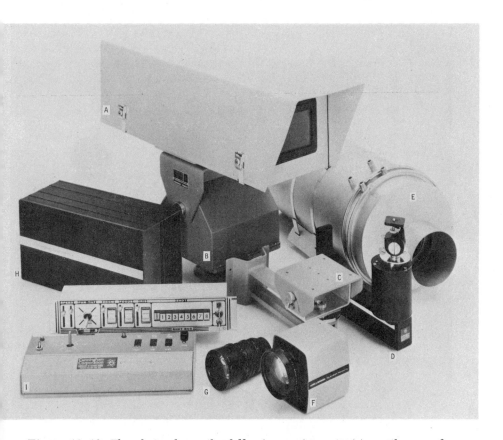

Figure 12-10 The photo shows the following equipment: (a) weatherproof housing; (b) pan and tilt mount; (c) an outside fixed mount; (d) an inside fixed mount; (e) a water-cooled housing; (f) a motorized zoom lens; (g) a fixed lens; (h) inside tamper-proof housing; and (i) remote controls. (Courtesy (Cunningham Corporation)

an explosion-proof housing, and Figure 12-10 shows a water-cooled housing and other accessories.

MONITORS

There are as many different types and qualities of monitors as there are television cameras. The size and type of monitor usually depends upon the number of cameras and whether or not a sequential switcher is employed in the system. The switches can be either manually or automatically operated and are used when more than one camera is monitored by a single receiver.

Figure 12-11 A Motorola TV monitor and control equipment. Note that the operator faces the direction of the monitors even if he is talking with someone. (Courtesy Motorola Communications and Electronics, Inc.)

Monitors or receivers that are commonly used in industrial or commercial applications have 9-inch screens measured diagonally. The number of horizontal line resolutions govern to a great degree the clarity of the image received. A good-quality 9-inch-screen monitor permits installation of many cameras in a console using a minimum of space (see Figure 12-11).

The location of a television receiver in relation to the position of the person monitoring the system is of critical importance. Generally, the system monitor or operator also has functions to perform not related to the surveillance system. These duties will usually include monitoring annunciators of fire, anti-intrusion, and process detection systems, answering telephones, answering inquiries from visitors, issuing passes or checking identification. If most of the operator's time is spent working or looking in a certain direction, the receivers should be located somewhere along his or her line of sight, even if the screens are observed only by peripheral vision.

I visited a plant recently where the guard was seated at a desk in an office and was controlling visitors, issuing bills of lading to truck drivers, checking employee identification, and answering telephones. He was also monitoring an eight-camera surveillance system through four 12-inch receivers. The receivers were installed 90 degrees from the guard's primary direction of activity and at a height that required him to raise his head to observe them. To make matters even worse, the persons he was doing business with could observe the monitors better than he could. Had these receivers been of the 9-inch type and were they installed in front of his desk, with the monitors shielded at the top and sides, he would have been able to observe them constantly, regardless of the function he was performing.

COMPONENTS OF A TYPICAL CLOSED CIRCUIT TELEVISION SURVEILLANCE SYSTEM

A closed circuit television surveillance system may utilize only a few components or pieces of equipment. The most simple, of course, is one camera and one receiver. Seldom can the cost of this simple system be justified in security applications. This type of camera-monitor system is often found when processes or hazardous operations are being monitored, but they do little to increase the security at any installation.

A typical system installed to increase the security of a facility and the safety of its occupants would probably be composed of at least the following items.

1. Several cameras. Depending upon the size of the area under surveillance, the majority of the cameras would probably be equipped with pan and tilt devices. Wherever possible, cameras should be located so that if

they are equipped to traverse horizontally (pan) or to be elevated or depressed (tilt), the greatest area possible can be observed through the system. Most security applications will require a combination of movable and fixed cameras. Fixed cameras are used to observe one point only.

2. Intercommunication capability. Often in security applications it is desirable to install two-way communication somewhere near the camera location and the monitor. This arrangement will make possible the operation of railroad or vehicular gates from a remote location at the monitor. In other applications, a closed circuit television camera forms a communication tunnel between a hospital and the nurses quarters. Two-way communication would alert the person monitoring the camera that a nurse or other person was entering the tunnel. Should an attack in the tunnel occur, the screams of a woman would immediately alert the guard and ensure that he not only observes the monitor but activates the video-tape recorder for possible use as evidence at a later date.

3. Time and date generator. This device is used to record the exact time and date that an incident occurred that was observed by the closed circuit television surveillance system and recorded on video-tape. The date and exact time that the incident occurred appears as a matter of record on the video-tape of the incident.

4. Sequential switcher. This device may be automatic or controlled manually. One sequential switcher is usually all that is needed for a single surveillance system; throwing a switch puts the system in automatic or manual mode. The switcher is used when more than one camera is being monitored with a single monitor. One monitor can effectively be used in most instances to monitor three cameras. When the sequential switcher is in the automatic mode and is preset to switch at specific times, usually about every 10 seconds, it will switch from one camera to the other. Thus, in the period of 1 minute, the person at the monitor will have observed twice all three areas observed by the camera.

5. Video-tape recorder. A video-tape recorder is used to record incidents that are observed on the television monitor. This does not necessarily mean that the only activity recorded on the tape would be illegal activity or activity that violates some rule or procedure. The recorder can also be used in plant traffic studies of vehicles or pedestrians. Video-tape recorders can be used with a time-lapse device so that the images picked up by the camera are recorded only for specific periods of time. Video-tape recorders are a necessity when covert television cameras are used. If the activity observed is illegal, a record of the activity will be needed in connection with legal or disciplinary action. The video-tape recorder can be attached to an ordinary home television receiver and the tape reviewed. However, the tape is normally reviewed on the same monitors that captured the pictures.

6. Split-screen monitors. Split-screen monitors are used when fixed-position television cameras are used to control personnel access. The personnel access control in this instance would require two cameras. One

camera is focused on the individual and the second camera is focused on the surface upon which the individual desiring access to the protected area places his or her identification card with the photograph upward. The guard on duty at the monitor is thus able to compare the photo on the identification card with the individual, because both appear on his monitor screen at the same time. With this type of system, a two-way communication system would also normally be installed, and obviously either the gate or the door where access will be authorized is remotely controlled from the monitor's position through an electrical lock or an electrical latch arrangement.

7. Monitors or receivers. As previously stated, the number of monitors will be determined by the number of cameras in any given surveillance system. The size of the monitors will depend upon the number of monitors, the size of the console, and the amount of room available for mounting the monitors. In most security applications, the 9-inch monitor is adequate. It is small and requires little room, and if the surveillance system is expanded at a later date and additional monitors are required, less overall space will be required, regardless of how expansive the system is. One camera or several cameras can be monitored from several different locations. For example, if a camera is used to monitor a certain process while operations are in progress, the monitor may be located in the foreman's office of that particular activity. When operations cease and the camera reverts to a security role, it is merely switched to the monitor at the guard station.

8. Zoom and fixed lenses. A zoom lens is often needed when a television camera is used in a security environment to observe certain details more closely. A camera located at a remotely operated vehicular gate may be zoomed in on the vehicle to read the name of the company printed on the truck or the license plate number. In other instances, it might be used to identify specific individuals in the area being observed. The zoom lens is rated on a ratio basis. For example, a zoom lens with a five-to-one ratio would mean that when the lens is fully extended, the image observed on the monitor would be magnified five times. Zoom lenses are available in a ratio up to twelve to one. In addition to the zoom lens, fixed lenses in various sizes are available. The focal length of the standard fixed lens normally used for indoor application is 16 millimeters; however, lenses are available in a range from wide-angle 3.5 millimeter "fish eye" lenses through telescopic lenses of 225-500-millimeter focal length.

9. Camera housings. Camera housings range from a relatively simple housing made of sturdy steel, with an impact-resistant glass-covered aperture, to environmental camera housings. The latter are waterproof, can be heated or cooled, and have windows that may be equipped with a windshield wiper. Shields can be installed on the front of the camera to protect the window against rain, snow, or sunlight. Available environmental housings include explosion-proof and water-cooled versions. The location and application of a particular camera will dictate the type of housing that is required. In some instances, perhaps no housing is required. This may

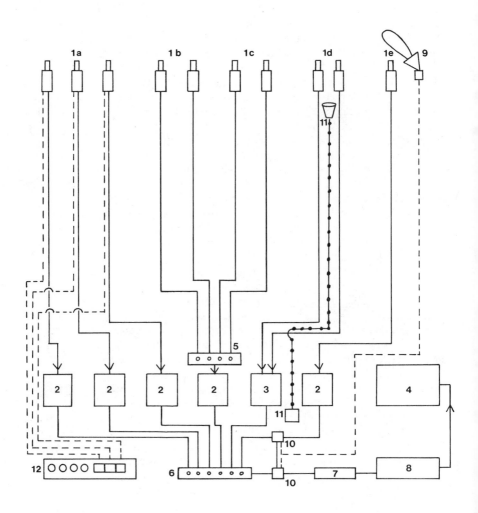

Figure 12-12 The drawing utilizes different types of cameras, lenses, environmental housings, applications, and allied components and equipment to illustrate that a closed circuit television surveillance system can consist of one camera and one monitor or, properly designed, can furnish a sophisticated system of surveillance and control. (Drawing by Caril Magdefrau)

1a. Low-light-level cameras, motorized zoom lens with automatic iris, environmental housing, and pan and tilt motor with automatic scan.
1b. Indoor cameras with standard lens and environmental housing.
1c. Indoor cameras, wide angle lens, and tamper-proof housing.
1d. Indoor personnel identification cameras, one with wide-angle lens to view ID card and one with standard lens to view the person.
1e. Indoor camera, standard lens, "hidden" installation.
2. 9-inch diagonal screen monitor.
3. 9-inch diagonal screen-split image monitor.
4. 19-inch diagonal screen to monitor video-tape recordings.
5. Four-position automatic sequential switcher with adjustable timing.
6. A six-position manual switch.
7. A date and time generator.
8. Reel-to-reel video-tape recorder.
9. Microwave intrusion (motion) detector activates camera 1e.
10. Automatic bypass and VTR activation relay.
11. Two-way speaker system used in conjunction with the ID cameras.
12. The camera control console with ability to pan and tilt, to zoom in and out, to focus near or far, to control speed, to scan automatically and/or manually, and to select cameras.

be the case when a camera is installed at an inside location to monitor
gauges or recording devices.

See Figure 12-12 for a schematic drawing of the relative position of
each component in a sophisticated closed circuit television surveillance
system.

Camera locations can often be improved by installing the camera on a
mount consisting of metal pipes, the configuration of which has been designed
to ensure proper placement of the camera for the most effective operation
and observation of the area to be monitored. Often, cameras mounted on
rooftops will be limited in the areas they can observe near the building
unless they are installed on a mount that is designed to permit the camera
to protrude beyond the walls of the building, making it possible to observe
almost directly downward on the vertical plane.

This chapter has been designed to familiarize the reader with the security value of a closed circuit television surveillance system and to acquaint
him or her with the various component parts of a typical system. If nothing
more, the reader should by now be acutely aware that regardless of the
type of facility and its operational or crime-suppression problems, there
is usually some area or point where the employment of a closed circuit
television camera will increase the effectiveness of the security plan and,
in all probability, reduce the cost of this increased security.

One security guard post manned 24 hours per day, 7 days per week under
the present rates charged by most private-contract security companies will
cost approximately $40,000 annually. In most areas of the United States,
a three-camera system can be installed for approximately the same amount
of money. Once installed, the system can be used for years at minimal
additional cost, usually only the cost of servicing, repairing, and maintaining the system.

The actual design of a closed circuit television system and the preparation
of a proposal should be left to the experts in the field. Remember, however,
that the primary task of these experts is to sell television equipment; they
may have little or no security expertise. It is the responsibility of the
security expert or surveyor to determine his needs and tell the television
technician what he needs to accomplish. The selection of equipment and
its location and installation are the television technician's responsibility.
Whenever and wherever possible, the installation of the system should be
frequently inspected by the security surveyor to ensure that his requirements are being followed and met.

A PROPOSAL FOR A CLOSED CIRCUIT TELEVISION SURVEILLANCE SYSTEM

To someone who has had no formal training in electronic engineering, the
first look at a proposal for a closed circuit television surveillance system
may be overwhelming. To "cushion" any such apprehension and to outline

items that should appear in any professionally prepared proposal, I have recreated below a complete proposal, including a price quote (which was factual at the time of writing). Note that the proposal commences with an explanation of camera location and a general outline of each camera field of view to pinpoint the actual structures or objects the security supervisor wants observed.

Camera Location #1

East of the vehicle road, south of rail track #2, near Dock #4. This camera should be mounted approximately 20 feet above ground level either on a pole or steel tower. The camera should be enclosed within an environmental-type housing, equipped with an auto-iris lens to compensate for all lighting conditions, and mounted on a controlled pan and tilt motor unit. This camera would scan 220 degrees, thus being able to observe the vehicle gate, Building #10, and the rail gates.

Camera Location #2

Immediately adjacent to the northeast corner of Building #14. This camera should be mounted 24 feet above ground level, either on a pole or steel tower. The camera would be enclosed within an environmental-type housing, equipped with an auto-iris lens to compensate for all lighting conditions, and mounted on a controlled pan and tilt motor unit. The camera would scan 180 degrees, thus being able to observe the area from Building #12 south along the west wall to the shipping area.

Camera Location #3

Approximately 100 yards west of the truck dock on the grass plot. This camera should be mounted approximately 25 feet above ground level, either on a pole or steel tower. The camera would be enclosed within an environmental-type housing, equipped with an auto-iris lens to compensate for all lighting conditions, and mounted on a controlled pan and tilt motor unit. This camera would scan 200 degrees, thus being able to observe rail gates #1 and #2 and the doors on Building #46. Planned future use would include the proposed employee parking area west of Building #19.

Specifications

1. Cameras. Panasonic Model WV261 cameras or equal with Newvicon S4075 image tube are recommended. The specifications for the camera should meet or exceed the following:

   Power source—117 VAC, 60 HZ
   Power consumption—Approximately 15 watts (with automatic iris lens)
   Tube type—2/3-inch separate mesh Newvicon S4075

Scanning standard—525 lines, 160 fields/30 frames
Synchronizing—Internal (line) random horizontal, line locked
    vertical; (INT) 2:2 interlacing
Horizontal resolution—550 lines
Video output—1.0 vp.p composite/75 ohms
Automatic light compensation—16,000:1 with automatic lens
Required illumination—Over 0.05 ft candle (0.5 lux) (f 1.4 lens)
Operating ambient temperature—14° F—113° F
Lens—Automatic iris, f 1.4, 16 mm, C—mount type

2. Environmental housing. Should be the side-access type designed
for maximum weather protection, Vicon 800 series.
3. Pan and tilt motor unit. Heavy duty, weatherproof, with adjustable
stops, auto scan capability and remotely controlled, 24 VAC or 115
VAC power source. Controls compatible with motor unit.
4. Video amplifiers. Video amplifiers required between cameras and
monitors to preclude line signal loss.
5. Monitors. The specifications for the monitors should meet or exceed
the following:

Power source—117 VAC, 60 HZ
Power consumption—Less than 38 watts
Video input—0.5-2.0 vp.p composite/75 ohms or Hi-Z looping
    through
Horizontal resolution—More than 700 lines at center
Video frequency response—10 MHZ
Maximum video gain—39 dB
C.R.T.—9-inch diagonal, type 230ADB4
Operating ambient temperature—14° F—122° F

6. Coaxial cable and connectors. Belden type RG11U and RG59U or
equal with standard PL259 coaxial connectors.
7. Estimated cost (installed). Three cameras, four monitors (see
Note 1) and all required components: $28,000.00.
8. Life expectancy. Not less than 5 years.
Note 1: While all cameras are to be monitored in the security guard
office, it is recommended that Camera #2 also be monitored in
the warehouse supervisor's office.
Note 2: The 9-inch monitors are specified not only because of their
excellent clarity, but more specifically because the monitors
may be mounted at the rear of the guard's desk to provide continuous viewing even while guards are performing other tasks
at the desk (for example, telephone, radio, or paper work).

If a service and maintenance contract is involved, it would normally be handled separately and would be presented to the customer only after the installation proposal had been accepted or approved. This contractual agreement is of no concern to the security representative, and he should not become involved in any of these negotiations.

13

Physical Security
of a Computer Area

In a 1976 U.S. Research and Development pamphlet, a key was proposed
for a security system designed to lock up vast quantities of information
stored in U.S. computers so that only authorized persons can get at the
information. However, this key is "too small" and "within 15 years will
be rendered totally insecure," in the opinion of two Stanford computer
experts.

The two experts, electrical engineering professor Martin E. Hellman
and graduate student Whitfield Diffie, criticized the computer key proposed
by the National Bureau of Standards and the National Security Agency in an
article in the March 1976 Professional Journal of the Association of Com-
puting Machinery. Hellman and Diffie had been working on related research
in data security under National Science Foundation sponsorship.

Numerous computer thefts of company secrets and even of money in
recent years have caused the industry to look hard for better methods of
securing their trade secrets and other private information stored in computers. At the same time, there has been wide public concern about the
privacy of individuals' computerized files held by the Internal Revenue
Service and other government agencies. So far, the only way to tell whether
computerized secrets are safely stored is to use trial-and-error methods
to find the code words or signals that will enable one user to read another's
files. Such eavesdropping already occurs now and then quite by accident.
The system proposed by NBS originated at IBM and consists of a kind of
combination lock called an "algorithm" which is an encoding computer program. When the user puts his key into the algorithm lock and feeds information into the machine, it is stored or sent to the recipient in coded form.
The same key must be used again by the sender to retrieve the information
or by the recipient to read the message. Any other key will produce only
garbled versions.

If approved, the algorithm lock will become a standard item of integrated
circuitry. It is mounted on a tiny silicone ship and manufactured in quantity
for installation in any computer whose users want it. The key to the lock
is a series of 56 digits, zeros and ones, arranged in any order. The large
number of possible arrangements of these digits, approximately 100 billion,
gives the appearance of a high level of security. However, Hellman and

Diffie hold that the so-called "56" key is not at all that secure—that such a
key could be broken in a day by anyone with enough money to build the trial-
and-error machinery to search the 100 billion keys. The machine would
cost about $20 million by their estimate. Such a prodigious search has only
become economically feasible within the last few years due to revolutionary
advances in electronics. They believe it significant that this would probably
be too much for a private firm to invest in prying into a rival firm's secrets,
but not too much for a government agency. The implication is that by setting
a 56-bit standard, the government wants to be able to pry in the name of
national security or on other pretexts but prevent others from doing so.
"While it well established that a large number of keys does not guarantee
security," says the Stanford pair, "too small a number of keys guarantees
insecurity."

It is widely held that computation costs will continue to decline by an
order of magnitude every 5 years. In 10 years, the $20-million machine
will cost approximately $200,000 and be within the reach of any large organi-
zation. If adopted, the proposed standard would have to be changed before
that time. "The cost of modifying terminals, systems, etc., to use the
new standard and the cost of 're-encoding' old files which are still deemed
private would be high. These costs seem unjustified since the cost of enlarging the key of the proposed standard would be minimal."

Enlarging the 56-bit key to 64 bits would escalate the cost of key-breaking
machinery to about $5 billion, they estimate. This cost might give pause
to governments today, but in 10 years the expected advances in technology
would reduce these figures to $50 million and $25,000 respectively. The
Stanford experts have urged a much higher standard with at least 128 key
bits which the computer users could employ wholly or in part. It would
then be impossible to break the key by trial and error. "We strongly
encourage NBS to consider modifying its proposed standard," they conclude.
"At least it should define the level of security it believes the proposed standard offers and make public the reasoning behind its belief. Adoption of a
standard with built-in obsolescence is not justified."

Computer crime is essentially a "white-collar" crime, and many of the
"blue-collar" security measures suggested by some members of research
projects are not accepted by individuals involved in the planning, programming, and operation of a computer system, whether or not the individual
is criminal or "legit." It is the people, not the machines, who are dishonest
and careless. There is, as I see it, no alternative to the control of personnel to minimize computer losses.

In June 1976 the following computer crime was uncovered and reported
by the public press. A former employee of a company supplying computer
services to the Federal Energy Administration was convicted of what has
been described as "the white-collar crime of the future"—that is, tapping
classified information from a government computer. The convicted employee admitted at his trial that he had extracted information from the FEA

computer on 15 occasions by using computer terminals attached to his Alexandria, Virginia, office phone and his Lantham, Maryland, home phone. Through this process he was able to accumulate 39 rolls of computer printouts on the nation's oil and energy resources before his unauthorized computer use was discovered by another employee of his company. The convicted employee claimed at his trial that he committed the theft only to show how lax security was at his company which had approximately 1300 employees who handled work, not only for the Federal Energy Administration, but for the Federal Trade Commission, Environmental Protection Agency, and Departments of State and Labor. The president of the company reported that the only reason this employee could tap the computer was because he "retained in his memory the keys to unlocking the information."

A Justice Department spokesman said the technique used could be used to gain access to many government and private computers including those of the FBI, the IRS, or even the CIA. The technology and the secret codes are all that are needed.

An article appearing in the public press reported that a computer programmer had been charged with stealing components of a minicomputer system. The programmer was arrested and charged with larceny of equipment that local police estimated was valued at up to $75,000. Most of the equipment was seized at a business operated by the programmer's father.

Police alleged that the programmer stole the system components from June to October 1974 from his employer and brought the parts to his father's business where he assembled the system.

Here we have two extremes of computer crimes. However, both crimes are alleged to have been committed by employees. In addition to outright theft of information and material, there exists the very real problem of sabotage by employees, vandalism by outsiders, and "scrambling of information" by professionals to delay, confuse, and alter records, often to cover up theft of information. There is also the threat of destruction or damage to the computer operation by natural hazards, fire, high winds, and floods. Therefore, the security program for the protection of a computer environment must weigh the cost of protection against the risks involved. One must keep in mind that "total protection" is necessary. Piecemeal security programs are often worse than none at all. Protecting a computer operation is no different than protecting a single building. All doors in the building must be considered, not just some. Data files, equipment, tape libraries, personnel control, and all phases of operations must be considered, and these considerations must include all human and natural hazards.

A recent study by a large computer manufacturer determined that about 95 percent of the hazards consisted of accidental errors and omissions, accidental water damage, fire damage to the equipment or area, deliberate falsification by employees, and irrational acts of employees. All other hazards combined result in about 5 percent of the total resource losses.

The destruction of or erasure of information from tapes has been bally-hooed in the press for the past 10 to 15 years. Stories were often started or circulated by manufacturers of devices that would furnish protection against this crime. One story circulated widely concerned the accidental erasure of "several tapes" by a computer repairman who placed his flash-light, which had a small magnet that permitted the light to be attached to a metal object, on the side of a metal cabinet used to store tape reels. A flashlight magnet, which is a permanent-type magnet, has an approximate magnetic "gauss" field at the pull edges of 800, an insufficient strength to erase tapes inside a cabinet. A permanent magnet of sufficient strength applied to a tape correctly can seriously degrade or erase data on the tape. Even though it has been exaggerated, this vulnerability does exist, but there are numerous more effective ways to sabotage computer operations.

If those security measures discussed in connection with access control are combined with other physical security techniques and incorporated into the security plan, the installation of magnetometers in the tape storage areas is unnecessary.

ELEMENTS OF COMPUTER SECURITY

The protection of information that is stored and/or processed in a computer system depends on the security that results from a combination of elements: primarily administrative security, personnel security, physical security, communications security, emanation security, and computer security.

In further analyzing these principle categories, we must consider the following elements.

Administrative Security

1. Supervision of the entire security program by the security chief or a member of management.
2. Accountability procedures, or as sometimes referred to, the audit trail. These procedures include determining how every record in the system got to its present state and when and by whom each change was made.
3. The responsibility of individuals given specific assignments.

Personnel Security

1. The proper selection of personnel that will be assigned to computer operations.
2. Developing the operational assignments for each of the individuals selected.
3. Procedures used in briefing and debriefing.

Physical Security

1. The initial selection of the site where the computer will actually be installed.
2. The selection of a particular area within a building or the construction of a separate building to house the computer operations.
3. The assessment of the necessary protective devices that will be used in the physical security program.
4. Power-supply protection, including an auxiliary power-supply source.
5. Air conditioning, humidity control equipment, and heating equipment protection.
6. Protection of peripheral openings such as windows and doors and protection of the walls, ceiling, and floors.
7. Lighting and water-supply protection—that is, the location of the water supply for the sprinkler system pipes and the electrical conduit that supplies illumination of the area.
8. Fire protection equipment.
9. Building design and construction, fire retardation materials to be used.

Communications Security

1. The area where connecting lines enter the building or the computer area must be considered for protection.
2. The location and protection of all electrical junction boxes.
3. Communications control in coding and input-output devices.
4. Protection of processing or telephone switchboard equipment.

Emanation Security

1. The identification of all users of the equipment.
2. The surveillance of processing accesses.
3. The isolation of hardware components.
4. The maintenance of the integrity of the system.

Computer Security

1. Security of all software systems, including security of the computer operating programs, file management, communications control programs, application programs, and resource accounting programs.
2. Protection of all hardware components against fire, theft, or vandalism.
3. The protection of terminals, card readers, punches, printers, paper tapes, and items of this nature.
4. The protection of remotely located printers, card readers, paper tapes, and video displays.

A word about protection against erasure or scrambling of magnetic tapes. It would be practically impossible to generate an electric or magnetic field outside a building that would have any effect on recordings on a tape inside a building. Furthermore, a large permanent magnet will have no measurable effect on a tape held 20 inches away. If the magnet is moved to within 6 or 8 inches of the material, it may begin to cause errors that might render records unreadable. At 3 inches away, a very strong magnet will, for all practical purposes, erase the data, and a powerful electromagnet would have an adverse effect from further distances.

A simple way, then, to protect against magnetic fields originating outside the building in which data processing facilities are located is to keep all magnetic media at least 20 inches from the outside walls of the building. That means that the tape library should not be immediately adjacent to an outside wall. It should be far enough away from the peripheral wall so that there is a walking space between the library container and the wall.

Radar signals, if strong enough, can interfere with the operation of some data processing equipment, but only if the signal that reaches the equipment is greater than 5 volts per meter. Masonry walls or any metal in the walls will reflect the signal from the building. A simple method of screening is to use aluminum mesh wire, and usually this is needed only at window openings.

Radiation and radioactive particles are not a threat to data processing installations except possibly to unexposed microfilm. Magnetic fields that are associated with X rays are insignificant in terms of the energy required to change the magnetic state and thereby destroy or scramble any data stored on the tape.

COMPUTER TERMINOLOGY

It has been said that computer personnel have created an entirely new and different language. My initial experience in the field caused some bewilderment because of this "language barrier." Total information security includes exposure assessment in the information-processing framework. This information is generally broken down into steps so that a determination can be made as to whether or not the information is human readable or merely computer interpretable. This framework is generally broken down into 11 steps in order to make this determination.

1. Data gathering. This is the manual creation and transportation of data that is still in a human-readable state.
2. Data transmission. This is the manual movement of source documents to the input area where they are converted to a machine-readable form. These documents are still human readable.

3. Data conversion. This is the physical conversion of human-readable documents to machine-readable documents. In this stage, quite obviously, the data are both human readable and computer interpretable.

4. Data communications input. This is the transmission of machine-readable data by telephone, mail, or messenger. In this form the tapes, cards, or disks may be both human readable and computer interpretable.

5. Data processing. This is the execution of application programs to reform intended computations; at this stage the information is only computer interpretable.

6. Data receipt. This is the receipt of data that are to be stored while awaiting processing. This information is on disks, tapes, or drums and is now only computer interpretable.

7. Output preparation. This is the preparation of the output media for dessemination to the users. It includes cards, disks, tapes, drums, or paper. These outputs are both computer interpretable and human readable.

8. Data movement. This is the manual movement of computer produced output in various forms to the output area to await user pickup. This information is on tapes, paper reports, and cards, and is both computer interpretable and human readable.

9. Data communications output. This is the transmission of the output from the computer to the user. This information is transmitted in the same manner as the input material and is both computer interpretable and human readable.

10. Data usage. This is the actual use of data by the recipient, which includes storage of data while being used. In this stage the data are human readable and may be in the form of paper reports, cards, microfilm, and so on.

11. Data disposition. This is the disposition of the data after usage and includes the methods of storage, length of time of storage, and/or final disposal. In this stage the data are both computer interpretable and human readable.

These various steps or stages in information processing must be known in order to reduce the potential exposure of the information.

There exists a certain relationship between the information exposure and other sources in the information system. The assessment of this exposure depends not only on the form of the information but also its relationship to personnel within the organization. These personnel resources are generally classified into ten groups.

1. EDP management
2. Data center management

3. Computer operations personnel
4. Input/output control personnel
5. Clerical personnel
6. Systems and programming management
7. Systems analysts
8. Programmers
9. Software specialists
10. User personnel

A comparison of the stages of information processing and the personnel within a computer organization who handle the information at various stages assessed properly will indicate where, within the organization, exposure is the greatest. This information is needed by the security surveyor because <u>indirectly</u> it will have an effect on the physical security plan established.

TYPES OF COMPUTER CRIME

Next, the types of computer crime should be examined because these will have a <u>direct</u> bearing on the degree of security established in specific computer operations or specific areas within a computer environment. Donn Parker, Senior Information Processing Analyst at Stanford Research Institute's Information Science Laboratory, and author of the book <u>Crime by Computer</u> (New York: Scribner, 1976), identifies five types of computer crimes.

1. <u>Financial crime</u>. This occurs when the thief takes money or negotiable instruments. Financial crime is performed best in systems where the computer is used for financial processing, including accounts payable and receivable or payrolls.
2. <u>Property crime</u>. This type of crime involves the taking of merchandise or other property for resale.
3. <u>Information crime</u>. Information crimes can be performed best by means of unauthorized access via a remote terminal or when the system services and physical facilities are available to employees during nonworking hours or when computer programs or files are <u>insufficiently protected</u>. This crime is best illustrated by time-sharing cases where copies of information (that is, valuable files, programs, or customer lists) are taken.
4. <u>Theft of services</u>. This crime is committed by using computer time at company expense for personal benefit. For example, it would be easy for a professor in most universities to obtain free computer time for teaching purposes and use it instead for research purposes. Such research could lead to publications or consulting jobs, the royalties or fees for which would come to the professor.

5. <u>Vandalism</u>. This involves intentional damage designed to deny the use of the computer to others or to cause the organization to spend time and money for repairs. An example cited by Mr. Parker is one that was reported in the <u>Wall Street Journal</u>. In this incident, which occurred several years ago, a computer employee at one company was given 2 weeks' notice before he was laid off. This individual promptly removed all the labels on some 1500 reels of tape, costing the company thousands of dollars to reidentify the data.

To further provide security guidance applicable to computer systems, it is necessary to identify other threats that exist. These threats, peculiar only to computer systems, are generally classified under three categories.

1. <u>Denial of service to others</u>. This may be achieved by blowing the system up, clogging the system with information that is worthless, or crashing the system. This is accomplished by overloading a particular computer operation with so many requests for tasks that are time–consuming that the computer service is, in effect, unavailable for use by others.
2. <u>Access to sensitive information</u>. This is the unauthorized disclosure, whether it is purposeful or accidental, of stored information, whether it be from a credit bureau or a classified operation.
3. <u>Unauthorized modification of contents of a computer system</u>. This is the most general of the three identified here. It usually implies assessing information so that one can modify it in a meaningful way. It is a much more insidious means of securing unauthorized information than the previous two discussed, because it may well be that the service will actually appear normal and yet will have been changed.

There are two other methods of securing unauthorized information that perhaps are not as common as those already discussed. These are the gathering of information either by aggregation or by inference.

By aggregation we mean gathering enough nonsensitive information and data that when combined with other nonsensitive data would become significantly more sensitive. For example, the names of individuals alone may not be considered sensitive information; however, when combined with their home address and Social Security number, it becomes significantly more sensitive.

By inference we mean securing information that is considered sensitive from data that is acquired through a series of inquiries into the computer. An example would be securing the cost of operating a department that is totaled on a weekly basis. When an employee leaves, and his or her salary is deducted from the operating cost of the department, the salary of that employee can be inferred from the data on weekly operating cost.

The physical plant security measures that are used for the protection of computer system do not vary a great deal from the physical security measures, personnel identification practices, and means used to classify and destroy documents that are used in securing any facility or area where sensitive information is being used or stored. The degree of security established for the protection of computer systems is entirely dependent upon the classification, sensitivity, and the privacy requirements of the information being handled by that particular computer system.

PASSWORDS

In the paragraphs above the term "passwords" was mentioned. To the military man, they mean the code word or words that are used to identify himself as a friend when challenged. To the computer community, it means the same thing; a word used to access a computer for information. Password use is not limited to time-sharing operations where they are generally employed to identify the user but can also be applied to increase the protection of terminals, data, files, and programs.

There are some weaknesses, however, that the reader should be aware of. These same weaknesses were prevalent in the military usage of passwords, and almost every former or present military man who ever was in a situation that required the use of a password has some humorous or tragic tale to tell.

The weaknesses stem from the fact that passwords can be given away, either intentionally or inadvertently. Because a complex password can be difficult to remember, there is always the threat that it will be written down and left somewhere near the computer terminal or carried in the operator's pocket or purse. It is not uncommon for a password to be loaned to a friend who has forgotten his and who requires immediate access to the system.

Another weakness is that passwords can be too trivial. For example, in order to make remembering the password easy, the user's initials or the day of the week or the month in which the user was born may be used. This is similar to using birth dates, wedding dates, and sequences of numbers that are already committed to memory to place on combination locks.

The third weakness in the password system is that entire lists of passwords may be acquired, either deliberately or accidentally, from the computer's memory. Obviously, anyone in possession of a password list has access not only to the full system but also to its associated files.

To increase the effectiveness of passwords and to ensure that they are not compromised, stern disciplinary action should be taken against offenders in the form of reprimands initially. If the compromise persists, more significant penalties should be imposed.

Because it is possible that the entire password list can be acquired from the computer, protection of the master list can be increased if the list is completely coded (encrypted). A simple two-complex algorithm may be used. The password would be processed by the algorithm before being compared to the previously encrypted master list. Therefore, possession of a master list would not provide a means of access to the system by the intruder. The use of an already encrypted password would cause it to be doubly encrypted, and, therefore, it would fail the comparison test.

DISASTER PLAN FOR THE COMPUTER AREA

The individual responsible for security of the computer operation and all its components must also remember that he or she is faced with certain natural hazards that can disrupt operations. In spite of all of the precautions and protection measures in location, construction, and design already employed in protection of the computer environment, disasters can occur. A disaster plan must be included before the plan for protection can be considered complete.

An effective disaster plan must provide for protection of all those items discussed; however, no matter how detailed the plan, how often the plan is tested, and how effective the equipment provided for the protection against natural hazards is, it does not take the place of (1) backup systems and (2) offsite duplicate record storage.

It has been found that for a backup system to be effective, it is necessary to test the system regularly after it has been designed. Unless this testing precaution is taken, the plan may prove to be unworkable in an emergency. Three types of backup systems should be considered.

1. Air-conditioning backup to ensure that the required atmospheric conditions can be maintained in the event of failure of the primary system.
2. Backup computer machinery must be tested to ensure that the computer hardware that will be relied upon for a backup system is compatible with the primary machinery.
3. Auxiliary power supply sources are needed. This involves merely the installation of a backup generator of sufficient capacity to keep the computer machinery operating should the primary power source fail. The generator should be run frequently to ensure that it is in working order, and measures should be taken to ensure that an adequate fuel supply is always immediately available.

I have frequently encountered situations where backup or duplicate tapes and drums are stored in a vault located across town at the site of another organization's computer operations. Although the backup information is thus being stored offsite, this system is not as nearly desirable as storage of this information elsewhere. After all, the tapes being stored in another company's vault may well be stolen or destroyed merely because of an attack upon that organization's computer facility. Depending upon the type of organization and facilities available, this procedure could well result in placing the information in an even more vulnerable location because that facility may be more subject to attack.

The tape libraries or storage vaults at the computer location should be accessible only to those individuals actually requiring such access. In some instances, I have found that the same card used in a card reader to gain access to the computer area by all personnel assigned to these operations would also operate the card reader, permitting all access to the storage vault. Obviously, this arrangement reduces drastically the protection of the tapes in the vault or tape library.

Offsite storage of computer information need not necessarily be nearby, because, it is hoped, these tapes may never be required. In the case of a fire at a telephone facility in New York that almost completely destroyed that operation, communications were almost completely reestablished within 72 hours through the use of computer backup tapes that were stored in a site in Arizona.

Numerous organizations are constructing computer tape depositories that offer excellent protection for offsite backup tape storage. Almost all large urban areas have such installations, some of which utilize underground storage facilities. In several cities, I have found that an individual or individuals have purchased Federal Reserve Bank buildings from the government that have been abandoned for newer structures. By redesigning the vault area and establishing identification and peripheral controls, excellent storage areas for computer backup tapes have been created.

PEOPLE ARE OFTEN THE PROBLEM

Early in this chapter I pointed out that people, not machines, were careless and dishonest and also noted that only 5 percent of all computer losses can be attributed to direct theft of information. Therefore, to summarize I will relate an actual experience that I had while I was assessing the security of a computer area of a worldwide conglomerate.

The secured area was on the seventh floor of the 31-floor building that housed the company's headquarters. Some of the floors in the building were occupied by tenant companies; therefore, ingress and egress to the building could not be restricted to the personnel employed by the client company.

I proceeded to the floor housing the computer operations and found a uniformed guard at a desk near an entrance door on which was printed in large letters "COMPUTER AREA—AUTHORIZED PERSONNEL ONLY."

I left the elevator and was able to walk completely around the service core of the floor by using a hallway that was not under the guard's control. Several doors opened off this hallway. I found two that appeared to be emergency exits from the computer area. Neither of these doors could be observed by the guard on duty, and both were locked so that ingress from the hallway was not possible.

I had waited in the hallway near these two doors for about 18 minutes when one door opened and a young lady came out. I could clearly see that inside the door she had used was a sign that read "Emergency Exit Only." I immediately stepped toward the door, and the lady obligingly held it open. She then proceeded to the ladies room located in the service core.

Once inside I engaged two keypunch operators in a conversation without being challenged by them or anyone else. I then proceeded to another desk where another person was working and used his phone to call our client. I did not ask to use the phone, nor was I challenged. When the client answered, I asked him to meet me in the computer area as soon as possible. In only a few minutes I was joined by my client who expressed astonishment that the guard on duty at the entrance to the area had let me in without asking for identification or logging me in on his register. When I explained that I had entered through an emergency exit that was held open for me by an employee, he was appalled.

A simple local alarm on the emergency exits would have eliminated the use of these doors for unauthorized purposes. Furthermore, the use of one television camera with a monitor at the guard's location at the main entrance to the computer area would have uncovered these unauthorized movements, and this hazard would have been soon completely eliminated.

14

High-Rise
Building Security

The Memphis, Tennessee, <u>Commercial Appeal</u> (June 24, 1976) carried a
story titled, "Rapist Strikes in Restroom," which read in part:

> A 28-year-old office worker was attacked and raped on the
> fourth floor of the Dermon Building shortly after 7:00 A.M.
> yesterday, police said. The sex crimes squad commander
> said the woman arrived at work at 7:00 A.M. and then took
> two coffee pots to a restroom to begin making coffee.
> When she entered the restroom she was grabbed from behind
> by a man who began choking her with what she said was a red
> bandana. She said she yelled out but the man threatened to kill
> her, and he put something over her head and raped her on the
> floor.
> Police fanned out in the building trying to find persons who
> might have encountered the man but the commander said no one
> could recall seeing a man fitting the description.
> He cautioned women about entering darkened offices or
> restrooms, particularly in early morning or evening hours.

In researching the subject of high-rise security, I read numerous articles
written by locksmiths, by manufacturers of locks and access-control devices,
by magazine editors who had interviewed security specialists, and by other
experts in the field. Each tended to slant the contents of the article to
"peddle their wares."

The magazine editorial staffs tended to write articles they themselves
did not fully understand which would, as likely as not, either confuse the
reader or misrepresent the information gleaned during an interview.

Some articles would quote building managers who had difficulty differen-
tiating between a "dead bolt" and a "dead beat." One two-page article on
high-rise building security contained such subheadings as "Long Bolt,"
"Pin Tumbler Cylinder," "Removable Core Cylinder," "Aluminum Doors,"
"Traffic Control/Security," and "Pared Doors." All of these subjects
certainly apply to securing the high-rise building, but they are an infinitesi-
mal part of the technique of securing a high-rise structure and present an
incomplete picture of the topic.

Other articles covered other aspects of building security that in some degree can be applied to high-rise building security. But most of these articles do not address themselves to the specific problems that are created by vertical occupancy of a structure by many tenants with unrelated business activities.

The basic principles of access control, the types of locks to use, the effect of door construction on security, and many other elements of physical security have been discussed in other chapters. Though these security measures apply to high-rise buildings, they will not be discussed again here. In this chapter, we shall examine primarily those hazards peculiar to high-rise structures and the action recommended to reduce or eliminate these hazards.

It is essential to determine what and where the problem areas are and exactly what operations need more protection than others. Here again, the assessment of the criticality and vulnerability of the building or parts of the building must be the first step in planning high-rise building security. The second step is the actual physical study of each area. The third is the analysis of the criticality-vulnerability assessment and physical examination. Fourth is the final plan based upon the analysis and upon the degree of security required in each area.

One thing to keep in mind is that no two structures are exactly alike; however, in most instances, the activities in basement levels, lobby levels, mezzanine levels, and elevator operations will be fairly similar. In other words, there are certain critical and vulnerable floors that by the very nature of the activity taking place there will require about the same degree of security whether the building is in New York City or in Houston, Texas.

We shall not discuss these in any particular sequence of importance, because, for example a computer operation of a certain corporation may be more vulnerable to attack than that of another. Therefore, a logical place to start may be either the basement or the penthouse area at the top of the building. We shall start with the security activities in the basement.

BASEMENT SECURITY

No matter how many levels there are below ground level, some or all of the following operations or areas will normally require some degree of security.

1. Docks. In most instances, unless the building is a part of a huge complex, the docks are usually no larger than that required to allow two trucks to service the building. These docks are used for both shipping and receiving, and, in most instances, because the activity in high-rise office buildings primarily takes the form of office operations, expensive office equipment, stationery, and other highly resalable items move across the docks. In high-rise office buildings, a great deal of waste paper is gene-

rated, and unless it is shredded and baled in the building, the removal of
the trash over these restricted dock areas makes it possible to unload a
truck, deliver items, secret items to be stolen in the trash, and load them
on the trash truck for removal without even having the item checked in by
the receiving clerk. When these transactions occur, it is extremely difficult
to investigate successfully to determine where the item actually disappeared,
whether it was in the area where it should have been loaded, whether it disappeared enroute, or whether it disappeared from the docks of the receiving
unit. The basic principles of dock security outlined in Chapter 7 of this
book should be followed.

   2. Storerooms. The size of the facility, the number of different organizations that occupy the facility, and the type of activity in the building will
determine the number of storerooms that will have been created in the basement areas. The very location of these storage areas makes attacks upon
storerooms very easy. Usually such an attack is totally or partially hidden
from others or could be hidden merely by moving material stored in outside
areas. The material being stored in any particular storeroom will determine the amount of security to be established. The principles previously
discussed in Chapter 6 should be tailored to each situation, and the degree
of security required in each individual storeroom should be established.

   3. Operational activities. By this we mean mail room operations,
printing operations, or perhaps even computer operations, even though
the basement normally is not the place to establish computer operations.
However, if any of these operational activities take place at the basement
level, they must be secured in much the same manner that they would be
regardless of where they are located, with one exception. Because of the
small number of personnel normally operating in a basement, the opportunity
for an intruder to enter these operations is greater. Therefore, personnel
operating in basement levels must be constantly reminded of the security
threat, and these areas should not be left unattended even for short periods
of time. Usually these operations, except for computer operations, can be
secured during the operational day with automatic pneumatic door closers
and latch-type locks to ensure that these doors remain secured at all times,
whether the operational area is occupied or not. Obviously, computer areas,
regardless of their location, should be secured as discussed in the chapter
on computer security.

   4. Scrap and trash removal. The hazards inherent in these operations
can be minimized if all scrap paper is shredded and baled and the bales
removed over the shipping dock. However, in many instances, particularly
in urban settings, if cafeterias are located on upper floors, trash and garbage removal is also accomplished by removing it from the building through
the basement dock area. All cafeteria garbage or trash should be placed
in plastic bags, and the bags should be secured with inexpensive seal-type
devices so that the dock supervisor or the guard can at a glance determine
whether or not the plastic bag had been opened after it left the cafeteria so

that other items could be secreted in it. If trash is removed from the building without being compacted or baled, it is an absolute necessity that these removal operations be supervised both at the time the trash is being discarded in the dumpsters or other container and at the time the container is removed from the building. If the trash is placed in plastic bags with special plastic seals where it accumulates on the various floors, the security of these operations may be improved, providing supervisors of the custodial crews check the bags and seal them personally.

5. Maintenance shops. Maintenance shops will always be found in high-rise building basements, and these must be secured from unauthorized entry, not only during periods when operations cease, but during operational periods as well. Otherwise, material and tools will certainly be stolen. The security treatment of doors leading to maintenance shops should be approximately the same as that created for the protection of other operational activities in the basement.

6. Auxiliary power equipment. Auxiliary power equipment normally will not be confined within an area and is somewhat exposed to being tampered with or sabotaged by practically anyone who is in the basement either legally or illegally. Ordinary industrial-type chain link fencing of about 9 gauge can be used effectively to enclose this type of equipment on all sides and at the top, thereby reducing its vulnerability to attack tremendously.

7. Basement operation offices. There are normally some offices, whether occupied by the maintenance chief, a shipping and receiving clerk, or other management personnel, located in the basement. These offices should be secured in a manner similar to that prescribed for any office where equipment and records cabinets are stored.

8. Restrooms. Restrooms in the basement, like those throughout the remainder of a high-rise building, should remain locked at all times, and the keys should be controlled. A more secure and convenient arrangement is to install a manually operated cipher lock, issuing the combination only to those personnel who will be authorized to use the area.

9. Air-conditioning and air-circulation equipment. This equipment may be found either in the penthouse or in the basement. If it is in the basement, the job of securing it may be a little more difficult than if it were located in a penthouse. The size of the area and the number of areas involved where this type equipment is installed will determine the method used to secure it. In most instances, constructing an enclosure similar to that used to protect power equipment, using industrial-type chain link fence and being sure to enclose the area completely to the ceiling, will adequately protect this type of equipment. If closed circuit television surveillance systems are installed in the building, it may be desirable to use a camera to monitor this equipment and the auxiliary power equipment.

10. Elevator terminal wells. The elevator wells for both freight and passenger elevators that terminate in any basement level must be secured to prevent unauthorized access to the elevator shafts or elevator equipment

at the terminal level. This can normally be accomplished by securing the
service doors merely by locking them with a dead-bolt-type locking device
and controlling the key.

    11. <u>Miscellaneous activities</u>. In all probability, there will be several
other activities in most basements at the various levels. The type and
degree of security that is established obviously will depend upon the type
of activity involved. For example, if civil defense dry rations, water, and
other supplies are stored in the basement, they will require no additional
security. However, they should be stored in such a manner that they do
not create places where property that is stolen in other areas of the building
can be hidden. Also, the design of the storage area must ensure that intruders entering the building during operational hours cannot secret themselves among or behind the storage boxes.

    In addition to the security measures discussed in the preceding list, the
installation of one or two "man-traps" should be considered. These could
consist of inexpensive microwave alarm devices properly directed toward
stairwells or photoelectric cells strategically located in the area to ensure
trapping an intruder or a "stay-behind." If a closed circuit television surveillance system does exist, possibly the only additional security precaution
required would be a strategically located camera protected with a tamper-
proof housing and equipped with a pan and tilt device.

GROUND OR STREET LEVEL

The ground or street level is sometimes also referred to as the lobby level,
and the effectiveness of the security established at higher levels will depend
upon the amount of security and <u>control</u> that is exercised in the lobby. All
elevators to the building—the high-rise, medium-rise, and low-rise banks—
will usually terminate at this level. All fire stairwells will usually terminate
also at this level. In some buildings, these fire stairwells may lead directly
onto the street; however, in the majority of high-rise buildings in highly
populated urban areas, the stairwells terminate inside the building lobby.

    In a multitenant-type building, it is extremely difficult, and in some
cases actually impossible, to establish any type of control over personnel
using the elevators to proceed to higher levels. If occupancy of the building
was properly planned, it is possible to establish some controls at the elevators in the lobby level. For example, if a tenant is a large organization
occupying several floors and if the tenancy was properly planned, controls
could be established at any of the three banks of elevators. That is, if
this organization occupied the top floors, perhaps it would be possible to
establish personnel control through the use of a regular identification system
used to screen all personnel using the high-rise bank of elevators.

    This has been done in the Time-Life Building in New York City where a
security force is able effectively to control all personnel moving to and from

the floors occupied by that organization. Visitors are cleared through a receptionist and after it has been determined that the visitor will be seen, the individual is issued a pass that authorizes him or her to see a particular individual on a particular floor. To make this system even more effective, the visitor's identification passes or cards could be color coded by floor, and the visitor could be required to wear the identification. Supervisory personnel and patrolling guards could then more effectively police nonemployees visiting the organization.

Often deliveries are made to the basement and/or upper floors from the lobby level through the use of the freight elevator. This elevator should be controlled by the security force to ensure that a security guard is present at the elevator entrance when the freight elevator is being used. If a higher degree of security is desired, control over the freight elevator can be effectively established through the use of a closed circuit television camera and remote control of the elevator at the monitoring position.

All doors at ground level that are exits from fire stairwells and are used only in an emergency should be secured so that entry into the stairwell is not possible. The removal of all hardware on the outside of the door should be considered. When conditions require a high degree of security, consideration should also be given to the installation of closed circuit television cameras to observe doors that are not in a direct line of sight of a guard positioned in the lobby or stationed at a monitor.

The main building lobby should be kept as free as possible of items that have no operational value. Large potted plants and other items that have an aesthetic value only should be kept to a minimum, reducing as much as possible any area where explosives or firebombs might be left. Often, particularly in the lobbies of banking institutions, management will allow displays of various kinds of art. These will range from various types of sculptures to paintings and drawings that are displayed by placing them on large boards. More often than not, these displays are between the main entrance doors and the banking floor, creating an excellent location for the criminal to case the bank, checking movement of personnel and observing operations, by pretending to be admiring this art. Security personnel should always discourage these types of displays.

Exterior lobby doors should be secured after the normal business day. There will usually be some traffic by tenant personnel up to, and occasionally after, midnight. A traffic flow study should be conducted for a period of 2 or 3 days to determine the approximate time when the majority of the personnel have departed the building. When this information is secured, a locking schedule for exterior doors should be established, and all doors should be secured, with the exception of one or two depending upon local necessity. The doors that are not secured must be controlled, and the size of the security force and the sophistication of the security hardware system will determine exactly how control over these doors will be established.

Needless to say, any type of security system for a high-rise building must start with an effective identification system. If an identification system does not exist, it is extremely difficult to convince building management that one must be established. The cost of establishing the system must be calculated based on the number of occupants in the building and the average annual turnover; this information can be secured from each of the tenants. Without some means of identification, the effectiveness of any security program that may be designed is drastically reduced. Probably the most effective means of convincing building management that an identification system is needed is to have top management visit a high-rise building where such an identification system is in effect.

MEZZANINE LEVEL

The mezzanine level may be closed or open. If the mezzanine level is closed (that is, if the lobby cannot be seen from this level), the security established on this floor would be similar to the security established on the majority of operational levels. If the mezzanine level is open so that individuals on the mezzanine level can look directly down into the lobby, additional security precautions should be taken. If the mezzanine level is open, perhaps the main guard post and monitoring stations with all of the security hardware controls should be located there. Installing the monitoring station at this level removes it from the general view of the public and affords some degree of privacy.

If the building has a mezzanine, whether it is open or closed, the configuration of the building lends itself to the installation of closed circuit television cameras located so that activities in the lobby can be observed from an overhead position. This could normally be done with two cameras located diagonally across from one another each being equipped with a panning device and a zoom lens. If overhead cameras are used and if the layout of the lobby permits, the number of lobby cameras can be reduced. This depends on whether all doors and areas in the lobby can be adequately observed by cameras mounted at the mezzanine level.

OPERATIONAL LEVELS

The degree of security that will be required on any given operating floor obviously depends on the activity in that particular area. There are some areas, however, that will require a higher degree of security than others. For example, the mail room for the building will require a higher degree of security than the building manager's office. If mail is delivered to various floors by a mail escalator or through an arrangement of dummy elevators with the controls to the various floors located in the mail room, certainly the degree of security established for the protection of this area should be greater than if the mail was hand delivered through the elevator system.

Numerous other operational areas may exist depending upon the size and type of the high-rise structure. These areas will require various degrees of security.

COMPUTER LEVEL

If large corporations occupy an entire high-rise building or the majority of the space in the building, computer operations will normally be found in the building. We have devoted an entire chapter to physical security of computers and computer areas, and matters discussed there apply equally well to computer operations in a high-rise structure. Therefore, rather than repeat these discussions, we refer the reader to Chapter 13.

EXECUTIVE SUITE LEVELS

I have often found in auditing the security program of a high-rise structure that adequate security existed in numerous areas; however, the executive suite level or levels lacked any semblance of security. As often as not, this was because management resisted any security being established.

The executive suite levels must be secured, and management must be convinced that security is required. There are numerous methods of securing an executive suite, and the method to be used will be determined by the configuration of the floor. However, in all instances these floors are serviced by elevators; therefore, the protection provided should start at the elevators. One method is to enclose the elevator doors so that a lobby is created. This can be done through the use of various types of material; however, the use of impact-resistant glass, with the receptionist controlling the door through an electrical latch arrangement has been found to be quite effective. The lobby should be constructed and the doors arranged so that the receptionist can observe the elevators from her position. Doors leading into fire stairwells and the lobby restrooms should be excluded from the protected area. Executive suites will contain restrooms, small kitchen facilities, and so on, that can be excluded from the lobby being created.

I once surveyed a building that had adequate security at the ground level, at the basement level, and at the various operation levels. It was obvious that a great deal of thought and planning had resulted in an overall effective program for building security. However, the executive suite was completely unprotected and directly above the executive suite was a large meeting area that could be used by various organizations in the city. Meetings and other activities were conducted both during normal business hours when the execu-

tives were present and after business hours. During the period of the survey, I spent some time on the executive level, and on three different occasions, unescorted nonemployees using the meeting area exited the elevator
on the executive suite by mistake. Needless to say, this created a great
deal of confusion, in addition to exposing the entire executive suite to unauthorized entry.

In another building occupied by a huge conglomerate, the executive suite
is located on the uppermost operational level. Security personnel are used
to monitor the elevators and control the executive floor during duty hours;
however, if an executive decides to remain after the normal business day
when traffic to and from the executive offices has ceased, the security guard
secures the elevator lobby from the remainder of the offices by closing a
tool-resistant steel gate, similar to a day gate in a walk-in bank vault. The
guard then assumes other duties, and the executives unlock the gate and
again secure it as they depart. Custodial personnel and their equipment
are searched by a member of the security force before they are authorized
to enter the executive suite office area.

The amount of security that is necessary for the protection of executive
personnel is normally determined by the size of the organization and its
activities. However, regardless of these two considerations, enough security must be established to ensure that personnel not authorized in the executive suite level cannot gain access to it.

GUEST AREAS

Many large organizations that have operations throughout the various countries of the world will provide guest accommodations in the office building
for either foreign dignitaries or their own executive personnel who are
visiting the corporate headquarters. These guest accommodations eliminate
the need for this category of personnel to remain in public hotels or motels
and furnishes the personal security necessary.

The security established for the protection of the personnel using these
areas should be similar to the electronic protection used in residential
security with the exception, possibly, that closed circuit television cameras
may be used to monitor lobby or corridor areas. The protection should
include point protection at all peripheral openings and, if necessary, "man-
traps" using motion detectors or photoelectric cell devices to further secure
elevator and fire stairwell openings at the core of the building after the
occupants have retired.

Obviously, all of the devices are monitored at the building security console or security headquarters, and the protection system should include
some "panic buttons" located in the bedroom or possibly the den area, and
one should certainly be located near the entrance door.

I have often wondered why motels and hotels at which dignitaries, enter-
tainers, and personnel with a high publicity exposure usually stay do not

install protective alarm systems in those suites that are normally reserved
for this category of personnel. A year or so ago, an actress staying at a
New York motel was raped in her room. The incident resulted in a lawsuit
being brought against the motel owners, and the actress was awarded $2.5
million by a Brooklyn federal court jury. I do not know whether or not the
suite used by the actress was protected with any electronic protection;
however, such protection would possibly have prevented the incident.

EQUIPMENT LEVELS

In many high-rise structures, air-conditioning, heating, and air-return
equipment is located in the uppermost levels of the building in an area
usually referred to as the "equipment penthouses."
    These areas are also often used as a spectator promenade, particularly
where the view from this level is attractive or unusual for one reason or
another. The establishment of the spectator promenade immediately reduces
the security in these areas, and often the operating engineer and his control
boards are purposely exposed so that visitors to the building may observe
within. In this case, only ordinary plate usually separates the spectators
from crucial building controls. If building owners and management insist
that the spectator be given a view of the sophisticated controls, impact-
resistant glass should be installed. However, because the majority of the
people who are permitted to view this equipment do not understand it anyway,
it would appear that the area should be completely enclosed by walls and
solid wooden doors and not even be labeled as the building equipment control
room.
    The spectator promenade areas are usually open during a specific portion
of a day, and the public is invited to visit the area and spend as much time
as they desire. Usually, the area is secured at a specific time, and all
spectators are asked to leave. If promenade areas exist, a specific elevator
should be designated to be used to reach this area. If the area is large,
and depending upon the number of spectators on any particular day, consideration should be given either to using a patrolling guard in the area
during the period the promenade is open or to installing closed circuit television to permit constant observation during the open period. In any event,
the area must be searched immediately after visiting hours to ensure there
are no "stay-behinds."

ELEVATOR SECURITY

Instances of attacks and robberies occurring in elevators appear to be increasing throughout the country, indicating that high-rise building security
perhaps needs to be increased.

There are two simple methods of increasing the safety and well-being of personnel using elevators. One is the use of a closed circuit television camera with a wide-angle lens that is monitored by the security force. Another is the installation of an impact audio device that would open the listening circuit and alert the guard at the monitor should a person scream or shout for help.

The freight elevator should be included in the closed circuit television surveillance system, and the fact that activity on the elevator can be observed should be openly advertised. In many instances, custodial service personnel use the closed elevator to secret items either on their person or in their packages. The use of closed circuit television in the freight elevator will completely eliminate this possibility.

EMERGENCY STAIRWELLS AND DOORS

Security procedures and policies should be established to prohibit tenants from using emergency stairwells for operational purposes. The use of emergency stairwells for operational purposes immediately reduces the effectiveness of the overall building security program, not only for the tenant using the stairwell, but for all of the tenants in the entire building.

If there is an operational necessity for personnel to move frequently between floors and if using the elevator would not only cause an inconvenience but would be extremely time-consuming, it is far better to construct stairwells inside the protected area from one level to the other. Sometimes, if the flow of personnel between floors is high, escalators are installed between the involved floors. Whether an escalator or an inside stairwell is used, building security will not be compromised.

All emergency stairwell doors should be equipped with locking devices so that they cannot be opened from the stairwell side. Free egress from the floors into the stairwell must, of course, be preserved. A newly constructed high-rise building I recently surveyed has electrical latches installed on every emergency stairwell door in the building. These can be controlled either individually or collectively by the security guard at the console. In addition, a two-way communication system between the security console and each emergency stairwell door has been installed. Should an individual not familiar with the building move into the stairwell and not be able to return to any of the floors, he or she can merely depress a button and have immediate communication with the security force. This arrangement also allows the use of the emergency stairwell for operational purposes by tenants who may require this access. The electrical latches are released on the doors at the levels being used, and the tenant assumes the responsibility for any security violations that may occur in their area as a result of the open doors.

RESTROOMS

Restrooms that are located in the service core of the building, as most of them are, are used not only by the tenants on that floor, but also by visitors. They may also be used by any who happen to have unauthorized personnel who happen to have gained access to the floor.

Incidents of criminal attacks, including rape and robbery, are on the increase in these areas, and the restrooms can no longer be left unlocked. This applies to both male and female restrooms. In a recent incident, two gunmen entered a male restroom at an industrial facility and, in the course of about 30 minutes, robbed and held captive 14 male employees. The incident occurred just prior to shift change, ensuring that the maximum number of employees would enter the restroom in a short period of time and affording the criminals an effective escape by permitting them to mingle with the employees departing the facility. Obviously, this facility at that time had practically no security program and absolutely no system for identifying and controlling personnel moving into and out of the facility.

Restrooms are usually secured with key-operated locks that had originally been installed on the doors or that are newly installed. To reduce the number of keys that would have to be issued in any given organization, the receptionist or switchboard operator will normally have the keys to both the male and female restrooms. In most cases these keys will be found lying on his or her desk, with a large metal or wooden tag labeled "male" or "female" attached to the key. The tag attached to the key is sufficiently large to reduce the possibility that personnel will place the key in their pocket or purse, thus causing inconvenience for others. However, the key is available and conveniently marked for anyone desiring to perpetrate a crime in the restroom. I have on numerous occasions distracted the receptionist and picked up both keys without being observed. Later I have replaced the keys without him or her ever having knowledge that they had been taken.

The use of mechanically operated cypher locks should be considered for securing all restrooms where the degree of security requires that they be locked. This eliminates the need for using any keys; should a visitor need to enter the restroom, he or she can either be escorted or given the proper sequence of numbers to disengage the lock. Combinations can be changed in a matter of seconds by building maintenance personnel.

CONTROL OF DOORS AND ELEVATORS TO PARKING DECKS

Because of the lack of ground-level parking areas, numerous high-rise structures are serviced by parking decks that rise to a specific level. Parking decks that are six to eighteen levels in height are not uncommon. In many instances, access to and from the parking decks in the building is through a door that remains open constantly during the operational period.

Obviously, this arrangement negates any security that may be established in the lobby or any other level.

Most of these parking decks are serviced by an emergency stairwell and an elevator, particularly if they rise above three or four levels. If elevators are available, consideration should be given to securing all of the doors that exist between the parking deck and the floor of the building, and procedures should be established that require all personnel to use the elevator and proceed to a given level and enter the building through a controlled entrance. The number of employees and perhaps the time of day will determine where this authorized access route to and from the parking deck elevator is established.

In one building I surveyed, there are only two entrances between the building and the 12 level parking deck. One entrance is controlled by the tenant and is used only by the personnel operating the mail room. The second doorway is located at the second level of the building, which is a shopping mall. This door is not controlled and is open during business hours for use by the public. However, because the remainder of the emergency stairwell doors on the shopping mall level are controlled by the security force, this opening does not create a security hazard for the remainder of the building.

CAFETERIAS AND DINING ROOMS

Many newly constructed high-rise buildings, particularly those that are occupied by huge corporations and that house their entire corporate headquarters, have been equipped with an employee cafeteria and dining rooms at various levels for executive personnel. When eating facilities exist, problems are created in the transport of foodstuffs to the preparation areas and the removal of garbage from the building. In addition, because the cafeterias are intended only for employees, problems may be created by unauthorized personnel attempting to use these facilities.

When a cafeteria exists, an identification system is required, and control must be established while it is open. Where the control is established and who executes the control depend largely upon the size of the eating facility. Unless it is extremely large, control can usually be exercised at the cash register or by operating personnel at the head of the cafeteria line.

A procedure and time schedule should be established to control the input of foodstuffs and the removal of garbage. These controls, although they will need to be tailored to specific situations, are basically no different than those controls discussed in previous chapters.

If the dining areas used by executives are on the levels that are already adequately protected, no further considerations are necessary, with the exception that personnel servicing these areas obviously need to be controlled. If the dining areas are on the same levels as the cafeteria and are adjacent to the employee cafeteria operations, further controls may be required.

Often meals and snacks are brought into the building by outside vendors after employees have called in an order. This is an extremely poor practice that probably should be discontinued. In most instances, employees are not authorized to eat at their desks, and if eating areas are furnished, food should be made available in vending machines.

GENERAL SECURITY MEASURES

From time to time, certain situations may require a change in security procedures. For example, vacant office space, regardless of its location, should always remain locked and should be checked during each patrol of the building or floor by the security force. Small offices that are vacated during the lunch period should be secured when the last occupant has departed. When secretaries or receptionists control access from elevator lobbies to the various floors, a relief schedule should be established to ensure that the post is not vacant. Often security guards will relieve receptionists during lunch periods and/or coffee breaks.

If it is not possible to have potted plants and other objects removed from lobby areas or the floors of the building, they should at least be kept to a very minimum and should be placed a considerable distance out from the wall. This is so that any objects foreign to the area can easily be seen by the patrolling security guards. Bombs are often left in lobby areas behind or in potted shrubbery, as well as behind waste containers or any other object that may be used to hide the bomb parcel.

Patrols of the building should be established, and the study and analysis of security requirements will indicate where and how often the guard should patrol. Sometimes it may not be necessary to patrol each of the floors after the first patrol of the building has been made. Security requirements may be met if only one additional patrol is conducted after the custodial personnel have completed their duties.

GENERAL KEYING PLAN

A building of any size will require that security personnel obtain the expertise of a locksmith to establish the locking requirements of certain areas in the building and the building as a whole, in order to obtain the highest degree of security at the most economical cost.

When construction of a new building has been completed and the contractor removes the contractor core or otherwise changes the locks so that the keys held by contractor personnel will no longer operate them, it is absolutely essential that key control be established immediately and assigned to one specific individual and maintained by him or her only. Certain policies and procedures regarding key issuance must be established, and the key control system must be inspected by either building management or the chief of the security force or any other disinterested party. The inspector must be completely familiar with the control established so that an effective inspection can be made. These inspections should be unannounced and should be made frequently enough to ensure that control is being maintained.

Security personnel should have a key to any area in which they will be authorized, and keys should be issued to the custodial force on a daily basis and recovered by the security force assigned to building protection. Outside contractors, such as concessionaires operating a cafeteria and/or dining rooms, should not be issued keys to any peripheral openings unless it is absolutely essential. Normally, if the security force is present and outside concessionaires need access to the building before it is opened for the operating day, procedures can be established to have the security guard present to admit these personnel.

Consideration should be given to locking not only restrooms, but also equipment rooms and storage rooms, with cypher locking devices rather than key-operated devices because the installation of a cypher-type lock eliminates the possibility that the lock will be picked.

MASS MOVEMENT OF FACILITIES

Police or security personnel will often be called upon for advice when a corporate organization intends to move from one location to another or from many locations to another. The current trend, one with which I do not necessarily agree, is to bring the corporate headquarters and all divisions together under one roof. Obviously this is being done for efficiency of operations; however, it appears to be placing "all of the eggs in one basket." In some instances, protection can be increased, particularly if security is given consideration during the planning stage. The relocation of administrative organizations continues to occur, and security personnel must become involved and consideration given to numerous situations.

I will cite an example of organizing the move of a large insurance company from five different buildings in the same city to a new high-rise building a few blocks away. The movement involved some 200 laborers recruited by the moving company from labor pools. These laborers had to be transported to the city where the move was being effected and had to be kept in this area until the move was completed. The move was scheduled for a weekend and was to be completed in approximately 48 hours.

The organization for the move consisted first of liaison with the local police department, which was asked to block off from public use the streets involved in the move. Because the move was to take place on a weekend, this restriction created no problems insofar as local traffic was concerned, and the area of the city being used was not used by through traffic.

Using rented cots and bedding, management set up a dormitory on some of the floors of the buildings being vacated. Specific restrooms were designated for use by the laborers, and portable showers were installed. A command post was established, and this was manned by the chief of security, a police liaison officer, certain representatives of the client, and communications personnel. A first-aid facility was also established and manned during the period by qualified personnel.

The company's employee cafeteria was used to feed the laborers who were operating in 8-hour shifts. That is, they worked 8 hours and were off 8 hours. The cafeteria was kept open all day and night, with food available at all times. The security force marked the routes to be taken by the loaded trucks from the buildings vacated to the new building and carried out a general surveillance of the operations from the roofs of certain buildings.

Special identification cards were printed by the company being moved, and all personnel authorized in either the buildings being vacated or the new building were issued one of these cards. No personnel were authorized in any of the buildings unless the identification card was produced. The cards were color coded so that personnel supervising the move and company employees could be distinguished from the hired labor force. Company employees authorized to be in the area or to take part in the move had been designated, and all other employees were required to remain out of the area until their normal work schedule on Monday morning. The only incident involving the identification and control system occurred when the president of the company attempted to enter the new building at about 2:00 A.M. Although he tried to gain access to the building at three entrances, he was not able to do so and was finally directed to the command post where he was issued an identification card.

The controls established resulted in the move being completed 12 hours sooner than scheduled, and, as far as the company was able to determine, the only item missing was a wall clock removed from the wall of the new building.

Planning for this move started some 4 months before the move was to take place. Attention to detail in every aspect of the move was the key to the success of the operation. The movement of any type of facility, whether it is a banking facility or a corporate headquarters, requires detailed advance planning, so that those portions of the plan that involve law enforcement authorities, the moving company, and other outside personnel can be thoroughly studied. Rehearsals, if worthwhile, should be conducted.

The information contained in this chapter will not solve all of the security problems that may face security personnel because some structures will require less security, whereas others may perhaps have critical areas that require tight security. The basic principles discussed in preceding chapters, coupled with the security planner's own ingenuity and the cooperation of building management, should result in an efficient, effective security program.

Once the security program has been formulated, procedures must be established to deal with any emergency that may occur. The emergency may be a bomb threat or a situation created by a natural phenomenon.

The security chief and members of building management should establish an emergency procedures manual to include building evacuation. The emergency procedures manual can be based upon information discussed in this and other chapters of this book that will assist in formulating the overall emergency plan.

It is important that all areas and activities in the building, particularly those discussed in this chapter, be given separate consideration. The plan should take account of the fact that only certain areas or the entire building may be involved in any particular emergency.

In planning the emergency procedures manual, for example, the actions, policies, and procedures to be followed should a bomb threat be received may be designed using information supplied in the chapter of this book dealing with bomb threats.

15

Hospital
and Health Care Security

The health care industry is the fourth largest industry in the United States and is probably the fastest growing segment of the economy today. There are almost 4 million people employed in the industry, which has skyrocketed in size in the last 10 to 12 years.

The material in this chapter will apply whether the surveyor is conducting a study of a hospital or of some other type of health care facility. The need to secure certain areas, departments, and operations is approximately the same, with the exception that some health care facilities, because of the primary type of care given patients and the size of the operation, will probably not require a study of as many areas as would a hospital, regardless of the size. The degree of security needed may vary. For example, the pharmacy of a small county hospital may not require the degree of security that is needed to protect a pharmacy in a hospital in a large metropolitan area. The criticalness of the area seldom changes, but the vulnerability may.

Prior to commencing the study, an analysis of the geographical location of the facility must be conducted, and the psychological and sociological outlook of the individuals or groups of individuals living or working in the area or in some other manner connected with it must be examined. Similarly, the location of a particular department within the hospital or health care structure will, in all probability, affect the overall organization of security in that particular area because the vulnerability to attack may be increased or decreased. For example, stronger security would be needed for a busy outpatient pharmacy that is <u>located on the street level</u> in a hospital building than would be required for an in-house pharmacy that is <u>located in upper levels</u> of the structure. Obviously, the pharmacy located at street level would, in all probability, be more likely to be attacked than would the pharmacy on the upper level. However, when analyzing the need of securing the area to prevent internal thefts and incidents, in all probability the degree of security that is required would be approximately the same at each location.

I once spent approximately 24 hours as an emergency patient in a very small county hospital in Mississippi. Because I was ambulatory, the pajamas and robe issued me by the hospital were all the authority I needed to roam at will throughout the building. I therefore conducted what can be considered a survey, although no report was rendered. Although the lack of security appeared appalling initially, after I considered the geographical location of the facility and the psychological and sociological outlook of the community, I soon realized that the degree of security required to adequately safeguard life and property was considerably less than that established when I conducted a survey of the largest privately owned hospital in the world with a bed capacity of (at that time) 1600.

Although the seriousness of the problems encountered varied drastically, the same basic problems existed. In the small hospital in Mississippi, I visited the boiler room area. I was greeted by the engineer on duty and was able to examine in detail these operations taking place in the basement without ever having been challenged. Apparently, the hospital pajamas and robe represented my credentials to be in the area. On the other hand, I was able to roam at will through the basement level of the large hospital with no more credentials than a suit and tie, carrying a very official looking clipboard containing a yellow legal pad. Perhaps an example will emphasize the different security needs of hospitals or health care facilities located in high- and low-risk areas. A speeder doing 60 miles per hour on local New York City streets creates the same hazards as a speeder doing 60 miles per hour in a rural community, but the degree of the problems created is certainly multiplied in New York City.

A detailed discussion of a hospital's security problems and techniques that may be employed to overcome them would take an entire volume by itself. This book is written to give the police department crime prevention unit officer and security surveyor sufficient information that, if tailored to a particular facility or area in the facility, will permit him or her to provide recommendations to management that will ensure that the degree of security required is established at the most reasonable cost.

In this chapter, then, we shall take an overall look at hospital organization by department. We shall highlight some of each department's likely security problems and briefly suggest remedial action to be taken. Detailed procedures for reducing or eliminating most of the major problems are also discussed throughout this book.

Those hazards that are peculiar to health care facilities only are discussed in some detail. The pharmacy, for example, is found in health care facilities with as much frequency as first-aid rooms are found in industrial plants. Because pharmacy operations pose critical problems, a good deal of time is spent discussing this area. Visitor control in health care facilities poses unique problems, and so a detailed discussion of the personnel control problem is presented.

TYPES OF PEOPLE LIKELY
TO BE ENCOUNTERED IN HEALTH CARE FACILITIES

Studying the types or categories of people that one deals with in a health
care facility will often result in eliminating many embarrassing situations
and creating a more favorable public relations image. There are five major
categories of people that are encountered in a health care facility.

1. <u>Patients</u>. This is the facility's commodity. Everything that occurs
in a health care facility evolves around improving patients' health. All
activity is directed at their comfort, their mental attitude, and their even--
tual discharge, not only in a better physical condition but with a favorable
attitude toward the hospital and its staff that will generate goodwill for the
facility and probably future business.

2. <u>Professional staff</u>. The people that make up this group are the doctors, surgeons, nurses, technicians, and the like. I do not intend to offend
any doctor, but doctors are more careless about security than any other
group of professionals I have had the pleasure to meet. Doctors still carry
the "black bag" that will contain drugs and expensive instruments. Yet, try
to convince doctors that they should place their instrument bag in the car
trunk and that they should lock their cars. To make matters worse, they
park nearest the hospital in an area marked for all to see, "DOCTORS
ONLY." This is like leaving the bank vault open on weekends, with the front
door unlocked. I have had surgery performed a couple of times and have
wondered who trusts who in a hospital when I am asked to remove all rings,
watches, and any other jewelry before being wheeled down the long corridor
to surgery.

3. <u>Administrative staff</u>. We have finally found a friend! The administrative staff is the first group of people in a hospital that anywhere closely
resembles any other group of workers. Here we are dealing with management in various levels of operations that make the health care facility "tick"
and keep it "ticking." This is where decisions are made although not necessarily approved. The administrative staff has to come up with answers
when a patient's personal belongings are stolen from his room. They must
ensure that cadavers have been properly disposed of, that there is sufficient
clean linen available, that food is nutritious and properly prepared. They
"run the facility," and they are the ones who will cooperate and give assistance to the individual who is organizing an appropriate physical security
program for the facility.

4. <u>Hourly employees</u>. These employees are not necessarily fourth in
importance, for they contribute their share to the successful operation of
the facility and without them the facility could not operate for any extended
period of time. But historically they are the creators of a great majority
of the security problems faced by health care installations. The greater
the population in this category, the greater the problem. Identification
techniques previously discussed can be applied to all personnel in a hospital,

but such techniques are especially important in the case of hourly employees. Apply, then, those principles of control already discussed and back up the regulations with stern disciplinary measures when infractions occur.

5. Visitors. This fifth group is made up of all sorts of people who visit patients in a hospital or health care facility. This group may also present serious security problems. I do not intend to imply that hospital visitors are thieves, but I do intend to make it clearly understood that a lot of thieves visit hospitals. And because of this, some sort of control must be established. The "kook" who dons a doctor's garb and examines female patients has never operated other than during visiting hours. To do otherwise would unnecessarily expose him.

We must also consider the attitude of the bona fide visitor. At work, the guard at an employee exit may require this person to open his lunch box or her purse so that the contents can be examined before they depart their place of work. Say this same individual visits the hospital later that evening, obviously to visit a close friend or relative. The attitude of this individual when approached by a security guard is completely different. At his place of employment he must comply with certain procedures; however, because he is visiting a loved one at a hospital, his attitude is completely changed. Therefore, a guard at a hospital must use methods that differ from those that would be appropriate at an industrial facility.

VISITOR CONTROL

After spending the better part of a day interviewing the administrator of a hospital who had been given the gigantic task of securing his building, which had, for starters, 57 peripheral doors at ground level, my first thought was to pack up my survey tools and go home. However, on second thought, the challenge revitalized my mental condition. Although absolute visitor control under these or similar circumstances is practically impossible, there are things that can be done to establish some degree of security. Even with 57 doors on the ground level, one can limit the employee and visitor entrances through peripheral door controls, enforce established visiting hours by training staff personnel to "police" visitors, train staff to challenge strangers found in areas where visitors should not be, and, if a security force is justified, and certainly under these circumstances it would be, patrol, patrol, and patrol.

In smaller hospitals where visitor control is possible, volunteers, rather than security guards, can often be used to effect this control. Volunteers can issue visitor passes to specific patient rooms and thereby control the number of visitors per patient at any given time. The passes can be color coded for each day of the week. Color coding and dating the visitor pass will ensure that, should a visitor depart other than through the authorized exit, the pass cannot be used on successive days without being immediately identifiable.

The patient, upon admission, should be thoroughly briefed on the periods during which visiting is authorized and should be requested to assist the hospital in enforcing these rules. Usually a patient will cooperate, but he or she must be made aware of the problems that exist if too many visitors are authorized in the hospital and if visiting hours are not enforced. The patient should be made aware that visiting hours are scheduled so that visitors do not interfere with patient treatment, patient feeding, or other patient care.

The nursing staff must be required to assist in policing visitors and in challenging strangers in their areas of responsibility in the hospital. This should extend to all supervisors of all departments, particularly supervisors assigned to the housekeeping and maintenance departments because they probably frequent more areas in the hospital than the supervisors of any other department. However, all supervisors must assist in personnel control in their immediate areas if any semblance of control of nonemployees is expected to be accomplished.

The control of emergency exits is necessary in larger hospitals where the issuance of visitor passes or other controls discussed are impractical. Emergency exit doors, particularly those nearest doctor offices or doctor lounges, are the ones most frequently violated. Emergency exit doors that are not to be used for operational purposes should be equipped with local alarms and signs indicating that the alarm will be activated if the door is used without authority. In construction of new hospitals, peripheral doors at ground level or that lead to ground level should be wired either to the guard headquarters or to the switchboard operator so that he or she can identify exit doors being used surreptitiously and can notify either the security force, if one exists, or a supervisor nearest the area. An electrically operated 10-inch bell should be installed above these emergency exit doors at the end of emergency stairwells and a sign should be put up announcing that the bell will be activated if the door is used. This will normally deter all but the person who has committed a crime in the facility and is using the alarmed door as a means of escape and younger people who have entered the hospital unescorted and are intent merely on creating disturbances.

While conducting a survey of a rather large hospital, I positioned myself outside an emergency exit door near a doctor's lounge that was clearly marked with a sign stating "Doctors—Please Do Not Use This As an Exit." I waited outside between 5:30 and 6:00 in the evening, and during that period there were seven violations. When the seventh doctor exited, I stepped in his direction and said, "Hey, Doc, hold that door." The doctor obligingly held the door open for me, and I was not only able to enter through an unauthorized opening but went directly to the doctor's lounge, picked up two expensive overcoats, and took them to the administrator's office, all this without being challenged by anyone, even though there were three doctors in the lounge preparing to leave.

This incident emphasizes the point that emergency exits must be controlled in some manner. The use of two "screw-eyes" and a railroad or similar type of seal to secure the door will often act as a deterrent, will not restrain rapid egress, and will certainly give the security chief after-the-fact information on whether or not the door is being used surreptitiously. Often, if door violations persist, the use of a tracing powder and an ultraviolet light may assist in determining who is approaching the door and from what direction.

In some instances, television cameras can be effectively used. These should be positioned outside the building where several doors and the area immediately adjacent to the building can be observed. However, in larger facilities, it may be impractical because of the expense involved in attempting to include individual emergency exit doors in a surveillance system.

One other security measure should be considered for control of emergency exit doors, particularly those that are remotely located or isolated from the corridors inside the building. In addition to installing a bell on these doors, an electrical line should be run to the nearest corridor or lobby, and should be attached to a red light that will be illuminated and remain illuminated if the door is violated. Often the emergency exits that are being used surreptitiously are so remotely located that even a 10-inch electrical bell at the location is unlikely to be heard by guards inside the building who are actively patrolling corridors and lobbies.

The next several paragraphs will discuss specific security problems in areas that are primarily found only in health care facilities. In other areas that have already been adequately covered, the discussion will pertain to only those techniques applicable particularly in health care facilities.

BUILDING SECURITY

We have already discussed controls that can be established to reduce the unauthorized use of emergency exit doors. The remaining peripheral doors must be examined individually to determine which of the doors can be secured so that entrance into the building is not possible. In all health care facilities, there are some doors that can be secured from about 5:00 or 6:00 P.M. and remain secured until approximately 7:00 A.M. Other doors cannot be secured until after visiting hours, when all visitors have departed the facility. Then these doors can also be secured. However, all peripheral doors must be considered to be emergency exits and must be equipped with the type of hardware that will facilitate speedy egress. Another point that must be kept in mind is that if a given door is to be secured against entry for specific periods of time, either the fire department must be notified and must approve the schedule, or security guards should be instructed to open the door should an emergency arise.

A study of each peripheral door, including a personnel traffic flow analysis must be made before any locking schedule for the peripheral entrances
can be established. However, surprisingly enough, the majority of the
peripheral doors at ground level at any health care facility can be secured
around 6:00 P.M. and remain secured until approximately 7:00 A.M. In
some instances, depending upon the location of the facility, these doors can
remain secured over the weekend when the majority of the operations are
considerably curtailed.

All hourly employees should be required to enter the hospital only through
authorized employee entrances and should be made to exit in the same manner. In some instances, more than one employee entrance will be needed
for the hourly employees because of the location of their work area or the
area to which they report initially. The best method I have found to ensure
that hourly employees enter and depart the facility through a specified doorway is to locate the time clock that is used by that employee in the immediate vicinity of the door. Those employees who work in the administrative
offices normally enter and leave through lobby areas and are usually quite
uncontrolled. Certain doors leading off the lobby area to the outside can
be designated for use by these employees to use, and, as a deterrent, a
security guard can be posted at the entrance at least at infrequent intervals
and to observe departing employees.

The use of anti-intrusion alarm systems and closed circuit television
surveillance systems, if not provided for during hospital construction, are
usually extremely expensive to install, and, in all probability, recommendation that such systems be installed will meet with little success. Consideration should be given, however, to the use of closed circuit television cameras
on the outside of the buildings and in operational tunnels that connect buildings.

Those principles discussed in the chapter on building security should be
considered while conducting the study of the building or buildings of a health
care facility. These principles should be tailored as needed to meet the
security requirements of each area of the facility.

AREA SECURITY

Except in the case of a large county hospital or a nursing home facility
where expansive real estate surrounds the facility's building, the establishment of any area security is usually not possible, with the exception of the
security furnished in the doctor's, visitor's, and other employee's parking
lots. Even in this area, the establishment of further security is not possible
because the parking lots are generally leased by professional operators
who, even though the property may belong to the hospital, have the responsibility of establishing security in the operation of the lot.

In instances where the parking lots are the responsibility of the health care facility, consideration must be given to proper illumination and the possible use of television cameras. Television cameras will not only increase the safety of individuals but will deter vandalism and theft from and of automobiles. If the health care facility is small and does not have a 24-hour-per-day security force, the cameras can be monitored at the switchboard. The operator should be instructed to notify local law enforcement authorities immediately if he or she observes any questionable incidents.

If a security force is used, an outside patrol using a motorized vehicle, probably a three-wheeled gasoline-driven vehicle, should regularly survey all outside areas and parking lots, with the patrol patterns being changed constantly. Obviously, when such patrols are used, communication between security force members will make the patrols that much more effective.

The nursing staff of most hospitals works shifts from 7:00 A.M. to 3:00 P.M., from 3:00 P.M. to 11:00 P.M. and from 11:00 P.M. to 7:00 A.M. The 11:00 P.M. shift change is the one that creates the most problems, usually in the form of attacks upon nurses as they move from the facility to their parked automobiles or from the facility to local bus stops. Patrols should be increased during this shift change, and security guards can be stationed along the route taken by the nurses from the facility to the bus stop or parking lot. This would immeasurably increase the safety of the nursing staff during the 11:00 P.M. shift change. When a security force does not exist or is so small that this service is impractical, local law enforcement agencies will often move their patrol cars into the area during the shift change and increase the personal protection of the nurses merely by increasing the patrol activities during a period from about 10:30 to 11:15.

In some of the more recently constructed hospitals, parking garages are available for the hospital staff and, in some cases, for visitors also. When such garages exist, a study should be conducted with a view toward reserving parking on the various levels or in areas of the various levels for certain categories of personnel that are employed by the hospital. The parking area for the nursing staff should be located as near as possible to the elevators or stairwells that they use, and the illumination of these areas should be sufficient to ensure the safety of the 11:00 P.M. shift change. The doctor's parking area should also be near stairways and elevators to increase the protection of their automobiles and any medical supplies or equipment that remain in the vehicles as well as to ensure that they can park quickly if they have to return to the hospital should an emergency involving one of their patients occur.

If the oxygen supply for the facility is stored outside the building, it should be further protected by an industrial-type chain link fence constructed according to the specifications previously outlined.

PROTECTIVE LIGHTING

The inspection of all outside and inside areas after dark will determine where illumination should be increased. Quite often, particularly in urban areas, all exterior illumination that can be considered a part of the protective lighting system is furnished by the spillage from existing public street lighting. In more rural areas, it may be necessary to install additional lighting to ensure that outside areas, at least those areas immediately adjacent to the facility's buildings, are adequately illuminated so that patrolling guards or the night staff can have observation for some 30 to 50 feet around each of the buildings. Inside lighting normally is reduced after visiting hours. However, sufficient protective lighting must remain to ensure that patrolling guards and the staff on duty can observe all areas inside each building still being used for operations.

PERSONNEL OFFICE

The personnel office ideally should be so located within the building that direct entrance into the area from the outside would be possible. This would ensure that applicants for employment do not wander through the hospital looking for the personnel office, perhaps creating pedestrian congestion in the lobbies and corridors. At the very least, the employment office should be located in an area where those individuals applying for employment are out of view of the public and do not interfere with patient care. On occasion I have witnessed applicants for employment securing applications at the personnel office and then completing the application in the main lobby of the hospital. This type situation should be avoided because, particularly in larger facilities, high turnover of hourly personnel would create a great deal of traffic into and out of the personnel or employment office. If at all possible, the employment office should be located away from the main facility; that is, in another building if there is one. Several of the larger hospitals have established employment offices away from the hospital, and all employment activities are conducted from these offices. Often this results in more efficient personnel operations and certainly means less confusion and fewer security hazards at the health care facility.

Probably because of the high turnover of hourly employees, very little background investigation of employees is conducted. Often only the person's name, address, Social Security number, and telephone number are listed on a simple 3-by-5-inch card. This is merely enough information to place the individual on the payroll. We have previously discussed background investigation and encourage those studying hospital security or in charge of hospital security to insist that adequate background investigations are conducted.

ADMISSIONS AND DISPOSITION DEPARTMENT

The name of this department has changed in certain areas of the country
in the past few years; however, the operations remain approximately the
same. This is the department that admits and discharges all patients that
move into and out of the hospital.

This department is also usually in charge of the patient's personal belongings, because unless a patient enters the hospital through the emergency
room, these are the first hospital staff members to come in contact with
the patient.

The safekeeping of personal belongings of patients obviously is a necessity, and the number of beds or patient capacity of the hospital will dictate
the type and size of security container necessary to protect these belongings
adequately. Security envelopes specially manufactured for use in hospitals
are available. They are serially numbered, and the depositor's check or
receipt and the identification label have the same identification number.
The patient's belongings are sealed in the envelope in his or her presence,
and he or she signs the identification tag on the envelope. It is then countersigned by the person receiving the belongings for deposit and dated. A
depositor's check or receipt is completed by the person receiving the belongings and also by the depositor and is dated. This check must be presented
to identify the depositor before the personal belongings are returned.

In some larger hospitals where patient turnover is considerable, I have
discovered the personal belongings of patients that have expired. On one
occasion, I found that cash in excess of $1600 and two obviously expensive
rings were still in the depository for patient's personal belongings 3 years
after the patient had died. Any personal belongings that are stored for the
patient in the admissions and disposition department or elsewhere in the
hospital should be inventoried at least semiannually. If a patient who has
deposited personal belongings with the hospital should die disposition of
deceased's personal belongings should be made as soon as possible. In
the instance cited above, a considerable amount of money had to be spent
in attempting to locate the next of kin of the deceased patient.

BUSINESS AND CASHIER'S OFFICE

These two offices or operations are discussed together because in most
instances they are very closely related. Either the business office will
handle cash and payments from patients, or, if the operation is large enough
to support a cashier's office, these transactions are conducted at this location.

The amount of cash handled normally is not very large because most
payments by patients are made by check. However, if the facility is very
large and if the gift shops, cafeterias that are open to the public, and the

vending machines throughout the facility are owned and operated by the hospital, the amount of cash that may be found at the cashier's office at any given time may be somewhat larger.

In one instance, I found that a hospital, a privately owned institution, operated all of the facilities mentioned above, and that after a normal week-end between $18,000 and $25,000 in cash was generated, including a few thousand dollars in coins. After the money had been removed from the vending machines and the safes in the cafeterias and the "shoe box" in the gift shop, it was counted, separated by denomination, and remained in the cashier's office until pickup by an armored car service between 11:00 A.M. and 1:00 P.M. on Monday. During this time the money was merely left on the floor in the cashier's office, which was unlocked and approximately 50 feet from the nearest lobby entrance. To make matters even worse, the individual responsible for this operation was the chief pharmacist who was already overburdened with work.

Obviously, when the cash being handled reaches figures in the hundreds or even thousands, additional precautions must be taken. Either bank deposits should be made, armored car service pickup scheduled more frequently, or secure money safes installed. A caution here: Never store cash in the same security container that is used to store the personal belongings of patients.

If hospital employees service vending machines and remove the money protection must be given to the cash as it is transported from one vending machine area to another and eventually to the cashier's office, regardless of the accounting procedures involved. Even though after a great deal of cash has been accumulated, the bags of coins become rather bulky and heavy and would be difficult to remove from the premises, further protection is required. Wheeling the bags of coins through a hospital corridor on one of the numerous types of hospital carts just does not get the job done. If necessary, a conveyance should be fabricated so that the money can be placed inside a metal container and locked, preferably with a combination-type lock. This arrangement will certainly deter an attack upon this individual, if not completely eliminate the chance that one will occur. However, the individual removing cash from the machines must be cautioned to be particularly alert when the security container is open while he or she is making deposits.

In larger hospitals, the cashier's office should be considered as a banking or financial operation, and the use of customer counters, impact-resistant glass, electrically operated doors, and holdup alarms must be considered. If the operation of the cashier's office still includes cashing employee pay checks on pay day, this procedure should be eliminated, even if it means giving the employee an additional 10 or 15 minutes to run across the street to the nearest branch bank.

ACCOUNTING DEPARTMENT

The accounting department requires very little additional security over that established for other administrative offices at the facility, with the exception that security personnel should be concerned with the security and the storage of blank checks used for both the payroll and accounts payable and the check signature plates for these two accounts. The blank checks should at least be locked in a file cabinet, and the payroll and accounts payable checks, if of different design, should be stored in two different containers. The check signature plates, if they exist, should not be stored with the blank checks; instead they should be given added protection by storing them in a safe or vault that is secured with a combination-type lock. If a walk-in vault is available, check signing machines can be located in the vault and secured automatically when the vault is closed after the business day. Remember that patient's belongings should not be stored in the vault unless they can be secured in safe deposit boxes. The envelopes containing personal belongings must never be exposed to access by unauthorized individuals.

PHARMACY DEPARTMENT

Almost all health facilities of any size have a pharmacy operation. In some instances, two or more pharmacies may be located in the same hospital complex. As previously discussed, the location of the pharmacy within a given building will determine the degree of security that is required to protect it against outside attack.

Robert J. Lee, Director of Security Services at St. Mary's Health Center in St. Louis, reported in the February 1976 issue of The National Locksmith that in October 1974 he had mailed questionnaires to 384 hospitals inquiring about the extent of criminal activity within hospital facilities. Of 19 items asked in the questionnaire, 14 concerned phony or altered prescriptions, internal theft, burglaries, and holdups. Two questions sought to identify the precautions hospital pharmacies are taking to meet these criminal challenges, and the last three were designed to categorize the respondents by bed size, by state, and by the type of neighborhood in which the hospital was located (that is, rural or metropolitan).

One hundred sixty-eight hospitals responded, and the results were analyzed by computer. Of the facilities that responded, 70 percent were located in metropolitan or suburban areas. These hospitals reported the largest percentage of criminal activity. Rural hospitals reported fewer crimes and fewer security precautions.

Altered or phony prescriptions were reported by 72 hospitals, with 81 percent of these incidents being reported by metropolitan hospitals having more than 200 beds. The 72 hospitals reported that 1,529 of these phony prescriptions were presented during the first 9 months of 1974, with most of the prescription blanks having been stolen from the hospital to which they were presented after being falsified.

Obviously, then, this is the first area that must be considered, and controls and procedures must be adopted to ensure protection of the blank prescription slips, not only at the pharmacy, but throughout the doctor's offices as well.

A second common occurrence that I have found, particularly in larger hospitals, is that salespeople representing various pharmaceutical companies are allowed to enter the pharmacy and inventory their own stock. This appears to be a common practice, and no control over these individuals is exercised. I will admit that in all instances the salespeople were identified prior to being authorized inside the pharmacy storage area; however, no determination was made whether or not these persons were in fact still employed by the pharmaceutical companies they were representing. This practice should be eliminated; there are many other simple methods that are not time-consuming that can be used by pharmacists in their resupply procedures.

One such method is to draw a colored line along the entire length of each shelf used for storage, the line being a set distance back from the front of the shelf; when the items stored on that shelf are used to a point where the colored line is uncovered, the clerk automatically requisitions a predetermined supply of the product. And when the requisitioned products arrive, the stock present on the shelf is moved to the front of the shelf and the new supply placed behind it. This same procedure or a variation thereof can be used to ensure that items having a predetermined shelf life are properly disposed of and replaced.

The pharmacy, like the cashier's office, should possibly be protected by anti-intrusion alarms, strict personnel control, and holdup alarm systems.

Regardless of its size, the pharmacy will normally handle a considerable amount of cash during any given period. In organizing the security of the pharmacy department, consideration must be given to cash handling, and proper safeguards must be included in the overall protection program.

One word about narcotics control. Because narcotics are federally regulated and federal examiners or inspectors frequently visit pharmacies, usually the security and control of these substances is adequate. However, I have found that often procedures that are used to transport narcotics between the pharmacy and the using unit should be changed. Adequacy of the storage cabinet at the using unit should also be examined. It is not unusual that nurses at a nursing station will use the narcotics cabinet to secure their purses, even though other secure areas are available.

In almost all health care facilities, particularly hospitals, an emergency supply of various drugs and antibiotics is available, usually to the head nurse, should an emergency occur and these items be required before the pharmacist can return to the hospital. When "reach-through" refrigerated and nonrefrigerated cabinets are used, usually there is no special security problem. However, "reach-through" cabinets should be located in a well-lighted area, and if security patrols are made of the hospital, a watch clock key should be located in the vicinity to ensure that the cabinet is under the observation of the patrolling guard.

If no such cabinets are available and the emergency supply is located inside the pharmacy, with the nurse being given a key to the pharmacy for emergency use, the routine used for the security of this key should be checked to ensure that it is not available to anyone except the head nurse or chief of nurses on any given shift. This can normally be accomplished and controlled merely by establishing a record that is maintained in the same place where the supply of narcotics is stored and that is inventoried during each shift change. The key is merely passed on during the inventory and signed for by the recipient.

GENERAL STORAGE AREA

Persons who are not thoroughly familiar with hospital operations often are not sure of the difference between the general storage area and central supply. To clarify this, the general storage area is that operation which receives and issues practically every commodity that is purchased and used by the hospital, including those items used in central supply. The only items that will not come through the general storage area are usually foodstuffs and some drugs, medications, and other items of this nature that are delivered directly to the dietary or pharmacy department.

Central supply, on the other hand, is that operation which supplies sterile equipment and material that is used in surgery and throughout the nursing operations.

The inspection procedures and security controls established in the general storage area are similar to those that apply to warehousing operations. Access to the area should be limited to authorized personnel, the method of accountability in receipt of material and in issuing this material to using units should be studied carefully. Physical security of the area is determined by its location, size, and the amount of material that will be stored at any particular time.

One method of determining losses of highly pilferable items such as silverware and china issued to the dietary department and sheets, pillowcases, blankets, and items of this nature issued to the laundry and consequently to the using units in the hospital is to set up a detailed list by item. For example, the list should indicate numbers of forks, knives, spoons, teaspoons, and so on, for the dietary department, and numbers of sheets, pillowcases, blankets, and other items of this type for the laundry department. Check the records in the general storage area over a specific period of time (I usually go back 1 year from the date the survey is being conducted) and list the number of each item received during that period and the number issued to the using department. Then check the number that are still on hand. It will be immediately obvious whether items are being lost or records are being maintained inaccurately. Using this list, check the dietary department and the laundry department to determine the number of each item they received, the number still on hand, and the number that have been destroyed, because in both instances items are either breakable or will wear out. This simple inventory of approximately two dozen items will indicate to the surveyor the probability of loss through thefts and carelessness in these two departments, which handle the majority of the pilferable items used at a health care facility.

CENTRAL SUPPLY

Central supply is normally located some place near the center of the building and is usually near the operating rooms. This area will normally be manned by only a small number of employees, and issuance of items is usually accomplished by use of a Dutch door. The central supply will normally be open 24 hours per day; if not, a key to the area will be available either to the chief of nurses or the security force so that access to the area can be gained should emergency supplies be required in the operating rooms. In the past 2 or 3 years, a great deal of the surgical hardware such as scissors, forceps, tweezers, and items of this nature have been replaced by one-time-use throwaway instruments, and this has lessened thefts of more expensive surgical equipment.

Usually central supply can merely be locked and secured with a good-quality key-operated lock, and if control of the key is established, the operation is adequately secured. However, the use of some inexpensive, effective anti-intrusion alarms may be considered to increase protection.

PURCHASING DEPARTMENT

The purchasing department is usually located near the general storage area, and all purchases made by the hospital, including drugs and medicine that may be delivered directly to the pharmacy, are normally made by this department, receipted for, and approved for payment. The purchasing department requires little more security than any of the other administrative offices in the facility, with the exception that records stored in the department should be placed in metal containers, preferably with a fire rating of at least 1 hour, which should remain locked after business hours.

Items that are returned to the supplier are normally processed through
the purchasing department, and the survey should include an examination
of the procedures used. The storage of the items being returned and the
reason why they are being returned should be recorded on the documents.
On occasion, I have found that items that have been removed from the
pharmacy or using units throughout the hospital because the shelf life had
expired are not being disposed of properly or being returned to the supplier,
whichever procedure applies. This not only invites thefts or removal of
property from the hospital without authority but also creates a potentially
dangerous health problem and subjects the hospital to a liability suit brought
against the facility because of negligence on the part of the facility's personnel.

LAUNDRY DEPARTMENT

We have already discussed the system that should be used to check the
major items issued to the laundry and dispensed to the using units. If the
spot inventory indicates major discrepancies, it might be necessary to
interview personnel from the purchasing department and supervisors from
the general storage area and possibly even accounting to determine where
the discrepancies lie. This should be resolved before the survey continues.
     The hours of operation, the number of employees in the laundry, and its
location in the facility will determine the amount of physical security that
should be considered for the protection of the building and its contents.
The surveyor must consider each peripheral opening through which items
that have been laundered can be passed from the building to personnel outside. This is particularly important in metropolitan areas where the laundry
facilities are immediately adjacent to a public street or public or private
alley.
     In some instances the health care facility administrator will authorize
certain employees, usually those that work in the laundry and the nurses,
to have their personal clothing laundered at the facility. This is an extremely
poor practice and establishes an excellent opportunity for the employee to
remove hospital property when they remove their personal laundry. If this
procedure exists, the security surveyor should recommend that it be stopped
immediately.
     Insufficient marking of various items of linen, including sheets and
pillowcases, will often create a problem of identifying an item if an employee is apprehended in possession of the item outside the facility or even
at his or her home. Marking a sheet, for example, along its hem does not
really suffice because only a small portion of the sheet, perhaps 2 or 3
inches, need be cut off to remove the marking; the sheet can be rehemmed
and still be usable. Similar marking of a pillowcase does not render the

pillowcase unusable if the marking is removed. Consider marking the
sheets across the corner at the top and at the bottom so that if the marking
is removed, the sheet is no longer usable. If this is done, and if pillowcases are marked on the inside in the center, theft of sheets and pillowcases
can be reduced greatly. In larger, more modern hospitals, the theft of
linens such as hand towels and washcloths can be eliminated through the
use of disposable paper items.

Regular blankets and thermal blankets are now being purchased with the
name of the facility permanently imprinted on the article, and this has substantially reduced the thefts of these more expensive items; however, one
cannot be complacent, and the overall controls established in the laundry
department and its operations must consider the possibility that these items
may still be stolen.

If linen is being used and the facility is equipped with soiled-linen chutes,
the opening at the using unit must remain locked at all times except when
actually in use, not only to ensure that clean linen is not placed into the
chute for later recovery, but also to ensure that items stolen on the various
floors are not wrapped in soiled linen and placed in the chute for later recovery at the chute termination point.

In addition to securing the chute opening, the termination point, which
usually is a rather large basement room in which one or more chutes may
terminate, must also remain secured, and the keys to the termination point
controlled. Consideration should be given to having a member of the security force inspect these soiled-linen rooms from time to time to determine
whether or not items stolen throughout the complex are being removed in
this manner.

In facilities where linen is still being used, the sewing and mending
operations should be included in the study. Determine who makes the
decision whether or not an item is no longer salvageable. If the item is
determined not to be of any further use, ensure that the procedures include
tearing the item into small enough pieces to ensure that the item in fact
does lose its identity and can no longer be used as intended. The procedure
used in accounting for the material being repaired in the sewing and mending
operations must also be scrutinized.

The security of new stock available at the laundry facility should be
examined, and this stock should receive at least the same degree of security
as that established while it is still in the general storage area.

DIETARY DEPARTMENT

If the dietary department in a hospital is concession operated, it probably
can be excluded completely from the security study. However, if the department is being operated by the hospital, it should be considered as vulnerable
to thefts as are the laundry and housekeeping departments.

The study of the dietary department should begin with an interview with the dietician and a review of the administrative procedures used in the receipt of perishables, dairy products, meats, and dry foods.

In most instances, these items are delivered on different days of the week directly to the dietary department over a receiving dock in the immediate area. Sometimes dry or canned foods may be received by general storage and issued on a requisition basis from that area.

The study of the department should include the type and frequency of inventory, the security of the meat lockers, and whether or not a running inventory is being maintained so that at any given time the type and amount of meat in the refrigerator is recorded and can be inventoried.

The method of issuing food to the head cook or chef should be examined, including the security of the food that is being left in the kitchen area overnight for the preparation of breakfast the following day. The procedure of making this food available to cooks and other dietary employees is necessary because they report for work 2 or 3 hours in advance of the time the dietician arrives.

The security of all refrigerators and the control of the keys used to secure them should be examined, as should any storerooms in the dietary area.

The method used to issue food from the storeroom to the kitchen should be examined. During the period of the survey, at least one meal should be checked by comparing the amount of food indicated on the master menu with the amount indicated as being issued by the storeroom. This check should include perishables, dairy products, and, in particular, meat products.

A checklist of silverware should be made, as previously discussed, and a determination made of the accountability of broken plates, saucers, cups, and items of this type. If food is moved from the kitchen area to the various using units by cart, the procedures used to account for all silverware, utensils, and number of meals should also be checked.

In newer hospitals, a device referred to as the Tray-O-Later is often installed; this device reduces the exposure, not only of food, but of utensils, dishes, and silverware to possible theft. This method of delivering meals to the various using units is similar to the operation of a mail escalator. Specific meals for patients are placed on a tray and are delivered to the proper using unit through a belt and lift arrangement. After the meal has been consumed, a reverse procedure returns the tray and items to the kitchen, and each tray can be checked individually to ensure that all items that were on the tray have been returned. If this method of serving meals is used, the surveyor should check to determine that trays are inventoried when they are returned.

Most garbage removal operations now consist of garbage disposal units which no longer require that any garbage or leftover food be removed by hand from the premises. However, in those areas where garbage is still removed in this manner, the procedure should be reviewed in detail, and the operation should be observed covertly to determine whether or not procedures are being followed. Often items such as hams, fowl, and other meats, more expensive canned products such as tuna fish, salmon, and asparagus, and other foodstuffs are stolen from the dietary department merely by placing them in a plastic bag and dropping the bag into the garbage container. The bag of food is recovered later, either off the dock or in collusion with the individuals that actually remove the garbage. In some rural areas, garbage at a health facility is still being picked up by local hog farmers. Close scrutiny of this operation will often reveal that food-stuffs are being stolen in this manner through collusion between hospital employees and the individual removing the garbage.

The overall physical security of the dietary area, including the kitchen and storerooms, should be reviewed, and a sufficient amount of security should be established so that the area cannot be entered by workers on the night shift who will often eat in the kitchen area simply because no other cafeteria facilities exist. If there is a practice of allowing these workers to use the kitchen facilities, an attempt should be made to discourage it; and if the procedure will continue, additional security may be needed in the area of the refrigerators and the storeroom. This additional security may be established merely by ensuring that an adequate locking device is installed and that the keys properly controlled or by installing a small microwave anti-intrusion alarm directed toward the entrances to these areas. The alarm can be set up to sound locally or it can be tied into an alarm console if one exists.

Often the dietary department will be issued silverware and china still in their cases. Because of the bulk of the material and the normally limited storage space in the storeroom, these items will be found stored in the kitchen area, often in the vicinity of the receiving docks. Procedures should be adopted to issue these items to the dietary department only when needed; if issued in bulk, they should be secured in a storeroom.

HOUSEKEEPING DEPARTMENT

The housekeeping department is usually located in one of the basement levels, and the size of the operation, obviously, will depend upon the size of the facility. In almost all instances, a storeroom of sufficient size is available for the storage of supplies that are required by the department during a week's period.

This department also has possession of keys to all areas of the hospital in order that the various offices, laboratories, and areas normally kept secured after business hours can be cleaned. Key control in the housekeeping department is always found to be a major problem, with control being extremely loose and in many cases with key accountability completely lacking. Therefore, the survey of this department should start with an examination of the security of the keys issued and the records maintained of those keys that were received; an inventory should be conducted of all of the keys that are used on a day-to-day basis. This will usually require only that the keys be checked at the end of the day shift because, normally, regardless of the size of the hospital, there are very few housekeeping personnel during second and third shifts. If there are second-shift and third shift housekeeping operations, these keys can easily be checked at shift change. Only those keys actually needed by late-shift personnel should be issued.

Because the housekeeping department will usually need keys to every area in the hospital, there is a definite need for a sturdy, lockable key cabinet, and procedures outlined for key control must be followed explicitly. Too often rings of keys are found merely hung on pegs or nails on a board installed on the wall and are even identified as to the lock the keys will operate.

Annual turnover among the housekeeping staff is almost always in excess of 100 percent, and, therefore, key control becomes all the more important.

The security of the housekeeping storeroom is probably the next area that should be examined. This study should include an examination of the records indicating the receipt, issuance, and quantity use of expendable cleaning materials. A comparison of the amount of material used by two or more individuals who are assigned the approximate same size areas with the same type of duties will immediately indicate whether or not some of these individuals are diverting the expendables to their own use.

The expensive machinery used in the housekeeping department, such as floor buffers and commercial-type vacuum cleaners, is usually stored on the floors on which it is used in what are referred to as "janitor rooms." The security of these rooms should be checked to ensure that they can be locked and that they remain locked except when items are being removed from the room or being replaced. The record of losses of these machines over the past year should indicate whether they are being stolen by employees or others who enter the hospital for the purpose of stealing such property.

In newer hospitals, trash chutes are installed on the various floors. They either terminate in the basement, where the trash is removed manually, or in a shredder and baling machine, in which case the trash is removed by an outside contractor. If shredders and balers are used, in all probability there will be no security hazard involved in trash removal. However, if it is necessary to remove the trash from the termination point manually, chutes must be locked at the user's end, and rooms at the termination of the chutes must also be locked and controlled in a manner similar to that described when we were discussing security of laundry chutes.

Finally, the surveyor should concern himself with the organization of the department and supervision of employees. These employees normally are issued color-coded uniforms; if so, they are easily identified. The surveyor should concern himself with the fact of whether or not supervisors are spending their time in the department offices or actually supervising their personnel. If adequate supervision over these personnel is exercised,

incidents of theft, misuse of equipment, and entry into unauthorized areas
can be greatly reduced, if not eliminated in some operations. The lack of
supervision in this department will usually result in a high rate of pilferage
and theft not only of hospital property, but of patients' property as well.
Because employees from this department are able to enter all areas and
because turnover and absenteeism mean that individual assignments may
be rotated or changed daily, it is difficult for security to receive the cooperation of the nursing staff and others in policing these employees.

CAFETERIA OPERATIONS

If the health care facility has a cafeteria that is operated on a concession
basis, the surveyor need not concern himself with it, with the exception
that, like a concession-operated dietary department, patrols by the security
force through the area will have to be conducted.

If the cafeterias are operated by the facility, the study of the area should
generally follow the same format used to determine the security requirements in the dietary department. However, because cafeteria operations
will require the handling of a certain amount of cash, additional precautions
to safeguard the cash will be required. A review of the procedures used
in cash handling and accountability should also be made.

Cafeterias that are operated by the facility will often be supplied through
the dietary department in the case of perishables and through the general
storage department in the case of nonperishables. In either case, the method
of issuance, security of storage areas, methods of inventory, and garbage
removal operations must be examined. The security of storerooms and
refrigerators after the cafeteria is closed or is only in partial operation
for the convenience of second- and third-shift employees should be included
in the study.

GIFT SHOPS

Gift shops at a hospital can be operated either by a concessionaire or by
management of the facility. If it is concession-operated, the security
responsibility as far as the hospital is concerned is a moral obligation only,
because losses sustained through employee theft or shoplifting are the problems of the concessionaire and not hospital management.

If the gift shops are hospital-operated, in all probability they will be
under the management of one hospital employee with volunteer sales personnel. Often these volunteers are inexperienced in retail store operation,
and the security surveyor may well be justified in recommending that some
training be given the volunteers regarding all the security hazards that exist
in this type retail operation.

An examination of the storage areas should include receipt of and issuance to the retail floor of all the material sold in the shop and the physical security and inventory procedures in the storage rooms. Often, no storage areas are available in the immediate vicinity of the gift shops, and storage rooms in one of the basement levels are used. Obviously a basement storeroom may require higher security than a storeroom immediately adjacent to or behind the gift shop. Furthermore, the study should also include the safety of the personnel (usually female) who will be transferring items from the storeroom to the gift shop.

The procedures used in handling cash will need to be examined, and procedures already established for the cafeteria and pharmacy will probably suffice for the protection of cash in the gift shop operations.

Sometimes the gift shops will also handle flower deliveries, even though the flowers are not sold by the gift shop. The volunteer workers take delivery of the flowers and carry them to the proper floor or person, rather than have the employee of the outside florist perform this task. If a flower service exists, every effort should be made to establish an area somewhat apart from the remainder of the gift shop operation, and the flowers should be delivered to the patient as soon as possible after they arrive.

In larger hospitals, flower deliveries are allowed only at specific times and are handled by a special department. These deliveries will normally be in excess of 100 per day, and the special department is, therefore, required. The department usually consists of two or three employees and may be the operational responsibility of any one of a number of departments. The security surveyor should concern himself with the control of these personnel because they also have free access to all of the patient floors. Deliveries by these individuals directly to the patient should not be authorized. All deliveries should be made to the nursing station; a member of the nursing staff should then make the actual delivery to the patient.

MAIL ROOM

Mail room operations usually do not present too great a security problem in a health care facility because only incoming mail is handled, and normally no postage metering machines are available. Stamp machines that are coin-operated may be available; however, they are normally not the responsibility of the mail room clerk but rather the concessionaire handling the vending machines. If the vending machines are facility-owned, the individual in charge of these operations usually cares for stamp machines.

If mail room operations combine handling of patient mail as well as all of the incoming and outgoing hospital mail, in all probability postage metering machines will be supplied. If so, the security of the operation should be similar to that established in the case of any other mail room operation, for example, in an industrial facility or a high-rise building.

The security surveyor should not overlook the fact that items, particularly smaller, more valuable items, could be stolen at the hospital and removed via the mails without mail room personnel being aware that they are mailing contraband. Because there is little need for parcel post operations at a health care facility, this practice, if it exists, should be discouraged. Items that will be shipped parcel post by a specific department, whatever the reason, would then be taken by a member of that department directly to the post office. Thieves very infrequently use the U.S. Postal Service to commit their crime, because once apprehended, very seldom does the criminal escape trial and possible punishment.

PATHOLOGY DEPARTMENT

A few years ago pathology departments that also operated the blood donor center created considerable problems in hospital security. However, in almost all instances, hospitals and health care centers now no longer accept donors off the street and pay for blood donation. This practice has been tremendously curtailed primarily due to the increased use of drugs and other controlled substances, which has resulted in a high percentage of the blood being contaminated by hepatitis and other diseases.

If blood donations are not taken, or rather purchased, from the general public, probably the pathology department security will consist only of quality locking hardware on the doors and checks by the patrolling guards.

If blood donations are being accepted, the problems to be encountered will be determined by the location of the area to which the donor reports. Certainly, if this practice exists, the donor operation should be as close as possible to a peripheral door to reduce the amount of this type of traffic within the hospital. It is more desirable to conduct the operation off premises in a manner similar to that previously discussed in the case of employment operations. The problems normally encountered at these donor areas are people problems. For example, persons who are intoxicated or under the influence of drugs may come to the area for the purpose of securing $5 or $10 by giving blood; because of their condition, they will not be accepted, and a disturbance may result. Often the only solution is stationing a security guard in the immediate area while operations are in progress.

EMERGENCY ROOM

Emergency room operations are a 24-hour-per-day, 7-day-per-week security problem. Here again we have a people problem, particularly in those larger cities where the police and fire department emergency squads deliver injured personnel who are under the influence of alcohol and/or drugs. In most instances, the only answer to controlling this problem, because it is practically impossible to eliminate it, is station an unarmed guard in the area to assist the doctors and nursing staff in handling unruly patients once the police or fire department personnel have departed.

The emergency room will in all probability have a supply of drugs and antibiotics on hand for emergency use; it is rare that the security of these items is lacking. The emergency room area (because it is historically plagued with people problems) will usually be adequately secured to prevent thefts of medicines or equipment by these type individuals.

The surveyor should concern himself with some of the procedures in the emergency room, particularly after the admissions and disposition department has been closed. Because only emergency cases are handled during the second and third shifts, medical records are started in this area and shipped to the admissions department the following day as are the clothing and personal belongings that have been taken into custody at the emergency room. If the patient is unconscious, at least two witnesses should be used to inventory and secure personal belongings, and all personal clothing to be shipped to the individual's ward or to the admissions department for further disposition should also be inventoried. The methods used by the admissions department to inventory and secure personal belongings should be duplicated in the emergency room operations. The security study of the area should include physically tracing the route used in transferring clothing and personal belongings from the emergency room for safekeeping.

Similarly, the surveyor should concern himself with the procedures used to inventory and safeguard the personal belongings of those individuals who are dead on arrival. He or she should also review the system of receipts and the handling of these receipts when items are removed from a cadaver by the police to be used as evidence. In this case, the signature of the officer retaining the item and his badge number should be recorded on the receipt along with the signature of the hospital employee who has authorized its removal.

Guards on duty in emergency rooms should also be charged with the responsibility of keeping the emergency access areas clear of all but emergency vehicles. If injured personnel are brought to the hospital by private or police automobiles, these automobiles should be moved from the unloading area as soon as the victim is removed from the vehicle.

MORTUARY OPERATIONS

Mortuary operations in a health care facility are not the most pleasant operations to examine; however, in order to complete the security program for the facility, an examination of these operations is mandatory.

The study of the mortuary operations must include the methods and procedures used to handle the personal belongings and clothing of the cadavers, whether they are dead on arrival or expire inside the facility. Normally, when a patient expires, items of personal clothing are removed from the nursing unit, placed in a plastic bag, and either placed on or attached to the stretcher that is used to move the body to the morgue. Clothing lockers or some suitable container should be made available to the morgue attendants so that the clothing can be inventoried, the receipt signed and returned to the nursing unit, and the clothing secured in a locker or other container. When the body is removed by an undertaker, the clothing should accompany the body, and the undertaker's employee should sign for the clothing; this receipt is then maintained in the morgue files.

Personal belongings other than clothes should be handled differently. Personal belongings of patients that expire in the hospital should be given only to properly identified next of kin. The personal belongings removed from the bodies of individuals dead on arrival should be inventoried by the emergency room staff and transported to the admissions and disposition department. The next of kin is then notified, and the personal belongings can be recovered after proper identification is made.

In larger operations where two or more cadavers may be awaiting disposition, the wrong body has been picked up by an undertaker. Procedures used to identify cadavers should be reviewed to ensure that every precaution is taken to prevent such an unfortunate circumstance from occurring.

GENERAL LOCKER ROOMS

Almost all health care facilities and definitely all hospitals have locker rooms located at the facility that are used by male and female employees. These lockers unfortunately are usually located in the basement or other remote areas, and this may endanger the safety of employees, particularly female employees. There have been many instances of employees being raped in locker rooms in larger hospital operations. When the locker rooms are located in remote areas of the hospital, the following precautions should be taken: First they should remain locked and a cypher lock should be used so that numerous keys need not be issued; second, the area outside the locker room should be under constant surveillance with a closed circuit television camera; third, frequent patrols of the area should be conducted by the guard force, particularly during the second and third shifts. Employees should be furnished with locks to the lockers, and occasional unannounced locker inspections should be conducted.

If locker rooms for female employees are remotely located, and the hospital itself is located in a high crime area, additional security can be established by installing "panic" buttons or holdup alarm buttons in out-of-the-way areas in the locker room. Thus, should an intruder successfully penetrate the area, a female under attack may be able to reach one of these alarm buttons and signal for help. If no anti-intrusion alarm system is installed or the distance between the locker room and the switchboard makes it economically unfeasible to monitor the alarm at this location, merely installing a 10-inch bell and a flashing red light outside the locker room or in a nearby area that is usually occupied is in itself an effective deterrent. If this system is used, a large sign should be placed on all entrances to the locker rooms announcing that the system is installed.

The identification and control of personnel, the establishment of key control, safety provisions for personnel, organization for emergencies, further theft controls, and security of the maintenance department will all need to be included in the physical security study and analysis of health care facilities in order to formulate the overall protection plan. However, these areas and topics are common to almost all facilities, and, in most instances, entire chapters have been devoted to them in this book.

THE DISASTER PLAN

Now that our hospital is secure as is humanly possible for everyday operations and still has the appearance of a health care unit that is cheerful, efficient, and responsive to the needs of the people, this same facility must be able to shift into high gear rapidly and with as much efficiency and care in handling the sick and injured when a disaster strikes the community. Even in an emergency situation, care must be taken to ensure that the "permanent patients" are not neglected and that their routine continues.

In order to accomplish this, a great deal of study is needed. The person charged with the responsibility of formulating the disaster plan must have intimate knowledge of the hospital's organization and personnel capabilities and capability of the physical plant itself.

A disaster plan should not be confused with the emergency and evacuation plan, the fire plan, or the safety plan of a health care facility.

A disaster plan is a systematic arrangement of details to provide organized guidance when a natural disaster or other event inflicts widespread destruction, distress, and injury and is not to be confused or made a part of other emergency planning. It is concerned wholly with the contribution the facility can make to the community in the event of an emergency and entails no self-preservation action or planning.

The format for, and a model of, a typical disaster plan for a hospital requires more space than can be devoted to the subject in this book. Another book soon to be published will contain these features as well as formats and models of emergency and evacuation plans for other type organizations.

As I reflect on the material covered in this chapter, I realize that not every area in a hospital or other health care facility may have been included. Likewise, when discussing the types of people encountered in a hospital, I was particularly remiss because I failed to include "us security folks."

16

Bank and Financial
Institution Security

Section 3 (a) of the Bank Protection Act of 1968* states in part:

> Within six months from the date of this act, each federal super-
> visory agency shall promulgate rules establishing minimum
> standards with which each bank or savings and loan association
> must comply with respect to the installation, maintenance and
> operation of security devices and procedures reasonable in
> cost to discourage robberies, burglaries and larcenies and to
> assist in the identification and apprehension of persons who
> commit such acts.

It also provided for penalties to be imposed on a bank or savings and loan
association should it be in violation of the act.

Today it appears that all federally regulated financial institutions are
in compliance to one degree or another. However these acts may have
affected attacks against banks and savings and loan associations, it appears
that robbery by extortion has increased. Extortion is not directed solely
against these money-handling businesses, because any business having
available large amounts of cash is subject to having its management attacked.
Therefore, this chapter is devoted almost entirely to the protection of
financial management against this growing menace.

The need for bank management to be alert against bank robberies by
extortion has never been greater. Adequate safeguards against the possibility of robbery by this means are as much a responsibility of financial
institution management as is the maintenance of a sound lending policy.

In recent years, the instances of bank robbery by extortion have increased tremendously. This means of robbery has not been confined to
any particular area in the United States. To the contrary, recent kidnappings of bank executives or members of their families have occurred in
the Bahamas, South America, and Latin American countries.

*Public Law 90-389, 90th Congress, H.R. 15345 July 7, 1968.

The demands of extortionists have ranged from $250,000 ransom payments for the return of a banker's daughter on Grand Bahama Island to as little as $40,000 demanded by extortionists of a 70-year-old bank president in Bath, Pennsylvania, to free his 68-year-old wife.

In Grandin, Missouri, a terrible tragedy occurred when a bank president, his wife, and 16-year-old daughter were slain by extortionists. This tragic episode involved a demand by the extortionists of only "about $10,000."

WHY BANK ROBBERY?

It is true that in the past some of the criminal element has succeeded in extorting, or has attempted to extort, money from banks by holding either a bank executive or members of his or her family as hostages. However, this type of heinous crime was seldom resorted to, possibly because the federal Lindbergh law mandated the death penalty for kidnapping.

Why, then, in the past few years has bank robbery by extortion become so much more common?

The increase in extortion may have been prompted by the passage of the Bank Protection Act of 1968 previously mentioned and The Minimum Security Devices and Procedures for Federal Reserve Banks and State Member Banks, Regulation P. In combination, these two measures increase drastically the possibility of positive identification of the bank robber and his or her subsequent apprehension.

Whatever has precipitated the increase in robbery by extortion, the fact remains that bank executives are faced with a very real problem and must establish security measures to cope with possible extortions and include them in their standard operating procedures and security measures for the facility.

KIDNAP, EXTORTION, AND PERSONAL SAFETY

Statistics indicate that between 1967 and 1970, the average hostage claim was $22,000. During the period from January 1971 to August 1972, the average claim increased to $77,000. During this period actual losses through extortion totaled to approximately $1,672,000. From 1973 to 1975, the average increased fourfold.

This alarming increase must be considered in the light of two additional factors. First, the most frequent target of the kidnapper/extortionist is the bank executive or his or her family. The safety and well-being of households of other bank employees must also be considered, because their safety and well-being has also been jeopardized. Second, the protective devices that have been installed in banks to meet the requirements of the Bank Protection Act of 1968 are avoided by the criminal when extortion robbery occurs.

The bank robber will physically enter the bank building, often taking hostages after robbing the bank in the hope of effecting a successful escape. In contrast, the banker or bank employee and/or his or her family is exposed to being kidnapped while driving in their automobile, walking down the street, leaving their community church, or even within the safety of their own homes.

Sometimes the extortionist will call the bank executive and claim that he has his family and is holding them hostage; at this time, he announces his demand for money. Or, the banker may be confronted by this type of criminal on the banking floor. The extortionist may have an accomplice who will pick up the money at the bank, or he may instruct the banker to deliver his ransom demand elsewhere.

In almost every instance, violence against a person or persons is threatened. Unfortunately, violence is sometimes resorted to whether or not cooperation is received.

The possibility of a bank robbery by kidnap/extortion is real, and the circumstances will be varied in almost every instance. Ways and means must be devised to ensure that employees react promptly and properly when faced with this type situation, and this information disseminated to all possible victims.

What procedures might be followed when a threat is received and what action may be taken to deter or prevent such occurrence is discussed in the next several paragraphs.

Several deterrent actions are helpful in approaching this problem. These suggestions will assist in the development of specific procedures. However, it must be remembered that they will have to be tailored to fit the particular banking facility and local conditions and situations.

TELEPHONE THREATS

Should the banker/employee receive a phone call informing him or her that a member or members of his or her family are being held hostage and that a ransom must be paid to ensure their safe return, some or all of the following actions may need to be initiated.

1. The recipient of such a telephone call should remain as calm as possible and try not to upset the caller.
2. Detailed notes covering the entire conversation should be made, with special attention being paid to the exact time of the call, the exact words of the person calling, any voice characteristics that may be noted, and a description of background noises, if any are heard.
3. Whenever possible, another person or the switchboard should be notified while the call is in progress, and an attempt should be made

to trace the call. (The telephone company should be consulted to obtain their recommendations relative to tracing such a call.)

4. The person receiving the call should always indicate his or her willingness to cooperate.

5. Be absolutely certain that any instructions received are noted in detail. Instructions received should be repeated back to the caller to ensure that they are correct, particularly where it involves a very sophisticated plan.

6. When the call is completed, immediately notify the nearest office of the Federal Bureau of Investigation and the local law enforcement department.

7. Attempt to keep the caller on the line as long as possible to facilitate tracing the call by asking some or all of the following questions:

    a. Ask who is calling.
    b. Ask whether the call is serious or merely a prank.
    c. Ask the caller why you should not think it is a prank.
    d. Ask any other types of questions that may come to mind or that have been prepared according to the emergency procedures manual.

8. If the caller has indicated that a hostage or hostages are being held, question the caller along the following lines:

    a. What is the person wearing?
    b. Is the person or persons all right?
    c. Ask permission to talk to the person to verify the call.
    d. Ask the caller exactly what he or she wants and make him or her repeat it in detail.
    e. Ask the caller what denominations of bills he or she wants.
    f. Ask where and when the money should be delivered and insist on details on how to arrive at the drop-off point.
    g. If the money is to be given to someone, ask how that person will be recognized.

9. If the caller indicates that a hostage is being held, arrangements should be attempted on the first call to effect simultaneous exchange of the money for the hostage.

10. If the caller indicates a drop-off point, try to arrange a person-to-person payoff, arguing on past occasions other parties recovered the payoff and turned it over to a police agency.

11. The ransom money should include as a minimum some "bait" money.

The bank security officer should design a form that contains a precise set of instructions to be followed if an extortionist calls to announce that a hostage has been taken. This form may be similar to the list of questions that already appear on the instruction forms that are used to interrogate the caller conveying a bomb threat. The wording on the form obviously will need to be tailored to fit the local situation, and the form should contain a sufficient space for bank personnel to make any additional notes on the call. The phone numbers of the local office of the FBI and the local law enforcement office should be included on the form, as well as the phone or extension number of the bank security officer.

IF THE HOSTAGE IS BROUGHT TO THE BANK PREMISES

If a bank officer or other employee has been taken hostage away from the banking facility and is brought to the bank by the criminal, with members of his or her family also being held as hostages elsewhere, several important items must be considered.

1. The holdup alarm must not be tripped.
2. A prearranged signal that can be completely disguised to the criminal should be given to ensure that another employee is aware that an extortion is in progress.
3. Employees recognizing the extortion signal should immediately contact the police and/or local FBI office and give them the address of the hostage employee's family. If this cannot be accomplished while the criminal or criminals are in the bank, it should be done immediately after they depart with the hostage.
4. All employees aware of the incident that is occurring should follow the robbery procedures regarding observation, description of the perpetrator, and preservation of the area for fingerprints.
5. The hostage should proceed to secure money as requested, being certain that decoy money is placed with the ransom money.
6. When a hostage is brought to the bank by the criminal, and he or she successfully secures the ransom demand, much more money than is actually given him or her should be publicized, because this type crime usually involves more than one individual, and this may create dissension between the criminals involved.

PERSONAL INFORMATION FILES

A personal information file should be maintained on each executive of the bank facility, and this procedure should possibly be extended to include chief tellers and certainly all bank branch managers. The file must be classified "Confidential" but should be immediately available to a designated officer of the bank, preferably the security officer. This file should be available to the security officer at all times, including weekends. The file should contain the following information, and the form may be tailored to fit the local situation.

1. The name of the official and the nickname if applicable.
2. The home address.
3. The home telephone number.
4. Wife's name and nickname if applicable.
5. Name of wife's employer if applicable.
6. Business name of wife's employer if applicable.
7. Address and telephone number of wife's employer if applicable.
8. Any children, listed separately by age, by name and nickname if applicable; the school they attend and its telephone number.
9. Automobiles owned by the family; including the year, make, color, license number, and the name of the person who usually drives each automobile.
10. The names, addresses, and telephone numbers of the neighbors living on each side of the employee or across the street.
11. The names, addresses, days and/or hours employed, whichever is applicable, of any domestic employees.
12. Any regularly scheduled social activities of the dependents by name, location, and telephone number of the activity. If the dependent usually attends this activity, include the name of a person at the activity who would know the dependent's whereabouts at the location.
13. At least two current color photographs of each member of the family.

This personal information and the photographs may prove invaluable to police agencies in successfully thwarting this type of robbery.

Should hostages be taken from the bank in a robbery attempt, similar procedures to those just outlined should be formulated. If an alarm is tripped during the course of a robbery, the police department that normally responds must be contacted immediately and notified that hostages have been taken. This should be done before the police arrive at the bank if at all possible.

When notifying the responding police agency, the identification of the hostages and the clothing they are wearing should be given to the police. This will assist in ensuring that innocent hostages are not fired upon should the police pursuit of the robbers lead to gunfire.

PREVENTION OF THE KIDNAP/EXTORTION ROBBERY

In conjunction with developing a plan of action to cope with possible kidnap/ extortion plots, effective methods must be designed to deter or prevent this type of incident from occurring. The primary way to prevent this type

of crime is by formulating safety precautions that should be observed by
all bank employees.

The safety precautions that are outlined in the following section are not
necessarily for protection only against kidnap/extortion plots. The preventive methods outlined, if practiced diligently, are also an effective deterrent
against armed robbery, burglary, rape, and assault.

SECURITY IN THE RESIDENCE

The security of bankers and their families in their home can be enhanced
by the installation of an anti-intrusion (burglar) alarm system. Properly
installed, the home anti-intrusion alarm system will protect all peripheral
openings of the building. That is, every window and exterior door of the
home should be included in the alarm system. If the alarm system is to
be considered complete, emergency or "panic" buttons should be strategically located throughout the residence. These buttons are normally installed
in the bedroom, near the front door and back door, and in the kitchen or
other area where a considerable amount of time is spent.

This alarm system may or may not be connected to an alarm company
central station or the police department. The usual installation will include
12-volt sirens on the outside of the residence that can be heard by the neighbors who, by prearranged agreement, will immediately notify the police
should an alarm occur.

The installation cost of such an anti-intrusion alarm system will depend
on the size of the residence, but in most instances the cost of installation
will be between $2,000 and $5,000. Obviously a great deal more protection is received from this type of anti-intrusion alarm system because it
furnishes an additional means of summoning help should an attack by a
kidnapper/extortionist occur.

Whether or not an alarm system is installed at the residence, the following measures will greatly assist in preventing or deterring a kidnapping.

1. Incorporate exterior protective lighting into the anti-intrusion alarm
    system, if it exists. This system should illuminate the entire exter-
    ior of the house should an intrusion be attempted.
2. If no anti-intrusion alarm system is installed, at least install a
    similar protective lighting system that could be manually illuminated.
3. Install viewers on all windowless doors so that anyone outside the
    door may be observed before the door is opened.
4. If outside doors contain glass windows, use a two-way key-operated
    security-type lock rather than a manually operated bolt or latch-type
    lock that can be opened by breaking the window and reaching inside.
5. If the home is equipped with an intercom, extend it to a speaker/talker
    device on the outside of all door entrances.

6. Under no circumstances should a door be opened to speak to anyone not personally known to the occupant.
7. Notify the police department of any suspicious persons or vehicles seen in the neighborhood. Write down license numbers and descriptions of vehicles and individuals whenever possible.
8. If someone is heard prowling outside the residence, do not leave the house to investigate. Instead, turn on all available outside lights to frighten the prowler off or leave the lights off and notify the police; leaving the lights off and notifying the police is the best procedure for apprehending a prowler.

INSURANCE COVERAGE

It is questionable whether or not existing blanket bond coverage would apply when a bank officer or employee acting under threat of bodily harm to himself or his family delivers bank funds to an extortionist or his confederates at a point outside the premises of the bank. In all probability there will be no coverage.

It is recommended that the bank's legal counsel be consulted during the formulation of the kidnap/extortion plan so that he or she may research the insurance coverage that exists and all other legal aspects of the bank security program, including the protection it offers.

In all probability when bank funds are turned over to an extortionist or his confederates on the bank premises, existing blanket bond coverages would apply.

The Surety Association of America announced a rider to the existing blanket bond coverage that will clarify this situation somewhat. Effective August 2, 1972, any bank funds paid to an extortionist on the bank premises would be considered as constituting a robbery rather than an extortion and therefore would be covered.

At the same time, two additional riders were also announced. The first such rider eliminated coverage when bank property or funds are delivered to an extortionist or an accomplice at a location other than the bank premises. The second rider provided the coverage that was eliminated by the first rider for an additional premium. The second rider covers the loss of bank funds delivered to an extortionist off the bank premises by a bank officer or employee as the result of a threat made against a bank officer, the bank's employees, or relatives of employees. An important part of this rider is a "notification clause" whereby the coverage becomes void unless the bank notifies, or attempts to notify, the FBI, local police, and bank security officer of the robbery.

If this coverage is not provided for or is voided as the result of non-compliance, the bank can either take the loss or file a claim with the bonding company under their fidelity agreement. In the second case, however, the employee involved would be classified as an embezzler and would be subject to immediate dismissal and criminal prosecution.

This is a serious problem, and bankers should give much consideration to this aspect of the problem of extortion by robbery. They should consult with their insurance company to ensure that adequate protection is provided for the establishment, its officers, and employees, but they should also consult the bank's legal counsel to ensure that proper coverage is maintained, so that the bank's officers and employees are properly protected against being classified as an embezzler, in which case they would be subject to dismissal and possible criminal prosecution.

PROTECTION OF MARKETABLE SECURITIES

A second area in which financial institutions are sustaining ever-increasing losses is in securities handling and storage. The Department of Justice announced on December 23, 1974, that it was issuing comprehensive suggestions to financial institutions to improve the protection of marketable securities. The suggestions were compiled through the joint effort of the financial community and the federal government. Three important areas are covered: (1) on-premise protection; (2) procedures to follow if theft or losses of marketable securities occur; and (3) checks that can be made to detect counterfeit or forged securities. A copy of the complete paper can be secured from the Department of Justice.

It is interesting to note that the then Attorney General* urged the financial community to make better use of the FBI and the NCIC (National Crime Information Center) to report lost, missing, stolen, and counterfeit securities and to use the NCIC to validate suspicious securities. The following are the suggestions in the three areas listed above. The suggestions in these three areas are not generally available and do present a definite deterrent to crimes involving theft and counterfeiting of marketable securities.

On-Premise Physical Security

1. All securities held by a financial institution should be kept in a vault or other highly secure area. This includes blank securities, as well as those held as collateral on loans, in trust, and in the institution's own portfolio. Special care should be given to bearer instruments.

*News Release, December 23, 1974. Released by the Department of Justice. Attorney General William B. Saxbe announced issuance of suggestions to Financial Institutions to improve protection of marketable securities. These comprehensive suggestions were prepared by the Justice Department in cooperation with public and private organizations.

2. Keep securities separate from the actual trust or loan file. Keep an up-to-date list of serial numbers of trust securities and collateral securities both in the trust or loan file and in the securities folder file which is kept in the secure area unless the trust asset ledgers and loan collateral registers are considered adequate. No person should have access to both sets of records. Do not destroy such inventory lists or similar records for a reasonable period after the termination of the account.

3. Establish practical procedures and records of accountability for each marketable security from the time it enters the financial institution, while it is passing through the various processes, and up through the time it is delivered safely out of the financial institution and into the custody of the next authorized holder.

4. Make scheduled and unscheduled periodic and spot checks of the stored securities.

5. Use an employee identification system which delineates which employees will be allowed to go to certain areas in the financial institution and which requires the use of ID badges or cards to indicate which employees are permitted access to given areas. Require employees and visitors who enter controlled areas to sign appropriate logs.

6. Control the movement of nonemployees by issuing, and keeping a record of, temporary badges for visitors, auditors, and others. Do not permit repairmen, service people, and janitors free movement within the premises, especially in the secured and restricted areas.

7. Control the points of entrance and exit to the secure areas where the securities are held. Records should be maintained which accurately reflect those securities brought into or taken out of the secure area and the persons doing so. The movement of securities should be accounted for on a daily basis.

8. Use a secure method of transmitting securities. It is advisable not to use the mails to transport securities unless absolutely necessary. However, if the mails are utilized, use registered mail, especially when mailing "bearer" instruments. Certified mail, which can provide proof of mailing and a receipt signed by the addressee, does not provide the protection and indemnity available through registered mail. Do not normally use ordinary mail! Maintain a record of the serial numbers of all securities sent through the mails. This record should include the registered mail number. A duplicate record of the serial numbers can be mailed separately to the addressee to provide independent notification of the mailing. This would assure prompt notification of nonreceipt. In situations where stock powers are being utilized, they should also be sent under separate cover, if possible.

In addition, the financial institution should consider the use of restrictive endorsements on those securities to be sent through the mail. Treasury Circular no. 853, which can be obtained from the Federal Reserve, contains helpful suggestions in this area.

Rather than incurring the high cost of using registered mail for nongovernment and nonbearer securities, financial institutions might consider utilizing blanket mail insurance coverage policies which are now generally available through various private insurers. These contracts require daily reporting to the insurance carrier of the number of items sent and the value of each on a single reporting form. It is then possible to mail these nongovernment and nonbearer securities by ordinary mail.

9. Keep a duplicate set of fingerprint cards of all present and former employees on file, unless state law prohibits such a procedure. Having two sets of fingerprint cards kept separately will guard against possible removal or substitution of a card by a corrupt employee, will serve as a possible prior deterrent, and will promote the progress of a criminal investigation if the need should occur. Also keep at least two current photographs of each employee in separate files.

Procedures to Follow When Theft or Loss of Securities Occurs

When any theft or disappearance of any securities occurs, whether it be through possible burglary, theft from the mails, misplacement, embezzlement, or loss, the following actions should be taken immediately.

1. Notify key people within the institution.
2. Identify what is missing by conducting a physical search and by back-tracking through audit trail, utilizing the assistance of internal auditors, the controller, and others, to check the institution's records in order to trace the movement of the securities from the time received and to determine if the securities might have been misrecorded or misrouted. All employees involved in the movement of the missing securities should be interviewed.
3. Immediately thereafter notify law enforcement, including the FBI and, if the securities were mailed, postal inspectors, in order that the securities can be entered into the National Crime Information Center (NCIC) and an appropriate criminal investigation initiated. Remember that the NCIC lists missing, embezzled, and counterfeit securities as well as stolen securities.
4. Insist that all officials and employees cooperate fully with law enforcement; identify for law enforcement those employees having access to the securities and provide law enforcement a flow chart of your operations for its investigative use.
5. Notify the New York Stock Exchange Clearing Corporation so that a "lost notice" will be prepared for circulation.
6. Place "stops" with the transfer agent for stocks and "notations" or "caveats" with the paying agent for bonds.
7. Complete appropriate Postal Service forms to assist in tracing securities by mail.

8. Notify the local Federal Reserve Bank and the Claims Section, Division of Securities Operations, Bureau of Public Debt, Treasury Department, Washington, D.C. 20226, if federal government bonds or securities are involved.
9. Notify a private securities clearing house computer facility, if you are a subscriber or can otherwise arrange to do so (that is, through a correspondent bank, for example).

Checks to Detect Counterfeit or Forged Securities

Any reasonable and prudent individual in a financial institution can assure himself or herself of the authenticity and genuineness of a stock certificate by a sight-and-touch examination. Although over-the-counter stocks will not have all the characteristics listed below, stocks selling on the New York and American Stock Exchanges will. Check for the following.

1. The engraved decorative border design is in a color other than black and has the feel of "slightly coarse" sandpaper.
2. The color design has a crisp look; it is sharp in definition and not washed out or flat looking. Even the finest white or color lines are clean and clear.
3. The hand-engraved "vignette" or picture, which is almost always printed in black ink, is sharp, and the flesh tones of the allegorical figure that is frequently part of the vignette are given careful attention. The vignette figure is well defined and almost always three dimensional, with eyes that are clearly visible. The background is clear, without any traces of fading or coarse broken patterns. The vignette feels like "very fine" sandpaper.
4. The face of the certificate shows a hand-engraved title and a script text which is clear and distinct. The name of the company is raised slightly higher above the surface of the paper than the script text which also feels slightly raised. Neither should feel flat with the paper.
5. The certificate is serially numbered in a provided number panel in a sharp, clear, distinctive type style. Although obvious, remember that no two certificates should have the same serial number.
6. No alterations should have been made to any of the features of the certificate, either in the preprinted portions of the certificate or in the later inscribed information such as the owner's name or the amount of shares represented. Any signs of erasures should be viewed as a danger signal.
7. The number of shares inserted must not exceed the limitations imposed by the certificate; for example, a "less than 100 shares" certificate is limited to 100 shares.
8. The paper has a substantial and good feel to it; it should snap and crackle when it is handled crisply.

9. If the certificate has planchettes (little dots of several different colors imbedded in the paper), they are not found in identical places on any two certificates and some should be able to be removed with a pin. If several certificates are placed together on top of each other in the same order, a pin pushed through a planchette on the top certificate should not go through a similar planchette in a certificate below because of the random manner in which planchettes are mixed into the paper mash as it is rolled.

10. The certificate may have an overprint, such as a correction of the par value, a change in company name, or a silvering out of the transfer agent or the registrar panel with insertion of a different bank's name or the name of the authorized corporate officer. Such changes do not mean that the certificate is counterfeit or fraudulently altered, but you should verify the changes by a telephone call to the corporate secretary or to the bank note company.

If the above checklist is followed and there are still questions about the authenticity and genuineness of the certificate, telephone the transfer or paying agent, the corporate secretary or other appropriate corporate official, and/or the bank note printing company to resolve these questions. If a certificate is counterfeit, immediately thereafter notify the appropriate law enforcement agency and retain the counterfeit certificate if possible.

BUILDING SECURITY

The physical security of the financial facility, whether or not it is federally regulated, should be established in much the same manner as it is for any other business entity. Certainly the electronic devices required of regulated facilities by the Bank Protection Act of 1968 should be used in nonregulated establishments as well. Overall security required is determined by an assessment of the criticality and vulnerability of the facility and by careful analysis of the security study. Previous chapters discussing door security, locks, electronic devices, and the like should be reviewed in formulating an adequate overall security plan.

In spite of all of the precautions taken in the protection of the physical plant, holdups are still likely to occur. I have discussed protection with employees of nonregulated and regulated financial facilities, and it is surprising the number of employees who are not familiar with the two categories of holdups and the procedures that should be taken in the event either occurs. This subject will be discussed in the following sections.

BANK HOLDUPS

Bank holdups usually fall into two categories.

1. <u>Armed robbery</u>. This is when firearms are openly displayed during a robbery, usually involving two or more bandits, although a so-called "solo bandit" may also make this type of an attempt.

2. <u>Secret robberies</u>. In this type of bank robbery, often referred to as "private," the individual or individuals do not display firearms or a weapon of any type and attempt to hold up the bank without attracting any attention. This method usually involves a prepared note that is simple and brief, and the robber may announce his or her intention by whispering to the teller as the note is passed.

Armed robbery is usually well planned and committed by experienced bandits. These holdups can take place at any time during regular banking hours or before or after banking hours. Many successful armed robberies have been carried out at the morning opening hour. Weapons are used openly, and usually these bandits are after vault cash. That is, they are seeking a great deal of cash rather than that stored at any one particular teller's cage.

Action to be Taken During an Armed Robbery

Most of the five directives that follow are generally observed by security guards on duty in the banking facility; however, they apply equally as well to any other employee of the bank who is present when an armed robbery occurs or to any individuals who should happen to walk into the bank when an armed robbery is in progress.

1. Always obey the bandits' commands, but <u>do not do more than told</u>.
2. Avoid any fast movement that may startle the bandits or cause them to start any violent action.
3. Concentrate on making mental notes of the description of the bandit or bandits. In particular, observe any distinguishing characteristics such as long noses, slanted eyes, high or large eyebrows, or short arms. Note the height and weight of the individual, whether he or she is left-handed or right-handed. Be especially careful to note any physical defects such as a stutter in speech, a limp, visible scars, cauliflower ears.
4. Sound the alarm at your first safe opportunity. Personnel should not attempt to move from the position they were frozen in when the bandits arrived until the bandits are well on their way out of the facility.
5. All personnel must be reminded that bandits are potentially very dangerous. Nothing should be done that might jeopardize the safety of <u>anyone</u> in the bank. A holdup demands a great deal of good judg-

ment on the part of the financial institution's employees. Extreme caution must always be exercised. Employees and security guards must be made to understand that they should attempt nothing heroic.

After the Armed Robbery Occurs

Immediately after the robbery has been committed and conditions are safe, several things must be accomplished by the employee.

1. Assistance must be given the injured if this is necessary.
2. All alarm switches must be activated.
3. The direction of the escaping bandits and a description of the vehicle and its license plate number should be noted whenever possible.
4. Security guards should close the lobby of the facility to the general public and admit only authorized personnel. However, this procedure, if adopted, should be included in the guard's special instructions.
5. All personnel must immediately jot down all of their descriptions and all other information concerning the holdup individually and not collectively before they become influenced by the questions asked by law enforcement authorities.

The fifth recommendation is probably the most important in the category of action after a robbery has been committed. Supervisors must ensure that each employee completes his or her own individual notes pertaining to the robbery, including, as near as possible, the exact time that their observations were noted and in the sequence in which actions occurred. It is of utmost importance that each employee remain at his or her assigned position. If necessary, a bank officer should distribute note paper or forms to these individuals to ensure that an individual is not influenced by another's observations and thinking.

In the training of employees in financial facilities, sufficient time should be devoted to the expected action of employees should a robbery occur. Even though the facility may be adequately covered with still picture cameras and/or closed circuit television cameras and VTR (Video Tape Recorder), the most detailed descriptions of the bandits and their actions are often furnished by employees. This subject should be covered during the initial training of employees and is of particular importance for all teller personnel. I recommend that each teller position and each desk position located on the banking floor be supplied with at least one copy of the form shown in Figure 16-1 or a similar form to ensure that the employee's memory is "jogged" and that the description of the bandits and their actions are as detailed as possible.

Figure 16-1

PHYSICAL DESCRIPTION
HOLDUP OR EXTORTION/KIDNAPPING

COLOR_____ SEX_____ NATIONALITY_____

AGE_____ HEIGHT_____ WEIGHT_____ BUILD_____
                                                             Thin, Stocky, etc.
COMPLEXION_____ HAIR_____ HAIR_____
               Light, Ruddy, etc.   Color   Straight, Curly, etc.
EYES_____ NOSE_____
        Color, small, large, etc.   Large, pug, broad, etc.
EARS_____ GLASSES_____
        Prominent, small, etc.   Describe frames
MOUSTACHE OR BEARD_____
                Color, shape
MASK OR FALSE FACE_____
               Type, describe
SCARS & MARKS_____
           Moles, birthmarks, blemishes, make-up, etc.

CLOTHING   MISCELLANEOUS

Hat_____   Weapon exhibited_____

Overcoat_____   (Revolver, automatic, color, etc.)

Raincoat_____   Speech_____
                                 (Any accent, stutter, etc.)
Jacket_____
                              Any names used_____
Suit/Dress_____

Trousers/Slacks_____   Mannerisms_____
                               (Left-handed or right-
Shirt/Blouse_____
                         handed, nervous?)
Tie_____
                       Physical defects_____
Shoes_____   Fingers missing,

Other Clothing_____   limp, stoop-shouldered, etc.

Does each piece described fit?
Is it too large? Too small?

PROMPTLY COMPLETE THIS FORM AND GIVE IT TO THE BANK
OFFICER IN CHARGE.

A Holdup Involving a Note Passer

This type of bandit can be of either sex, although they are usually males.
More and more frequently, the note passer robber, although male, may
be disguised as a female. Personnel should be particularly watchful of all
strangers entering the bank floor in smaller establishments or branch banks,
during periods when teller lines are short. The mannerisms and/or characteristics that usually mark a <u>note passer</u> are as follows.

1. Invariably he or she will be a stranger.
2. The individual will often wear dark glasses or other obvious disguises.
3. He or she will normally be carrying a briefcase or other container,
    possibly a paper shopping bag or a folded paper bag that is withdrawn
    from the clothing.
4. In all probability, the note passer will loiter around the bank without
    conducting any business. He or she is awaiting the best moment to
    approach a teller, usually when there are few patrons and when the
    robber will be able to exit the bank quickly without drawing attention.

Approaching Suspicious Strangers. If strangers are noted in the facility
and their actions are very suspicious, an employee of the bank or the security guard should approach the individual and ask him or her if they need
assistance. This type of simple greeting is usually quite disarming and
not inconsistent with good customer relations. If the person approached
does have improper intentions, he or she realizes they have been detected,
and this will usually discourage any further activity. Should the individual
depart the facility without conducting any business or presenting any reasonable explanation, he or she should immediately become a suspect. The
description and activities of the individual should be jotted down immediately
even though no further action may be taken. In these instances, it is often
desirable to activate the holdup camera to photograph the individual. A
copy of the photograph should be given to law enforcement officers for
possible identification and should be kept on file should the individual return
at a later time and perpetrate a robbery.

The Suspected Note Passer in Line at a Teller's Window. If an individual
that is a suspect moves in line before he or she can be approached by an
employee or security guard, the suspect should be watched closely. A
possible note passer will usually commit some of the following actions.

1. The individual may remove a note from a pocket, purse, or some-
    where else on the clothing as he or she nears the teller's window.
2. Very likely the individual will become extremely nervous and will
    look around continuously, because this type bandit is usually a rank
    amateur.

3. The individual is likely to look frequently at the person in line behind him or her. If a very likely suspect enters the teller's line, one of the bank officers or another employee should get in line behind the individual. This often is enough to discourage the attempted robbery.

4. The individual may leave the line and move away to one of the service tables if a person gets in line behind him or her. If this occurs, the individual should definitely become a suspect, and the photographic equipment should be activated. Perhaps even the police should be called and made aware of the situation. The police would then stop the individual <u>after</u> he or she has left the facility for routine questioning.

5. Employees of financial facilities and security personnel who regularly operate on the banking floor should regularly scan the faces of the tellers, particularly those nearest the exits, because the expression on the face of a teller will usually indicate that a holdup is taking place. If a suspect under observation reaches the teller's window, the teller's facial expressions should indicate whether the suspect in reality is a bandit.

Holdups in Progress

Once employees or security guards are either notified or observe that a holdup is taking place, timely decisions must be made to determine the appropriate action to be taken, remembering that every holdup is in all probability different. Every individual during training must be cautioned to use their own good judgment.

One very important consideration is <u>whether or not the bandit is armed</u>. This should be determined before any attempt is made to apprehend him or her. If both hands of the individual are visible, and no weapon is seen at that particular moment, perhaps a move can be made to apprehend him or her. However, if a hand is in a pocket, it must be <u>assumed that the bandit is armed and has a gun in hand</u>. Extreme caution must be used in any attempt to apprehend the bandit. A call to the police would probably be more wise. <u>The safety of all bank employees and customers</u> in the bank at the time a robbery occurs should be the prime concern of security officers and bank employees.

Other Precautionary Measures

I have often recommended that financial institutions, particularly private loan companies or even insurance companies whose agents collect cash on specific days of the week, design the operational entrance to the facility in such a manner that it will slow up departure of an intended robber and therefore act as a deterrent. There are two basic methods that may be considered: (1) the installation of a revolving door that will slow up the speedy exit of a bandit; and (2) constructing the exit lobby in such a way that a person must pass through two doors that are at a 90-degree angle from each other.

I have also often recommended, without much success, that a financial facility have a decal printed and placed on each entrance or exit door announcing that when a holdup occurs and the silent alarm is sounded, all doors are automatically secured to prevent anyone from leaving the facility. Obviously, financial officials are horrified by such a thought, always remarking that they want the bandit to get out of the bank before any violent action occurs. However, I still feel that even though exit doors may not be equipped with an automatic locking device, such a sign would be an effective psychological deterrent.

17

The Retail Industry
Protection Plan

Five major types of criminal acts are especially detrimental to the retail industry. These are shoplifting, employee theft, burglary and robbery, fraudulent checks, and credit card fraud. The next largest cause of losses to the retail industry is vandalism. Although not always considered a cause of major loss, in some instances, for individual stores, at least, loss through vandalism in any particular period may very well be the major loss.

SHOPLIFTING

Inventory shortages occur when the value of all merchandise on the retail store's shelves and in their storerooms is below the book value of the inventory. These shortages result from many causes; however, the major cause is external and internal thefts.

In a release by the U.S. Department of Commerce in September 1975, the Director of the Consumer Goods and Services Division reported that one of the largest corporations in America had "sales" of $20.3 billion. This company's venture was crime, and the report went on to state that crime against business in the next year could very well increase to $23.6 billion. To put these figures in perspective, total sales for the three largest department store retailers totaled $22 billion in 1974. Crime, the report stated, makes more money than Sears, Roebuck, Montgomery Ward, and J. C. Penney combined. Shoplifting offenses alone between 1960 and 1973 rose over 22 percent; however, these figures represent only those crimes that are reported to law enforcement agencies. Some experts have estimated reported crime represents only approximately 50 percent of the crimes committed.

The report went on to state that the rates at which retail stores are victimized are startling and cited an example in Detroit where the burglary rate of retail stores was 72 percent, whereas the robbery rate was 37 percent. The rates in other large cities ranged downward from these highs. The report indicated that in 1975 retailers lost $6.5 billion due to ordinary crime. In 1975, this figure rose to approximately $6.9 billion. The bulk of these losses are borne by general merchandise and apparel stores.

The losses sustained by retailers are completely out of proportion to their place in the economy. Retailers contribute only about 10 percent of the Gross National Product, whereas their crime-related losses make up about 25 percent of the losses of all business. Small firms suffer more from crime than larger businesses, because small businesses are the criminal's major commercial target. The rate of crimes against small firms is 35 times greater than that against firms with receipts of $5 million or more.

Although shoplifting is very highly publicized as the number-one crime for retail stores, many security experts believe that losses from theft by employees are substantially greater. Although concrete evidence to substantiate this assumption is not available, retailers in a major urban area recently reported that over 3,000 employees had been prosecuted for theft or had been terminated after admitting that they had committed thefts. The value of the merchandise stolen by this group was $857,000.

Shoplifters come from all walks of life; however, they can generally be broadly categorized as ordinary customers and professionals who steal for a living.

The incidence of shoplifting increases and decreases depending upon the season of the year. For example, shoplifting is probably at its prime during the Christmas season because of large crowds of people, the employment of part-time sales personnel, and the general overall rush of legitimate customers to complete their Christmas shopping. Another time of the year when increases will occur is when department stores hold their large "end of season" sales. Approximately the same atmosphere exists as is found at Christmas and other holiday rush periods. However, during these seasonal sales, the period for the shoplifter to operate is considerably shorter.

Some observers find that the majority of the shoplifters who are apprehended are female, and in some areas of the country, records will indicate that this is true. However, many professional shoplifting teams consist of both males and females, and, even though there are more women shoplifters than men, the dollar value of merchandise stolen by men is usually considerably higher than the value of the items stolen by women.

Shoplifters have been categorized by type, and these types are generally accepted as being valid by management of retail stores, retail store security directors, and the law enforcement agencies. Six of the most common types of shoplifters are listed below with a thumbnail description of that category of individual and the generally accepted reason why these individuals steal.

1. The professional. This individual is probably the most difficult to detect. The professional, regardless of sex, steals for a living and is intimately familiar with general retail store security measures and with the particular program of the specific establishment they intend to victimize. Professionals often work in teams and have been known to move from shopping mall to shopping mall or city to city. This category usually steals

expensive merchandise that has a high resale value and rapid turnover.
Obviously, these individuals have a ready outlet for the merchandise they
steal. The professionals, because this is their "occupation," take very
few chances, one of the reasons they are so difficult to detect.

2. The narcotics addict. Obviously this individual steals to support
his or her drug habit, which costs staggering sums on a day-to-day basis.
Because addicts are physically dependent on drugs and quite often under the
influence or partially under the influence of drugs, they will take greater
chances than any other category of shoplifter and, therefore, are fairly
easy to catch. However, it must be remembered that, because of their
present condition and the fact that they are desperate to obtain more drugs
to sustain their habit, addicts are extremely dangerous to apprehend. Sales
personnel should not try to apprehend this type of shoplifter unless they have
received special training.

3. The vagrant. This group usually has no funds and steals because of
physical need. Quite often, they are under the influence of alcohol, because
a high percentage of vagrants are also incurable alcoholics. They will
usually steal only what they need and immediately attempt to leave the
premises. Vagrants are very easy to detect, simply because of their
physical appearance, dress, and furtive manner. Vagrants seldom resist
if apprehended because being apprehended is almost a way of life to them.

4. The amateur. Amateurs steal on impulse, and usually the item
stolen is one that the shoplifter personally desires and will, in all probability,
if successful, keep rather than try to resell. Items most frequently stolen
by amateurs are various types of jewelry, clothing, or special types of
gourmet food that the shoplifter wants but cannot afford. Amateurs are
quite easy to detect by an experienced security guard, detective, or sales
person. These individuals normally will not resist apprehension and will
maintain their innocence to the very end. Obviously, if amateurs are not
apprehended or if they are apprehended and released, they enjoy the success
and will often, over a period of time, turn professional.

5. The juvenile. Juveniles most often steal for thrills or because they
are forced into the act by another individual or a group to which they may
belong. The items stolen will vary; however, they are usually inexpensive
small items that receive little protection in the store and are easiest to
obtain and to hide. Often, particularly in large urban areas, juveniles in
groups will descend upon a particular store, and while some are creating
a disturbance as a diversion, others will steal and depart. Juvenile shoplifters are fairly easy to detect, and if apprehended, handled firmly, and
released to their parents at the store, they will often never repeat this
offense.

6. The kleptomaniac. The kleptomaniac is discussed last among categories of shoplifters because he or she has the financial means to purchase
whatever they need or want but are compelled to steal for some inner psychological satisfaction. Kleptomaniacs usually appear very nervous and often

shy; regardless of the number of times they are apprehended and possibly convicted, they will usually repeatedly steal. Therefore, kleptomaniacs are fairly easy to detect. If persons in this category are known to live or operate in a specific area, photographs should be made available to all sales personnel and security personnel. These personnel, if they recognize a known kleptomaniac in the store, should approach the person and let him or her know that he or she is being watched. In some instances, klepto-maniacs have been barred by courts from frequenting a specific store; if such a person enters the store, he or she should be asked to leave the store immediately.

The Memphis, Tennessee, <u>Commercial Appeal</u> reported in its October 11, 1976, issue that an administrative city court judge favored "some type of crackdown" on businesses that do not follow through to prosecute shoplifting cases. The judge said in part:

> We have far too many cases where the security guards, particu-larly those at downtown stores, are catching shoplifters, are getting the warrants and getting the people arrested, and then just dropping the matter.
>
> They seem to fear being sued for prosecuting. According to the law, they have already accepted liability by obtaining the warrants. It's a terrible practice. It leaves the courts and the police in bad positions and I want it stopped.

In a later article, the same city court judge estimated that it cost the taxpayer $60,000 per month for court costs and other costs for the "no-shows."

Retailers also assume a part of the costs involved when individuals apprehended in stores are not prosecuted; but in addition to that, retailers should realize that a shoplifting loss of $50 can be the equivalent to losing the net profit after taxes on sales of $2500 if the store is operating on a net profit margin of 2 percent. That is, the $50 profit made on $2500 worth of merchandise sold is negated by the $50 item stolen. If shoplifting during a given period amounts to losses of $5,000, this would be equivalent to losing the net profit after taxes on $250,000 worth of merchandise if the store was operating at a 2 percent margin.

Recognizing a Shoplifter

Shoplifters will usually rely not only upon the fact that they are hidden from direct view of anyone but also upon the assumption that <u>the hand is quicker than the eye</u>. Next in importance to the successful shoplifter is a speedy but not too obvious exit.

Unfortunately, most permanent sales persons and almost all part-time sales persons hired seasonally are not at all familiar with the characteris-tics of shoplifters. In addition to those actions and attitudes discussed

earlier, shoplifters have several other characteristics that sales persons
should be alert to. Listed here are some of the types of people who are
likely to be potential shoplifters. Obviously, some of these items will apply
to many shoppers. The person who fits into many of these categories is
the one to watch.

1. Individuals wearing outer garments that quite obviously are too
   large or inappropriate—for example, a raincoat on a sunny day.
   Male shoplifters favor trousers and coats or jackets that are large
   and baggy; and women favor full skirts.
2. Individuals who appear to be roaming aimlessly looking at items
   and who, when approached, claim to be waiting for a friend to shop
   with.
3. Individuals who enter the store carrying bundles, boxes, shopping
   bags, or topcoats and other outer garments over their arm. Quite
   often newspapers and umbrellas are used to hide small items that
   are stolen, and, therefore, individuals with these items should be
   suspect. Some shoplifters have been apprehended wearing bogus
   plaster casts on their arms and carrying their arm in a sling. Any
   individual wearing any paraphernalia of this sort should also become
   a suspect. Obviously, if the store has a policy of depositing all
   boxes, bundles, bags, and items of this nature at the front of the
   store, a good percentage of these individuals can be eliminated.
4. Individuals who constantly keep one hand in an outer pocket.
5. Individuals who appear to be nervous, who walk in an unusual manner,
   or who are constantly adjusting their clothing or even rubbing the
   back of their neck should be suspect, because these and similar
   actions might be used in secreting items that have been stolen.
6. Individuals who, after being approached by a sales person, continually pick up and replace a variety of articles on the pretense that
   they are undecided or confused as to which item might be the best
   gift for a friend or loved one.
7. Individuals who walk behind a sales counter or reach into a display
   case; these persons should be approached immediately and asked
   if they need assistance.
8. Individuals who have requested assistance from a sales person and
   then show little or no interest in the articles they have inquired
   about; quite often, this ploy is used to cover up the actions of another
   person nearby who is attempting to steal.
9. Individuals who are extremely nervous, have a flushed look, are
   continually wetting their lips, or perspiring freely could well be
   a narcotics addict or a kleptomaniac.
10. Individuals who frequently use washrooms or dressing rooms and
    then leave the area hastily have, in all probability, already stolen
    some item.

There are numerous other indications that will assist retail store security and sales personnel in recognizing the shoplifter; however, those listed above are the most obvious surreptitious actions of individuals with a plan to steal.

Shoplifting Methods

An untold variety of methods are used by shoplifters to remove merchandise stolen from a store. The method used depends upon whether the individual is professional or amateur and is limited only by his or her talents and ingenuity.

Professional shoplifters, because shoplifting is their occupation, have perfected their techniques and adopt methods that correspond to the kind of merchandise they are planning to steal. Their very livelihood depends upon not being apprehended, and so they plan ahead, know exactly what they will steal and where to find it, and then adopt the technique used to secure it and move it from the store.

The amateur, the juvenile, or even the vagrant is not as ingenious and talented as the professional shoplifter, and the methods used by these individuals are usually quite obvious and crude. Store security personnel and sales personnel should be trained to be alert for and recognize the method of operation of shoplifters. Listed below are some of the most common methods of operation and those that are probably the easiest to detect.

1. An individual may wear a long outer garment or, if a female, a full skirt, concealing articles between the legs. Some female shoplifters who have been apprehended have confessed that they practice removing items in this manner by using two or three telephone books and practicing hours to perfect the method.

2. An individual who wears a skirt, slacks, trousers, or other garment that has an elastic waistband will usually wear also some type of "shoplifter bloomers." The item is merely dropped through the stretched waistband and deposited into large bloomers with tight leg bands that act as a receptacle.

3. Sometimes shoplifters remove their outer garments to try on another garment. They then place the outer garment over the item to be stolen, pick up the outer garment along with the item, and depart from the store. Cleaning personnel operating in stores after hours should be required to place their outer garments in a specific area before they are allowed to move into the various areas throughout the store. Often custodial service employees use this method to steal. I once conducted a survey of a large department store. After it was closed for the day I observed the custodial crews entering the building and moving throughout the various departments and floors to clean their assigned areas. The majority of the fifteen

male and female personnel wore outer garments when they arrived
at the store; however, when they left, the majority were carrying
their coats and jackets. Obviously they had had another successful
night.

4. An individual will enter the store without wearing jewelry or other
   accessories and in the course of trying on these types of items will
   leave a bracelet, ring, or some sort of neck piece on and depart
   the store. I once surveyed a retail store and discovered that numerous individuals entered the store barefooted but fewer departed
   barefooted. When this was reported to the store manager, he said
   that "he could care less" because the shoe department was concession operated.

5. A shoplifter will palm an article and then place it in a newspaper,
   a package, under a coat carried over the arm, or even in gloves
   if they are worn. Individuals who carry small children in the store
   often use the children's clothing to hide small articles that have been
   stolen, and adults who bring babies into the store in strollers create
   a special hazard and must be observed closely.

6. Garments such as raincoats that have slits in the pocket are used
   to secret small items in the trousers or to drop them in "shoplifter
   bloomers" by reaching completely through the outer garment. Often
   the shoplifters will slit the outer pockets of their garments so that
   they can place their hand through the slit and hold a large item stolen;
   it merely appears that their hand is in their pocket.

7. Obviously, the individual who inadvertently displays hooks sewn
   inside a coat, around a waistband, or in some instances inside long,
   full sleeves, hangs small items on these hooks and transports them
   from the store in this way.

8. Some bold shoplifters simply walk rapidly to an unattended section
   of the store near an exit, grab those items nearest, and depart
   hastily from the store.

9. If such items as popcorn, beverages, or foodstuffs are sold in the
   store, and the customer is allowed to remove them from the immediate area where they were purchased, the boxes, cups, or bags make
   convenient containers to remove small items from the store.

10. If price tags are not securely fixed to articles, they will often be
    switched, allowing the shoplifter to purchase an item for much less
    than its actual cost. Such items can be carried from the store in
    full view of the security force.

Numerous other methods are used to remove items from the store, some
of which are probably not yet known even to store security personnel, because the professional shoplifter works constantly to improve methods and
techniques.

Combating the Shoplifter

The preceding discussion may make it appear that the shoplifter has the
upper hand and that, regardless of what management may do to improve
physical security and to increase the degree of training of their employees,
shoplifting cannot be combated. In all probability, in most areas of the
United States it is impossible to eliminate shoplifting completely; however,
store management, security personnel, and sales persons can discourage
shoplifters if they are properly trained and alert and if effective detection
techniques recently developed are used to improve security against the
shoplifting menace.

Unfortunately, marketing techniques have been developed to display the
merchandise and make it desirable to a potential buyer. However, at the
same time, these techniques tempt the potential thief and offer greater
opportunities for the theft to be committed. It is a recorded fact that both
sales and thefts increase when imaginative displays of goods at check-out
counters suggest to the customer that they are needed and can conveniently
be selected. It appears that when customers can handle goods displayed
in this manner, an impulsive theft is often triggered by the combination of
opportunity and temptation that has been created.

The following paragraphs will suggest some measures that may be taken
to discourage or deter shoplifting. However, these measures will be effective only if practiced and supervised by alert sales personnel.

1. All customers should be served as quickly and as efficiently as
    possible. Usually customers who are approached immediately will
    appreciate the service. Potential shoplifters will be discouraged
    because they will realize that sales personnel are properly organized,
    properly stationed and properly trained. (I dislike being approached
    immediately by sales personnel, probably because of my infrequent
    shopping trips and because I am consciously checking security
    techniques immediately upon entering a store. Therefore, it bothers
    me when I am immediately approached by a sales person, although
    I appreciate the fact that the store is truly security conscious.)
2. Always be alert for individuals who appear only to be loitering or
    wandering around.
3. Sales personnel should never turn their back on a customer being
    served, because this is an open invitation to a shoplifter to steal.
    Management should organize and arrange display counters and
    supplies so that their sales personnel need not turn their back on
    a customer. If a telephone is in the area, the sales person should
    turn and face the customer while talking on the phone.
4. Never leave a department completely unattended, for this obviously
    gives the shoplifter an opportunity to conduct his or her business.
    All too often in large department stores, particularly where self-

service is expected, there are too few sales personnel or supervisors to cover the entire area adequately.

5. Sales personnel should always acknowledge the presence of individuals accompanying the presumed customer to let them know their
presence is noted. While waiting on one customer, the sales person
should acknowledge other customers that are in the area with some
type of polite phrase for the legitimate customer but a disarming
warning for the potential shoplifter.

6. All expensive merchandise that has a high use or resale value should
be secured in showcases or other display cases, and these displays
should be arranged in such a way that they can all be watched by the
sales personnel assigned to the area. These counters are usually
referred to as "NBC" counters (national brand counter), meaning
that national brand products are grouped in this more protective
area.

7. Never stack merchandise so high that sales personnel cannot see
over it. If necessary, provide mirrors so that sales personnel may
see behind displays and always keep counters and tables neat and
orderly so that removal of an item can be noted immediately.

8. Merchandise should be arranged so that customers have to pick it
up. If merchandise does not have to be lifted up, it can more easily
be pushed off the counter into some type of container. Sometimes
two items can be pushed off, one to be stolen and the other to be
returned to the merchandise display.

9. When merchandise is normally marketed in pairs—for example,
shoes or gloves, put only one item on display if the items are easily
removed.

10. If merchandise has been taken from the stock room at a customer's
request and the customer has not purchased the item for whatever
reason, return the merchandise immediately to the secured stock
room and do not remove more items for inspection by the customer
than can be effectively observed and controlled by the sales person.

11. Every transaction should be covered by a receipt, and a policy should
be established that no cash refunds will be made regardless of the
circumstances unless the item returned is accompanied by a valid
receipt.

12. The area where sales are consummated whether at the cash register
checkout counter or elsewhere in the store, should be kept entirely
clear of discarded sales checks or cash register tape, because the
shoplifter can recover them and use them as evidence of a sale.
The shoplifter, having observed a cash register receipt or sales
slip falling to the floor when a particular item is purchased, will
pick up that receipt, steal an item of the same value, and remove
the item from the store with impunity.

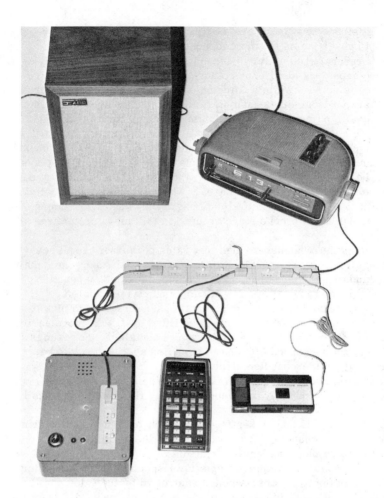

Figure 17-1 The SGM Display Alarm System will effectively reduce shoplifting. It consists of four components, a control box, a jumper cord, a
connector strip, and display cords. The control box is located in the lower
left of the photograph and shows it connected to the connector strip with
the jumper cord with protected items connected with the display cord.
(SGM Corporation)

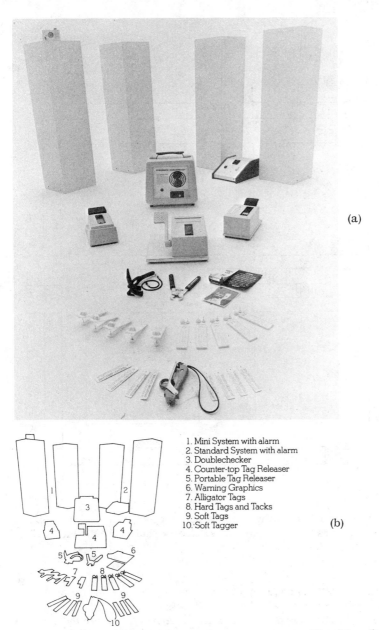

1. Mini System with alarm
2. Standard System with alarm
3. Doublechecker
4. Counter-top Tag Releaser
5. Portable Tag Releaser
6. Warning Graphics
7. Alligator Tags
8. Hard Tags and Tacks
9. Soft Tags
10. Soft Tagger

(a)

(b)

Figure 17-2 The Sensormatic System uses a sensitized tag that is attached to every article to be protected. When a sale is made, the tag is removed. If the item is stolen, and an attempt is made to remove it from the store, strategically located sensors detect the tag and trigger an alarm. (Sensormatic Electronic Corporation)

341

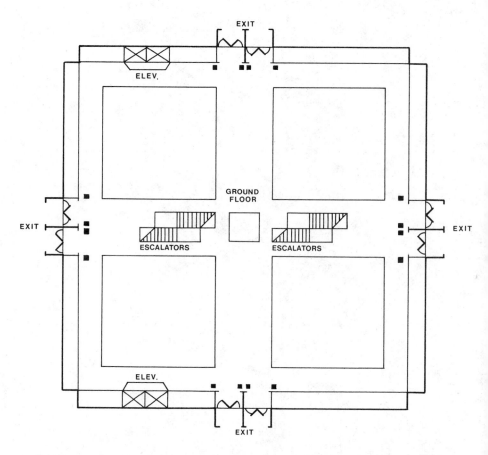

Figure 17-3 A schematic drawing showing possible locations of the Sensormatic System detectors used to scan exits. (Sensormatic Electronic Corporation)

13. A warning system should be devised to alert all employees when a suspected shoplifter is in the store. This can usually be accomplished by a code word or phrase that is announced over the PA system. This should include developing a method by which sales persons and other employees can notify the store office of the presence of suspected shoplifters.

14. Definite procedures must be established to deter "till tappers." The cash register should be opened only once, and that is when the sale is rung up. The cash register drawer should be closed before the merchandise is wrapped or bagged, and the cashiers must be

trained not to be distracted while the cash register drawer is open.
If for any reason the cashier must leave the immediate area of the
cash register, the responsible cashier should be required to lock
the register, even if other cashiers are at registers in the same
area. This will prevent adjacent cashiers from being tempted.

There are effective detection devices on the market today that can be
considered in the overall security program of the store. These will not
only deter or even possibly eliminate shoplifting, but will also reduce thefts
by employees. One such device is shown in Figure 17-1.

Another field-tested, highly effective system known commercially as the
Sensormatic System is completely flexible and can be efficiently and effectively employed within departments of a store or in stores of practically
any size. The equipment employed in this security system is shown and

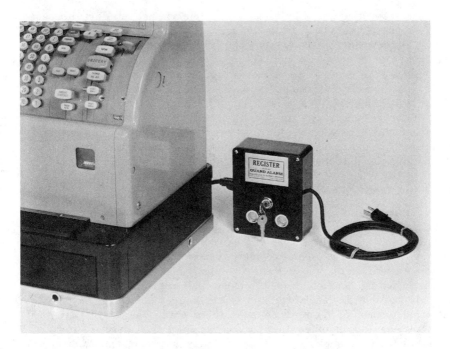

Figure 17-4 This device is installed by simply plugging it into the register,
turning the register guard alarm key to the on position, and removing the
key for safekeeping. Any unauthorized operation of the register motor
switch will lock up electronic circuits, and the alarm will sound continu-
ously. (Bernard Ephraim, Electronic Manufacturing & Consulting Engineer)

identified in Figure 17-2, and a typical installation is shown in the sketch in Figure 17-3.

Another device on the market is effective in cash register security. When installed and activated, this device sounds a loud electronic horn and disconnects any power from the cash register so that the drawer cannot be opened (see Figure 17-4).

Mirrors are effective and inexpensive deterrents to help curb shoplifting. Store maintenance personnel can usually install the mirrors after management has determined the hazardous "blind spots" and insured that the mirrors are correctly located and properly adjusted, so that otherwise clandestine activity can be exposed (see Figure 17-5).

THEFTS BY EMPLOYEES

Although shoplifting was the first type of crime against retailers discussed and receives a great deal of attention from retailers, employee theft is as great a cause of inventory shortages, as we indicated in the opening paragraphs of this chapter.

Employee thefts may involve the theft of cash and the theft of merchandise. However, in my opinion, the losses sustained through thefts of merchandise by employees is far greater than those sustained through theft of cash. This is so even though in retail establishments there are often as many employees handling cash as there are employees handling merchandise, and those involved in cash-handling operations often are subject to an irresistible urge to steal simply because the opportunity exists.

Employee Theft of Cash

Retail store employees will use various techniques to perpetrate thefts of cash, and the technique used will always depend upon the opportunities that are presented and the looseness of the procedures established in the area of cash handling. The type of registers used today will range from the old wooden cash drawer to the modern sophisticated minicomputers. The more sophisticated the machinery used in these cash transactions, the more unlikely that thefts of cash by employees will occur. However, even with the sophistication of the minicomputer, there are techniques that are used by employees to supplement their paychecks. We shall list here some of the more common techniques still in use today that retail management and security personnel should be aware of.

1. The failure to record purchases that have been returned and stealing an equal amount of cash.
2. Ringing up less cash than the item cost. The cashier will usually not give the customer a sales slip and in some instances will retain the sales slip indicating the amount of cash underrung so that the

Figure 17-5 Mirrors used in retail store protection are good deterrents. Motorized mirrors are even more effective. Properly installed, they enable clerks actually to observe around a post or like obstruction. (Courtesy A. J. Lehmann Co., Inc.)

money can be pocketed later. An effective deterrent is to establish
a procedure that does not allow the cashiers to empty their own
registers.

3. Failing to ring up a sale properly. This is accomplished when the
cashier leaves the register drawer open, places the money directly
into the register, and does not ring up the sale. The money is later
removed.

4. Voiding a sales check after the customer has departed by ringing
up "no sale" on the register and pocketing the money then or later.

5. A common method used, particularly when customer activity is
heavy, that is to overcharge customers, ring up the correct amount,
and steal the extra cash.

6. If cashiers are authorized to cash checks, they may cash bad checks
for friends or accomplices.

7. If the cash register contains two or more drawers that are assigned
to different clerks, thefts from adjacent drawers will often be made.

8. Falsification of store records to conceal thefts.

9. Processing fictitious refunds or simply giving fraudulent refunds
to accomplices, with the money being divided later.

10. Outright stealing of checks that a customer has been told to make
out to cash.

In the area of administrative handling of the store's cash, employees
in the accounting department will often use some of the following techniques.

1. Pocketing any unclaimed wages or forging names to unclaimed salary
checks.

2. Issuing checks on returned purchases that were never returned and
pocketing collections made on presumably uncollectible accounts.

3. Paying a creditor's invoice twice and keeping and cashing one of
the checks.

4. Padding a payroll through the use of fictitious names or entering
incorrect rates or times worked for an actual employee and dividing
the overpayment with that employee.

5. Forging checks and then destroying them when they are returned
with the periodic bank statement.

6. Increasing the total amount of invoices, checks, or vouchers after
they have been officially approved.

7. Receiving kickbacks from a supplier by invoicing goods above the
established prices.

Employee Theft of Merchandise

The theft of merchandise by employees can take many forms and can be
accomplished by many methods. The merchandise may simply be removed
from a counter using basic shoplifting techniques or more sophisticated

plans involving several employees may be developed. These may include account manipulations that will conceal large-scale thefts or merely organizing a small group of employees who, in collusion with outsiders, remove merchandise in large quantities. This method is referred to as systematic pilfering. Many methods have been developed by employees to steal from their employer; however, in the retail field the following are considered by some experts to be standard.

1. Simply passing merchandise across the counter to an accomplice.
2. Trading stolen merchandise with friends employed in other departments.
3. Hiding merchandise in the store for later removal or hiding merchandise for removal by friends or relatives who may be assigned to the shelf-stocking crews or the custodial service organization.
4. Merely hiding merchandise on the person or elsewhere and removing it from the establishment during breaks or at the end of the day.
5. Stealing unlisted packages from the stock room or from the delivery truck.
6. Stealing from the company's warehouse in collusion with warehouse employees or stealing directly from the store stock room by concealing the goods on the person or in a package.
7. Stealing merchandise from the lay-away area or the returned goods room.
8. Giving friends or relatives employee discounts.
9. Shoplifting during authorized breaks.
10. The theft and use of property passes to remove stolen articles from the store.
11. The outright theft of trading stamps or pocketing trading stamps that should have been given to the customer.
12. Falsifying inventories to cover up shortages.
13. Using sales receipts that were not given to a customer and placing them on stolen goods which will either be kept or returned later for a cash refund.
14. If sales slips are used in the training area or are available in the supply area, they can be attached to merchandise that will be removed from the store.
15. Intentionally damaging or soiling merchandise that the employee desires, particularly if there is a policy of discounting the merchandise for sale to the employee.
16. Persons in the marking room may print incorrect tickets to cover stolen goods.
17. Shipping merchandise to friends' addresses or to the employee's own disguised post office box.
18. Smuggling stolen goods out of the store through the trash removal operations.

Reducing Employee Thefts

All of those security measures discussed in previous chapters will apply
in one degree or another to establishing security measures to prevent or
deter thefts from occurring in the retail establishment. The high annual
turnover among employees in retail stores about equals that of hourly
employees who work in hospital and other health care institutions. However,
retailers have greater problems in employee turnover because they must
substantially increase the number of employees during holiday shopping
periods and when large sales occur. This further dictates the need to establish some "hard-nosed" policies that will discourage employee theft from
occurring. The following measures may be taken to assist in curbing employee thefts.

1. Complete a detailed background investigation of all employees and
   check out references.
2. Do not hire individuals who appear to have serious financial or
   personal problems. If individuals already employed find themselves
   facing such problems, they should be given assistance where possible, and supervisors should be alerted to the possibility that the
   employee may attempt to relieve personal financial problems through
   theft.
3. Establish one employee entrance and exit and insist that all employees
   use this exit any time they enter and exit the store while on duty.
4. Employees who stay late or arrive early for no apparent reason
   should be confronted and asked to explain these actions.
5. Never permit an employee to make a sale to himself or herself.
6. Establish a procedure that requires all employees to check their
   packages in a specific location where they will be picked up when
   they depart at the end of their shift.
7. Whenever possible, each sales person should be given a separate
   cash register or cash drawer and should never be allowed to make
   his or her own final tally.
8. Do not allow free access to any of the storerooms. If the storerooms are not manned, procedures should be established so that
   only department heads or other management personnel enter the
   storeroom areas.
9. If an employee makes frequent errors on sales checks or otherwise
   appears to be inefficient, he or she should be retrained.
10. Establish a strict refund system and follow through to ensure that
    it is not circumvented.
11. Have the security force or members of management make frequent
    checks of the delivery platforms, loading docks, and similar
    locations to ensure that packages and merchandise are not left
    unguarded. At the same time, shipping labels should be checked
    to ensure they are correct.

12. Deal with dishonesty firmly and be consistent in handling dishonest acts and disciplinary problems.
13. Any inventory shortages that are uncovered should be investigated thoroughly to determine as nearly as possible where the shortages occur.
14. When losses are uncovered, regardless of the size, an investigation should be made immediately.
15. Establish a systematic means of inventorying all merchandise sold by the store and supplies used by the store.
16. Deposit cash receipts on a daily basis or have an armored car service pick them up.
17. Require two people, preferably one of them being the manager, to sign all pay disbursement checks.
18. Ensure that the accounting department reconciles bank statements monthly and compare cash receipts with deposits indicated on the statement.
19. Occasionally, particularly during the first few days of the month, the manager should receive and open all incoming mail.
20. Secure the cash registers so that the cashiers cannot read the totals.
21. Serially number all sales checks and all receipts used for refunds.

This list does not cover entirely all of the remedial action that may be taken to reduce or deter employee thefts from the retail establishment; however, if all of these recommended actions are included in the security program, considerable progress will have been made in that direction.

ROBBERY AND BURGLARY

Probably the most violent crimes against the retail business are robbery and burglary.

Robbery, potentially the most violent crime to occur in a retail establishment, consists of thefts in the presence of the victim and others through the use of threats or force. The robber is usually interested only in obtaining cash, and if he or she is interested in obtaining merchandise, it must have a very high value-to-weight ratio because the very nature of the situation requires a speedy departure from the scene.

On the other hand, burglary is the illegal entry of premises with an intent to steal. In the retail industry, the crime will usually occur after store hours or in unattended storerooms where there is very little likelihood that the burglar will come in contact with any employees. Burglars, because they have more time at their disposal, can be more selective in the goods they steal and usually steal in large quantities.

We shall not discuss burglary in detail because the best way to deter burglars is to establish physical security of the premises through locks, alarms, and security personnel. All of these precautions have been discussed in previous chapters. If the building is properly and adequately secured, burglary should be only a minor threat compared to other possible crimes against retail establishments.

The threat of robbery is much greater. The robber strikes during business hours and is usually armed with a firearm of some type. He or she will usually attack the cash register area or the customer service desk (particularly if check-cashing services are offered) or will attempt to steal cash deposits as they are being taken from the store by store personnel at the end of the business day. Obviously, the answer to eliminating this last threat is to engage an armored car service for the transport of cash to the bank. If store employees transport the cash, it should be done during daylight hours and following no set pattern. The times and routes should be varied so that it would be practically impossible for one or two individuals to make a predetermination of the time or the route. Even the exits used from the store should be changed on a daily basis.

Cash losses due to robberies can be considerably minimized by frequently removing excess sums from the cash register and by making frequent bank deposits. Consideration may be given to making more than one bank deposit on any given business day.

Almost all robberies occur only after the robber has had ample opportunity to study the activities of the retail store he or she intends to rob and has made a fairly accurate determination of the amount of money that is on hand at any given time. Therefore, if only small amounts of money are in the cash registers or in the store, the store is a less tempting target and is less likely to be robbed.

If a great deal of cash is allowed to accumulate in the store, the cash room requires high security and should be protected through the use of electrically controlled doors and holdup alarms to make it unattractive for a robber to attempt a holdup. The cash room should not be in an isolated location in the store but preferably in a well-traveled area.

During the training of store personnel, they should be instructed to comply with the demands of robbers, turning over whatever cash or other material they demand. The robbers, in all probability, will be armed and are likely to be nervous and perhaps desperate. If a robber is under the influence of alcohol or drugs or a rank amateur at the trade, he or she will be far more dangerous than a professional. Store personnel, including security guards, must be made to understand that no heroics are expected of them and that any attempt to capture or apprehend a robber is likely to result in serious injury or death.

All suggestions for training and counseling to employees and security guards in banks should be applied in counseling retail store management and employees (see Chapter 16).

Similarly, still cameras activated either electronically or by radio signal and closed circuit television cameras and video-tape recorders will be as effective deterrents in a retail establishment as they are in a financial institution and should be considered for use in the protection scheme.

FRAUDULENT CHECKS AND COUNTERFEIT MONEY

Losses due to the cashing of bad checks or the acceptance of counterfeit certificates can be controlled by a well-planned, rigidly enforced procedure for accepting checks to pay for merchandise or to be cashed in check-cashing operations.

Supermarkets offer cashing services more frequently than do department stores. Several national firms operating supermarkets will issue check-cashing courtesy cards after a simple application has been completed. Seldom is this application very comprehensive, and the background check usually is made merely by calling the banks listed and the local credit bureau. It has been my personal experience that the only information required in applying for check-cashing privileges is the name and address of the individual and the serial numbers of one or two credit cards or perhaps a driver's license.

The basic rule for protection against fraudulent check passers is to secure adequate identification from the person wanting to pay by check. A charge plate or credit card is often used to identify the check casher only by the signature on the credit card. However, in most instances after the signature has been on the credit card for any period of time, it is quite unreadable. Also, the surface of the card on which the signature is written gives a signature considerably different characteristics than the same signature written on paper.

A system manufactured by Veriprint Systems Corporation utilizes impregnated paper to produce a highly readable fingerprint that is kept on file after the individual has been properly and positively identified. Subsequent identification is made when checks are cashed by placing a small piece of the paper on the rear of the check being cashed and asking the check casher to place a fingerprint on this paper. Verification is then made using an instrument commercially called the Vericomp. The original card and fingerprint are inserted in one slot, with the check and fingerprint in a second slot. Fingerprints are automatically read by the electronic device, and a light shows that the print is either verified or not. This system is an excellent means of identification, providing the check casher was properly identified originally.

The use of photographic equipment that is capable of photographing the check and the individual at the same time, thus creating a permanent record of the transaction, is also an effective means of deterring fraudulent check cashers. See Figure 17-6 for a photograph of this equipment.

In addition to establishing the identity of customers who will be authorized to cash checks at a retail establishment, only first-party checks should be

Figure 17-6 This dual-lens camera records the person and the check simultaneously on a single frame of film to produce a record that can be used for investigative purposes. (Regiscope Corporation of America)

cashed. In addition, a limit should be placed on the amount of the check, the amount of purchase, and only personal checks made out to the store should be cashed.

When the Treasury Department becomes aware that a particular batch of counterfeit money is being circulated, this information is almost immediately disseminated to all businesses in the area where cash transactions are made. The information will normally contain the denominations of the

Figure 17-7 This device is known as the Q-Alert. It is battery operated, and when the sensor is rubbed across the face of a genuine certificate, the indicator will light. The light is activated by black engraving on genuine bills but not black printing used for many counterfeits. If the light does not go on, the certificate is presumed to be counterfeit.

counterfeit certificates and possibly more detailed information on the serial numbers or other detectable flaws on the face or the back of the bill that will distinguish it from a legitimate certificate. A device known as the Q-Alert is said to be a fast, simple method to detect counterfeit currency (see Figure 17-7).

CREDIT CARD FRAUD

Most retail stores accept credit cards that are issued by banks and other financial institutions rather than issuing their own credit cards. However, the trend of late has been for stores to issue their own credit cards. Losses can be minimized if certain procedures and precautions are taken.

First, applicants must be closely screened to ensure that their credit is good, and this background and credit check will by itself minimize losses. It should be remembered that this credit screening must be performed within the limits that are prescribed and permitted under Fair Credit Legislation. Firms that operate their own credit plans must ensure that clerks are trained to follow exactly the prescribed screening procedures for the store's own charge cards.

Probably the greatest advantage of the point-of-sale computer terminal used by many large retail firms at the present time, instead of cash registers, is that it can be programmed to verify the credit card in the case of every credit sale that is made. Immediate notification of the status of invalid cards can be programmed into the computer within minutes after the store is made aware by a card holder that the card was lost. Store personnel should be trained to return cards to the customers immediately after they have been used to record the purchase to avoid any confusion or innocent switching of cards and to prevent theft of the cards.

Larger credit card organizations supply their member firms with lists of cards that have been lost or stolen and of fraudulent cards of which they are aware. This list is continually updated. In addition, in most instances, sales personnel can phone a toll-free number to receive up-to-the-minute credit data on the individual presenting the card.

VANDALISM

Vandalism in a retail establishment can occur during business hours or after business hours. During business hours, vandalism can be reduced by properly trained, alert store personnel, because vandals prefer to create damage when they are unnoticed and will usually leave the establishment without doing any damage if they realize they are under surveillance by store personnel or uniformed guards.

Vandalism at night creates quite another problem. In many large cities, this is a major problem, and high loss of assets is involved. Burglary prevention techniques previously discussed will offer good protection against vandalism attacks at night, as will a well-illuminated exterior and the removal of shrubbery and other materials that vandals can use to hide their movement. Frequent police or private security patrols of the area at unannounced times and physical security techniques discussed in the chapter on building security will drastically reduce the losses due to vandalism after the normal business day.

Early in this chapter, we presented statistics on retail crime contained in a release put out by the Consumer Goods and Services Division, U.S. Department of Commerce. This same release ended with the following comment.

> The real question to be settled is whether (1) business wants to bear the cost of subsidizing crime by treating it with kid gloves or (2) wants to invest in a gloves off strategy which, although not without cost, promises to earn a much higher return over the long run.
>
> The first strategy tolerates crime, places responsibility at the doorstep of law enforcement agencies, and abdicates responsibility for self regulation.
>
> The second strategy leads to development of aggressive policies and procedures that (1) anticipate and combat crime within any given business; (2) weed out through individual and collective action problems common to an industry or profession; and (3) forge a cooperative relationship with law enforcement.
>
> Reducing crime loss presents a challenge to which the American business community must respond constructively and competitively. This challenge must be met with dispatch.

18

Reducing Vulnerability
of the Construction
Site to Thefts

Washington – June 23, 1976

Construction Industry Plagued with Heavy Thefts and FBI Help
is Sought

Construction industry officials have asked the FBI for help
in curbing an alarming number of apparently organized thefts
of heavy equipment – bulldozers, loaders and even large cranes.

The highly priced but poorly documented vehicles are generally trucked to auctions hundreds of miles from the site of the
theft or are cannibalized for parts or sold overseas.

Vandalism and theft of materials and hand tools have long
plagued the construction industry, but theft of heavy equipment
is a relatively recent development. Many millions of dollars
worth of equipment is not being recovered. Unlike automobiles,
heavy equipment generally is not licensed and registered. A
bill of sale is proof of ownership, and the police, once a theft
is reported, often do not know what they are looking for. One
contractor reported the theft of a wheel–mounted loader to Cook
County, Illinois, police, only to have the officer ask, "What's
a wheel–mounted loader?"

Recently the Associated General Contractors and Associated Equipment
Distributors collaborated on a pamphlet now being given to local police.
This pamphlet illustrates what various pieces of equipment look like, who
makes them, and where the serial numbers on the equipment are located.

Top officials of the Associated General Contractors (AGC) recently met
with the FBI Director to ask his assistance. One likely outcome of that
meeting may be a special listing for construction equipment in the National
Crime Information Center. The AGC lists the value of all construction
thefts in 1976 at $100 million, a figure that the AGC readily admits is guess
work.

One contractor recounted what, perhaps, is a typical theft. A week
before a scheduled auction of heavy equipment in Kansas City, a man phoned

the auctioneer to say he was bringing in a 1974 Caterpillar high loader to
be sold.

Two days before the auction, the high loader was stolen from a job site
in Calhoun County, Georgia. The thief brought the high loader 800 miles
to Kansas City aboard a rented trailer. The high loader, worth $40,000,
was duly auctioned off.

This theft was brought to light only because a Caterpillar Company official
became curious at what seemed like an attempt to deface the serial number
and checked it back through the company. In the meantime, the thief had
unloaded an illegally acquired bulldozer at another auction in Illinois.

I have always felt that if I were to commit a theft from a guarded construction site, the greatest probability of success would lie in stealing
something of very large size. My reasoning would be (1) that the larger
the item being stolen, the more profitable for me, and that (2) hauling a
Caterpillar tractor off the site on a flatbed truck through the guarded gate
creates less suspicion than does driving out with one or two pieces of plywood. Try stealing $200 worth of tools from a "gang box" on a quiet Sunday
afternoon. You will almost certainly get caught by the weekend guard, whose
primary means of livelihood is probably teaching school. You will be
stopped, questioned, and "turned over to management" every time.

The really big thefts occur this way: Rent a flatbed trailer or steal one
and drive to the site. Greet the guard, give him a cup of coffee or a cold
drink, depending upon the weather, and gripe about having to work on Sunday. Move into the site, load a bulldozer or perhaps two onto the flatbed,
and depart the site without even stopping at the gate. A friendly wave of
the guard's hand will probably indicate that you had a very profitable day.

During the Alaska pipeline project, one could read almost every day
reports that earth-moving equipment, huge dirt trucks, and the like were
disappearing from the project and were being recovered in the United States,
particularly in California and Washington. This entails actual movement
of the machinery, not manipulation of paper work. As indicated in the
article cited at the beginning of this chapter, federal laws should be established to require the registration of all heavy equipment, not only construction equipment, but farm equipment as well at the time manufacture is
complete. I see no need for the use of a registration plate and no need of
a charge to the buyer or owner beyond the administrative cost of processing
titles or ownership papers as the vehicle passes from one owner to another.
If such legislation is enacted, it should provide for retroactive registration
of equipment for a period of at least the past 5 years, because the longevity
of the equipment we are discussing is often considerably greater than that
of an automobile or over-the-road truck.

I believe that if this were accomplished, thefts of this type of equipment
would be reduced and in some areas possibly eliminated, which should
result in lowering the cost of construction of everything from housing to
interstate highways. I include heavy farm equipment in the registration

process because it appears to me that if only construction equipment is registered and controls exercised over its ownership, thieves will automatically slide down the scale and start stealing farm equipment. Farm machinery is nearly as valuable as construction equipment, and yet it is seldom, if ever, protected by any type of security force or physical security device except, perhaps, during tomato and similar harvests on the west coast of the United States when equipment is grouped together and guarded on days that it is not being used. However, in these situations guards are employed primarily to prevent vandalism to the equipment or theft of parts and fuel.

If something positive is not soon done to reduce thefts and vandalism at construction sites, the already increased cost of labor and material will bring all but the most needed construction of new homes, commercial facilities, and public structures to a virtual halt, because all losses during construction and any subsequent losses are eventually paid for by the consumer.

Some experts feel that 20 percent of the cost of construction is due to losses sustained by the contractor. Based upon my experience with surveying construction sites to establish security programs, I feel that this estimate is low. There is no firm figure of the annual national cost, but when one considers the $10 to $15 billion loss to all industry through thefts, the figure of $100 million quoted above appears to be small.

What, then, do these losses mean? To the building contractor, they mean additional expenditures to secure the job site, equipment, and material. To the contractor's company directors, officers, and stockholders, they mean that adequate protection must be provided at the most economical cost to preserve profits. To the customer, they mean that the completion of construction on time and at the predetermined cost will depend to some extent on the contractor's security program.

Many measures that can be incorporated into the security plan to reduce losses merely involve application of those principles already discussed. Control of personnel and vehicles at a construction site is paramount in formulating the security plan.

PERIMETER SECURITY

The establishment of a perimeter barrier is accomplished by installing an industrial-type chain link fence at least 7 feet in height around the entire site. The only openings should be those needed for operational or emergency purposes. Because such a barrier is only a temporary one, the installation of the barbed wire cleavage normally found at permanent installations does not appear to be necessary. The contractor must also consider the value of such a barrier should labor disputes lead to strikes during the construction phase. Designating certain gates in the barrier for use by specific trade union personnel reduces the possibility of site shutdown merely because one union strikes and other union members refuse to cross the picket lines.

All gates that are used operationally should be controlled while they are in use and should be secured with a good-quality padlock when inactive. Railroad-type seals should be used on all inactive gates, and the security force should inspect them on a daily basis.

SPECIAL AREAS INSIDE THE BARRIER

Certain areas inside the barrier, particularly on the larger sites, may require additional protection. If so, an additional or secondary barrier should be erected. The following are some of the areas that may be considered for additional protection.

1. Service areas that contain the gasoline dump, equipment and vehicle repair facilities, and other operations of this sort.
2. Construction material storage areas.
3. Construction site offices of the prime contractor and subcontractors.
4. Gang boxes. These should be grouped in two or three areas rather than allowing them to be scattered throughout the sites. Securing these gang boxes inside one of the secondary barriers will increase the protection; however, it does not negate the necessity for locking each box individually. Small gang boxes may be chained to heavy equipment when operations are not in progress—for example, during the night and on weekends and holidays. Those supplying security guards to construction sites may consider securing the gang boxes with their own padlocks to supplement the padlocks used by the contractor. The boxes may also be sealed in such a way that if they are opened during the period that the security force is on duty, this will be immediately evident. Often a claim of theft is registered, even though the tools were never placed in gang boxes.
5. Open trucks. The installation of industrial convex mirrors on poles at a height of about 14 feet and angled downward permits guards to observe the inside of open-bodied dump trucks, the canisters on "cherry-pickers," and equipment of this sort without requiring the guard to mount the vehicle. Some authorities estimate that 85 percent of the losses of small tools and equipment can be attributed directly to employees of prime contractors and subcontractors who have access to the site.

The establishment of secondary barriers will not only assist in securing specific operations, equipment, and material, but will also assist in controlling access to this equipment during periods that operations are in progress. Obviously, these areas should be secured when operations cease and watchman watch clock key stations should be installed either at the gate to the secondary barrier or inside the area, depending on whether the guard can observe the entire area from the gate.

In road construction or other types of construction that involve vast areas, the establishment of a perimeter barrier to protect the entire site may be impractical. In this case, perimeter barriers of sufficient size should be erected around the logistical areas. Another barrier should be erected for construction equipment, and all equipment should be moved inside the protective barrier at the end of the operational day. These barriers are temporary and can be moved as construction progresses from · one point to another.

GENERAL AREA SECURITY

In addition to those principles previously discussed relative to area security, some specific techniques may be used that will increase the overall security of a construction site.

1. Minimize the number of places that stolen items can be hidden during the day and recovered later, particularly during the hours of darkness.
2. Locate dumpsters used for the removal of trash in areas that can be observed by the security force or by contractor's employees.
3. Whenever possible, eliminate any areas containing a considerable amount of undergrowth that are immediately adjacent to the site, particularly if they are inside the protective barrier. ·
4. Be particularly watchful of excavation areas near the perimeter, and eliminate those that are not necessary as soon as possible.
5. Avoid parking equipment near the perimeter barrier, particularly during the hours of darkness and over weekends.
6. Do not allow trash, salvage material, or other rubbish to remain strewn around the area for an extended period of time. This will not only reduce potential fire hazards but will reduce the places where stolen items can be hidden and recovered later.
7. When equipment is not protected by any type of perimeter barrier, group all of the equipment together during the hours of darkness and on weekends to give the guards an opportunity to protect it adequately.
8. Whenever possible, require employees to park as far from the construction site as possible. If necessary, furnish these parking areas.
9. Establish area patrols, and control these patrols by installing watch clock key stations. Require patrols to be conducted regularly; however, ensure that no pattern is established. When large areas are involved, the security force should be furnished a vehicle capable of negotiating the terrain involved.

BUILDING SECURITY

Building security at a construction site can be considered in two phases. Initially, the protection of the job site offices and later, as construction progresses, security of the partially completed or completed buildings. The security of job site offices can normally be accomplished by grouping the temporary buildings or trailers in a central area so that they can be better observed, patrolled, and protected by the security force. Ensure that the maximum amount of security is furnished these temporary office buildings, because the construction of trailers and prefabricated buildings leaves a great deal to be desired as far as physical security is concerned.

Locking devices installed on trailers by the manufacturer should be supplemented with additional locks, the hinge pins on the doors should be welded in place so that they cannot be removed, and the windows should be covered with additional protection.

Completed or partially completed buildings, in addition to being patrolled by the guards, can be further protected by the temporary installation of protective alarms of the portable type that can be moved on a day-to-day basis. Most of these alarms can be either AC or DC powered. These alarms may be trip wire, photoelectric, or microwave intrusion detectors. If some buildings or portions of buildings are complete and the site is still under construction, temporary alarms such as photoelectric cells, pressure mats, motion detectors, or local audio alarms may be temporarily installed. All alarms, when activated, should produce an audio and visual signal to indicate to the security guard on duty that the area is being violated.

PROTECTIVE LIGHTING OF THE CONSTRUCTION SITE

Temporary protective lighting should be installed at all perimeter gates or avenues of approach into the site and along the entire perimeter barrier if one is installed. If no primary or secondary barriers are installed, then a protective lighting system assumes even greater importance. Protective lighting should be installed in the areas where equipment is grouped, in service areas, and in material storage areas. This lighting should be installed whether or not a perimeter barrier is erected.

PERSONNEL PRACTICES

There is no doubt that most of the thefts from construction sites, as indicated earlier, are internally generated, whether they take the form of day-to-day pilferage or the theft of large items by workers who return to the site after darkness. Sometimes these thefts from construction sites can lead to greater losses later on. For example, one bank construction site was entered and a copy of the plans to the safe deposit and cash storage vaults were stolen.

The only effective way to prevent thefts on the job during working hours is through a good program of identification and control of personnel. Security must begin with top management of the construction company and must include every one of the contractor's employees, subcontractors and their employees, and visitors and salespeople that will be authorized on site. Given the large number of employees involved in any project, including subcontractor employees, no individual can personally recognize those authorized or not authorized to enter the site. Therefore, the cost of manufacturing identification cards and issuing and recovering them from those personnel who will be authorized inside the protected area will be a minor cost compared to the losses that could be sustained if personnel control is not established.

Most of the techniques discussed here apply especially to establishing an effective security program at a construction site; however, again we remind the reader that all those basic principles of security discussed in other chapters can be applied in one manner or another in the overall protection plan.

FIRE PROTECTION AT CONSTRUCTION SITES

There is no doubt that second only to the losses sustained through the theft of equipment and material are those losses sustained through fires that occur at construction sites. In the majority of the cases, these fires occur before construction is complete; because permanent fire fighting equipment, such as sprinkler systems, is not yet installed, construction sites must rely upon local fire departments, who must lay hose from the nearest hydrant to the fire scene.

It is of utmost importance that all-weather roads are provided, water mains installed, and other underground work completed prior to the start of major construction. Access roads furnished for fire fighting equipment can also be used by construction equipment, and the water supply can be used for both construction and fire fighting purposes.

A day-to-day inspection of the construction site should be conducted to ensure that no open trenches may delay or altogether prevent vehicular access to the fire scene. If open trenches are unavoidable, alternate routes to the structures should be provided, and the servicing fire department should be informed of these routes.

Combustible or flammable materials should be stored some distance from the structures being constructed as well as a safe distance from the construction site's temporary offices.

If construction is in progress during cold weather, additional precautions must be taken to ensure that heating equipment in the temporary offices is safe to operate and properly functioning. Site foremen and supervisors should constantly be alert to ensure that heating equipment such as "salamanders" used to heat work areas does not create unnecessary fire hazards.

The early selection of a project fire chief or fire warden is essential. This individual should have some previous experience and should be knowledgeable in the area of fire protection and prevention techniques. He should be required to formulate and distribute rules for the protection of the project and should be given the authority to enforce them. He should also act as liaison with the servicing fire department and should keep that department advised when any particularly hazardous work is being conducted. He should advise the servicing fire department of planned completion dates of the various phases, particularly those which, in his opinion, make the structure unusually susceptible to fire.

This fire chief or fire warden should be charged with the responsibility of organizing fire fighting teams assigned to specific buildings or areas, including assignment of specific individuals to man emergency equipment and open and close hydrants or automatic sprinkler risers, as the situation may dictate.

Provision should be made for convenient fire department access to the area and all buildings at all times. In any building, at least one stairway should be carried up with construction so that it is available for use by the fire department to gain access and as an emergency escape for workers.

The probability of total loss obviously is greater in the absence of precautionary measures. Therefore, it is necessary to increase fire protection as work progresses toward completion. As the need for combustible form work, scaffolding, material storage, temporary buildings, and other hazardous materials diminishes, they should be removed from the site. Temporary ladders and catwalks installed for construction and fire fighter access should be removed when permanent stairways, stairway enclosures, firewalls, and other features of the completed structure will retard the horizontal and vertical spread of fire.

OTHER SECURITY MEASURES

Another security measure that may be considered is the storage of material away from the construction site in a more secure warehouse; the material can be moved to the site on a day-to-day basis only as it is needed. Usually this type of storage area is available within a few minutes' transportation distance of the construction site, and use of a warehouse should be seriously considered if the construction site is not protected with a perimeter barrier, adequate lighting, and a security force.

Construction sites may be protected through the use of dogs that are allowed to roam inside the perimeter barrier inside partially completed buildings during periods when operations have ceased. In one instance at a construction site in Texas, rattlesnakes were placed in excavations near the perimeter, and this fact was widely publicized. Admittedly, these two practices will definitely deter the vandal and in all probability serve as an effective deterrent to the thief; however, they serve as greater deterrent to the police and the fire departments that may be required to enter the site. Therefore, I personally would not recommend the employment of dogs, reptiles, or any other type of animal that is not under the specific control of an individual.

19

Individual
and Group Theft Controls

Well, I left Kentucky back in '49, I went to Detroit working an assembly line.

The first year they had me put the wheels on Cadillacs.

Every day I'd watch them beauties roll by and sometimes I'd hang my head and cry, 'cause I always wanted me one that was long and black.

One day I devised myself a plan that should be the envy of most any man.

I'd sneak it out of there in a lunch box in my hand.

Now gettin' caught meant gettin' fired, but I figured I'd have it all by the time I retired and I'd have me a car worth at least a hundred grand.

I'd get it one piece at a time,

And it wouldn't cost me a dime.

You'll know it's me when I come through your town.

I'm gonna ride around in style,

I'm gonna drive everybody wild,

Cause I'll have the only one there is around.

So the very next day when I punched in with my big lunch box and with help from a friend, I left that day with a lunch box full of gears.

I never considered myself a thief, but GM wouldn't miss just one little piece, especially if I strung it out over several years.

The first day I got me a fuel pump, and the next day I got me an engine and a trunk, then I got me a transmission and all the chrome.

The little things I could get in my big lunch box like nuts and bolts and all four shocks, but the big stuff was snuck out in my buddy's mobile home.

This is the beginning of a song by Johnny Cash and The Tennessee Three entitled "One Piece at a Time." It appears under the Columbia label on a record cut in 1976 by CBS, Inc.

This song should awaken those who still are not convinced that employees steal. Regardless of the type business, if it requires hiring people, the business will sustain losses. The severity of the loss will be based upon many factors: type and size of the commodity or material being handled; number of employees; mode of transportation; personnel controls in force; and many other conditions, all of which will have some effect upon the loss of assets.

Some people steal and do not feel it is actually stealing. There is a story of a proud father who had just completed reading a fine report card given him by his young son. While still praising the boy, he looked through his pockets for a pen to sign the card. Finding none, the son offered him the one that he had in his pocket. The father took the ballpoint and, seeing the name of the school inscribed on the pen, said, "Son, where did you get this pen?" "From school, dad—the teacher has a lot of them in her desk," the son replied. The father severely admonished the boy and said, "Don't take any more pens that don't belong to you, son. If you need any, I can get plenty at the pen factory where I work."

It is a fact that many employees take small items without thinking they are actually stealing. Yet these same people will place these items in their pockets, so that the gate guard will not discover them. Perhaps the place for management to start is asking, "How many criminals do I really employ?"

In the chapter on identification and control of personnel, I point out that identification of a potential employee should be established before accepting him or her as an employee and that this identification requires that a thorough background check be conducted.

If the background investigation covers all periods of time employed or unemployed of 30 days or longer for the past 15 years, or, in the case of young people, beginning with high school entrance, plus those other areas recommended, management can be reasonably certain that those applicants with a recorded history of theft or instability can be eliminated and will not become a part of the work force.

Jacob Guzik, who was at one time Al Capone's bookkeeper, is reputed to have said, "I can steal more with a pencil then ten men with guns." Remember that all losses do not necessarily go out over the dock or through the employee exit or the front door.

ELECTRONICS USED TO STEAL

Today's businesses face not only loss of assets through fraud, embezzlement, and physical removal of raw and finished products; the problem of theft of proprietary information during the research and development stage and subsequent loss of assets is increasing almost daily. George Orwell, in his novel entitled 1984, predicts a society under constant surveillance by "Big Brother." Today, electronic surveillance can legally be used by law enforcement agencies under a system of regulatory statutes, but it is Cousin Charlie who is also using these devices and techniques to steal company secrets ranging from development of new products to marketing schedules and strategies.

We shall concern ourselves in this chapter with employee thefts and physical controls to deter or eliminate them. However, thefts using electronic devices are a real hazard in many instances. When this possibility does exist, I would recommend that management secure the services of an accredited professional electronics engineer specializing in the area of locating these hidden eavesdropping devices.

Those readers who desire to expand their knowledge in this field should secure a copy of "Utilization of Electronic Surveillance Equipment in Crime Countermeasure Programs," by Samuel W. Daskam, General Manager, F. G. Mason Engineering, Inc., Fairfield, Connecticut 06430. Mr. Daskam's discussion of electronic surveillance sweeping techniques (pp. 7-8) can be easily understood by the layman and is complete in all details.

WARNING SIGNALS OF INTERNAL DISHONESTY

Many lists of signals that may indicate that internal stealing is being committed have been compiled. There also have been many occasions when honest employees were treated unjustly because management misinterpreted or overreacted to some of the signals.

Mr. Saul D. Astor, President of Loss Prevention Institute, Inc., an affiliate of the New York-based Manpower Safeguards, Inc., points out that, "Too often signals pointing to internal theft, even when noticed, are mistakenly ascribed to chance, eccentricity, coincidence, or some other benign happenstance . . . and the signals are therefore ignored." Astor's list of signals is as complete a list as I have ever found published, and, with his permission, they are listed here.

Signals from Merchandise, Files, and Equipment

1. Merchandise or materials missing from boxes or containers.
2. Merchandise or materials in unusual place—such as near an exit, on top of phone booth, in rest room, or in concealed corner.
3. Merchandise wrapped in a package or bag for no good reason.
4. Merchandise in wrong box.
5. Merchandise in trash.
6. Partially empty cartons where only full cartons are supposed to be kept.
7. Ladders, fixtures or piled up boxes located to give access to windows.
8. Equipment which can be used for theft (magnets, crow bars, etc.) found in areas where they have no legitimate purpose.
9. Something out of position or missing between night and morning.

10. Extra merchandise in receiving or shipping areas.
11. Merchandise wrappings or labels in rest room, locker room, trash, etc.
12. Packing or wrapping materials out of place.
13. A critical document found in the trash or discarded elsewhere.
14. Missing files or documents; files or documents out of place.
15. Frequent damage to containers of desirable or expensive goods.
16. Documents, authorization stamps, etc., in possession of employee who does not need such items to perform his job.

Signals from Locks, Alarms, Doors, Windows, and Perimeter

1. Signs of forced entry at perimeter doors and windows, such as scratches near lock, damage to door jamb, broken panels, etc.
2. Gates, window screens, fences, etc., bent out of shape.
3. Signs of tampering on interior doors, cabinets, transoms, etc.
4. Windows found broken or unlocked.
5. Emergency exit lock broken or open.
6. Alarm system wires or contacts broken, damaged, or jumped.
7. Security seals and locks seemingly locked are actually unlocked.
8. Truck seals missing.
9. Footprints or signs of activity in remote external perimeter areas.
10. Keys missing or keys found in possession of unauthorized persons.
11. Key that does not fit a lock for which it was intended (indicating lock was switched).
12. Broken locks.
13. Frequent "false" alarms or frequent inability to close premises because system shows a "break" somewhere.
14. Electronic security devices frequently in need of repair and inoperable.
15. Evidence of pre-opening or after-closing unauthorized entry to warehouse or stockroom.
16. External perimeter lights frequently broken or inoperable.
17. Indications of prowling on the roof or on emergency staircase.
18. Unscheduled opening shown on central station alarm report or time lock record, not satisfactorily explained or authorized in advance.
19. Disappearance of time lock or central station alarm records.

Signals from Records and Documents

1. Discrepancies between inventory records and physical counts.
2. Inability to ship out same number of units received or manufactured because some units are missing.
3. Controlled documents missing or out of sequence.
4. Excessive number of "voided" documents.
5. Decline in employee purchases.

6. Discrepancies in cash funds.
7. Daily bank deposit does not correspond with receipts.
8. Bad checks frequently accepted or approved by a particular employee.
9. Frequent need to replace tools and equipment, not consistent with normal wear.
10. Unusual rise in consumption of supply items.
11. Frequent payment for merchandise or materials based on vendor's "proof of delivery" rather than normal receiving documents.
12. Cost of raw material per unit of production is higher than previous averages.
13. Unexplained drop in gross profit percentage.
14. Unusually high percentage of refunds or credits.
15. Figures are different on original and carbon copies of a document, although all should be prepared in one writing and should be the same.
16. Erasures, changes, pencil entries on documents which are not supposed to be altered.
17. Unexplained alterations in inventory records.
18. Documents not properly signed or countersigned.
19. Excessive use of substitute records because originals are "lost."
20. Employment application cannot be checked out.

Signals from Personal Behavior

1. Double talk or inconsistencies by an employee who is explaining discrepancies or "errors."
2. Violent temper or other unpleasant behavior which tends to discourage people from asking questions.
3. Symptoms of a drug user.
4. Heavy gambling on horses, cards, numbers, sports, etc.
5. Borrowing, particularly from loan sharks, but also habitual borrowing of any kind.
6. Expensive habits such as heavy drinking, drugs, extramarital affairs.
7. Having more money or spending more than earnings could support:

   a. Flashes big roll.
   b. Buys expensive items—jewelry, car, house, boat.
   c. Has expensive hobby.
   d. Always picks up check at restaurant.
   e. Dresses expensively.

8. Disgruntled, dislikes boss or company, and complains about being underpaid or overworked.
9. Admission of theft from prior employer.
10. Abnormal fear of, or antagonism toward, security or executive personnel.

11. Possession of illegal knife, gun, brass knuckles, etc.
12. Terrorization of one employee by another.
13. Espousing violent revolution.
14. Never takes time off or vacation, or comes in during vacation or day-off.
15. Concealed family relationships among employees.

Signals from Employee Activities

1. Secretive conversations among employees; secretive phone conversations; sending or receiving cryptic messages.
2. Coming in too early or staying too late for no good reason.
3. Frequent errors due to "carelessness" or deliberate intent.
4. Frequent short-cuts in procedures to "expedite" procedures.
5. Habitual carrying of gym bags, shopping bags, etc.
6. Habitual wearing of unusually loose-fitting clothing.
7. Coming out of rest rooms or secluded areas with clothes bulging.
8. Attempting to distract or hold the attention of a supervisor for no good reason.
9. Repeated violations of such security regulations as:

   a. Use of unauthorized entrance or exit.
   b. Keeping personal packages or handbags at work station.
   c. Violation of employee purchase procedures.

10. Using or wearing merchandise just received or manufactured and not yet available for sale.
11. Using or wearing stock merchandise without authorization.
12. Suspicious damages to merchandise (if employees can buy damaged goods at discounts or get damaged merchandise for nothing).
13. Signalling by hand, whistle, etc., when supervisor approaches.
14. Rapid loading of a truck while other trucks loaded more slowly.
15. Signing another employee's name or initials.
16. Return to work area after others have left to retrieve something forgotten or for some other pretext.
17. Security personnel overly friendly with employees, customers, or outside servicemen.
18. Complaints by employees that personal belongings are being stolen.
19. Presence of employee in an area where he has no legitimate business.
20. Too much time taken by truck driver to cover delivery route (indicating possibility of illegal drops).
21. Offering items for sale to employees at unrealistically low prices.
22. Punching time cards or signing out for other employees.

Signals from Customers and Outsiders

1. Frequent customer complaints of shortages or substitutions in shipments.
2. Unusually large or frequent credits to a customer for returned merchandise, especially as a ratio to sales.
3. Anonymous phone calls or letters concerning theft.
4. Unusually friendly relationship among employees and such outsiders as truck drivers, repairmen, trash collectors.
5. Frequent contact among employees and visitors, expecially those visitors who carry shopping bags or other containers.
6. Contact by employees with such unsavory characters as gamblers, pushers, loan sharks, etc.
7. Many customers always deal with one employee and refuse to buy from anyone else.
8. Stock being sold in outlets that never buy from the company.
9. Gifts or favors to accounts payable employee from suppliers or to accounts receivable employee from customers.
10. Reduced purchases by customers who deal closely with warehouse or shipping personnel.
11. Presence of outside personnel (telephone repair, building service, salesmen, etc.) in areas where they have no legitimate business, or in unbusinesslike communication with employees.

Security personnel, consultants, and advisors can add to each of the above lists those signals peculiar to their particular environment. However, to compile and possess a list will do little to reduce thefts and pilferage unless some determined remedial action is incorporated into the security plan.

THE EXTENT OF THE PROBLEM

I dislike statistics, first, because when dealing with thefts and crime in general, most are merely estimates and, second, because any figures quoted are soon outdated and tend to change almost daily. However, the U.S. Department of Commerce in a release in early 1976 estimated American business was losing between $5 and $20 billion annually (the National Council on Crime and Delinquency in February 1975 released a figure of from $5 to $15 billion annually).

The U.S. Chamber of Commerce estimates an annual cost of $40 billion. This figure includes cost of other crimes in addition to employee thefts. The total value of U.S. securities stolen from securities handling institutions in 1975 was estimated to be in excess of $20 billion. Whatever the estimate, from whatever source, it is <u>safe</u> to assume that the cost of employee theft is tremendous, and it is an accepted business practice to pass this cost on to the consumer in the form of increased prices.

THE ROLE OF THE UNDERCOVER AGENT

The employment of an undercover agent usually supplied by a private investigative company can be an effective aid in determining the amount of losses sustained and how the property is being removed from the facility.

The services of undercover agents are secured through the facility's regular employment procedures, and they are placed either in the affected department, office, or area, or on maintenance or custodial crews to afford them a wider range of activity and, therefore, the opportunity to contact more of the employees.

Undercover agents will usually be highly trained specialists in their area and, as often as not, experts in a particular trade or activity. The primary reason for any failures on the part of undercover agents can usually be attributed to the fact that too many individuals in a particular facility are aware that an undercover agent has been employed and placed in a particular area. In most instances, a member of top management will make the decision to use an undercover agent, and he should maintain this secrecy. There is no reason to notify even the personnel office, the department to which the agent is assigned, or any other individual. If there is an opening in the company and the agent has the proper qualifications for the job, the personnel department will treat the agent simply as a qualified applicant for employment.

The undercover agent can be employed either prior to, during, or even after a physical security survey has been conducted; however, it is best to employ an agent prior to the survey, so that the means used to remove property from the facility can be determined in advance. This information will help the security analyst to develop the best techniques to remove the hazard.

After an undercover agent has been placed in the facility, it is possible that the information he or she develops requires that the agent be moved into another area and/or department. This is usually accomplished with considerable ease, because the agent has probably been a good worker, capable of performing many functions. So long as the transfer is not considered a promotion, the transfer can usually be effected without anyone becoming suspicious. If a union organization prohibits such transfers or if longevity is involved, a second agent may have to be employed.

The greatest obstacle to hiring an undercover agent occurs when the work force is tightly organized, and some of it has been laid off. In these instances, it is practically impossible to place an undercover agent in the organized group until the original work force returns to work. However, other pretexts can be used. If more than one facility is owned by a particular company, the agent could be placed in a plant as an observer or to study certain methods to be used at a plant elsewhere. If the services of an undercover agent are required, the professionals furnishing this service will certainly devise a means of having their agent placed in the operation.

USE OF LIE DETECTOR IN COMBATING EMPLOYEE THEFT

The use of lie detectors in detection and prevention of employee theft was unheard of until a few years ago, and in many states the use of such devices is outlawed. However, these laws vary; some prohibit the use of a polygraph examination in pre-employment practices but do not restrict its use during investigations, providing, of course, that the subject submits voluntarily.

Sometimes the law merely prohibits the use of information gained as a result of a lie detector test in a court of law. Security personnel should research local laws as they apply to the use of this device.

For the benefit of those readers not familiar with the polygraph machine or the technique employed in its successful use, I shall briefly discuss the pertinent salient factors that, when properly accomplished, make the lie detector a valuable instrument in theft investigation and a valuable deterrent as well.

THE INSTRUMENT

In an article entitled "The Lie Detector Technique: A Reliable and Valuable Investigative Aid" (American Bar Association Journal, vol. 50, no. 55, May 1964), by Fred E. Inbau, who then was a professor of law at Northwestern University, and John E. Reid, of John E. Reid and Associates, described the machine as follows:

> The instrument that is used in the proper application of the lie
> detector technique is essentially a pneumatically operated mechani-
> cal recorder of changes in respiration, blood pressure and pulse.
> These basic features may be supplemented with a unit for record-
> ing what is known as the galvanic skin reflex (based, supposedly,
> on changes in the activity of the sweat pores in a subject's hands)
> and another unit for recording muscular movements and pres-
> sures. Any instrument that does not include respiration and
> blood pressure-pulse tracing is totally inadequate for lie detector
> testing in actual case situations. A galvanometer, used alone
> may function quite well in experimental testing in a psychology
> laboratory but its utility in actual cases is rather negligible.

Obviously the results obtained from lie detector tests depend upon the expertise, education, and training of the examiner and his or her ability to interpret the results of the test. In these interpretations, the examiner must be able to determine when he or she receives truthful answers and when the answers are obviously false.

The accuracy of the technique of interpretation is often difficult to estimate. Errors are made, but the relatively few errors that do occur will usually not harm the innocent, because mistakes in diagnosis almost always involve a failure to detect lies of guilty subjects rather than the attribution of lies to a person who is actually telling the truth.

In the past few years, the operation of lie detection equipment has become more sophisticated, and hundreds of competent professional operators are available. Private investigative companies will normally employ polygraph operators either on a per-person or daily basis. In large companies, they are often placed on annual retainers and used as the need arises.

THE MAGNETOMETER IN THEFT CONTROL

The magnetometer is the device that is so familiar at almost all of the nation's 530-odd airports. The device has proved to be a valuable deterrent to aircraft hijacking by disclosing metal objects larger than a certain specified mass that are carried by individuals. My own personal experience in having supervised airport operations using these devices in cities as large as Chicago, through medium-sized cities such as Memphis, and down to smaller cities such as Roanoke, Virginia, have indicated that if the personnel are properly trained in its use and the sensitivity of the machine is properly adjusted, the device is absolutely reliable.

In addition to being used at airports, these machines are used by industrial plants, museums, court houses, and computer installations, and by a long list of other facilities, including hospitals and narcotic centers.

Magnetometers designed for general use come in two basic designs. One is the configuration that is referred to as the walk-through detector; the second is the hand detector. The latter are hand-operated instruments used to search the entire body electronically by passing the device along the sides, under the arms, and along the legs and the front and back. This device is normally used when only a small number of personnel need to be searched. Figure 19-1 shows a walk-through magnetometer that would normally be used in searching employees departing a facility or a certain area within the facility.

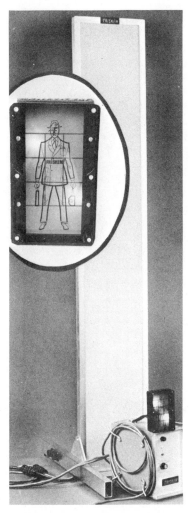

Figure 19-1 A walk-through magnetometer with its detector in the lower left of the photo. The blowup of the monitor shows lights on the screen indicating on what part of the body metal was detected. (Courtesy Infinetics, Inc.)

MECHANICAL DEVICES

In addition to the various types of locks, there are numerous mechanically
operated devices that will assist in reducing thefts by employees and others.
For example, a tamper-proof nut will foil theft of wheels from an employee's
automobile in the parking lot (see Figures 19-2 and 19-3); another device
will deter, if not eliminate, theft of truck trailers and tandem trailers
parked at the industrial facility or the terminal (see Figure 19-4).

In addition to these items, one must always consider the effectiveness
of reducing thefts by individuals through purse and lunch box inspections,
the package pass systems, and other methods that have been practiced for
many years.

Paper shredders should be considered for the protection of documents.
These shredders, or pulverizers, range in size from those that fit any
ordinary wastebasket to large machines that will pulverize huge amounts
of paper in minutes. These waste paper destroyers should not be overlooked
if protection of proprietary information is important. If huge quantities of
paper and other writing or printing material are generated, it may be economical over a longer period of time to bale the waste and sell it rather

Figure 19-2   Tamper-proof nuts that can be utilized to increase the secur-
ity of automobile wheels and other exposed items that are bolted to a surface.
The uppermost item is the lock, and the lower item the key to operate it.
(Courtesy Torque Locks, Inc.)

Figure 19-3 The same type tamper-proof nut applied to secure a spare wheel and tire. (Courtesy Torque Locks, Inc.)

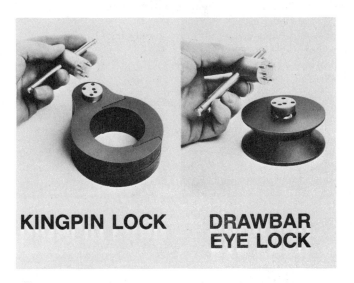

KINGPIN LOCK **DRAWBAR EYE LOCK**

Figure 19-4 The kingpin lock on the left and the drawbar eye lock on the right are easily installed and almost impossible to remove without the keys shown in the model's hand. Such devices may not eliminate thefts of trailers but will certainly ensure a considerable delay in removing the items. (Courtesy Torque Locks, Inc.)

than to dispose of it through trash removal operations that move it to a
public dump or an incinerator.

Now, up to now everything went all right 'till we tried to put it
all together one night and that's when we noticed that something
was definitely wrong.

The transmission was a '53 and the motor turned out to be a
'73 and when we tried to put in the bolts all the holes was gone.

So we drilled it out so that it would fit and with a little bit of
help from an adapter kit, we had that engine running just like a
song.

I got it one piece at a time,
And it didn't cost me a dime.
You'll know it's me when I come through your town.
I'm gonna ride around in style,
I'm gonna drive everybody wild.
'Cause I'll have the only one there is around.

Uh, yeah, Red Rider, this here's the Cotton Mouth in the
psycho-billy-Cadillac, c'mon. Huh?

Uh, this here's the Cotton Mouth, and negatory on the cost
of this machine, there Red Rider.

You might say I went right up to the factory and picked it
up - it's cheaper that way.

Uh, what model is it?

Well, it's a '49, '50, '51, '52, '53, '54, '55, '56, '57, '58,
'59 automobile.

It's a '60, '61, '62, '63, '64, '65, '66, '67, '68, '69, '70
automobile.

This may not necessarily be the only car in the world that was built
piece by piece with stolen parts. It seems to me that I have seen several
strange-looking automobiles on the road during the past few years.

20

Minimize the Bomb Threat — Plan Ahead

The FBI reported that during the first 5 months of 1976, 23 persons were killed, 108 persons were injured, and an estimated $6 million in property damage occurred as a result of a total of 549 bombs being exploded in the United States. The death toll during the period equaled the number killed during the same period in 1975. However, the injury toll was higher by 50 victims.

In May 1976, there were 100 bombings or attempted bombings which resulted in 5 persons killed and 22 injured. Over 95 percent were written bomb threats or hoaxes. The chance that a threat may be real requires that some plans be prepared to ensure the safety of building occupants and the public. To reduce property damage, the plan must include search procedures by occupants, usually employees, and they must receive some training in these procedures. Responsibility for action rests with building or facility management initially, and through management it rests with the security force or local police or fire department bomb squads.

Decisions must be made quickly when the threat is received, and search teams must be able to move rapidly to their areas and conduct their searches systematically and thoroughly, even though the caller may have specified that the bomb was placed in a certain area. On some occasions, a caller claimed that a bomb had been placed in a certain area and was set to be detonated at a specific time when, in reality, the bomb was actually located in a remote area some distance from the area specified. Obviously, the intent here is that should the caller decide on a second threat some days later, he will in all probability cause an evacuation of the facility, because management must assume that there actually is a bomb located in the facility and not necessarily in that area indicated by the caller.

Before any bomb threat procedure is implemented, a meeting should be held with all personnel in the building or facility. In a high-rise tenant-occupied office building, this may mean that the building management may be required to conduct several meetings to instruct the majority of the occupants. Personnel should be fully informed of the plan and the reasons for the plan, because their full cooperation is needed if the plan is to be successful. Without this cooperation, there is little chance that any plan will succeed.

It is best that those who would be most affected by a bomb threat plan
be given the information straight from management rather than to receive
bits and pieces of information through rumor or employee gossip. Furthermore, if all occupants are aware that an effective bomb threat plan is in
existence and that evacuation will not necessarily be made, it could have a
deterrent effect on hoax calls from within or even from former disgruntled
employees. All personnel should understand the seriousness of conveying
bomb threats by phone or mail and should be aware that the penalties are
severe.

WHY DO PEOPLE CALL IN BOMB THREATS?

Numerous categories of individuals may telephone a bomb threat, ranging
from former employees, competitors, thrill seekers, criminals, political
extremists, and the like. The list of possible suspects would be quite long.
As in police work, the rule generally is that everyone and anyone involved
in an investigation is a good suspect. The security manager, when attempting to ferret out a suspect in a telephoned bomb threat, should not exclude
anyone in the initial investigation, either friend or a possible enemy.

The desire to create publicity is probably among the first reasons that
bomb threats are conveyed. This is particularly true when the activity is
a part of a scheme of the political extremist or the revolutionary. Either
individually or collectively, they are seeking recognition. In almost every
instance in the past when a bomb was actually exploded inside or outside a
building, newspaper offices and radio and television stations would receive
a call within minutes of the explosion—sometimes they received calls almost
at the moment of detonation.

The extortionist often uses a bomb threat to extort money or for other
reasons. The extortionist, however, will usually on the first call tell the
party upon whom the extortion attempt is being directed the true location
of the explosive device and the time that the device is scheduled to be
detonated. These calls usually allow sufficient time for a search for the
bomb to be made, and the device is usually found and dismantled. On
occasion, dummy bombs have been used, merely to prove to the individual
or individuals being threatened that the very real possibility exists that
the bomber can and will actually place a real explosive device. These
tactics are used to convince the person being threatened that the bomber
means business and that if his or her demands are not met, an explosive
or incendiary device will, in fact, be detonated.

Some individuals construct and place bombs in facilities for no other
reason than to kill or injure people. Obviously, this individual is a sadist
and is probably among the most dangerous among the group that are capable
of planting explosive or incendiary devices. The sadist will, in all probability, plant his device where the most people are located to ensure himself
that people are killed and maimed.

At the other extreme is the bomber who does not want anyone killed or injured and therefore calls after he has planted his device and warns that the device is to go off at a certain time. If his call is taken by an individual who treats it as a hoax, the bomber may have to plead with the individual who answered to believe him and evacuate before someone is killed or injured.

Sometimes police officers are killed by a bomb that has been placed for the express purpose of killing a policeman. This will quite often be done by placing an explosive device that is set to detonate the moment it is moved. These devices are similar to the booby traps used by the military. In other instances, bombs are constructed to detonate when normal dismantling procedures are started. This type of bomb was placed in a locker at New York's La Guardia Air Terminal in September 1976. The bomb was constructed and placed in a cooking pot and was apparently wired to detonate when the cover of the container was removed. In this instance, police bomb squad officers were killed and injured.

There is also the individual who wants to become a hero of sorts and plants a real or fake bomb in a facility and then claims to have received a bomb threat, including notification of where the bomb was located. Rather than notifying the individuals in management who are charged with the responsibility of handling bomb threats, our "hero" discovers the bomb or fake device and, in all probability, will remove it from the facility. However, frequently these faked calls are perpetrated by security guards, particularly during late night shifts, who claim to have received the calls. They find the device and notify local bomb squad officials who arrive on the scene to remove or dismantle the device. The security guard receives a hero's tribute in the local paper the following day. Fortunately, these individuals are almost always apprehended through good police investigations.

Fortunately, persons who telephone a bomb threat are apprehended, arrested, and prosecuted, and, in most instances, convicted and incarcerated. The high incidence of prosecution and conviction has somewhat assisted in deterring bomb threats. For example, it is a federal crime for an individual even to imply at the airline check-in counter or at the search point that he has a bomb or will destroy the aircraft. In numerous instances, individuals have been arrested and investigated merely because these empty threats were conveyed as the result of having spent too much time in the airport lounge awaiting flights.

PREPARING THE PLAN

Plans and organization to cope with bomb threats must be made in advance, and such plans must be clearly identified as being designed to cope with bomb threats and are not bomb removal plans.

A well-organized bomb threat plan using the organization as it is already established will minimize any risks taken, and if the information is properly disseminated, it will instill confidence and should assist in the elimination of panic should a threat be received and the plan implemented.

Planning should start with a designation of a control center that should normally be near the focal point of communications, usually telephone, but may include radio in some instances. This control center may be located at the switchboard or at the central guard headquarters if the organization has a security force. The control center should be isolated from adjacent activities, and no personnel should be authorized in the center who are not assigned some specific duty.

In preparing the bomb threat plan, the local police or fire department bomb squad officials should be consulted, because these bomb disposal units will be directly involved not only in any actual bomb removal and subsequent deactivation of the device, but also in searches of the facility when threats are received.

In developing the plan, the planners should consider the current identification system used for control of personnel and whether or not the identification system could be made more secure and the controls more restrictive. The need for the bomber to have access to the area where he will place his device immediately indicates that if he is successful, more restrictions and tighter controls must be established at the points of ingress and egress. Without these controls, the plan almost immediately loses a great deal of its effectiveness.

The planners should have floor plans of the entire building, and these plans must be up to date. In high-rise office buildings, almost each time a new tenant is accommodated, the configuration of the floor is changed. The floor plans of each level should be studied in order to determine those areas where a bomber could most easily hide a device. These areas should be marked on the floor plans, and when the search teams are organized and trained, the floor plans with these areas designated must be furnished them, because obviously these are the first areas that should be searched.

Second in importance only to the study of the floor plan is a detailed inspection of the entire building with particular attention to those areas already designated on the floor plan as possible bomb device sites. The building inspection is made not only to verify that the floor plans studied are correct, but to survey other areas on each floor where a bomb device may be secreted in the ceiling or at the ceiling level. The inspection of the building should involve a detailed inspection of the ceiling, the air ducts, the potted plants, and other likely hiding places, including wastebaskets or large ashtrays in the common areas on each floor. The walls should also be inspected, and the location and size of paintings, pictures, or plaques that could be used to hide an explosive device should be noted. Using an explosive compound, a small pocket or wrist watch, and a small battery, an explosive device small enough to be placed behind a picture or painting could be fashioned; it would be impossible to detect such a device without removing the art object. It is entirely possible that a bomber could photograph a painting or picture, duplicate it, install his explosive or incendiary device, and then plant the device merely by switching the pictures, without even having to remove the original from the facility.

The inspection of the building must include ceiling lights with removable covers, easily removable ceiling panels, fire hose cabinets, and all equipment rooms. This inspection should also include a check of all doors that should remain locked except possibly when in actual use; if violations are found, immediate remedial action should be taken.

The physical inspection of the facility should also include an inspection of the activities taking place above or below a computer area or an executive office. Accessibility of these areas must be assessed, and possibly some changes may be required. In one instance in which I was involved in organizing the bomb threat plan, we were able to increase the safety of an executive immeasurably by rearranging his office so that his desk was located some distance away from an exposed wall that could otherwise not be protected.

In the preparation of the plan, consideration should be given to the training or retraining of all security and maintenance personnel to ensure that in their tours through the building they are ever alert for suspicious looking or unfamiliar items or unauthorized personnel. Because they normally move throughout the entire facility, security and maintenance personnel should make periodic checks of such areas as stairwells, closets under stairwells, and rest rooms. Regardless of the type of structure, all personnel should always remain alert for any individual who appears to be reconnoitering an area or obviously studying a particular area. Suspect persons should either be approached and asked for identification by the individual observing them or reported to the security force, management, or even the police.

The preparation of the plan should include, whenever possible, personnel who man the telephone switchboard and those individuals that have direct outside telephone communications. As a minimum, receptionists, telephone operators, and those individuals with direct outside lines should be given special training on how to respond to a bomb threat call, and each should be furnished with the form that is devised to record in detail the context of the threat.

If the facility has a mail room, individuals assigned to this operation should be given special training in the recognition and handling of a possible letter bomb and/or suspect package that appears to be out of place or that is being forwarded to an individual not normally receiving such packages. If mail room operations are large enough, consideration could be given to securing X-ray-type inspection devices and/or metal detecting devices so that mail room personnel can examine without opening any suspect package or letter (Figures 20-1, 20-2a, and 20-2b).

Figure 20-1 This device, known commercially as the Letar-Gard, is an electronic instrument used to screen envelope-size material in mail rooms, which emits an audio signal when metal is detected in the envelope. This is usually used only when letter bombs are suspected. (Hoteltron Systems, Inc.)

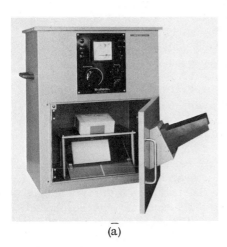

(a)   (b)

Figure 20-2 This multipurpose X-ray system is an effective means of
inspecting suspected parcels without opening the package. This device is
a fluoroscopic system that is simple to operate and offers excellent security
against packaged or letter bombs. (Baal Teau Electric Corporation)

EVACUATION

Without a doubt, the most serious decision that management must make in
the event of a bomb threat is whether or not to evacuate the facility. A
decision to evacuate may be exactly what the person making the threatening
call has in mind. He or she may want to not only disrupt normal activities,
but to ensure that all personnel are involved and know of the bomb threat,
thereby reducing their efficiency. The goal of the threat may be to have
the company incur the high cost of the evacuation and loss of productive time.

   In planning the procedures that will be used during an evacuation, consideration must be given to maintaining adequate security over the evacuated
area to ensure that material, documents, and property is not left exposed.
This is so particularly if only partial evacuation takes place, because the
threat that was conveyed may be designed to have an area evacuated so that
it is subject to easy intrusion.

   Evacuation should not occur automatically whenever a bomb threat is
received. This policy would almost certainly result in bomb threats being
continued, even though a decision not to evacuate may involve a calculated

risk. Consideration should be given to the fact that the vast majority of bomb threats conveyed in the past have turned out to be hoaxes. The likelihood that a bomb threat is real should be assessed in the light of the type of organization and the type of material being manufactured.

Past investigations have revealed that targets of terrorist bombers are not selected at random. The target or targets and the actual planting of the explosive device appears to follow a fairly well set pattern. The target selected usually has symbolic political or personal meaning for the terrorist. It is kept under close surveillance to determine possible avenues of ingress and egress and the type personnel control in use. Even individual security guard activities and personal behavior on specific shifts may be studied. A specific period may be chosen by the terrorist to plant the bomb merely because a single guard at a control point is lax in the performance of his functions.

When evacuation plans and procedures are being studied, consideration should be given to organizing and training an evacuation unit that consists of key management personnel. When high-rise buildings with many tenants are involved, the organization and training of this unit must be coordinated with all of the tenants in the building. The unit should be trained in how the building should be evacuated, the priority of evacuation, and the routes from the area being evacuated to the outside or to other safe areas in the building. All evacuations need not necessarily involve the removal of all personnel from the entire building. For example, if a threat is received indicating that an explosive device is on the fifth floor, the decision may be made to evacuate only the fourth, fifth, and sixth floors, assembling these personnel either on another floor or in the lobby until the search has been completed. Whenever possible, partial evacuation should not involve movement of personnel outside the building so that they can be seen by the bomber. The evacuation units should always precede the personnel being evacuated and should be trained to observe ahead on the route of evacuation and through any doorways they may pass. This should be done because if the bomber is of the sadist type, he may have knowledge of the evacuation route or of the specific exit that must be used because of the configuration of the building, and he would have placed his explosive device along the route or at the exit door.

BOMB SEARCH TECHNIQUES

Training teams or units in bomb search techniques is undoubtedly one of the most important functions of the bomb threat planning committee. A great deal of material is available to the planners concerning bomb search techniques by rooms or areas and entire buildings, including searches of outside areas immediately adjacent to the building involved.

The physical construction of buildings and their surrounding areas vary so widely in the problems that search teams will encounter that all items or areas could not possibly be covered. However, if an effective security program has been formulated and is being executed according to plan, the number of areas that need be searched can be considerably reduced because the number of areas accessible to a bomber in any building will be in direct proportion to the degree of security that has or has not been established.

It is imperative that all personnel, particularly those that are involved in directing evacuation and building or area searches, not touch or move any suspicious object regardless of how innocent it may appear. If an object in an area is obviously out of place, it should be considered suspect and reported to the bomb removal personnel. The removal and/or disarming of an explosive or incendiary device must be left to the professionals who have received training in these areas. Whenever one of these lethal devices is handled by amateurs, injury or death is likely to occur.

The preceding information will assist security and managerial personnel in preparing a bomb threat plan. However, all of the circumstances that could occur must be considered, and alternate plans must be formulated. For example, what if the threat is received by mail or by telephone during lunch or when there is no means of notification through the use of a public address system? Special plans need to be prepared to cope, not only with each specific situation, but for any eventuality. What if a power outage at a high-rise facility puts the elevators and the public address system out of service? Alternate methods must be formulated and/or emergency power equipment made available to ensure that any alternate methods being used will have the same assurance of success as the primary plan.

I would suggest that those planners who are faced with complex situations and are charged with the responsibility for formulating a bomb threat plan secure additional, more detailed data on the subject. There are two fine sources that have this material available: International Association of Chiefs of Police, The National Bomb Data Center, 11 Firstfield Road, Gaithersburg, Maryland 20760; and Motorola Teleprograms, Inc., Suite 26, 4825 North Scott Street, Shiller Park, Illinois 60176. A valuable pamphlet may be obtained from the Department of the Treasury, Bureau of Alcohol, Tobacco, and Firearms. Its title is "Bomb Threats and Search Techniques"– Publication ATF P 75502 (874).

21

The Emergency
Control Plan

In addition to formulating and testing a plan to cope with bomb threats, another plan should be formulated to control personnel and the actions of personnel in any type of emergency situation, should it be a civil disturbance, a labor dispute, or even sabotage that has disrupted normal daily activity. The individuals responsible for developing the emergency control plan in all probability would be the same individuals who have planned actions to be taken should a bomb threat occur.

These individuals will need some information and guidance not only in developing a plan, but also in presenting it to management. The plan will have to be "sold" to management so that it will back the plan with whatever "clout" is needed to ensure that it becomes a reality. Otherwise, it will be just another document that someone put together years ago that is generally referred to as an emergency plan and that since its formulation has not been updated, adapted to account for personnel changes, or tested.

Management must insist that the plan be sound, that it be tested, that it be updated as frequently as required, and that it is disseminated to those involved in the plan. Without this constant pressure on those who would be involved in the execution of such a plan, it becomes merely a piece of paper.

Once a plan is developed, management or security, or management through security, must ensure that it is foremost in the minds of those responsible for implementing it. How can this be accomplished? Call meetings? Management may feel these are too expensive. Call in individuals responsible for executing portions of the plan? Again, management may feel this is too time-consuming and consequently too expensive. However, the fact remains that the plan must not be left to gather dust and wither. What about new personnel who have joined the organization and whose organizational slot requires him or her to participate in the plan? How will they be notified of their responsibility in the event an emergency occurs? Merely having a plan on a shelf or in a drawer will be of little value when the emergency occurs. It takes constant surveillance, follow-up, and follow-through if the plan is to function properly and succeed should a real emergency occur.

What should be considered an emergency? What better place to turn to than the dictionary. "An emergency is a situation or occurrence of <u>a serious</u> <u>nature developing suddenly and unexpectedly and demanding immediate</u> <u>action</u>." How, then, should an emergency plan be developed? The format of the plan and the plan itself is relatively simple to develop. The overall conditions or situations that may occur are assessed, the vulnerability of the facility being protected is determined, and the assessment is analyzed to determine what preplanning needs to be accomplished. Let us then discuss how the plan should be presented to management and also to those who will be responsible for its execution.

INTRODUCTION

In most large metropolitan areas today, picketing, demonstrations, civil disobedience, and rioting are growing more and more common. The reasons for this are a matter for research beyond the scope of the emergency plan. However, the groups or individuals who cause, direct, or participate in such activities require some broad definition. Generally, the groups or individuals who precipitate the kinds of activity mentioned are labor organizations, terrorist groups, or political extremists.

Although the possibility exists that any number of activities could occur spontaneously and, in some instances, may not even be directed against a particular facility, management must still set up a plan to cope with such activities should they interfere with normal business processes or the movement of employees to and from the facility. Even though these activities may be directed against a neighboring building or facility, the size of the crowds in the area may disrupt normal activity. The circumstances surrounding such activities vary so greatly that it is virtually impossible to set down steadfast rules to be followed in each separate instance. The emergency procedure, however, should deal for the most part with those areas which lend themselves to advance planning. The activities of management and the implementation of the plan will have to be accomplished within the guidelines of good common sense.

SECURITY OF THE PLAN

The knowledge that an emergency control plan exists and knowledge of its specific contents must be restricted to only those persons who are responsible for formulating policy in connection with the plan and its implementation. Knowledge of the contents by unauthorized personnel could very well defeat the effectiveness of the plan and possibly create otherwise avoidable problems.

The plan itself should be handled as company proprietary information, and its reproduction, in whole or in part, should be strictly limited by management. The plan should be stored in a manner which would preclude unauthorized access, and each person possessing a copy should be held strictly accountable for its control. The plan should be serially numbered and issued by number to only those personnel involved in the plan. The plan should remain in the facility and not be allowed to be removed, even to an individual's home merely for study. Individuals to whom the plan has been issued should be provided with some type of security container so that the plan can be adequately safeguarded.

PURPOSE OF THE PLAN

Management of every corporation, company, institution, or of high-rise building should keep uppermost in mind that in dealing with unusual occurrences such as natural disasters, strikes, demonstrations, or civil disobedience it has certain responsibilities to its employees, owners, tenants, clients, and suppliers. These responsibilities can broadly be placed into the following categories in their order of importance.

1. The safety and well-being of the employees, tenants, and visitors.
2. The protection of all company property from damage or destruction.
3. Continued operation of the facility, with as little disruption of normal activities as possible.
4. A peaceful and equitable solution of the problem in question if the company itself is involved in the demonstration.

EMERGENCY PLANNING COMMITTEE

Once a decision has been made by management that an overall emergency control plan should be formulated and the basic plan has been designed, an emergency planning committee should be established. This committee will have the overall responsibility for any necessary advance action, from changing or adding to the physical security of the facility to providing for the necessary administrative tools to implement the plan.

This committee should be composed of the facility manager, the security manager, the safety, fire, and control manager, the personnel and labor relations managers, the public relations official, and a transportation representative if this position exists. Lower-level managers or supervisors can be advised of management's decisions at the appropriate time, when this is necessary. The above organization includes a wide cross section of management personnel in those areas that will be most affected by an emergency situation.

INTELLIGENCE SOURCES

Some of the activities with which the plan will deal may become general
knowledge before they occur, particularly strike activity after unsuccessful
labor negotiations. Other activities, such as wildcat strikes or civil rights
demonstrations, may occur almost spontaneously.

In either event, advance knowledge of the scope and duration of the activity
will be most beneficial in helping management to cope with the problem.
Information can be gathered from supervisors, department heads, and
cooperative employees. Every level of management must be alert for any
indication that such activities are being planned and should try to determine
the scope and details of any such activities.

In some extreme cases, it may be desirable to cultivate individuals in
the facility who are in a position to provide firsthand information of planned
spontaneous emergency situations. This should, of course, be restricted
to a situation wherein the possibility exists that to do otherwise might result
in serious injury to persons or damage to the facility. Serious repercussions
can result from this kind of intelligence activity unless it is handled with
extreme care and diligence. It should also be remembered that any information received in this manner must be carefully assessed for its validity and
confirmed by other sources whenever possible.

Advance information concerning a possible wildcat strike or civil rights
demonstration may allow management to counteract the activity or correct
the situation and thereby prevent the incident.

One management official should be assigned the responsibility of gathering and disseminating intelligence information to predetermined individuals.
However, all managerial and supervisory personnel must be made aware
that they also are responsible for reporting information concerning activities
that may be detrimental to the best interests of the company or the institution.

LIAISON WITH LOCAL GOVERNMENT OFFICIALS

Responsibility for maintaining peace and for protecting citizens and private
property is vested in the local police department, sheriff's office, and highway patrol. Fire protection is, of course, the responsibility of the local
fire department.

Due to the increased number of public disturbances in the past few years,
most police departments have initiated riot control plans and have trained
some of their officers in the control of riots. However, most police agencies are reluctant to become involved in labor disputes and may refuse to
act unless directed to do so by the courts.

The security manager of every facility should maintain liaison with local
law enforcement officials who are responsible for riot control planning to

take advantage of their knowledge in this area. The manager should learn what action is necessary to obtain the assistance of these law enforcement departments in the event an emergency should occur.

Management should not hesitate to alert local officials whenever they feel that this is warranted or to call upon them for assistance as necessary. If law enforcement agencies have formulated emergency action plans, they will usually make available information concerning that portion of the plan that involves a specific area and will also usually assist in providing guidance to private industries desiring to establish an emergency control plan.

PHYSICAL SECURITY

This portion of the plan should describe such actions as the erection of pre-fabricated window protection and the securing various peripheral doors or openings. It should also include instructions to the security force concerning additional posts that will need to be set up for each of the conditions that might occur—for example, strikes, civil disturbances, and water or wind damage. Also included should be a description of action to be taken during and after a fire emergency.

These plans will in all probability require that additional security personnel be assigned to the security force. This increase in manpower is usually accomplished by securing uniformed guards from a private security company. If the plans include these procedures, the security company that will be asked to supply the manpower when needed should be contacted. The local manager of the security company should visit the facility, should tour those areas where personnel belonging to his company will be posted, and should be given an orientation on only that portion of the plan that pertains to his functions. Should an emergency occur spontaneously, the private security company will be contacted, and its local manager will proceed to the facility and immediately post his personnel as they arrive.

DEFENSE AGAINST CIVIL DISTURBANCES

In large metropolitan areas, demonstrations occur for a variety of reasons. Some are spontaneous and occur without warning; others develop more slowly as the result of an isolated incident and can possibly be dealt with before any violence results.

A spontaneous disturbance will almost always be violent to some degree and often will result in attempts to commit arson, bombings, and assaults, some of which may be successful. Local, state, and federal law enforcement agencies will normally furnish the intelligence necessary for management to make a decision on what part of the emergency control plan should be executed or whether the entire plan should be brought into action.

When civil disturbances occur in urban areas, they are handled by local and state law enforcement agencies. The businessperson or manager should first make a decision on whether to open for business, stay open for business, or reduce business activities in only some areas. Second, he or she should make a decision on whether or not to execute physical protection by boarding up or otherwise protecting displays and other peripheral windows and by securing peripheral doors.

However, particularly in suburban or rural areas, businesses may be required to formulate plans that provide overall self-protection to include furnishing its own security forces. When these conditions exist, any emergency plan must be very detailed.

A great deal of information has been circulated concerning ways to prepare for, and cope with, civil disturbances; however, it has been my experience that too few facilities in all categories have any plans in existence. Even worse, there has been no exchange of ideas or thoughts on this protection among management, employees, and local law enforcement.

There are three basic plans, all closely interfaced, that must be a part of every management's planning. These are the emergency evacuation and disaster plan, the plan to deal with labor disputes that may become violent, and the plan to deal with civil disturbances. The first and last are absolute musts; the second is needed only if employees are organized and if labor negotiations have been difficult in the past. It may become necessary as the result of civil disturbances to initiate the emergency evacuation plan; therefore, one plan complements the other. All plans finally formulated and reduced to writing then become the overall emergency control plan.

SABOTAGE BY EMPLOYEES

Sabotage is the destruction or wrecking of property by subversive means. In this case, the saboteurs will be employees, and the target generally sought is critical, vulnerable, accessible, and at least partially conducive to self-destruction. Frequently acts of sabotage will result in just enough damage to close down critical machinery or processes temporarily in an attempt to gain some demands from management.

Six categories or forms of sabotage are generally used by the saboteur to disrupt operations in one degree or another.

1. Chemical. This form usually takes place in facilities where chemicals are readily available. Production is sabotaged by using improper mixtures, or chemicals are used to damage or destroy equipment or the finished products.
2. Electronic. Interrupting or interfering with the electrical power process or by jamming communications.

3. Mechanical. This is committed simply by breaking or omitting parts, failing to lubricate machinery or maintain it properly, or using improper or inferior parts in the manufactured product.
4. Fire. Using incendiary devices that are ignited by either mechanical electrical, or chemical means or setting a fire in some other way.
5. Explosive. The use and detonation of explosive substances that may range from dynamite through the various types of plastic compounds to the more readily available nitrates and combustible fuels.
6. Psychological. This method of sabotage includes inciting strikes, creating unrest or personal animosities, threatening the families of employees, or the deliberate destruction of an employee's automobile or parts of the automobile to gain the demands being sought.

The first five methods are most often used. The type of facility being attacked dictates the method most likely to be used. The protection plan must be designed to furnish the most protection in those areas that have been assessed as being most critical and vulnerable for that particular organization.

How, then, can sabotage be prevented? Remember that sabotage is usually committed before an actual work stoppage, when the employee has freer access to the facility. This is one reason why any check list of ways to reduce sabotage and violence during strikes gives priority to increasing manpower on the security force. (We shall give such a checklist shortly.) Since this additional manpower will in all probability be supplied by a private security guard organization, these personnel need to become thoroughly familiar with the facility and the psychological impact that the additional security manpower will have on employee population. It certainly is an indication that management is preparing for trouble. Sabotage can effectively be combated by reducing target accessibility and vulnerability. This may involve tightening personnel controls in the potential target area and re-screening and placing employees in accordance with the new security requirements. For example, any janitorial personnel who are likely to be disloyal might be reassigned from their regular areas to other areas where less critical processes are housed.

Managers should consider redesigning, reconstructing or modifying equipment to provide built-in protection against sabotage. (Much earlier we discussed a transformer that was sabotaged by rifle fire because it was protected only by a chain link fence.) Supervisors and security force personnel should be alerted to the possibility of sabotage and should be briefed on their role in preventing it. Finally, there should be a plan for handling the potential or actual saboteur. Will he be prosecuted if apprehended, or merely terminated? If the plan is to be able to deter or prevent sabotage by employees, charges should be immediately filed and vigorously pursued.

PREVENTING STRIKE-RELATED SABOTAGE AND VIOLENCE

In those facilities that are unionized and are subject to strikes, the possibility of violence has to be an accepted fact. Several preventive measures should be considered. Perhaps not all those discussed below will apply in any given situation, but certainly all should be considered to determine whether or not, if adopted, they would contribute to the protection plan.

1. Augment the existing security force with sufficient manpower to observe all outside areas immediately adjacent to the property. In some instances, it may be desirable to double the security guards on already established posts.
2. Station all security guards on company property, not on public property.
3. Do not arm security guards with any type of firearms. This will serve only to antagonize the strikers and turn them against the security force that usually plays a more or less neutral role between management and the striker. Properly trained security guards may be issued a baton or nightstick should they be required to defend themselves.
4. Establish observation posts to ensure that all outside areas can be adequately observed. Consideration may be given to establishing some posts at roof level or inside the building on the second or third floors.
5. Seldom can management be justified in using guard dogs if these had not been employed prior to the strike. When guard dogs are used, the handlers may be insufficiently trained, and there is a possibility that the dog will attack anyone nearby.
6. Once the strike has occurred, the security force should be notified of identification cards that are still in the possession of striking employees. The individual's name and the identification card number should be given.
7. The padlocks on all perimeter gates and locks on all peripheral doors of the building should be changed if employees that are now on strike have keys to these locks.
8. Secure all peripheral doors and gates that are no longer required because of the strike and keep them secured. These doors and gates should be inspected regularly to ensure that no entry or attempted entry has occurred.
9. Prior to the strike, recover keys issued to all employees who are a part of the bargaining unit.
10. If identification cards are issued to employees, consideration should be given to recovering them when the last paycheck prior to the strike has been issued.

11. Issue special identification cards or other identification media to employees who will not go on strike to ensure that they are readily admitted, particularly if contract security guards who are not familiar with the employees are used.

12. Conduct a meeting with those employees who will continue to work and advise them generally of the conditions that exist. Issue instructions to them concerning recommended actions to be taken while moving through picket lines, such as keeping the windows of their automobiles rolled up and the doors locked. They should also be told what action they should take if a picket steps in front of their automobile or if some other incident of this type should occur. The security chief should be available at this meeting and subsequent meetings to brief the company employees on actions they should take from time to time to ensure their own personal safety.

13. Consider changing automobile decals temporarily for those employees who will be continuing to work. Place these decals in another location on the vehicle and consider removing the decal originally issued. In numerous instances, nonstriking employees' automobiles have been damaged when strikers found them parked on the street and identified them through the company decal.

14. Remove all combustible trash from both inside and outside the property prior to the strike.

15. If underbrush and high weeds have been allowed to grow in outside areas, particularly near the perimeter barrier, cut and remove all of this ground cover to reduce the possibility of sabotage by fire.

16. For the same reason, empty all outside trash receptacles containing combustible materials and move them at least 50 feet from the perimeter barrier.

17. If conditions warrant, hoses should be attached to yard hydrants for immediate use should sabotage by fire be attempted. Any wrenches that normally are kept on post indicator valves should be removed.

18. Immediately after a strike has begun, all standpipe hoses should be checked over their entire length, and all fire extinguishers and other fire fighting equipment should also be checked to ensure that it has not been sabotaged.

19. Automatic sprinkler systems and other automatic fire protection systems should be tested immediately after the strikers have left the facility to ensure that OS&Y valves or post indicator valves have not been closed.

20. If the facility being struck is subject to having incendiaries thrown on the roof, provision should be made to lay water lines to the roof or to have hand portable extinguishers available.

21. If it appears very likely that sabotage may be attempted by hurling firebombs onto the roof, consideration may be given to erecting a

temporary barrier constructed of inexpensive chicken wire or other wire with a small mesh in those areas where firebombs could be thrown effectively from areas outside the protected property.

22. Similar precautions should be taken to increase security against possible firebombing of window openings that are near or face on the street. The use of plywood covers on the outside of the window is probably the most effective protective measure to use.

23. Protect company vehicles and vehicles of employees who are still working by parking them well inside the protected area. If there are several company vehicles and no perimeter barrier exists, the vehicles may be parked elsewhere.

24. Ensure that all lights in the protective lighting system are properly operating and inspect all outside illumination on a daily basis by illuminating the system just prior to darkness.

25. If applications for employment will be taken during a strike, establish a temporary employment office elsewhere. This will ensure that striking workers or individuals in sympathy with the strikers do not penetrate the protected area and possibly cause sabotage.

26. Arrange for a vehicular shuttle service to and from out-of-the-way bus stops and other points of public transportation used by nonstriking employees; possibly consider a temporary shuttle service to and from nonstriking employees' homes or specific areas where several employees may meet.

27. Compile a list of the names and telephone numbers of law enforcement and fire department officials and key personnel of the facility and make this list available to the security force and place it near telephones that are being used by nonstriking employees.

28. In advance of the strike, contact all vendors who will still be needed to service the facility to determine whether or not truck drivers will continue to service the plant during the strike or if they will honor the picket lines and refuse to deliver shipments. Also make provisions to divert any incoming shipments to locations away from the struck facility if it is felt necessary.

29. Review all emergency plans and, in particular, procedures to be used by telephone operators when annoying or threatening calls are received. Be sure operators know what actions should be taken and what records need to be maintained in the event of such calls.

30. Consider renting or purchasing a portable television camera monitor and video-tape recorder to be used by management personnel only, not the security force, to record infractions of company rules or acts of violence by the strikers.

31. If supervisors and other salaried employees will be "locked in," make available communications so that these individuals can communicate freely with their families.

32. If the facility is serviced by rail, consider removing all empty railroad cars prior to the strike and, if necessary, delay incoming rail shipments. Ensure that the railroad understands that any incoming shipments are not to be left immediately outside the perimeter barrier railroad gate but should be kept in the freight yards.

33. In recent strikes, strikers have used hunting-type slingshots to damage employee automobiles by either denting the metal body or breaking windows. Slingshots have also been used to knock out protective lighting, to break windows in the facility, and to commit other acts of vandalism. Employees observed using the slingshots should be arrested, because these weapons will inflict great injury and possibly even death, depending upon where an individual is struck.

The strike procedure plan should be considered highly proprietary and should be closely guarded against compromise, particularly to hourly employees. Only those supervisory and administrative personnel who will be affected by the plan should know its provisions or even that one exists.

If the security force is to be augmented by a contract security company, the supplier should verify that none of the personnel he furnishes is a relative or neighbor of any of the employees out on strike. This arrangement will prevent compromise of any plans necessarily revealed to the security force and will ensure that each man and woman on the security detail is not unnecessarily exposed to intimidation.

It is of utmost importance that all security personnel be briefed by company management regarding the property lines, company policy regarding the strike, what security personnel should and should not report, the importance of taking detailed notes of illegal activities engaged in by the strikers, what this illegal activity is, and any instructions that pertain particularly to that specific situation.

I have attempted in this chapter to cover the various types of emergency conditions involving people that could occur at various types of facilities being protected. This chapter deals with those situations in which large groups of people are likely to be involved and therefore does not include actions to be taken in the event of a bomb threat, which has been treated in a separate chapter. However, the development of an evacuation plan to be activated in the event a bomb threat may be one of the tasks of the emergency control plan committee.

22

The Employee Security Education Program

One of the vital parts of any security protection plan is the employee education program. It is almost impossible for security personnel to accomplish their mission effectively without the active interest and support of the majority of the employees in the facility.

To make changes in an existing security program or to begin a formal security plan at a facility requires careful planning by management as well as by security personnel. The security protection plan to be implemented should be studied in detail to determine how each aspect will affect each group of employees. Definite plans and outlines of the security education program for employees should then be drawn up.

The goal is the same in every employee security education program. All employees should be acquainted with how and why the security measures are being planned and implemented. Employees must see the need for the program and be encouraged to assist and comply with the plan.

The specific reasons for beginning a security protection plan vary sometimes but generally fall into similar categories. Employees, however, tend to think that security measures are personal. That they are being implemented because employees can no longer be trusted. With this justification, they will often resist new security measures. To overcome this possibility, a well-planned education program is important. It should be emphasized to employees that there is no lack of trust in them, but that the security procedures are to prevent the unauthorized person or persons from entering the facility. Keeping out undesirable persons will help to prevent acts of theft, sabotage, and vandalism.

The education program should stress the specific security problems to be handled, the consequences if the problems are not solved, and the advantages to employees of having a secure facility. If such acts as theft, sabotage, and vandalism are allowed to occur, the employees' work performance can suffer and harm to employees may result. If damage is done to machinery or to the building, employees may be laid off while repairs are being made. The effects of theft can be directly felt in the employees' paychecks. Thefts obviously have an effect on the company's ability to make a profit. Profits, in the long run, are required to increase wages, salaries, and other benefits, including company profit-sharing programs. If such con-

399

siderations are pointed out to employees in the security education program, they will then understand that security measures are required by the situation, not because of a lack of trust in them.

Another consideration in explaining a planned change in security procedures is that the average employee is not security conscious. This attitude must be acquired through security education. Most employees—from top management to hourly workers—are inclined to trust fellow workers. Because they themselves would not commit unlawful acts, they believe that others also would not. Therefore, in some security education programs, it is necessary to go over current theft statistics in the facility in order to explain the reasons for the security measures.

Experts estimate industrial theft amounts to between $8 and $15 billion each year. The magnitude and impact of such losses often must be explained, at least generally to employees, through a security education program. In national organizations, if decisions to institute security programs in all plants are made at corporate headquarters, management at the local level must be brought in on the decision and must also be made to see the reasons for the decision.

A successful employee education program depends on receiving the support of local management. In one case recently, plans for a new security program were sent to a plant from national headquarters without consulting local management and without showing them the reasons for the changes. The program was instituted, but when employees began to question and complain about the changes, local management placed all the blame on corporate management saying, "We don't want the changes; this is what 'they' said we had to do." Such an attitude damages not only employee morale and performance but undermines confidence in corporate policies. It also minimizes effectiveness of the security program, because it is quite obvious that security personnel will not get the backing of local management. Such problems can usually be avoided if local management is included in corporate security planning.

Consideration must also be given to how to explain security plans to various categories of employees. One group of employees might require a more detailed explanation than another. If, for example, one group of employees is only being inconvenienced by the sealing of a door in a security program, this group will need less explanation than will another group who must change their lunch schedules or parking routine.

If the security program requires switching from an internal security force to contract guards or from maintenance personnel to a larger uniformed guard force, additional precautions must be taken in the employee education program. Employees must be told what is happening to the personnel whose jobs are being changed or are being replaced. It is often damaging to morale to make employee changes or replacements without a satisfactory explanation.

Effective long-range planning can help greatly to increase the effectiveness of a security education program. Security measures often require such inconveniences for employees as moving employee parking farther from the building, restricting employees from going to their autos to eat lunch, and limiting ingress and egress to certain doors. These inconveniences can be allayed somewhat by special measures that to some extent overcome or reduce the inconvenience.

Inconveniences can also be balanced by announcing them at the same time as advantages and benefits are announced. If, for example, company officials are considering adding a hot-line cafeteria for employees, they could do so at the same time that changed or additional security measures are put into effect. In this way employees feel that they are getting a benefit along with a change of habit or routine.

Group psychology is another important consideration in making changes in security at a facility. For example, if a large portion of the employees at a plant are of a particular group—say, females—it is very important that detailed planning sessions be held in advance with supervisors. If new security measures include such things as handbag and parcel inspections before leaving the plant, great care must be taken in explaining the reasons for this. Otherwise a number of good employees may be lost, as classes of employees tend to quit in groups. Hiring of a psychologist might be justified to explain group dynamics and the effects of changes before instituting new security measures.

How, then, are all of these considerations to be put into effect in an employee security education program? One of the most effective methods is through the house publication, such as an internal newsletter, newspaper, magazine, bulletin boards, and orientation conferences.

Another effective method of employee security education is including announcements about the program in paycheck envelopes or other mailings to employees. Information can be spread through supervisors, local union leadership, or through workshops, group meetings, or other types of gatherings. Combinations of these and other numerous methods can make up an employee security education program which gets the job done. The methods used are limited only by the resourcefulness of the security director.

An employee handbook of security guidelines should be published and issued to all new employees (and to old employees if the project is just getting started). The handbook should contain all of the information essential to creating the same security atmosphere as the safety program does in the area of personal safety. The handbook must be written in language that can be understood by all employees.

Once the program is developed, conduct a security orientation of all present employees and arrange such orientation for all employees hired in the future. Don't conduct employee security education in a haphazard manner and be certain to review criminal laws that could be violated in that particu-

lar industry or individual job and the possible penalties for violators who
are apprehended, tried, and convicted. Continuing security education programs will develop and perpetuate security consciousness among all employees from top management to the janitorial crews.

A final thought to keep in mind when beginning new security measures:
People can accept and understand most changes that are made with good
reason if they are explained effectively and well in advance. Problems
arise when changes are made suddenly and with no apparent consideration
for those affected by the changes. An effective employee education program
will help to avoid these problems and to ensure that an effective security
plan can be implemented.

23

Design to Reduce
School Property Loss

In February 1977 Senator Birch Bayh said, before a meeting of the National Education Association, "It is estimated on a national scale we are currently spending almost $600 million each year as a result of vandalism in our schools."

When the figures are compiled for 1978, they will certainly surpass the $600 million mark.

In July 1976, the National Association of School Security Directors meeting in Alexandria, Virginia, announced that they were seeking $300 million from the Justice Department to assist in combating school crime, violence, and vandalism. Joseph Grealy, the President of the National Association of School Security Directors, and Chief of School Security for Broward County, Florida, stated: "It's not only the crime but the fear of crime that is the problem." By this Grealy was referring to the fact that because of violence that occurs during school hours, many children are horrified by the thought of having to go to school.

This chapter will be concerned with architectural design that will assist in reducing—and, in some instances, eliminating—public and private school property losses through vandalism that is committed both during the period that school is in session and after the buildings have been secured.

Acts of vandalism are committed by students attending school and by outsiders who may be unwanted intruders or invited spectators at athletic and other public programs. Their acts may be intended to cause harm to the school facilities, but casual acts of misuse, not deliberately intended to cause destruction, may have the same results. The larger the metropolitan area, the more severe and damaging are these attacks. School vandals are both male and female, with almost as many preteen and teenage girls being apprehended as boys. A school system can ignore the problem, live with it, or take action to reduce its effect and even eliminate the potential for such losses.

A great deal of the material appearing in this chapter was used by the author to address the Seventh Annual Conference of The School Planning Laboratory, College of Education, University of Tennessee, Knoxville, Tennessee, during January 1976, when the author participated in the Conference titled "Strategies for School Security."

ALARM AND SURVEILLANCE SYSTEMS

In recent years, sophisticated anti-intrusion alarm systems have been
developed that are activated for use only after activities within a group of
buildings, a building, or a part of a building have ceased. Even more
sophisticated closed circuit television surveillance systems have been made
available that have the capability of being used independently or in conjunction with the anti-intrusion alarm systems. These systems to detect unauthorized entry or activity obviously have to be monitored. When an alarm
is tripped or an unlawful act is observed on the television monitor, an immediate response by people, either guards or police, must be initiated. This
requires a rapid movement into the area being violated.

The cost of such protection will depend upon the equipment employed in
these two systems and the area being protected. In addition to the cost of
the equipment, three other cost factors must be considered. First, this
type of equipment must be installed by experts in each particular field.
The installation cost usually amounts to approximately <u>five times the cost
of the equipment</u>. Second, these systems are of little deterrent value by
themselves. In order to be effective in the property protection role, each
must be monitored, and a response capability must be immediately available.
This means people, <u>at least two of them on duty at all times the systems
are in operation</u>, whether the systems are monitored locally or from a
remote location. Third, it is necessary to establish communications between the persons monitoring the systems and the person responding. This
means radios, which are also extremely expensive, and, in all probability,
the responding guard will need to have some type of transportation.

IMPORTANCE OF FACILITY DESIGN

Anti-intrusion alarms and surveillance systems provide protection during
the time schools are not in session. What about vandals pursuing their
particular pleasures while the education facility is in operation, either
during the day or during a reduced evening schedule? <u>Vandalism, the
destruction and damaging of property</u>, in the public school system, can
be substantially reduced by carefully planning building design <u>prior to the
commencement of construction</u>. Giving facility design first consideration
in the protection plan can not only reduce the cost of vandalism, but can
dramatically reduce the cost of the inevitable protection plan. Alarms
and other such systems must not be considered as the total answer to the
reduction of vandalism. The measures initiated during the planning stage
are comprehensive and <u>start beyond the walls of the school facility</u>.

SITE SELECTION

Site selection for school facilities is extremely important, just as important as it is for a fire house, police station, or shopping mall. Here are some things to look for.

1. Consider the environment of the potential site. The psychological outlook of residents in the immediate area must be considered. The economic status of the area must receive consideration as well as the present and past crime rate as it relates to attacks against both persons and property.
2. Plan considerable distances between academic and administrative facilities, athletic buildings, and athletic and play fields.
3. The site should provide for adequate visual observation of all buildings and facilities by outside patrols or closed circuit television surveillance systems.
4. The site selected should be remotely located from high-speed approaches and away from public throughfares to limit opportunities for physical attacks.

PERIMETER BARRIERS

Perimeter barriers erected during the construction phase will substantially reduce costs in any cost-plus contracts because a barrier will present a physical and psychological deterrent to innocent entry. This barrier also provides an effective means of directing the flow of personnel and vehicles, establishes control points, and provides for an effective and economic employment of security forces. In addition, it is a physical deterrent against unauthorized entry.

Perimeter barriers at any construction site should be erected not only for reasons already stated but because they will be instrumental in meeting construction deadlines. Often when cost overruns occur on fixed-price contracts, security considerations or security plans are reduced because it is almost impossible for a contractor to cut costs by skimping on aspects of construction covered by fire codes, safety codes, and building codes. However, security codes are generally nonexistent, and because doors, windows, locking hardware, and other peripheral equipment and construction are the last installed or constructed, they tend to be at the mercy of the project purchasing agent's pencil.

After construction is completed, consider either industrial chain link or masonry barriers for the protection of parking lots, athletic fields, utility installations, and service areas. In many instances, cleverly planned building construction including sidewalks and masonry constructions (walls or screens) can establish effective foot and vehicular control <u>without being</u> <u>objectionable or even obvious in some instances</u>.

DRIVES AND PARKING

Parking areas and intrafacility roadways are most important, not only in establishing the overall protection plan, but in reducing the risk of destructive attacks from outside. Properly planned control points or moving patrols at the junction of the streets or patrols through the streets and areas will reduce the calculated risk assumed whenever there is vehicular or pedestrian movement.

WALKWAYS

Walkways should be planned to facilitate direct and logical access to specific areas and building entrances. Walkways should be planned whenever possible away from buildings and, rather than being <u>constructed parallel with the</u> <u>building, should be constructed between buildings with a spoke or spiderweb</u> <u>configuration</u>.

ATHLETIC FIELDS

Athletic fields should be located so buildings do not form a part of the perimeter and where a perimeter barrier of chain link construction would not be objectionable.

Spectator parking should be planned to ensure that direct access from the parking area to the seating area is possible. Access routes between the parking area and stadium stands should be quite <u>clear</u> and <u>planned</u> so that they do not necessitate cross-pedestrian traffic. Similar planning must be applied to the entry and exit from vehicular arteries. Deviations from the prescribed pedestrian routes by individuals or groups should be obvious to the security force. Scoreboards, time clocks, and electronic display boards should be located as high as possible above ground level to reduce damage by vandals or "enraged or rapturous spectators."

EXTERIOR LIGHTING

Exterior lighting must be considered in planning the overall protective plan. If a closed circuit television surveillance system is planned, sufficient illumination to ensure adequate observation of outside areas must be pro-

vided. Light fixtures should be no less than 14 feet in height, and the luminaire should be protected by a globe or shield manufactured of polycarbonate
or other impact-resistant material. Walkways, roadways, parking lots,
building doors, and any other area must be illuminated.

Outside light fixtures installed on buildings should be as high as possible,
flush mounted, and protected by impact-resistant material. Light fixtures,
as a general rule, should illuminate the horizontal rather than the vertical.
Exterior lighting should not be mounted at or near ground level and should
be automatically controlled. Either sodium- or mercury-vapor lamps
should be utilized. Finally, lighting controls should be inside the facility
and should be key controlled or otherwise protected to eliminate intentional,
unauthorized blackouts.

INTERIOR LIGHTING

Inside lighting will depend a great deal upon the decor of a particular room
or area just as the intensity of illumination will be dictated by the activity
in progress. Lighting of hallways, corridors, stairwells, rest rooms,
student service rooms, and areas commonly used by the students and the
faculty population should be accomplished by flush or near-flush wall or
ceiling-mounted fixtures protected, again, by impact-resistant shields.
The fixtures should be high enough to thwart all but the most determined
vandal.

LANDSCAPING

Landscaping is probably the most controversial subject that can be discussed
in any security preplanning conference. As was mentioned earlier in this
book, plants, shrubbery, trees, and hedges can obscure the view of cameras
and people. The cover provided by vegetation can be used to advantage by
the intruder. Some considerations in planning may include (but are not
limited to) the use of thorny shrubs or bushes (such as pyracanthea and
certain varieties of holly) along buildings and along walkways to channel
or prohibit foot traffic. No tall trees or trellises on or near buildings
that could be used for surreptitious entry into second-floor levels should
be planned. Attempts should be made to keep doorways clear of growth
that can be used as cover.

Where trees and shrubs cannot be avoided, attempts should be made to
increase the protective lighting to deter use of this material as cover by
an intruder.

GENERAL BUILDING DESIGN

General building design should include, but is not necessarily limited to, the following considerations.

1. Finished wall surfaces in common corridors, rest rooms, and athletic building interiors should be of a nearly nonporous material which resists writing material except, perhaps, grease pencils and paint, which are fairly easy to remove without damaging the surface.
2. Minimize ornate, nonfunctional items and aesthetic building material to reduce replacement costs if it becomes necessary.
3. Wherever possible, have the public use facilities in gymnasiums, auditoriums, pools, and libraries on the first floor, with entrances clearly visible throughout the interior and exterior areas.
4. Locate business and administrative offices near building entrances to assist in supervision of activities at these points and to ensure monitoring of ingress and egress.
5. Install locking hardware on all interior doors.
6. Design exterior walls to deter easy access to the building roof.
7. Use hard, mar-resistant wall materials.
8. Avoid any exterior wall-mounted fixtures which might be used to assist in climbing the building.
9. Avoid walls and half walls within 8 feet of any building.
10. Covered walkways near buildings should be avoided or made difficult to climb if this type of construction is necessary.
11. Avoid false building fronts or wide roof overhangs.
12. No transoms should be installed on any interior or exterior door.
13. Avoid skylights everywhere.
14. Keep the number of peripheral windows to a minimum and consider longer (higher) windows and sacrifice width. Windows that are no wider than 10 inches will normally prevent entry through these peripheral openings.
15. Provide substantial locking devices for movable windows and any glass sliding doors.
16. Keep windows at least 40 inches from any peripheral door to prevent opening a door by reaching through a nearby window.
17. Avoid putting windows in gymnasiums except when they can be constructed at an extremely high level.
18. Consider using impact-resistant or polycarbonate material for windows in libraries, fine arts buildings, laboratories, research projects, duplicating machine rooms, and other critical and/or vulnerable areas.
19. Protect windows at lower levels by constructing a decorative masonry screen about 1 foot from the building to offer effective protection yet permit natural light inside (see Figures 23-1 and 23-2).

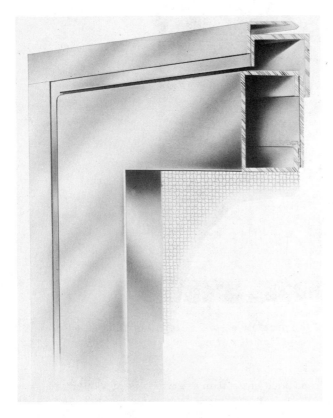

Figure 23-1 A cutaway view of the frame used on steel screen window protection. (Courtesy Kane Manufacturing)

20. All windows should be glazed from the interior.
21. Attempt to keep windows at least 6 feet from ground level and without sills that could be used by an intruder to gain access.
22. When screws are necessary in window installation, use only one-way screws.
23. Plan computer areas above the first-floor level, away from every day traffic, and consider using windowless rooms.

DOORS

The peripheral doors of a building are obviously intended for use in entering or exiting that building or portion of the building; however, they are also intended for the use only of authorized personnel. Yet, they are more

Figure 23-2 A view of the protective steel screen installed as window protection. (Courtesy Kane Manufacturing)

often used to gain surreptitious entry than are windows or skylights. Normally, unauthorized entry is gained merely by opening the door and walking in. Therefore, door security starts with the door locking schedule that is executed by an individual or group of individuals that have a sense of responsibility and can be depended upon to secure the doors on the established schedule.

It is quite possible that locking can best be accomplished through the use of a number of solenoids and electrical strikes, electromagnetic door-holding devices, and electromagnetic locking devices so that the locking devices can be electronically secured and/or electronically released.

Some features desired in peripheral and other high risk doors are the following.

1. Doors should be of solid wood rather than the hollow-core type.
2. Door hinges should be concealed with inside hinge pins.
3. Avoid exterior doors to rest rooms if there is an <u>interior door to that rest room as well</u>.
4. Avoid recessed doorways or vestibules located outside the doorway.
5. Place no windows in any peripheral door.
6. Sliding doors should be minimized because they are extremely easy to defeat and require great expanses of glass.

7. Roof hatch doors should be constructed of metal and should be fastened to a metal frame with cross members to resist twisting.

Satisfactory locking devices on doors are a necessary step in securing the building and building area against intrusion by the vandal.

1. No lock in the knob combination should be used. If such a device must be used, it should be supplemented with a double keyway dead-bolt lock also installed on the door.
2. Where the degree of security demands more protection a vertical dead bolt should be used.
3. Use padlocks on such doors as roof hatches.
4. Use locks with at least six pin tumblers.
5. Removable-core locks provide rapid lock changes and economy in changing the locking system and should be considered.
6. Consider card-operated electronic locks in high-risk areas such as libraries, computer areas, telephone equipment rooms, and duplicating equipment rooms.
7. Any door to a computer or telephone equipment area or any similar area should remain locked at all times. Mechanical cipher locks offer ample keyless locking protection for small one-door operations.
8. Combination padlocks should have serial numbers removed.
9. The use of bar locks on interior doors to high-risk areas should be considered when personnel safety permits.
10. Secure panic hardware on double doors by locking the doors together with a chain or cable when these areas are void of personnel.

MECHANICAL ROOMS AND UTILITY SYSTEMS

Mechanical rooms and utility systems must be considered for increased protection.

1. Air-conditioning and ventilation duct covers should be secured with one-way screws.
2. Conceal water and steam lines rather than installing them overhead.
3. Install sturdy lockable metal grills or gates to secure utility tunnels.
4. Secure all telephone and electrical switch junction or fuse boxes with sturdy locking devices (use hasps and padlocks rather than rely on the lock installed by the manufacturer).
5. Secure storm sewer covers, manhole covers, vents at ground level, and other such openings in building side walls within 18 feet of ground level.
6. Protect all thermostats with metal, not plastic, lockable covers. Conceal thermostats wherever possible. Thermostat locations may be recessed to offer better protection.

INTERIOR WALLS AND CEILINGS

Interior walls and ceilings are often the first areas where vandalism occurs, particularly in common corridors, hallways, and public use buildings or areas. Rest rooms are frequent targets for the vandal at any time of day or night.

1. Use no fabric or absorbent material to cover walls in corridors, hallways, and so forth. For example, flocked wallpaper is easily damaged or destroyed and extremely expensive to replace.
2. Plan use of hard-glazed epoxy surfaces throughout common areas.
3. Use no sheetrock, wood, or simulated wood paneling in exposed high-traffic areas.
4. Concrete block and cement construction covered with acrylic, ceramic, or glazed clay tile should be used in all rest rooms, kitchens, vending machine areas, and laboratories.
5. Avoid suspended acoustical ceilings and carpeting in rest rooms, kitchens, and other such areas.
6. Apply only flame-retardant paints on combustible surfaces.

REST ROOMS AND LOCKER ROOMS

These are high risk areas for damage and destruction by vandals. Consider these recommendations during the construction planning phase.

1. Fixtures in locker rooms, rest rooms, and the like should be of heavy-duty construction, and locks should have separate keying systems.
2. Install partitions in restrooms with floor and ceiling mounts or at least within 1 foot of the floor and ceiling. Screws of one-way design or those which require special tools for removal must be used.
3. Consider only self-closing faucets and concealed plumbing fixtures throughout the rest rooms as much as possible.
4. Recessed shelves, electric hand dryers, sanitary-napkin dispensers and fire-resistant commode seats should be installed.
5. Locate utility cutoff valves or switches for each rest room or shower area in protected locations to facilitate immediate damage control should the need occur.
6. Plan fewer restrooms with larger capacity wherever possible rather than more restrooms with less capacity in each.
7. Use stainless steel mirrors in place of glass or plastic ones.
8. Consider floor-mounted or recessed urinals and only floor-mounted commodes. Plan floor drains and scuppers in each restroom area

with sufficient capacity to handle effectively flooding from intentionally ruptured or damaged water lines.

9. Unless a special need exists, expose no electrical receptacles in
    rest rooms. If receptacles are necessary, cover them with a lock-
    able metal cover and recess the receptacle in the wall.

10. If containers for combustible trash will be supplied in any rest room
    or other common-use area, provide only the flame retardant type.

SOME GENERAL SECURITY MEASURES

The subject of educational building design preplanned for security cannot
be covered in minute detail because of space limitations. However, here
are a few hints. Consider the use of bucket-type seating permanently
fastened together and sturdily anchored, rather than benches. This will
discourage lying down or sleeping; secure picnic tables to the ground; for
patio surfaces and walkways, avoid loose or easily removed ground cover
material that could be used as missiles; roof-mounted flagpoles rather than
ground-mounted ones will deter incidents. There are literally hundreds of
other small details that should be considered in the formulation of building
design to increase the protection of the school building, its contents, and
the safety and security of the personnel who use the building.

It is the intent of this chapter to provoke thought in this area which should
be valuable for future school construction planning. The security industry
is organizing to develop building codes for security which will be offered
to public officials and the architectural and construction industries. It is
hoped that within a few years these security codes will be enforced as effectively as are today's fire and safety codes.

24

The Executive
Protection Plan

The September 24, 1975, issue of <u>The Security Letter</u> reported, as did
hundreds of public newspapers, that Lynette (Squeeky) Fromme, arrested
early in September 1975 for the attempted assassination of the president
of the United States, gave the Associated Press a list of over 80 people in
various organizations marked for death. However, the Associated Press,
for obvious reasons, decided not to release more than a few names, and
subsequently the entire matter was suppressed by the public press. However, Robert McCrie, editor of <u>The Security Letter</u>, was able to obtain a
copy of the list and also was able to read comments made by a member of
the Manson entourage concerning the death list candidates. It appears that
individuals and organizations were put on the list because they were involved
in activities that were presumed to be endangering the environment. The
list included petrochemical companies, food processors, high-technology
concerns, and even lumber and paper concerns. No persons or organizations were connected with any banks, retailers, transporters, or other
service organizations. Fortunately, individuals and organizations named
have, as of this writing, not been overtly attacked.

Whatever importance may be attached to this list of individuals and
organizations, it is of extreme importance that all security advisors,
corporate security directors, and the key executives of corporations adopt
a plan to cope with this comparatively new and extremely dangerous "avoca-
tion." It is also extremely important that security personnel and those
individuals responsible for the protection of corporations and their executive
personnel establish and continually update programs that will identify the
specific threats to their organizations and the organization's executives.
An analysis of the news reports of terrorist operations certainly is not
enough. Terrorism tends to be unpredictable and irrational, even though
individual terrorists may be quite rational, the only fear being that they
will not be able to achieve their final goals.

As important as developing the plan itself is the liaison that is established
with law enforcement agencies who would be called in for assistance should
a threat or an actual physical attack be made. This liaison, once established, must be maintained by the security personnel, and close working
relationships with their counterparts or representatives of the law enforce-

ment agency must be maintained. The law enforcement agency with whom liaison has been established must be consulted in the formulation of the plan, because planners can benefit immeasurably from the expertise they can offer. Once these plans have been formulated, they must be reviewed constantly and updated as required, and the law enforcement agency must be advised of all updates that change those plans that have already been known to them.

Terrorists select targets on an individual basis, and they are careful and meticulous in their selection, concentrating on those individuals or organizations who will furnish them the greatest political propaganda value. They will select the time for attack that will be most advantageous to them and will give them a strong likelihood of success. The moment of the attack will usually be when their adversary does not expect it. Quite obviously, the advantage of surprise is on the terrorist's side, and every protective plan must consider this.

In all probability, security directors and advisors will find that the most difficult portion of formulating a plan is selling the executives being protected on the need for such protection. Once this obstacle has been overcome, formulation of the plan itself is relatively simple. The fact that a plan must be tested to ensure that the goals and objectives set can be achieved must again be reemphasized.

A great deal of the information contained in previous chapters, particularly Chapters 16 and 20, contain a great deal of information that is relevant to formulating a plan for the protection of executive personnel. In these and other chapters, discussions covered such areas as executive office accessibility, installation and use of alarms and physical protection devices and techniques, after-hour access to executive offices, visitor control, executive suites, executive office area rest rooms, closets, screening of incoming mail, types of key control, and emergency plans for the executive and his family.

This chapter will deal with those other precautions that should be considered in the executive protection plan. Much has been written on this subject in many other sources, and some of these comments and recommendations are valid, whereas others are questionable. I will cover those areas often overlooked, perhaps because they do not apply generally to all executive protection plans or perhaps merely because authors lacked a sufficient amount of research and analysis on this particular subject.

UNLISTED TELEPHONE NUMBERS

In many instances, executive personnel will have direct telephone lines that are not routed through the headquarters switchboard. For obvious reasons, the telephone numbers to these lines and all home telephone numbers should be unlisted. Security planners should consider not even listing the names and addresses of any close relatives of the executives in the telephone books that are published and used locally. There is usually no need to have the names and addresses of executive personnel and close relatives listed in the telephone directory, because most calls to the residence are from selected individuals, organizations, or business establishments. If a direct-line telephone is used by the executive at the office, it should be equipped with tape-recording capabilities so that in the event a threat is communicated, a record of the conversation is made.

AUTOMOBILE PARKING

Too often, merely by driving through unguarded parking lots or observing parking lots with field glasses from the street or other vantage points, I have discovered the specific parking stalls used by individual executives. Executive parking areas must not be conspicuously identified, and even though the location near the headquarters entrance and the model of automobile parked would tend to indicate that it is an executive parking area, individual stalls should not be marked. If any parking area should be guarded, certainly the executive parking area should be protected by the installation of a perimeter barrier, protective alarms, adequate illumination, and control by the security force.

SAFE ROOMS

Although it may not be a necessity in the United States, in foreign countries there should be a room in the interior of the building that is designated as the room to which executives or others being protected would move to in the event an attack by a terrorist or a group of terrorists. This area should not be accessible from the outside and should be secured in such a manner that it is almost impossible for entrance to be gained without the use of some explosive device. This <u>safe room</u> should be equipped with communications, preferably a telephone and radio with radio communication capabilities to outside law enforcement agencies, first-aid equipment, rations, bathroom facilities, AM-FM radios, television sets, and items of this nature. Thus, if executives need to be cloistered for any period of time, they can be made relatively comfortable and can keep abreast of the situation through radio communications and can monitor press coverage. Such communications capability will be an asset and will assist the executive should he or she desire to direct that certain actions be taken. Planning for safe rooms in overseas headquarters nowadays seems to be a necessity.

MAINTAINING LOW EXECUTIVE PROFILE

The executive protection plan should include a plan for screening public relations and public announcements on a day-to-day basis, not only of the activities of the corporate headquarters and the executive personnel, but of the families of executive personnel as well. The terrorist today will often select his target and formulate his plan of action by information he has secured from the society pages of the local newspaper. Executives, particularly in overseas operations, must maintain a low profile, and corporate policies should limit day-to-day advertising of the company or its products in these overseas operations.

TRAVEL PLANS AND PROTECTION WHILE TRAVELING

In establishing and maintaining a low profile, executive personnel should not announce or release to the public news of any activity that involves travel or appearances at public events. Even though this type of publicity may sometimes not be avoidable, security personnel can effectively ensure that any item appearing in the public press is not accompanied by a photograph. Personal affairs of an executive's family, his or the family's club memberships, their social activities, and his or his family's travel plans should never be made known.

A great deal has been written concerning the specific tactics that can be taken while an executive is traveling in an automobile. Specific actions can be taken to avoid ambush attacks and to counter an attack should an ambush actually take place. This type of information can be secured by legitimate security personnel, but I feel that such information should not be made public in a book such as this for reasons that certainly are obvious to the reader.

Travel on commercial airlines, particularly within the United States, does not present the hazards common some 4 years ago, because ground security protective measures and other anti-hijack techniques have eliminated most of the hazards that involve personal safety of everyone when using commercial airlines.

Travel by company-owned aircraft presents quite another problem as compared to travel by commercial aircraft. First, physical security safeguards for the protection of the private aircraft and aircraft hangars and identification and control procedures pertaining to personnel and vehicles previously outlined must be established and written into the protection plan for company aircraft. Second, measures must be adopted to ensure that aircraft are adequately protected when they are away from their home base. This can usually be accomplished by securing the services, in advance of the flight, of local private security agencies at intermediate points along the route where the aircraft will be parked and unattended for any length of time.

In addition, if the situation is tense enough, consideration should be given to moving the executive from the corporate headquarters to the aircraft takeoff point by using different routes and possibly different means. The use of helicopters, for example, from time to time may foil plans for an attack.

All distinctive organizational markings or even organizational colors should be removed from the aircraft so as to make it particularly difficult to identify while it is in an air park.

Pilots and crew must receive special security training, and their bags, including the bag used to carry the air charts, should be checked by security personnel if they have been left in an area where it might have been possible to place an explosive or incendiary device in the baggage.

It may be desirable, particularly in overseas operations, to customize automobiles with a certain amount of armored plate to provide maximum ballistic protection of the individuals using these vehicles. This includes using transparent armor material for all windows, including the front, rear, and sides. This protection consists of 1-1/4-inch-thick laminate of tempered glass and plastic. Other protection used in customizing these automobiles is opaque armor plate material that offers a combination of strength, toughness, and hardness sufficient to withstand a direct impact with a jacketed 30.06 bullet. This protection is usually installed in the firewall, all doors, the rear seat, the roof, and all posts, columns, and panel sections. Floor protection usually is optional, depending upon a particular individual's needs, as is engine and radiator protection. Further information in customizing security automobiles can be secured from Tetradyne Corporation, Carrollton, Texas.

In concluding this chapter, I must emphasize that security personnel should never attempt by themselves to bargain with a terrorist who has successfully seized the hostages and should never attempt to deal with the abductor or physically attempt to effect their release of hostages. If the hostage is to be freed unharmed, negotiations should be conducted by personnel trained in the behavioral sciences.

Bibliography

REFERENCES

AELE Law Enforcement Legal Liability Reporter, Law Enforcement Legal Defense Center, Americans for Effective Law Enforcement, Inc. 960 State National Bank Plaza, Evanston, Ill., 60201.

Babaco Warning Bulletin, Summer-Fall 1975.

"Bank Protection Act of 1968." Public Law, 90-389, 90th Congress H.R. 15345, July 7, 1968.

"Bomb Threats and Search Techniques." Department of the Treasury, Bureau of Alcohol, Tobacco, and Firearms, 1976.

"A Brief Guide to Electronic Security Alarm Systems." Mosler Safe Company, 1561 Rand Boulevard, Hamilton, OH 45012.

Bund, Melvin. "Security in an Electronic Data Processing Environment." VCPA Journal, February 1975.

"Cargo Security Handbook for Shippers and Receivers." Pamphlet DOT P5200.5, U.S. Department of Transportation, September 1972.

Computer Security, September-October 1975.

"The Considerations of Physical Security in a Computer Environment." International Business Machines Corporation, Data Processing Division, 1133 Westchester Avenue, White Plains, NY 10604.

"Crime: Are You Next?" The Engineering Division, The Travelers Insurance Companies, Hartford, CT 06101.

Fire Control Digest. Washington Fire News Service, 7620 Little River Turnpike, Annandale, VA 22003.

"Fireproof." The Engineering Division, The Travelers Insurance Company, Hartford, CT 06101. Vol. 8, no. 3 (November 1975).

George, Harold. "Master Keying for a Small Industrial Plant." National Locksmith Magazine, June 1973.

"Guidelines for Automatic Data Processing, Physical Security, and Risk Management." Federal Information Processing Standards, publication no. 31, U.S. Department of Commerce/National Bureau of Standards (Washington, DC: Government Printing Office).

Imbau, Fred E., and Reid, John E. "The Lie Detector Technique." American Bar Association Journal 50, no. 5 (May 1964).

419

Industrial Security 15, no. 3 (June 1971). 2000 K Street NW, Washington,
    DC 20006.
Irwin, Frank G. "Final Report of Findings and Recommendations." School
    Planning Laboratory, University of Tennessee, August 22, 1975.
Lee, Robert J. "Study of Pharmacy Crime Reviews Need for Tighter Physi-
    cal Security." The National Locksmith, February 1976. Published by
    The National Publishing Co., Suite 505, 433 West Washington Avenue,
    Madison, WI 53703.
The Locksmith Ledger. Published by Nickerson & Collins Company, 2720
    Des Plains Avenue, Des Plains, IL 60018. 1975 and 1976 issues.
National Fire and Security Report, P. O. Box 1067, Silver Springs, MD
    20910. 1975 and 1976 issues.
National Retail Merchant Association, 100 West 33rd Street, New York,
    NY 10001.
The National Locksmith. 1975 and 1976 issues. National Publishing Com-
    pany, Suite 505, 433 West Washington Avenue, Madison, WI 53703.
News Release, U.S. Department of Commerce, September 10, 1975.
News Release, U.S. Department of Justice, December 23, 1974.
Phillips, Anne Wight, M.D., Surgical Research, Harvard Medical School,
    Cambridge; Youville Hospital, Cambridge; and Massachusetts General
    Hospital, Boston. Factory Mutual System Record, May-June 1973.
    Reprinted in Civil Defense Preparedness Agency Pamphlet MP-71,
    May 1975.
"Portable Fire Extinguishers−1975." National Fire Protection Association,
    470 Atlantic Avenue, Boston, MA 02210.
Porter, W. Thomas, Jr. "Computer Raped by Telephone." New York
    Times Magazine, September 8, 1974.
Post, Dr. Richard S. "Campus Security," January 1971.
"The Proposed Key for Security System Designed to Lock Up the Vast
    Quantities of Information Stored in U.S. Computers." U.S. Research
    and Development, Pamphlet p−2835, 1976.
"Protection Management." Man & Manager, Inc., 799 Broadway, New York,
    NY 10003.
"A Report to the President on the National Cargo Security Program."
    Secretary of Transportation, Washington, DC, March 31, 1976.
"School Security Survey." School Product News, 614 Superior Avenue W.,
    Cleveland, OH 44113.
"Security Guidelines for Business, Industry and Other Organizations;
    Prevention of Terrorist Crimes." Private Security Advisory Council,
    Law Enforcement Assistance Administration, United States Department
    of Justice. Security Letter, 475 Fifth Avenue, New York, NY 10017.
Security Systems Digest 6, no. 21 (October 8, 1975). 7620 Little River
    Turnpike, Annandale, VA 22003.
Sinha, Jessica. "Entry Control Systems: the Automated Doormen."
    Administrative Management, April 1975.

"Sprinkler System Guide." The Viking Corporation, 210 North Industrial
   Park Road, Hastings, MI 49058.
Taghaferri, Louis E. "Plant Operations During a Strike." Management
   Review, July 1972.
Thorsen, June-Elizabeth. "Computer Security, Equipment, Personnel and
   Data." Security World, 1974.
Trotter, Charles E., Jr. "Strategies for School Security." School Planning
   Laboratory, University of Tennessee.
Vardell, Larry G. "Lighting for Crime Prevention." Speech delivered
   at University of Wisconsin—Extension, August 1975.

Sources

Advance Devices Laboratory, Inc., 316 Mathew Street, Santa Clair, CA
   95050.
AirLocke Dock Seal (Division O'Neal Tarpaulin Co.) 549 W. Indianola Ave-
   nue, Youngstown, OH 44511.
Air Space Devices (a Norton Company), Safety Products Division, P. O.
   Box 197, Paramount, CA 90723.
Applied Metro Technology, Inc. 66 East Gloucester Pike, Barrington,
   NJ 08007.
Avant, Box 88, Concord, MA 9172.
A.V.I.D. Enterprises, 206 Bon Air Center, Greensbrae, CA 94904.
Babaco Alarm Systems, Inc., 1775 Broadway, New York, NY 10019.
BMR Security Products Corporation, Product Design, Research, and
   Manufacturing, P. O. Box 786, U.S. 25 S, Richmond, KY 40475.
Cardkey Systems (a Division of Greer Hydraulics, Inc.) 20339 Nordhoff
   Street, Chatsworth, CA 91311.
CFI Camera Division (a Schirmer-National Company) 100 Portland Avenue,
   Bergenfield, NY 07621.
Computer Security, 43 Boston Post Road, West Main Street, Northboro,
   MA 01532.
Cunningham Corporation (subsidiary of Gleason Works) Honeoye Falls,
   NY 14472.
Detex Corp., Security and Safety Equipment, 120 Marietta Street, N.W.,
   Atlanta, GA 30303.
Dominion Lock Company, U.S.A., Inc., Air Industrial Park, Plattsburg,
   NY 12901.
Elan Industries, Inc., Security Systems Division, St. Paul, MN 55114.
Emhart Corporation, (Hardware Division) Berlin, CT 06037.
Bernard Ephraim, Electronic Manufacturing and Consulting Engineer,
   4450 North Clark, Chicago, IL 60640.
Federal Western Parking Controls, Federal Sign & Signal Corporation,
   136th & Western Avenue, Blue Island, IL 60406.

Fox Police Security Systems, 46 West 21st Street, New York, NY 10010.

General Electric, Lamp Business Division, Hendersonville, NC.

Graviner, 100 Industrial Road, Berkeley Heights, NJ 07922.

Grinnell Fire Protection Systems Co., Inc., 10 Dorrance Street, Providence, RI 02903.

GTE Sylvania Incorporated, Electronic Systems Group—Western Division, P. O. Box 1-8, Mountain View, CA 94042.

Eddie Hamilton, Memphis Fire Department, Retired Chief. 4737 Mint Drive, Memphis, TN 35117 for valuable assistance in the field of fire prevention and protection.

Hoteltron Systems, Inc., 135 New York Avenue, Huntington, NY 11743.

International Bureau of Investigations, 1911 S. Shepherd Drive, Houston, TX 77019.

Jefferson Screw Corporation, 691 Broadway, New York, NY 10012.

Kane Manufacturing Corporation, P. O. Box 641, Kane, PA 16735.

A. J. Lehmann, Co., Inc., 1860 Broadway, New York, NY 10023.

Loss Prevention Institute, Inc., an affiliate of Management Safeguards, Inc., 2 Park Avenue, New York, NY 10016; Saul D. Aston, President.

Caril F. Magdefrau, 5218 Dunnellon Avenue, Memphis, TN 38134, for technical assistance on closed circuit television surveillance systems.

m.a.g. Engineering & Manufacturing, Inc., 13711 Alma Ave., Gardena, CA 90249.

Master Lock Company, Milwaukee, WI 53210.

P. O. Moore, Inc., Glen Riddle, PA 19037; Bulletin no. 67, 1958.

Motorola Communications & Electronics, Inc., 1301 E. Algonquin Road, Schaumburg, IL 60172.

Omni Spectra, Inc., Security Products, 1040 West Alameda Drive, Tempa, AZ 85282.

Pelco Sales, Inc., 351 E. Alondra Boulevard, Gardena, CA 90248.

Pyrotronics (a Division of Baker Industries, Inc.), 2343 Morris Avenue, Union, NJ 07083.

Raycon, Inc., Boeing Field International, 8490 Perimeter Road, South Seattle, WA 90108.

Raytek, 1277 Terra Bella Avenue, Mountain View, CA 94043.

RCA Closed Circuit Video Equipment, Newhowland Avenue, Lancaster, PA 17604.

Regiscope Corporation of America, 7 East 43rd Street, New York, NY 10017.

Sargent and Company, 100 Sargent Drive, New Haven, CT 06509.

Schlage Electronics (a Schlage Lock Company) 1135 Kern, Sunnyvale, CA 94086.

Security Distributing & Marketing, Security World Publishing Company, P. O. Box 272, Culver City, CA 90230.

Security Management, American Society for Industrial Security, 200 K Street, NW, Suite 651, Washington, DC 20006.

Security World Publishing Co., Inc., 2639 South La Cienega Boulevard,
    Los Angeles, CA 90034.
SGM Corporation, P. O. Box 401, Cranbury, NJ 08521.
The Shwayder Company, 2335 E. Lincoln, Birmingham, MI 48008.
The Silent Watchman Corporation, 4861 McGaw Road, Columbus, OH 43607.
Simplex Security Systems, Inc., Collinsville, CT 06002.
Smith & Wesson (a Bangor Punta Co.), P. O. Box 2208, Springfield,
    MA 01101.
Sonitrol Corp., 4251 University Boulevard, Jacksonville, FL 33216.
Stellar Systems, Inc., 315 Brokaw Road, Santa Clara, CA 95050.
Teledyne Geotech, P. O. Box 28277, Dallas, TX 75228.
Tork Time Controls, Inc., Mount Vernon, NY 10551.
Torque Locks, Inc., 23970 Clawiter Road, Hayward, CA 04545.
United Securities Products, Inc., 6843 Dublin Boulevard, Dublin, CA
    94566.
The Viking Corporation, 210 N. Industrial Park Road, Hastings, MI 49058.
Visual Methods, Inc., Box 644, 200 Birchwood Road, Westwood, NJ 07675.

Index

Access control, electronic, 165
  levels of, 156–175
  personal recognition, 156
  visitor, 166–169
Accounting departments, 297
Admissions and dispositions
  departments, 295
Alarm systems, schools, 404
  types of, 216
Anti-intrusion alarms, their
  capabilities and limitations,
  217–231
Area or space protection, 216
Area security, 25
Areas requiring special attention,
  83–89
Armed robbery, action to be taken
  during, 325, 326
  occurrence, after, 326
Arson, 14, 15, 178, 179
Assassination, 15, 16
Athletic fields, 406
Audio alarms, advantages and
  disadvantages, 228–231
  description of, 227, 228
  microphone systems, open,
    closed, or impact, 227, 228
  sound discriminators, in con-
    junction with, 228

Background investigation, 148
Bank robberies, categories, 325
  reasons, 313
Barrier construction, types of, 27

Bombings, 16, 17
Bomb threats, 379–387
  evacuation, 385, 386
  plans to cope with, 381–385
  search techniques, 386, 387
  telephone, reasons for, 380, 381
Building master key, 143
Building security, construction
  sites, 361
  financial institutions, 324
  health care facilities, 386–311
  high-rise, 269–385
Buildings on the perimeter, 42, 43
Burglary, 349–351
Buried line sensor system, 38
  magnetic stress, 38, 39
  pressure system, 38, 39
  seismic device, 38, 39

Cafeterias and lunch areas, 84–86
  operations, 306
Camera housing, 241–246, 249–251
  environmental, 245
  explosion-proof, 246
  mounting of, 241
  tamper-proof, 245
  water-cooled, 246
Camera, television versus still,
  239–241
Capacitance or capacity alarms,
  advantages and disadvantages
  of, 218, 219
  description of, 218
Carbon dioxide extinguishers, 184

Cards or badges, identification,
  157–161
Carelessness, 12
Cargo security, 104–109
Casual pilferer, 10, 11
Central supply, 300
Chain link fencing, 27–29
  cleavage, 28
  culverts or troughs, 28
  galvanization, 27, 28
  gauge, 27
  mesh openings, 28
  personnel or vehicular gates,
    29
Change key, 143
Checks, fingerprinting for, 351
  fraudulent use of, 251–353
  identification for, 351
  limiting amounts for, 352
  photographic equipment, 351
Civil disturbances, defense
    against, 392, 393
Clear zones, importance of, 41,
    42
Closed circuit television (CCTV),
    237–255
  components of a typical, 247–
    252
  lighting requirements for, 238,
    239
  proposal for, 252–255
  service and maintenance con-
    tract, 225
  use of, 162–164
Cold, 8
Collusion between drivers and
    employees, 103
Color coding, 161, 162
Combination locks, 138–141
Company stores, 87, 88
  relocation of, 91
Computer area, backup systems
    for, 266, 267
  disaster plan for, 266, 267
  elements of, 259–261

passwords, 265, 266
physical security of, 256–268
relocation of, 90, 91
tape libraries and storage, 267
Computer crime, financial, 263
  prevention, 264, 265
  information, 263
  property, 263
  thefts of service, 263
  vandalism, 264
Computer rooms, relocation of,
    90, 91
Computer security, administrative,
    259
  communications, 260
  elements of, 259–261
  emanation, 260
  personnel, 259
  physical, 260
Computer terminology, 261–263
Concessionaires, 84, 85
Construction sites, building secur-
    ity for, 361
  fire protection on, 362, 363
  general area security, 360
  other security measures for,
    363, 364
  perimeter security for, 358,
    359
  personnel practices, 261, 262
  protective lighting of, 361
  reducing thefts on, 356–364
  special areas inside barrier,
    359, 360
Counterfeit money, 352, 353
Credit card fraud, 354
Credit unions, 89
Criticality and vulnerability, 2
  assessment, 23, 24
Customer pickup areas, 91, 92

Darkness, 6
Data gathering, 261
  communications input, 262
  communications output, 262

conversion, 262
disposition, 262
movement, 262
processing, 262
receipt, 262
transmission, 261
usage, 262
Dietary department, 302–304
Disloyalty and dissatisfaction, 12,
    13
Display areas, 87
    relocation of, 91
Dock area, housekeeping in, 100–
    102
Dock doors, 73, 74
Dock security, 97–100, 270–273
    basement, high-rise, 270–273
    closed, 98, 99
    isolated, 99
    nonisolated, 99, 100
    open, 98
Docks and piers, illumination of,
    67–69
Door controls, 132–134
    electrical strikes, 132
    sequential locking, 132
    time-recording locks, 132
Doors, 71–80
    between working and idle areas,
        75
    danger areas and restricted
        areas, 77, 78
    dock, 73, 74
    employee entrances and exits,
        71, 72
    fire, 73
    locking schedules, 79
    production and office areas,
        separation of, 76, 77
    school facility, 409–411
    security areas, 78
    studying use of, 71
    tool rooms, storage areas, and
        supply rooms, 78
    vault, 78, 79

warehousing and production
    department, separation of,
    74, 75
warm working areas, 75, 76
Double cylinder locks, 134
Dry powder extinguishers, 184

Earthquakes, 9
Economic status of area, 1
Electrical strikes, 132
Electronic access–control sys-
    tems, 121–130, 165
    card-operated mechanical lock,
        130
    command key, 122, 123
    control unit, 123, 124
    cipher, 129
    electromagnetic locking device,
        130
    interrogation system, 121, 122
    printer, 124
    sensor, 123
    systems programmer, 124
Electronic devices, perimeter
    protection by means of, 32–40,
    216
    security through, 214–236
Electronic key, 132
Electronic padlock, 131
Electronics (use of in theft), 366,
    367
Embezzlement, 17
Emergency control plan, 388–398
    intelligence sources, 391
    introduction to, 389
    physical security, 392
    planning committee, 390
    purpose of, 390
    security of, 389, 390
Emergency gates, 41
Emergency key, 143, 144
Emergency planning committee,
    390
Emergency room, 308, 209
Employee entrances, 71, 72

exits, 71, 72
locker rooms, 84
Engineered extinguisher systems,
    210
Espionage, 13, 14
Executive protection plan, 414–418
    automobile parking, 416
    low profile, 417
    safe rooms, 416
    telephone numbers, unlisted,
        415, 416
    travel plans and protection while
        traveling, 417, 418
Existing breaches at the perimeter
    barrier, 43, 44
Existing hazards, defining and
    analyzing, 4–24
Explosions, 8, 9
Extinguishers, Halon 1211, 184
    Halon 1301, 184
    marking and placement of, 189–
        191
    operation, method of, 189
    portable hand, 182–188
    types of, 182–188
Extortion, 18, 313, 314
    prevention of, 137, 318

Fence assault system, 33
Financial institution security, 312–
    330
    precautionary measures, other,
        329–330
Fire, 8, 9
Fire alarm stations, 196, 197
    department telephone jacks, 197
    local, 197
    remote, 197
Fire, classification of, 181, 182
    elements that contribute to
        starting, 179, 180
    other elements of, 210
    protection plan, 175–213
    zones and codes, 197

Fire detection devices, 191–197
    air duct, 194
    air pressure supervision, 196
    fire alarm stations, 196
    infrared flame, 193
    ionization, 192
    photoelectric, 192, 193
    post indicator valve supervision,
        196
    supervisory, 194
    temperature supervision, 194
    thermal, 193
    valve supervisory, 196
    water level supervision, 196
Fire doors, 73, 210
Fire pails, tanks and barrels with
    pails, 182
First-aid facilities, 89
Flood lights, 65
Floods, 9
Foam extinguishers, 183, 184
Fraud, 18, 19
Fresnal luminaires, 66

Gift shops, 306, 307
Government classified operations,
    88
Grand master key, 143
Great-grand master key, 143

Hazards, heinous, 14–23
    human, 9–14
    natural, 5–9
    recognition of a security, 4–24
    security, definition, 4
Health care facilities, disaster
    plan for, 311
    types of people encountered in,
        288, 289
Heat, 6–8
Holdups in progress, 329
Hostages and kidnapping, 10, 20
Housekeeping, 46
    departments, health care facili-
        ties, 304–306

Human hazards, 9–14
Hurricanes, 9

Identification,
    areas to investigate for, 151,
        152
    background investigation for,
        148
    corroborating information for,
        152
    general guidelines, 150
    objectives, 150, 151
    outline for, 150
    personnel, 147–169
    supporting information, 152
Identification cards or badges,
        157–161
    color coding, 161, 162
    laminated, 157
Identification system, closed cir-
        cuit television, 162–164
    exchange, 162
    initiating, 154–156
    multiple, 162
    single, 162
Illumination in the protection plan,
        53–69
Illumination techniques, 66
    perimeter barrier, 66
    waterfronts, piers, and docks,
        67–69
Individual guard key, 144
Industrial building security, 70–92
Insurance coverage, 319, 320
Intelligence sources, 391
Intercommunication capability, 248
Interior areas of the building, 26
Internal dishonesty, warning
        signals of, 367–371
    employee activities, 370, 371
    locks, alarms, doors, windows
        and perimeter, 368
    merchandise, files, and equip-
        ment, 367, 368

    personal behavior, 369, 370
    records and documents, 368, 369
Interrupted beam system, 33–38
Isolated barrier (definition), 27

Key control systems, 144–146
Key systems, 141, 142
Keys,
    important terms, 142
        key change number, 142
        keyway, 142
        paracentric, 142
    parts of, 141, 142
        bow, 141
        post, 141
        shank, 141
        shoulder, 141
    types of, 141, 142
        barrel, 141
        bit, 141
        construction, 142
        corrugated, 142
        double bit, 142
        flat, 142
        push, 141
        warded, 142
Kidnapping, 19, 20
    prevention of, 317, 318
Kleptomaniac, 333, 334

Labor conditions, 2
Lamps, 59–63
    incandescent, 59
    mercury vapor, 59, 60
    quartz, 60
    sodium vapor, 59
Landscaping, 46
    school facility, 407
Laundry department, 301, 302
Liaison with local government
        officials, 391
Lie detector, 373, 374
Lighting, continuous, 64
    effective protective, 54–56
    emergency, 64, 65

inspections and outages, 55
movable, 64
shields, 54, 55
standby, 64
supplementary, 55
Lighting system controls, 56–58
emergency illumination, 58
manual device, 57
photoelectric device, 56
timing device, 56, 57
Line supervision, 235, 236
Loaded-stream extinguishers, 184
Location of fire and police departments, 2
Lock and key systems, 111–146
Locker rooms, general, 310
Locking developments, recent,
131, 132
Locking devices, apartment-house-
type cylinders, 136
emergency key box, 135
miscellaneous, 135, 136
Lock mechanisms, 116–118
disc tumbler, 116
lever, 116
mushroom pin tumbler, 117
removable-core, 117
single control key, 117
Lock picking, 136–138
extractors, 136
lock-pick gun, 138
picks, 136
rakes, 136
tension bars, 136
Lock selection, 113
Locks, 113–115
cylindrical, 114
maximum-security, 119–121
mortise, 114
sequential cylinders, 115
unit, 115

Magnetometer, 374, 375
Mailroom, 307, 308
Manpower requirements, 3

Man traps, 165
Masonry barriers, 29
barbed wire, broken glass or
nails, topped by, 30, 31
chain link fencing, in conjunction
with, 30
double purpose (sea wall), 30
geometrical pattern, size of, 31
Master key system, 142–144
building master, 143
change, 143
emergency, 143, 144
grand master, 143
great-grand master, 143
individual guard, 144
master, 143
sub-master, 143
Maximum-security locks, 119–121
interlocking pin tumbler, 119–121
Mechanical devices, use of for
theft control, 376–378
Microphone systems, 227, 228
closed or impact, 227, 228
open, 227
Model shops, 87
Monitoring or annunciator systems,
231–235
central station, 231, 232
local, 232
methods of, 231–235
proprietary, 231
remote, 232, 233
telephone dialer, 233–235
Monitors, 246, 247, 249
size and type of, 246
split-screen, 248, 249
Mortuary operations, 309
Multipurpose dry chemical extinguishers, 184

Natural phenomena, 2
Nonisolated barrier (definition),
27
Nuisances, attractive, 43

Open areas, security of, 45–52
Openings in the perimeter barrier,
    40, 41
  gates, emergency, 41
    operational, 41
    railroad, 41
Operational flow plan, 2
Operational gates, 41
Output preparation, 262
Outside storage and production
    areas, 47
Over, short, and damaged depart-
    ment, 102

Packaging for security, 94, 95
Padlocks, 118, 119
  car seal, 118
Parking lots, controls of, 49–51
Pathology department, 308
Patrols, foot, 51
  security, 51, 52
  vehicular, 51
Perimeter barrier, 25
  during construction phases,
    405, 406
  existing branches at, 43, 44
  illumination techniques, 66
  openings in, 40, 41
Perimeter protection, effective-
    ness of, 26, 27
  electronic devices, by means
    of, 32–40, 216
Perimeter, securing of facility,
    25–44
Peripheral walls of buildings, 26
Personal information files, 316,
    317
Personal safety, 313, 314
Personnel and vehicle identifica-
    tion, 147–174
Personnel offices, high-rise
    facility, 294
  relocation of, 90
Photoelectric alarms, advantages
    and disadvantages of, 220, 221
  description of, 219

Piers and docks, illumination, 67–
    69
Pilferage and theft, 10–12
Pilferer, casual, 10, 11
  systematic, 11, 12
Pilot operations, 86
Power sources, types of systems,
    63–65
Premise alarms, advantages and
    disadvantages of, 217, 218
  description of, 217
Private vehicles, 170–174
  color coding, 172
  decals, control of unused, 171,
    172
  decals, identification, 170–172
  design, 172
  numbered, serially, 172
  other, 173, 174
Protective lighting, effective, 54–56
  health care facilities, 291, 292
Protective lighting system equip-
    ment, 65, 66
  flood lights, 65
  fresnal luminaires, 66
  searchlights, 66
  spotlights, 66
  street lights, 65
Pump-tank extinguishers, 182
Purchasing department, 300, 301

Quality control, 86, 87

Radar or microwave alarms, advan-
    tages and disadvantages of,
    225–227
  principle used in, 225
Radio frequency space protection,
    advantages and disadvantages,
    224, 225
  description, 224
Railroad gates, 41
Real estate, excess, 48, 49
Recreational facilities, 48
Relocation of activities, 89–92
  computer rooms, 90, 91

customer pickup areas, 91, 92
display areas, sales areas,
    company stores, 91
personnel offices, 90
Residence, security in, 318, 319
Retail industry, protection plan
    for, 331-355
vandalism of, 354, 355
Robbery and burglary, 349-351

Sabotage and espionage, 13, 14
by employees, 393, 394
preventing strike-related, 395-
    398
Sales areas, relocation of, 91
School facility design, doors for,
    409-411
drives and parking, 406
exterior lighting for, 406
general building design, 408,
    409
general security measures for,
    413
importance of, 404
interior lighting for, 407
interior walls and ceilings for,
    412
mechanical rooms and utility
    systems for, 411
perimeter barriers in, 405
restrooms and locker rooms
    for, 412, 413
site selection for, 405
walkways, 406
School property loss, design to
    reduce, 403-413
Search lights, 66
Sea wall, 29
Secondary barriers, 32
Securing the facility's perimeter,
    25-44
Securities, counterfeit or forged
    checklist, 323, 324
on-premise physical security,
    320-322

procedures for theft or loss of,
    322, 323
protection of marketable, 320
Security classification of locks, 115
maximum security, 115, 119-
    121
pin tumbler, 115, 116
warded, 115, 116
Security education program,
    acceptance and effectiveness
    of, 401, 402
employee, 399-402
explanation of, 400
goals of, 399
implementation of, 399
reasons for beginning, 399
Security hazard (definition), 4
recognition of, 4-24
Security of open areas, 45-52
Security patrols, 51, 52
Security requirements, evaluating,
    1-3
Security through electronics, 214,
    236
Shoplifting, 331-344
combating, 338-344
methods of, 336
recognition of, 334-336
types of, 333, 334
Smoking areas, 85, 86
Sociological conditions and psycho-
    logical outlook, 1, 2
Soda acid extinguishers, 182
Sound discriminators, 228-231
audio alarms, in conjunction
    with, 228
Space alarms, 221-231
Spotlights, 66
Spot or point protection, 216
Sprinkler head, parts of, 204
types of, 204
Sprinkler systems, automatic,
    198-200
component of, 199, 200
cost of, 203
types of, 200-203

Street lights, 65
Stored extinguishants, 210
Sub-master key, 143
Surrounding terrain, 1
Switcher, sequential, 248
Systematic pilferer, 11, 12

Telephone threats, 314–316
Terrorists, 22, 23
Theft controls, extent of problem,
    371, 372
    individual and group, 365–378
    magnetometer, use of, 374, 375
    mechanical devices, use of,
    376–378
Thefts, by employees, 344–349
    lie detector, use of in combat-
    ing, 373
    of cash, 344–346
    of merchandise, 346, 347
    reducing, 349, 384
Time and date generator, 248
Time clocks, location of, 83, 84
    double carding, 72, 83
    time stealing, 72, 83
Tornadoes, 9
Trash removal, 102
Truck park security, 109, 110
Types of protection, 216

Undercover agent, role of, 372
Underwriters' laboratories, 215,
    216

standards (pamphlets or bulletins),
    215, 216
Ultrasonic space alarms, advantages
    and disadvantages of, 224
    description of, 221–223
    doppler effect, 221

Vault doors, 78, 79
Vehicle identification and control,
    169, 170
Vending machines and servicemen
    85, 86
Video motion-detection systems,
    240, 241
Visitor control, 166–169
    control point, 167
    escort service, 168
    logs, 167, 168
    health care facilities, 289–291
Vulnerability to theft and pilferage,
    3

Warehouse, dock and cargo secur-
    ity, 93–110
Warehouse, security in, 95–97
Waterfronts, piers and docks,
    illumination of, 67–69
Water motor alarm bell, 210
Window security, 80
    bullet proof glass, 82
    impact-resistant plate glass, 82
    one-way screw head, 83
    seals, 82